HISTORICAL AND BIOGRAPHICAL RECORD

OF

DOUGLAS COUNTY

ILLINOIS

COMPILED BY

JOHN GRESHAM

U. S. A.

Southern Historical Press, Inc.
Greenville, South Carolina

This volume was reproduced
from a personal copy located in
the Publishers private library

All rights reserved. No part of this publication may be reproduced,
stored in a retrieval system, transmitted in any form, posted
on the web in any form or by any means without the
prior written permission of the publisher.

Please direct all correspondence and book orders to:
SOUTHERN HISTORICAL PRESS, Inc.
1071 Park West Blvd.
Greenville, SC 29611

Published Logansport, Indiana 1900
ISBN #978-1-63914-627-7
Printed in the United States of America

PREFACE.

After several months of tedious work, I present this volume of Douglas County Biography and History to its subscribers. Like all local works of its nature there will be no doubt criticisms, as it is impossible to please everybody. I have endeavored to do the work conscientiously. The biographies were all carefully written and submitted in type to each individual and the errors consequently reduced to the minimum. Hoping the book will fully come up to your expectations,

I am yours respectfully,

JNO. GRESHAM,

June, 1900.

Logansport, Indiana.

EARLY SETTLEMENT

OF

DOUGLAS COUNTY.

CHAPTER I.

EARLY SETTLEMENT OF THE COUNTY.

ORIGINAL INHABITANTS.

Archæologists tell us that the white race is the third, and perhaps the fourth, race that has possessed this land. The evidences of the presence of the earlier races are not abundant in all parts of the country, but sufficient is learned of their habits, numbers and power to lead to the conclusion that they dominated the region within which the territory of Douglas county lies. Robinson Crusoe's unexpected discovery of a human footprint upon the sands of his deserted island was hardly more startling than have been the discoveries of antiquarians in Europe within the past twenty-five years. Scientific followers of Usher and Petarius had placed the various migrations of men, the confusion of tongues, the peopling of continents— the whole evolution of human society—within the narrow compass of a little more than forty centuries, when the discovery of the geologist and ethnologist developed the trace of human existence dating back to a possible period of 30,000 years. Nor are confirmatory evidences wanting to show that the "elder man" had found a place in the New World. The gold-drift of California has supplied abundant testimony to the high antiquity of man, and notably the "Pliocene skull," the popular conception of which is derived more widely, perhaps, from a characteristic poem by Bret Harte than from scientific publications. Explorations in Illinois, Missouri and South Carolina have yielded similar testimony, and while it should be stated that in many cases these evidences rest upon the testimony of single observers, and that there is not that recurrence of "finds" which would render "assurance doubly sure," yet there seems no room to reasonably doubt the presence here of that "oldest inhabitant."

MOUND-BUILDERS.

Descending to a later time, and one probably falling within the historic period, the more tangible traces of an early race of men are found. Of this race, named from the character of their remains, the Mound-Builders, the evidences are found vastly multiplied, and of such a character as to afford means of a reasonable conjecture as to their mode of life, their advancement in civilization, and final destiny.

These evidences, though first accepted with great distrust, have been so amplified and confirmed by more recent researches as to leave no room for intelligent dissent to the former existence of this race. The remains upon which this conclusion is based, "consists," says Mr. Foster in his "Pre-historic Races of the United States," "of tumuli, symmetrically raised and often inclosed in mathematical figures, such as the square, the octagon and circle, with long lines of circumvallation; of pits in the solid rock, and rubbish heaps formed in the prosecution of their mining operations, and of a variety of utensils, wrought in stone, copper, or moulded in clay." To the uninstructed mind the mounds, doubtless, seem a very slight foundation upon which to rear the fabric of a national existence, and yet to the archæologist they furnish "proof as strong as Holy Writ;" in them they find as distinctive characteristics as mark the pre-historic remains of the Pelasgi, the wall-builders of Europe, a not dissimilar race in many respects, and one which long ago found a place in the realities of history; and while they differ in external form, and are scattered over a wide scope of country —characteristics in marked contrast with those of the aboriginal race found here in possession of the county; yet the scientist finds in each mound the never-failing marks of a race peculiarity.

The widest divergence from the typical mound is found in Wisconsin. Here, instead of the circular or pyramidal structure, are found forms, for the most part, consisting of rude, gigantic imitations of various animals of the region, such as the buffalo, bear, fox, wolf, etc.; of the eagle and night-hawk, the lizard and turtle, and in some instances the unmistakable form of man. These, though not raised high above the surface, and even in some cases represented *intaglio,* attain the largest dimensions; one, representing a serpent, extending seven hundred feet, and another, representing a turtle, had a body fifty-six and a tail two hundred and fifty feet long. The significance of these peculiar forms has not been determined, but unmistakable evidences have been discovered which mark them as the wor kof the same race whose structures are found elsewhere so numerous throughout the Mississippi Valley.

Typical Structures are sometimes classified with reference to their purpose, as Inclosures —1, for defense; 2, sacred; 3, miscellaneous. Mounds—1, of sacrifice; 2, for temple sites; 3, of sepulture; 4, of observation. Of the first class, the inclosures for defense seem to have been constructed simply for protection against hostile attack. The locations chosen are those best adapted naturally to repel a military approach. The inclosure is gained usually by a steep and narrow way, requiring the assailant to place himself at immense disadvantage, while the garrison, provided with parapets often constructed of rubble stone, could fight under cover, and perhaps found in these stones his store of ammunition. The sacred inclosure included within its lines the mounds of sacrifice, temple sites, and sepulture, as all of these uses were sacred to the Mound-Builders, and yet in the "American Bottom" where the mound system reached its highest development, the mounds of these classes is not inclosed. The mounds of sacrifice, or altars, as they are variously termed, are generally characterized by the fact, "that they occur only within the vicinity of the inclosures or sacred places; that they are stratified; and that they contain symmetrical altars of burned clay or stone, on which were deposited various remains, which in all cases have been more or less subjected to the action of fire." (Squier and Davis' Ancient Monuments.) In relation to this later characteristic, it should be said that it is not at all plain that the use of fire was intended for cremation. A thin coating of moist clay was applied to the body, nude or wrapped in cloth, and upon this a fire was maintained for a longer or shorter period, but in most cases the heat was not sufficient to destroy the cloth, sometimes found in a good state of preservation. This evidently did not result from a lack of knowledge, as cremation and urn burial was also practiced.

Temple mounds are described by Squier and Davis as "distinguished by their great regularity of form and general large dimensions. They consist chiefly of pyramidal structures, truncated, and generally having graded avenues to their tops. In some instances they are terraced, or have successive stages. But whatever their form, whether round, oval, octangular, square or oblong, they have invariably flat or level tops," and upon these were probably constructed their temples, but which, constructed of perishable materials, have left no trace of their existence. This class of mounds is not found alon the lage region, or that line which seems to mark the farthest advance of this people. The principal structures of this class are found at Cahokia, Illinois; near Florence and Claiborn, Kentucky; at Seltzertown, Mississippi; at Marietta, Newark and Chillicothe, Ohio, and St. Louis, Missouri. The mound at Cahokia, "the monarch of all similar structures in the United States," may well serve as a type. When in all its integrity, this mound formed a huge paralelogram, with sides at the base, respectively five hundred and seven hundred feet in length, towering the height of ninety feet. On the southwest there was a terrace, one hundred and sixty by three hundred feet, which was reached by a graded way, and the summit was truncated, affording a platform two hundred by four hundred feet. This structure, upon which was probably reared a spacious temple, perhaps the principal one in the empire, covered an area of about six acres, while in close proximity were four elevated platforms varying from two hundred and fifty to three hundred feet in diameter. The great mound at St. Louis reached a height of thirty-five feet, and that at Marietta to about the same height.

"Sepulchral mounds," says Mr. Foster "consists often of a simple knoll, or group of knolls, of no considerable height, without any definite arrangement. Examples of this character may be seen at Dubuque, Merom, Chicago and La Porte, which, on exploration, have yielded skulls differing widely from the Indian type. * * The corpse was almost invariably placed near the original surface of the soil, enveloped in bark or coarse matting, and, in a few instances, fragments of cloth have been observed in this connection. Sometimes a vault of timber was built over it, and in others it was enclosed in long and broad flags of stone. Sometimes it was placed in a sitting position, again it was extended, and still again compressed within contracted limits. Trinkets were often strung about the neck, and water jugs, drinking cups and vases, which probably contained food, were placed near the head. Over the corpse, thus arrayed, a circular mound was often raised, but sometimes nothing more than a hillock." Other mounds have been found that favored the theory that many of these structures were used for miscellaneous burial. Mounds of observation is rather a fanciful classification intended to mark mounds found on elevated points of land. The authors of this classification think that these may have been used as platforms on which to build signal fires, and such are their elevation and outlook that such signals could have been seen at a great distance. This theory of special purpose, however, has not been accepted as supported by any speciol evidence. They may have been so used, or simply as an eligible site for resirence.

There is, in addition to these mounds, a large number of which are not embraced in this classification, which, following Mr. F. W. Putnam, whom Mr. Foster quotes at length, may be called "habitation mounds." A large number of these are described as located at Merom, Indiana, and a group of fifty-nine mounds at Hutsonville, Illinois, a few miles above the former place and across the Wabash river. These mounds were carefully examined, to ascertain if they were places of burial, without discovering a single bone or implement of any kind, but, on the contrary, the excavations showed that the mounds had been made of various materials at hand, and in one case ashes were found, which had probably been scraped up with other material and thrown upon the heap. In the ancient fort at Merom, in depressions found within the earth works, were found striking evidences of food having been cooked and eaten there, and the conclusion drawn by Mr. Putnam is that these pits were the houses of the inhabitants or defenders of the fort, who were probably further protected from the elements and the missiles of assailants by a roof of logs and bark, or boughs. Another writer, (Hon. William McAdams, Jr., Otterville, Illinois), in a paper read before the American Association for the Advancement of Science, at their Boston meeting, August, 1880, says: "There is in this region a peculiar class of mounds, that was for a long time a puzzle to me. They are usually found in groups of from two or three to twenty or thirty, and even more, and are generally on some pleasant knoll or rising ground in the vicinity of a spring or water-course, especially in the vicinity of our prairies or level areas of land. The mounds are from one to three, and in a few instances even four feet in height, and from twenty to fifty feet in diameter. One mound of the group is always larger than the rest, and always occupies a commanding position. Sometimes the group is arranged in a circle; other groups have no apparent design in arrangement. Numbers of these mounds can be seen in the cultivated fields. Although I have made excavations in them, and dug trenches entirely through them, I have found nothing but ashes, charcoal, decayed portions of bones of fishes and animals partially burned, shells from adjacent streams, flint chippings, and in one or two instances a flint implement of a rude character.

"After examining many of these structures, I am induced to believe that they are possibly the remains of ancient dwellings, made by placing in an upright position the trunks of young trees in a circle, or in parallel rows, the tops of the poles inclining inward and fastened together, the whole being covered with earth and sod to form a roof, or in the same manner as many Indian tribes make their mud lodges; as, for instance, the Mandans and the Omahas. Such a structure, after being repaired from time to time by the addition of more earth on top, would finally, by the decay of the poles, fall inward, and the ruins would form a slight mound. Consant and Putnam describe such mounds in Missouri and Tennessee, some of the largest of these ancient towns being provided with streets and highways. They are also found in southern Illinois, Indiana and Ohio. Putnam has described an inclosed town in Tennessee, in which were many low mounds, or rather, as he calls them, earth circles, that he has pretty conclusively shown to be sites of the lodges or houses of the people."

These are the main evidences brought forward to show that the Indian was the author of the mound system, and probably describe the character of the mounds found in Douglas county. On the farm of Wesley Blaase, in Bourbon township, some mounds have been found, from one of which human remains were taken. Other elevations, evidently formed by human hands, are found elsewhere in the county, but no proper investigation has been made of them to determine their relation to this race, if indeed they are true mounds. There is no presumption against the facts; but the data given are so insufficient as to leave no ground to base an intelligent opinion. This region was undoubtedly within the range of their influence, and doubtless these mysterious beings roamed over the place now possessed by successive races of red and white men.

THE INDIAN.

The obvious inquiry suggested by these conclusions is, Who succeeded this extinct race? To this question science offers no complete answer. Two hypotheses are entertained as to the origin of the Mound-Builders here. The one supposes them to be of autothionic origin, and that semi-civilization originating here flowed southward, and culminated in the wonderful developments of the Toltecs, of Mexico; the other supposes them to have originated in the South American continent or in Central America, and to have emigrated northward from natural causes, and later to have returned to Mexico, driven from their northern empire by an irresistible foe, or by a powerful political eruption among themselves. Upon any theory, the line of their most northward advance is pretty clearly defined, and writers upon this subject generally agree that the line of defenses, "extending from the sources of the Allegheny and Susquehanna in New York diagonally across the country, through central and northern Ohio, to the Wabash," accurately indicates the region from whence attacks were made and expected, and marks the farthest extent of the Mound-Builders' empire. But what was the character of the foe, what his action on the retreat of the Mound-Builders, and what his final destiny, is an unwritten page of science, for which there exists little data. It is a later sugestion that the North American Indian may be a degenerate but legitimate descendant of the dominant race, or even the Mound-Builders themselves, but there is a broad chasm to be bridged before these early races can be linked with the aboriginal tribes. Without making any such attempt, however, the Indian naturally succeeds this people in regular historical order, and, passing over the vexed question of his origin, it is sufficient that the whites everywhere found him in full possession of the country.

The natural habitat of the Indian is in the timber, and Douglas county possessing but little, there are few or no local traditions concerning them. The early French explorers found the tribes of the Illini nation along the banks of the Illinois river, where, under La Salle's influence, they were re-enforced by other tribes or remnants of eastern savages. Subsequently the Iroquois devastated the upper waters of the Illinois, and the land was occupied by other tribes, among which were the Kickapoos. The later treaties of the general government brought a number of other tribes to this vicinity, which remained until the general removal from the state about 1832. The grand prairie, however, served only as a great hunting ground to the various tribes located in the state, and seldom afforded a site for a village, save in the heavily timbered margin at some points. In Douglas county there were no such sites, and while there are evidences of their having been here, it was probably only for the purpose of hunting. There is a tradition that the government surveyors were attacked by a roving band in the eastern part of the county, and while it is quite possible there is no definite information in regard to it. But few of the early settlers saw any here, as they had generally left before the date of the earliest arrivals. John Hammet, who came to Camargo township in 1830, was visited by a large number of Indians during his first winter here. Harrison Gill came to Camargo in the same year, and it is related that on one occasion he visited a camp of the natives at Hugo, where his uncle jocosely informed the chief that the younger man was in quest of a wife. The announcement created some commotion among the fair sex, and there was "gathering in hot haste." There was no objection to color, provided he could hunt, and so pressing was the interest manifested by these untutored maidens, that Gill was forced to escape under the plea that he was a poor hunter. During all the intercourse of the savages with early settlers, the Indian showed himself a good citizen, and did not exhibit his usual propensity to steal or molest the whites in any way.

THE PIONEERS.

The open prairie country of Douglas county greatly retarded the settlement of this section of Coles county. A few came here previous to 1850, but the great bulk of the public lands was occupied by actual owners subsequent to that date. The first settlement in Coles county as originally formed was about 1824, and subsequent additions to the white population found homes at widely separated points, from the Cumberland road on the south, to Camargo on the north. The original pioneer of Douglas county was John Richman, who, in 1829, settled in Camargo township. He was a native of Greenbrier county, West Virginia, and came with his father when a lad of sixteen years to Vermilion county, Illinois. The journey was made over the tedious roads of the frontier in wagons accompanied by a drove of sheep, horses and cattle. Here the family lived on and worked a rented farm for two or three years. In the meanwhile the father, accompanied by a friend, made a visit to the Embarrass timber in quest of honey. Here in eight or ten days they secured several barrels of honey, and in the course of their rambles became so enamored with the country that Mr. Richman determined to remove to this region.

In May of the following year, 1829, the family removed and took up their residence a mile and a half from the present site of Camargo village in the timber skirting the Embarrass river. At this time there was not another white family within the present limits of Douglas county, and none in Coles north of Charleston. For upward of a year the Richmans lived in this solitude, when they were joined by Harrison Gill, and perhaps some six months later by Isaac Moss, who settled about a mile east of the present village of Camargo. The Indians were in the neighborhood for three years after the advent of these pioneers, their village occupying the present site of Bridgeport. The savages came in the fall for hunting, and stayed through the winter, and in the spring went north to their corn-fields. The first summer, the Richmans lived in a temporary camp built of logs split in twain, while the male portion of the family devoted their efforts to breaking the prairie, and securing a harvest, but they soon found their team power inadequate for the undertaking, and resorted to the timber. The work of clearing and putting in the crop consumed the time until the 10th of July, when they had the satisfaction of seeing fourteen acres planted in corn. Their next care was to provide a permanent shelter from the rigors of the winter. Logs were procured and partly hewed, when the grim terror of pioneer life, the ague, laid seven of the eleven members of the family prostrate. For several months the family were obliged to give up further work on their improvements, and the winter found them still occupying the original cabin. On the following year the hewed-log house was finished and occupied, and still remains a landmark of the olden time.

Harrison Gill, who may be noted as the first purchaser of land in Douglas county, was a native of Kentucky, and belonged to the family noted in that state. Other branches of the family came to Palestine in Crawford county about 1812, and found refuge in old Fort La Motte for some time. At the pacification of the Indians, the Gills settled on the Sandy Prairie, but James Gill a few years later moved further north and settled on the Embarrass, near the northern lines of the present Cumberland county. On reaching the age of twenty-one, Harrison Gill found himself possessed of a few hundred dollars, and upon the advice of his father proceeded to Illinois to invest his capital in land. Visiting his family relatives in the state, he found his uncle in Cumberland county busy in shingling his first permanent cabin, and at once engaged to assist in completing the job. This done the two made a tour northward in search of lands for investment. The first point above Charleston where a settlement had been made was at the mouth of Brushy Fork, where Maj. Ashmore had begun an improvement. He was pleased with the appearance of the country, and selected land in the northwest quarter of section 35, and the west half of the southwest quarter of the same section, in township 15 north, range 10 east, and at once repaired to the land office at Palestine, where the entry was properly recorded. The patents, which are still retained as a souvenir by the family, were signed by Andrew Jackson, as President, on the 8th of March, 1830. Mr. Gill has not been a citizen of the county, having returned to Kentucky soon after his purchase of the land.

John Hammet was scarcely second to Gill in his entry of land in this county; he visited

Illinois in 1828, and entered eight hundred acres of land north of the present site of Camergo village, in company with Gill. Mr. Hammet was a native of Virginia, from whence he moved to Kentucky, where his son, James R., was born. It was not until the fall of 1830 that he moved to his new purchase. The household goods were brought from Kentucky by teams of horses and oxen—Mrs. Hammet and smaller children coming in a carriage. It was November before the family reached the site of their new home, and before the cabin could be erected winter was at hand. The family was therefore obliged to find shelter in a tent with a large fire before the opening to keep off the cold. The under bed ticks had been filled with blue grass seed in Kentucky, and upon these the feather beds were placed and drawn near the fire. This winter was very severe, as was the following one, which is known as the season of the great snow, and many of the Indians in the vicinity made frequent visits to this new addition to the white settlement. At the time of the arrival of the Hammets, there were only two families of permanent settlers in the territory of Douglas county, though some squatters had taken up their residence in the southern part and who removed soon afterward. The family suffered great privations during the first years. No provisions had been brought from Kentucky, and everything during the first winter was only to be procured at a point on the Vermillion river, near the present site of Indianola. Their milling was afterward done at a still greater distance, at Eugene, Indiana, some forty miles away. John Hammet died in the winter of 1834, leaving the care of the farm and family to his widow, who discharged her responsibilities in a way to show how great a debt the country owes to its pioneer women.

Eli Sargent was a settler in Douglas county in the same year. He was a native of Maryland, but had subsequently emigrated to Ohio where his children were born. Anxious to avail himself of the cheap lands in Illinois, he made a journey here, accompanied only by his son, Snowden. They left home on the 18th of March, and proceeded down the Ohio river to Evansville, Indiana, on a flat-boat. Here they continued their journey overland, crossing the Wabash at Vincennes and directing their course to Paris. Mr. Sargent's original intention was to seek a location in Buffalo Heart Grove in Sangamon county, a point he had greatly admired when he passed through it, returning from a trip to Missouri two years before. Coming through Walnut Prairie, some fifteen miles below Marshall, Clark county, Illinois, he learned of Walnut Point, on the Embarrass river, where Ashmore had made a settlement. The favorable reports of this location determined him to visit it, and so pleased was he upon examination, that he entered four hundred acres here when he returned to Palestine. The household goods were promptly brought forward in wagons, and arrived at the new location in April, 1830, Mrs. Sargent arriving soon afterward. A wigwam in the Indian fashion was the first erected, and later the usual cabins which served the family as homes for several years. Maj. Ashmore was the only settler in this township (Sargent). In 1834 Mr. Sargent died, leaving his son, Snowden Sargent, to care for his family.

William Brian, a native of Ohio, came to Douglas county in 1834, and entered one hundred and sixty acres of land in section 18, township 16 north, range 7 east. He arrived at this point in June and erected a cabin, returning then to bring his family, consisting of his wife and four children. He returned to Illinois in the following September, and cultivated his farm for about a year, when he removed to the farm which is known as the old homestead. For several years he was the only resident of what is now Tuscola township. Jacob Taylor was probably the first settler in Garrett township. Soon after him came James Drew, who came to the territory of Douglas county in 1839, having, with his father, a job to split rails for Taylor. Land was cheap here at that time, and Drew being only eighteen years of age, thought it a favorable opportunity to secure a start by entering land. He first entered eighty acres, borrowing one hundred dollars of Taylor to make the purchase, and contracting to discharge a portion of the debt by day's labor. He put up a split-log house in 1840, and lived with his brother-in-law. At this time, for thirty miles west in the direction of Decatur, there was not a single house. Jacob Mosbarger was among the earliest settlers in Garrett township. He was a native of Ohio, settled subsequently in Indiana, and in 1845 started with the intention of settling in Iowa. He found it impossible to reach his proposed destination in time to secure a crop before the coming winter, and therefore stopped here to raise one crop, proposing to continue his journey the next season. He was so favorably impressed with the country, however, that he gave up his idea of proceeding to Iowa. He first settled in the edge of the timber on Lake Fork, and rented land. Two years later he settled on Congress land, pre-empting one hundred and sixty acres, which still remains in the family. Nathan Garrett was another early and prominent man in Garrett township; he was newly married when he came here in April, 1845, and began life on a capital of forty dollars in cash, and two horses and a wagon; he began by renting land until 1852, when he entered eighty acres, and has been successful in amassing considerable property. Benjamin Ellars, a native of Ohio, came to Illinois in 1835. In 1849 he moved to Douglas county, and settled on the west side of the east Okaw timber, just south of the Campaign county line. The family was one of the first to locate in that vicinity. To the west of their improvement on the prairie there was not a single settler. John D. Murdock, for whom a township in Douglas county was named, was a prominent settler in that section of the county; he was a native of Ohio, but had made a settlement in Fountain county, Indiana, but, dissatisfied with the health of the section, he sought a home in a prairie country. His attention was called to this region in 1853, and in July of that year came here to "spy out the land." Pleased with the outlook he would have purchased land, but did not meet with a satisfactory opportunity. On returning home he sold his farm, and in January, 1854, returned, coming to Georgetown, and then by way of Hickory Grove, following the ridge to Camargo. At this time he met with a man of whom he bought some three hundred and forty acres at eleven dollars per acre. In the following April he brought his family. A split-log house stood upon the tract at the time of its purchase, but being insufficient for the accommodation of his family, Mr. Murdock prepared a frame house in Indiana, and hauled it to his new purchase where he put it up in readiness for his family.

William W. Young came to Douglas county in the fall of 1853, and was one of the earliest settlers in Newman township. He was a native of Indiana, and lived for a few years after his marriage on rented land in his native state. He then came to Douglas county, accompanied by two of his wife's brothers. After entering one hundred and sixty acres of land he returned to Indiana, and a year later came with his family to the place chosen for his new home. On their arrival they boarded for a week in the neighborhood, while Mr. Young erected a frame dwelling into which the family moved directly it was completed. J. M. Cooley, one of those accompanying Mr. Young, took up one hundred and sixty acres on a land warrant in November, 1853. B. C. Nelson came to Douglas county three years later, and bought three hundred and twenty acres of railroad land on section 4, township 16 north, range 8 east. With the exception of one or two families there were no neighbors nearer than Okaw timber, and the site of Tuscola was a wild prairie covered with tall grass and resin weed.

There was nothing in the character of the country or in the history of the emigrants to this section to lead to the early formation of villages or thickly settled communities. The pioneers of Douglas county came singly or by twos and threes, and fixed upon an eligible site for farming, and there pitched their tabernacle. Up to the coming of the railroad influence in 1850, Camargo was the only village even on paper, and there was therefore no disturbing influence to divert the even settling up of the country. Camargo dates earliest among the townships of the county in settlement, and counts among the early settlers the Richmans, Hammets, Gills, Braggs, Watsons and Murdocks. Tuscola claims William Brian, the Hacketts, O. J. Jones, J. W. Smith, G. P. Phinney, B. F. Boggs, B. C. Nelson and others. Garrett claims the Garretts, Otters, Mullens, Lesters, Goodsons, Mosbargers, Drews, Howes and Ellars. Newman incudes among its early settlers Enoch Howell, the Winklers, the Hopkinses, Cooleys, Youngs, Skinners and Shutes. Sargent numbers the family from which it took its name, Ashmores, Gwinns, Reddens, Allisons, Maddox, Casebear and others. Bowdre claims Isaac Davidson, Breedens, Davises and Barnetts. Arcola, the Shaws, Henrys and McCanns; and Bourbon the Moores, Deharts, Weltons, Nelson Shaw, the Drews and others. In the latter township are quite a number of Germans who came in about 1852 and the years immediately following, and in 1864 the first of a considerable number of the same nationality generally known by the "Amish," a name commonly bestowed upon this sect of religionists.

NATURAL RESOURCES.

The country which these pioneers has thus chosen was a hunter's paradise. The prairie and timber were thronged with game of all kinds, and without this the early settler's fare must have been hard indeed. The first comers to this region were considerably in advance of those pioneer industries which mitigate the severities of pioneer life and were forced to make long journeys for the common necessities. Thus cut off from the natural sources of supply, the pioneer was forced to depend upon the resources of the country alone, which, even with the abundance of game, proved but a meager support for the family. Deer were found in unlimited numbers, and the first settlers found no trouble in killing more than the needs of the family required, right at his own door. Droves, reaching to the number of a hundred, were often seen, and settlers were in the habit of carrying their guns on almost all occasions, and seldom returned from any expedition without an evidence of the abundance of these animals in the shape of a haunch or ham of venison. Wild hogs served also to vary the frontier fare. These were animals that had escaped from the older settlements, and, subsisting upon the nuts and roots of the woodland, had gone wild in the course of nature. They were of a long-legged, gaunt species, and kept the timber pretty closely. They were no particular damage or annoyance to the settlers, but furnished capital hunting sport, and gave a relief to the monotonous recurrence of venison upon the table of the settler. Wolves were of the coyote species and were found in the open prairie. These were of more annoyance to the settlements, attacking sheep, young pigs and sometimes cattle. They were miserable cowards, never attacking a person, and were hunted and killed as a nuisance. They were small and undersized, making the night dismal with their howling, and when overtaken by the dogs would fall on their backs and fight much like a cat. On frozen ground, and when filled with a recent meal, they were run down with little difficulty on horseback, as they seemed to avoid the timber and would risk capture rather than go into it. Pinnated and ruffed grouse, better known as prairie chickens and partridges, were everywhere found in inexhaustible numbers and furnished a touch of delicacy to the early fare. Wild geese and ducks were to be had in considerable numbers, while in the rivers were found some fine edible fish. With this abundance of what are even now considered luxuries, it would seem at a casual glance that the pioneer life was a life of ease rather than hardship; but when it is considered that these were the sum of their early luxuries, that what we deem the common necessities and find so cheap as to pass almost unnoticed in our estimate of family supplies and expenses, were to the early settlers almost inaccessible and the most expensive, a great change is wrought in our estimate. Salt was more expensive than sugar and more difficult to procure. Flour could not for a time be procured at any price, and even meal, such as is provided to-day, was unknown on the frontier. And even the variety of game provided soon failed to answer the purposes of beef and pork. The system exposed to ravages of disease, and subject to the trying experience of early farm labor, demanded something more substantial than this. Nor could all give their attention to hunting. The prime reason for the presence of most of the pioneers in this country was to build up a home and lay the foundations for a future competence, and to accomplish this the larger part of the community centered here had only their hands with which to accomplish their mission. It was no uncommon occurrence to find men surrounded by this profusion of game who never shot a deer, and occasionally one who never owned a gun.

LIFE ON THE PRAIRIE.

The pioneers who formed the early settlements in this county were generally familiar with the isolation, and inured to the hardships and privations of frontier life, but with all this the open prairie presented difficulties to which they had hitherto been a stranger. From the standpoint of this later day, when the adaptability of the prairie has been so abundantly proven, it seems unfortunate that the early experiences of these pioneers led them to cling to the timbered portions of the country where foul water and miasma aggravated the inevitable discomforts of frontier existence. Life in a new country is everywhere subjected to the misery of malarious diseases. The clearing off of timber or the breaking up of prairie sod, involving the rapid decay of large quantities of vegetable matter, gave rise to the inevitable miasma, which wrought its sure work upon the system. Such sickness was generally confined to the last of the summer and fall. There was but little sickness in winter, except a few lingering fall cases that had become chronic; there were but few cases after severe frosts, and the spring and early summer were perfectly healthy. It was commonly remarked that when the bloom of the resin weed and other yellow flowers appeared, it was time to look for the ague. The first spring flowers on the prairie were mostly pink and white, then followed purple and blue, and about the middle of August yellow predominated. High water in spring, flooding the bottoms and filling the lagoons and low places along the streams, and then drying off with the hot sun of July and August, was a fruitful cause of disease, and in such localities it was often quite sickly, while the higher prairie was comparatively exempt. With these evils the pioneer was generally forced to struggle alone. Physicians were very few, and often so far situated from the scattered settlements that it took a day's ride to reach them. But where they were found within practical distance, the urgent necessity for the practice of every economy led the settlers to depend upon their own skill. Boneset, Culver's physic (root), and a long list of teas and herb decoctions were to be found in every cabin, and most of the ailments incident to a frontier life were generally made to yield to them. To have a severe case of malarial fever or several season's run of the ague was expected by each new-comer, and none were considered as having been fully inducted into all the mysteries of citizenship until they had had the regular malarial experience.

THE CABIN.

The early settlers brought with them nothing but what the necessities of the situation demanded. One wagon generally sufficed to bring the family, household furniture, farming implements and frequently two or three months' supplies. It requires no great amount of consideration to conclude that luxuries, or even comforts, could find no place in such an outfit, and so the pioneer, after constructing a shelter for his family, found his skill and ingenuity taxed to their utmost to supply this deficiency. It was necessary to manufacture tables, chairs and bedsteads before they could be used, and some of the most striking incidents of frontier life are founded upon this universal dearth of ordinary comforts. Hand tools were always a part of the load when possessed by the emigrant, but in the absence of these the ax accomplished all that was necessary. A section of a good-sized log, smoothed with an ax and furnished with a rough back, or often without a back of any sort, and legs, took the place of chairs. A rude bedstead was often constructed in the corner of the cabin with a single leg, the two sides of the structure supporting the rest of the bedstead which was framed in the logs. Upon this the bed cord, which could be easily brought, was arranged, or in its absence, deer-hide thongs. This or simply a heap of brush supported the "tick," which was brought with the family, and filled with leaves and dried grass until the first crop supplied a better substitute in the husks.

The cabin itself displayed the ingenuity of the pioneer and the poverty of his resources. A log pen, with a single door and window, the latter closed with greased paper or left open, and the door provided with a simple blanket, the fireplace constructed of such loose stones as could be found, and the chimney built up of sticks protected with a covering of mud; the roof of "shakes" split from a straight-grained tree, and held in place by weight poles, completed the *tout ensemble* of the early homes. At first there was often no floor but the ground, but generally slabs split out from the unseasoned timber were smoothed with the ax and made to do good service as a protection from the bare earth. When the door was constructed, these "puncheons" served as the material from which it was constructed, wooden pins taking the place of nails, and wooden hinges, latch and bars serving the purposes of the modern builder's hardware.

THE FARM.

These preliminaries accomplished, the most urgent necessity was to secure a crop. The plows were crude affairs, strong and serviceable but requiring great team power and considerable mechanical skill in the plowman. The sod was found tough, not easily "tamed," and very uncertain in producing a first crop. So tenacious was the turf, that the furrow turned out one unbroken strip of earth, and occasionally, when not especially careful, the plowman had the disappointment of seeing yards of this leathery soil turn back to its natural position, necessitating the tedious operation of turning it all back again by hand. The expenditure of all this labor was generally well repaid the first year, if the sod became thoroughly rotted, even though it produced but a small crop. Oftentimes the second and third plowing showed the soil stubborn and unkind. Few, even among farmers, know much of the labor involved in "breaking prairie," unless they have experienced its obstacles and overcome them. Corn was the only crop planted at first, and this furnished food for man and beast. A few years later, it was a mark of unusual prosperity to be able to furnish wheat bread to especial guests. The first crop was generally planted by cutting a gash in the inverted sod with an ax, dropping in the corn and closing it by another blow beside the first; or it was dropped in every third furrow, and the sod turned on it; if the corn was so placed as to find the space between the furrows, it would find daylight; if not, the result of the planting was extremely doubtful. Of course cultivation in this case was impossible, and if the crows and squirrels gave the crop an opportunity to mature, it generally proved a satisfactory return. Later the culture of wheat was begun, and with the increase of markets has grown to larger proportions.

Most of the settlers brought in horses and cows, but the former pretty generally gave way to oxen for working purposes. Hogs and sheep were occasionally brought in at first, but generally they were a later importation. All these animals were supported with little cost. The wide range of wild grass afforded excellent pasture and hay. With the range the early settlers had, their cattle would put on more flesh and in less time than on any other pasture. The sedge which grew along the sloughs was the first to start in the spring, and furnished the earliest pasture. The bent or blue-joint, which was principally found along the sides of the sloughs, or, in the vernacular of the pioneer, "between the dry and wet land," was preferred by stock to all other varieties, especially when mixed with the wild pea-vine. This made the best hay, and, as its yield was very large, was generally selected for this purpose. But the combined ravages of stock and scythe rapidly exterminated it, so that in many cases the ground where it grew became almost bare of vegetation. The stock and the farmer then resorted to upland grasses, but before the settlers multiplied so as to limit the range of the stock, the older and more experienced of the herd would go long distances to find their favorite pasture, often necessitating on the part of the pioneer a hunt of several days to recover them.

The native grasses were scarcely less marked for their medicinal qualities. Cattle and horses seemed to be remarkably free from disease so long as they could find plenty of wild grass and hay to feed upon. Horses raised upon the prairie were said never to be afflicted with the heaves, while horses brought here, suffering with this malady, were speedily cured by simply feeding on the native grasses. This advantage, however, was somewhat offset by the colic which this rank grass frequently produced in horses with fatal effect.

MILLS AND MARKETS.

No sooner was a crop secured than the lack of any proper means to reduce it to the necessities of the household was made painfully apparent. So long as the corn was soft, it was grated on rude graters made by punching holes through a piece of tin. After it became hard, it was sometimes parched and ground in a coffee mill, and at other times pounded in a rudely constructed mortar. A stump was hollowed out by burning and scraping to serve as a mortar. Over this was suspended from a "sweep" a pestle, to the end of which was fixed an iron wedge, and with this rude machinery bushels of corn were broken sufficiently fine to use in the various ways common to pioneer days. The finest was used in cornpones and dodgers, while the coarser was used as hominy, the separation being effected by means of a sieve made of a perforated deerskin stretched tightly over a frame. Corn-crackers were put in various settlements at an early date, but these did but little better work than the mortar. They did the work quicker, and such a mill was kept running night and day, while the patrons coming from distances of fifteen or twenty miles would wait patiently for a day or two to get their grist. But for flour, the only resort was to Eugene, Indiana, where an older settlement had secured the advantages of a flouring mill. The demand for groceries was limited to the means for purchasing, which were generally of the most slender sort. There was but little to sell, and then the only market was at Chicago, where the settlers hauled hundreds of bushels of shelled corn to sell at thirty cents per bushel. Coonskins, however, were almost land-office money. Fur buyers were an institution of the early times here, and many a quarter-section was purchased with the price of these skins.

There were some luxuries, however, that could be secured without money. Bee trees were, in many parts of the country, found in great numbers, and no piece of timber was entirely devoid of them. It sometimes required an expert to find them, and some united pleasure and profit in this sort of hunting. An experienced hunter would go out in a bright, warm day in winter or late fall and burn some honey comb, which seldom failed to attract the game to the honey, which was provided for them. Loading up with this, the bee would rise, circling in the air, and then fly straight to its tree. It was then the hunter's business to follow the fleet-winged insect closely, and thus pert, and there were few who were marked discover its secret. To do this required an expert for their success. Sometimes a number of bees from a single tree, at no great distance, were attracted. These do not rise in circles, but darting to and fro in a straight line, make the course plain enough to be easily followed, but this is rare. In other cases, the best that can be done is to discover the direction of the bee's flight, and taking this—against the sun if possible—to stumble along with upturned gaze, scanning every tree for the telltale hole or crack. But when the tree was found the battle was but half won. This must be felled and the occupants dispossessed of their stores. When the hollow extended down to the point where the ax must penetrate it, the hunter was often obliged to decamp in hot haste as soon as the blows had aroused the swarm.

The bee was easily domesticated, and many of the settlers captured swarms, placed them in sections of hollow logs, and in a little while possessed a constant source of supply for the table and the market. In some cases this was the principle source for the sweetening used in the culinary work of the cabin, and was the basis of a favorite drink. "Metheglin" was made of steeped honey-comb, and honey fermented. It was counted an excellent drink, and much preferred to cider, and when strengthened by age became a powerful intoxicant. This, however, has passed away with many other of the homely joys of pioneer days.

The ready tact of the pioneer housewives, and the unpampered tastes of that early day, found a good substitute for fruit in the pumpkin. When frozen, they were prepared and stewed down to a sirup, which furnished a very acceptable substitute for sugar or molasses in the absence of honey, and mixed with fresh stewed pumpkin formed a desirable sweetmeat. They were planted in considerable numbers, and stored in a vault constructed underneath the haystacks to be fed to the cattle during the winter. Well may this "fruit loved of boyhood" be apostrophized by the poet, and honorably be placed in a state's coat of arms.

PRAIRIE TRAVEL

Neighborhoods extended over a wide area of country, and a journey of fifteen miles was not considered a great undertaking for an afternoon's visit. Roads were few, and the prairie, easily cut up, often presented at points where lines of travel were obliged, by the conformation of the land, to unite, bog holes, that proved almost impassable. So long as the paucity of settlement allowed a pretty free selection of route, mud holes could be generally evaded and a worn track avoided. But this practice had its disadvantages. In a country without continuous fences and few landmarks, save the groves, it requires some skill and an intimate knowledge of the country to successfully cross even a small prairie in daylight. Crossing the uncultivated prairie at night was a very uncertain venture even to the most expert. If the night was clear, the stars were a reliable guide, and the pioneers became quite proficient in the simpler rudiments of astronomy. In a cloudy night, and a snowy or foggy day, their resources were less sure. A steady wind often proved the only guide. The traveler, getting his bearings, would note how the wind struck his nose—the right or left ear—and then, keenly alive to these sensations, would so maintain his course as to keep the bearing of the wind always the same, and regardless of all other guides, would generally reach his destination without difficulty. To do this required no little skill and a steady wind. If the latter changed gradually, the better the skill, the wider the traveler diverged from his true course. Without these guides, it was a mere accident if a person succeeded in crossing even a small prairie. The tendency is to move in a circle, and when this is once begun and observed by the traveler, the only resource is to camp in the most convenient place and manner, and wait for morning. Each family had its signal light, which served to mark the place of the cabin. It was a frequent practice to erect a pole by the chimney, upon which a lighted lantern was placed. Others had a light in the window, which often saved a dreary night's experience on the open prairie.

Such experiences, unpleasant in mild weather, were too often fatal in the winter season. The trackless prairie, covered with a deceptive expanse of snow, and swept by a fierce blast, which pierced the most ample clothing and the hardiest frame, made the stoutest heart waver. Journeys were seldom undertaken in such circumstances, save under stress of the most urgent necessity. But nearly every early settler can remember some experience in winter-season traveling, while some never reached the home they sought, or the end of the journey reluctantly begun.

With the settlement of the prairie, and the regular laying-out of roads, traveling became less dangerous, though scarcely less difficult. The amount of labor which could be devoted by the few people in the scattered settlements, made but little effect upon the roads of the country, which seemed particularly exposed, by the character of the soil and the conformation of its surface, to the unfavorable action of rain, and even now the farming community pays a heavy annual tribute to muddy, impassable roads.

HISTORICAL SKETCH

OF

DOUGLAS COUNTY.

CHAPTER II.

HISTORICAL SKETCH OF DOUGLAS COUNTY.

BY HENRY C. NILES.

By the treaty of peace between the French and English in 1763, the Illinois country was ceded to the latter. It remained in their hands until 1778, in which year Virginia troops under Gen. Clark conquered the country. A county called Illinois was then organized, and had been considered hitherto a part of the territory included in the charter of Virginia. Virginia ceded it to the United States in 1787, and it was called the "Northwest territory." In 1800 it received a separate organization and a territorial government in conjunction with and under the name of Indiana. Another division took place in 1809 when the distinct territories of Indiana and Illinois were formed.

The name of Illinois is derived from that of its great river, an aboriginal appellation, signifying the "River of men."

When Illinois territory was a part of Indiana, the seat of government was at Vincennes, and when the territory was set off from Indiana in 1809 the whole state was made into two counties, St. Clair and Randolph. From St. Clair Madison was made; from Madison, Crawford; the state then had about fifteen counties. In 1819 Clark was set off from Crawford, and extended to the northward indefinitely. Coles county was organized in 1830-31; Cumberland parted from it in 1842, and Douglas in 1859.

Illinois was admitted into the Union of states in 1818, with an area of fifty-five thousand, four hundred and ten square miles, about four hundred and nine of which belong to Douglas county.

Coles county, from the area of which Douglas was taken, once comprised within its bounds all of Cumberland county as well, and was named in honor of Edward Coles, the second governor of the state, elected in 1822.

Amongst the smallest counties in the state, though not the least by some seven or eight, Douglas county is geographically in the east centre of the state, and lies below the fortieth parellel of latitude, Tuscola the county seat, being in latitude thirty-nine degrees, forty-five minutes, north. The county is bounded on the north by Champaign county, on the east by Edgar, upon the south by Coles, and on the west by Moultrie and Piatt.

The election for and against the new county was held in Coles county on the first Monday in March, 1859, and the clerk was ordered to make his returns to Coleman Bright and Joseph B. McCown, of Camargo.

Coles was a large county of some twenty-four congressional townships, and containing about eight hundred and eighty square miles. New towns, demanded by the rapidly increasing population of the north part, were springing into existence, the principal of which, Tuscola and Okaw (for so Arcola was originally called), upon the line of the Illinois Central Raliroad, had been laid out, the latter by the railroad, upon its own lands, and the former upon railroad lands by private enterprise.

The tedious trip, over the prairie of twenty or twenty-five miles, to Charleston, the county seat, laid out in 1831, and the almost universal disposition of the people toward concentration, carried still farther, eventually, by township organization, were amongst the inducements that brought about the division.

Origin of Douglas.—In date of formation, Douglas county precedes Ford by one day only, and lacks so much of being the latest-formed county of the state, but though late in asserting its independence, it has not been unknown to the geography of the state, under other titles. In October, 1778, it was included in the county of Illinois; in 1790, it became a part of St. Clair county; in 1816 a part of Crawford; in 1819 a part of Clark; in 1823 a part of Edgar, and in 1830 a part of Coles. During all this time the territory now included within the limits of Douglas county was a wilderness, without the habitation of a single white man, with the exception perhaps of one family in 1829. The county of Coles was originally a part of Edgar, and as first formed included the territory of the present counties of Cumberland, Coles and Douglas. At this time the settlement at Charleston was strong in numbers and influence, and became the county seat. Later, as the southern portion of its territory began to settle up, an agitation was begun for a division of the large territory included in Coles and while the interests of Charleston were not hostile to this movement in the abstract, there was a very decided preference manifested for the way it should be divided. The leaders of the new county movement preferred to have the whole territory equally divided, but in such case it appeared certain that the county seat interests of Charleston would be put in jeopardy, as it would be located too far south in the reconstructed county to long hold the seat of justice. The question was soon forced into politics, and three campaigns were fought on this issue, the candidates for the General Assembly announcing themselves in favor of one or the other party. The Coles county people proposed the formation of a small county on the south, and eventually another on the north, and the issue was defined in the vernacular of the stock marks of the time as a crop or a split. Twice the Charleston people defeated the split at the polls or in the lobby, but finally a candidate was elected upon the platform of "first a split, second a crop, but in any case a new county," and in 1843 Cumberland county was formed. Another county would have been formed from the north end of Coles, but this part of its territory settled up slowly, and by the time that a movement was made for a new county, the necessity for its erection was no longer recognized by the older community. Coles county contained twenty-four congressional townships, enough to form two counties of the required area, and the tedious trip of twenty or twenty-five miles over the prairie to the county seat, located considerably south of the geographical center, intensified the determination to divide it. Public-spirited men organized the movement, and a bill was introduced in the General Assembly to form the new county. The name occasioned no little difficulty at first. W. D. Watson, of Camargo township, was in the senate and a Republican. The proposed county was politically in sympathy with him, and the petition for the new county asked for the name of Richman, that of the first white inhabitant; others proposed and pressed the name of Watson, and the subject was discussed at local meetings, with a good deal of excitement. There was a disposition on the part of the legislature to reject both names, and honor the name of Stephen A. Douglas with its designation. Dr. Pearce, of Camargo, and others strongly resisted this suggestion, and the vigorous opposition was not relaxed until it appeared certain that a bill could not be passed with another name, and even then it is said that promise was given by certain responsible persons, that the name should subsequently be changed. The name, however, has long since lost its political significance, and is worthily bestowed in honor of a brilliant and patriotic statesman. The peculiar spelling follows that adopted by Senator Douglas.

The act of organization.—The bill introduced for the purpose of organizing Douglas county provides as follows:

"Section 1. *Be it enacted by the People of the State of Illinois, represented in the General Assembly,* That all that portion of the county of Coles lying within the following boundaries, to wit: Commencing at the northeast corner of the county of Coles; thence west on the line between said county and the county of Champaign, to the northwest corner of the county of Coles; thence south on the west line of Coles county to the southwest corner of section eighteen (18), township fourteen (14) north, of range seven east; thence east on the section line to the southwest corner of section eighteen (18), township fourteen (14) north, range ten east; thence north to the township line between townships fourteen (14) and fifteen (15); thence east on said line to the east line of Coles county; and thence north on the east line of Coles county to the place of beginning, be and the same is hereby created into a new county, to be called the county of Douglas: *Provided,* that a majority of all the voters of said county of Coles voting on the question, shall vote for the same in the manner hereinafter prescribed.

"Sec. 2. The qualified voters of the said county of Coles may, at an election to be held in the several precincts of said county, to be held on the first Monday of March next, vote for or against the creation of the said new county of Douglas by ballot, upon which shall be written or printed, or partly written and partly printed, 'For the New County' or 'Against the New County.'

"Sec. 3. The clerk of the county court of the county of Coles shall give notice of said election in the several election districts in said county, in the same manner as general or special elections are given, as nearly as may be; and the judges of election and clerks thereof shall conduct said election and make returns thereof in the same manner as is now provided by law for conducting elections. In case of vacancies in the board of election, or failure to attend, such vacancies of absentees shall be filled in the same manner as is now provided by law in relation to elections. Returns of said election shall be made by the several boards of election to the clerk of the county court of Coles county, who shall be governed by the general election law then in force in opening and canvassing the same. The clerk of the county court of Coles county shall make return of the votes to Coleman Bright and J. B. McCown within six days after the same have been canvassed; and the said clerk shall also within ten days make return of said votes to the secretary of state.

"Sec. 4. If it shall appear that a majority of all the voters in said county of Coles voting upon the question have voted for the creation of the new county of Douglas, then, and in that case, there shall be held a special election in the several precincts within the limits in this act described for said new county of Douglas, on the second Monday in April next, for county officers. Said election shall be conducted by the judges of elections then holding office under appointment in the county of Coles, and at the usual places of holding elections; at which election the qualified voters of the new county of Douglas shall elect all county officers for said county, except such as are hereafter excepted, who shall be commissioned and qualified in the same manner as such officers are in other counties in the state, and shall hold said offices until the next general election for such officers, and until their successors are elected and qualified, and shall have all the jurisdiction and perform all the duties which [are] or may be conferred upon or required of like officers in this state. In case there shall be portions of precincts or election districts within the boundaries of the new county, then the voters within the same may, at the first election for county officers, as herein provided for, vote within such precinct or election district as they may deem most convenient within said new county.

"Sec. 5. All the justices of the peace, constables, or other officers who have been heretofore elected and qualified in the county of Coles, whose term of office shall not have expired at the time of said election, and whose place of residence shall be embraced within the limits of said county of Douglas, shall continue to hold their said offices and exercise the jurisdiction and perform the duties thereof until term of office shall expire and their successors shall be elected and qualified.

"Sec. 6. For the purpose of fixing the permanent county seat of said new county of Douglas, the voters of said county shall, at said election of county officers, vote for some place, to be designated upon their ballots, for a county seat; upon said ballots shall be written or printed, or partly written and partly printed, 'For county seat'—after which word shall be written or printed the name of the place intended. The place receiving the majority of all the votes polled upon that question shall be the county seat of the said county of Douglas; but if no one place shall receive a majority of all the votes polled upon that question, then it shall be the duty of the county court of said county to call another election, within sixty days thereafter, at the several places of holding elections in said county; at which time the voters of said county shall choose from the two places having the highest number of votes at the previous election, and the place having the majority of all the votes cast shall be the permanent county seat of said county of Douglas.

"Sec. 7. Notice of said election for county officers shall be given by the clerk of the county court of Coles county, in the same manner as notices of general elections are given in other cases; which notices shall specify that a vote will be taken upon the location of the county seat; and returns of said election shall be made to said clerk of said county court, the same as is provided by law in other cases.

"Sec. 8. All suits and prosecutions that have been, or may be commenced in said county of Coles, including all proceedings in the county court of said county in matters of probate before the organization of said county of Douglas, shall not be affected by this act, but all such suits, prosecutions and proceedings shall be prosecuted and conducted to their final termination in said county of Coles; and the officers of said county of Coles are hereby authorized to execute all writs that may be necessary for the completion of said suits, prosecutions and proceedings within the limits of said county of Douglas; and all judgments that may have heretofore or that may hereafter be obtained under the provisions of this section shall have the same lien upon all property within the limits of said county of Douglas as though the said territory had not been erected into a separate county.

"Sec. 9. As soon as the county officers shall have been elected and qualified, the said county of Douglas shall be considered organized, and the clerk of [the] circuit court of said county shall give notice thereof to the judge of the fourth judicial circuit, who shall hold court at such places as shall be designated by the county court, until the county seat is located, as herein provided, said circuit court to be holden at such times as said judge shall direct, until otherwise provided by law.

"Sec. 10. The school funds belonging to the several townships embraced in the limits of said county of Douglas shall be paid and delivered over by the school commissioners of the county of Coles to the school commissioner of the said county of Douglas as soon as he shall be elected and qualified

"Sec. 11. The county court of the said county of Douglas may, at any term of said court, by an order to be entered of record, appoint some competent person a commissioner for the purpose hereinafter expressed, who shall take an oath of office before some person authorized by law to administer oaths. Said court shall, at the same time, provide a sufficient number of blank books and deliver to said commissioner, who shall receipt for the same to the clerk of said county court.

"Sec. 12. As soon as said books shall be delivered to said commissioner, he shall record in each a copy of the order of his appointment, and of his oath of office, and shall thereupon proceed to transcribe into such books all such deeds, mortgages and title papers of every description, with the certificates of acknowledgment thereto, of lands lying in the county of Douglas, which have been recorded or may be recorded hereafter, before the organization of said county of Douglas, be recorded in the recorder's office of the said county of Coles; and there shall be allowed him, the said commissioner, such sum as his services aforesaid are reasonably worth; to be paid out of the county treasury of the county of Douglas.

"Sec. 13. When the said commissioner shall have completed his work he shall make return of said books to the clerk of the circuit court of said county of Douglas; and they shall thereupon be taken and considered, to all intents and purposes, as books of record of deeds, mortgages and title papers for the county of Douglas; and copies of said papers, certified by the officer having custody of said books, shall be evidence in all courts and places in the same manner that copies of records are evidence in other cases, and with like effect.

"Sec. 14. The county of Douglas shall be responsible for and bound to pay one-fourth of the county debt of the county of Coles, incurred for stock in the Terre Haute & Alton Railroad Company, and shall be entitled to one-fourth of the stock held by said county of Coles in said railroad company; and it shall be the duty of the county court of the county of Douglas, after the 1st of January, A. D. 1860, to pay the interest on the bonds issued by the county of Coles for that purpose, numbered from No. 1 to No. 25, inclusive, semi-annually, as the same shall become due; and also to provide for and pay the principal of said bonds, numbered as above, the same being one-fourth of the said debt of Coles county.

"Sec. 15. That the county of Douglas shall, until otherwise provided for by law, at this or a subsequent session, be attached to and constitute a part of the twenty-fifth representative district, and of the eighteenth senatorial district.

"Sec. 16. The secretary of state shall forthwith furnish the clerk of the county court of the county of Coles with a copy of this act, certified under the seal of state.

"Sec. 17. This act to take effect and be in force from and after its passage.

"Approved February 8, 1859."

A supplementary bill.—This bill was drawn up by A. G. Wallace, assisted by Dr. McKinney, Martin Rice, Coleman Bright, J. B. McCown, W. H. Lamb, J. R. Hammet and others. In its description of boundaries, township 14, of ranges 10, 11 and 14, were omitted in some way, and it soon appeared that the county as described in the act did not contain the required area "of not less than four hundred square miles," whereupon a supplementary act was asked for to cover their deficiency. The defective bill had passed both houses before this vital error was discovered, and only three days of the session remained. Dr. J. W. McKinney, of Camargo, at once started for Springfield, wrote out a supplementary bill adding eighteen sections of land. This was accomplished between ten and twelve o'clock in the morning, and after a deal of hard work the bill was considered in the house, under a suspension of the rules, and read a second time and passed, reported to the senate and again passed, under a suspension of the rules; the bill was signed by the governor at four o'clock and the Doctor, with a copy of it in his possession, was on his way home by six o'clck P. M. the same day. This bill also postponed the day of election and is as follows:

"Whereas it is represented that the county of Douglas, as created by the act to which this is supplementary, does not contain the number of square miles required by the constitution; therefore, in order to perfect the same, and that said county may contain the requisite number of square miles,

"Sec 1. *Be it enacted by the People of the State of Illinois, represented in the General Assembly,* that the folliong described territory, to wit: Sections one (1), two (2), three (3), four (4), five (5), six (6), seven (7), eight (8), nine (9), ten (10), fifteen (15), sixteen (16), seventeen (17), eighteen (18), township No. 14, range No. 10, and section six (6), in township No. 14, range No. 11, and sections four (4), five (5) and six (6), in township No. 14, range No. 14 west, be and the same are hereby declared to be a part of the county of Douglas, as fully and completely, for all purposes whatsoever, as if they had been contained within the boundaries set forth in the act to which this act is supplementary.

"Sec. 2. The election required by the act to which this is supplementary, to be held on the first Monday in March next, shall be held on the third Monday of March, in the manner therein provided.

"Sec. 3. This act shall be in force from and after its passage.

"Approved February 16, 1859."

The partition left the new county with regular outlines, save in the southeast corner, where some fifteen square miles of territory was not included to accommodate the citizens of Oakland an vicinity, who preferred to remain in Coles county, and by this concession the managers of the partition secured their co-operation. As finally formed, Douglas county contained four hundred and eight sections, the area amounting to between four hundred and nine and four hundred and ten square miles, the sections varying in this county considerably in size, the smallest being as low as two hundred and thirty acres, and many running somewhat over one thousand acres. These and other irregularities are occasioned by the inaccuracies of the government surveyors, and the practical limitations of the system.

The new county was now born and christened, and being admitted, the next thing in this case was to see that she was properly clothed, and to this end the first nominating convention for the selection of county officers was held in a board shanty on the McCarty farm, two and one-half miles east of Tuscola. The men put in nomination were selected without regard to party, and the officers who were then elected were:

County judge—James Ewing, still living in Arcola, and the associates were John D. Murdock, now a large land owner in Camargo township, who was again elected in 1861. He filled the position for six years, and had been active in the formation of the new county. And Robert Hopkins, one of the pioneers of Newman township, who was, at the birth of the new county, an associate justice of Coles. Mr. Hopkins died in the spring of 1863, leaving a large unincumbered estate.

The first county clerk was John Chandler, who was a good officer. He was re-elected in 1861, serving in all about six years. Mr. Chandler was one of the most active in the partition, and by reason of a large experience in public business was altogether depended upon for statistics in the interest of the new county. He served in the war with Mexico.

The circuit clerk and recorder, elected at this time, was Andrew G. Wallace, who was re-elected in 1860, 1864 and 1868, holding the office by re-election for over twelve years. Mr. Wallace was one of the first settlers, having arrived in Coles county in 1834, and was one of the first in Tuscola. He died in Tuscola in 1877.

Samuel B. Logan was the first sheriff. Mr. Logan is now a resident of Bourbon, Illinois, and is a large land owner. He was a captain in the Fifty-fourth Regiment, Illinois Volunteers, in the war of 1861.

The office of assessor and treasurer was taken by William Hancock, of Newman township. Mr. Hancock was engaged in banking in the city of Newman, and was a large farmer in Sargent township. He came to this vicinity in November, 1839.

The first county surveyor was Henry C. Niles, who was re-elected in 1861 and again in 1871. Mr. Niles came from Baltimore in 1857.

The first meeting of the county court, as it was called, was held in Camargo, so that the minds of the people might not be prejudiced as between Arcola and Tuscola.

The selection of the county seat, as was to have been expected, was the occasion of much excitement. The cities of Tuscola and Arcola, from their comparatively central position, and both being situated on the only railroad in the county, were the leading contesting points. The village of Camargo had claims to the honor which were strongly advocated, and the well known Hackett's Grove, not far north of the geographical centre of the county, was also talked of. The aspiring embryo cities of Tuscola and Arcola, at the first election, polled probably ten times their legal vote, and the count in these two places being so glaringly preposterous, neither was considered at this time, and the unwritten history of this canvass for county seat will probably remain unwritten during the present generation. At this first meeting of the county court—a special term—April 28, 1859, it was ordered that a special election be held May 30, 1859, to choose a county seat as between the two rival towns, which election resulted in the choice of Tuscola.

Camargo was made county seat *pro tem*, and Mr. W. H. Lamb was appointed commissioner to transfer from Coles county records those necessarily belonging to Douglas. Mr. Lamb had arrived in Camargo in 1853; was a merchant there until 1862, when he became adjutant of the Seventy-ninth Illinois Volunteers in the war of the Rebellion. He was elected county clerk, or clerk of the county court, in 1865, and at the expiration of his term accepted the cashiership of the First National Bank of Tuscola, but now resides in Santiago, California.

The people having, at an election held in November, 1867, decided to adopt township organization, Lucius McAllister, of Arcola, Jos. B. McCown, of Camargo, and Henry B. Evans, of Tuscola, were appointed Commissioners to divide the county into townships, which duty they performed by making the sub-divisions as they now stand. Jos. B. McCown served honouably in the war with Mexico, as also in the Civil war of 1861, when he was colonel of the Sixty-third Illinois Infantry. Col. McCown stood high in the estimation of the people and consequently exercised considerable influence in politics and public business generally. He possessed all the attributes of good citizenship, and his death, November 21, 1869, was much lamented.

H. B. Evans was elected assessor and treasurer in 1865 and re-elected in 1867; as assistant United States marshal in 1870 he procured the Douglas county data for the ninth census, and was postmaster of Tuscola for a number of years.

The first meeting, under township organization, of the board of supervisors, was held in Tuscola, on Monday, May 11, 1868, and the supervisors were: Caleb Garrett, of Garrett; Lemuel Chandler, of Bourbon; Asa T. Whitney, of Arcola; Oliver C. Hackett, of Tuscola; Geo. W. Henson, of Camargo; Benjamin W. Hooe, of Newman; Isaac W. Burget, of Sargent, and Benjamin Bowdre, of "Deer Creek" township, but upon being informed by the state auditor that there was a "Deer Creek" township in Tazewell county, the name was changed to "Bowdre," in honor of its first representative.

In September, the same year, a petition to the board of supervisors was circulated, to which a great many signatures had been obtained, wherein the petitioners endeavored to show their belief that a majority of the voters of the county desired the abolition of township organization.

Camargo township was formerly called Albany precinct, Newman was once Brushy Fork, Garrett township was a part of Bourbon, Bourbon was once North Okaw, Bowdre, once called Deer Creek, was a part of Collins precinct, and Sargent belonged to Oakland precinct.

Joseph G. Cannon came to Tuscola in 1859, the year of the new county; was elected state's attorney in 1861 and again in 1864. He was elected to congress in 1872 and is there now. He resides in Danville.

The first session of circuit court was held in the then just finished depot building of the Illinois Central Railroad, and the first civil case on the docket was Button vs. K. B. Johnson, default of defendant and judgment for three dollars and twenty cents. This was an appeal from Dr. J. T. Johnson, a magistrate in the village of Bouron. Dr. Johnson removed from Bourbon to a point south of Newman, and after a few years went west.

Afterward court was held over J. M. Maris store, on northeast corner of Parke and Sale streets, in which building Mr. Wallace had his office as recorder; at that time this was the largest available room in Tuscola, and after that, until the present permanent court house was built, in the large two-story wooden building which stands opposite the court house on the north. Judge Harlan presided and heard all cases, whilst busily engaged in carving curious toys from soft wood, a habit he rarely laid aside during business hours.

For a while the county clerk's office was in the east end of the hotel, burned in 1864, which occupied the site of the "Stanley House." The original hotel was built by the Town Company, and there seems to be good authority for the statement that the Illinois Central Railroad Company had agreed to put the depot about opposite the site of the court house, say Houghton street, but under a mistake of the person in charge, it got its present location.

The court house was begun under the administration, as a county court, in 1864, of Judge Francis C. Mullen, of Garrett township, assisted by John D. Murdock, of Camargo, and Caleb Bales, of Bourbon, as associates. Judge Mullen was the second county judge of Douglas county; was born in Delaware and came to Garrett township in 1850. Mr. Bales was elected in 1861 associate justice, and in 1872 represented his township as supervisor.

The court house was a brick building of two stories and basement, and contained the jail and living rooms for the sheriff or jailer. It was situated in Block "C," a roomy enough plat of ground, 216x320, in about the centre of Tuscola. The plat was deeded to the county by the original Town Company for the consideration "that a court house of a substantial character should be erected upon it within four years from March 7, 1864. The grounds to be used exclusively for county buildings, and also conditioned that when it ceased to be used for such purposes it should revert to the grantors."

The architect of the building was O. L. Kinney, of Chicago. The original accepted bid for the masonry was fifteen thousand dollars, and the carpenter work was offered for seven thousand and seven hundred dollars. The contractors for the masonry failed to perform their agreement, even after two or three extensions of time, and an advance of twenty per cent. on their contract, which advance was also made to the carpenter. The county board finally took charge of the work and in conjunction with Mr. J. M. Smith, of Tuscola, employed the same builders and others, and brought the work to a conclusion. The entire original cost of the building and furniture was forty-two thousand dollars, the painting, glazing and iron not having been included in any of the bids.

County Officers of Douglas County from its Organization in 1859.

COUNTY CLERKS.

John Chandler, elected April, 1859; re-elected 1861.

William H. Lamb, elected November, 1865.
John C. Parcel, elected November, 1869.
Daniel O. Root, elected November, 1873.
D. A. Conover, November, 1880, died in office February 2, 1899.
E. W. Jeffers, appointed, and is the present incumbent.

CIRCUIT CLERK AND RECORDER.

A. G. Wallace, elected April, 1859.
P. C. Sloan, elected November, 1872.
John N. Outcelt, elected November, 1882.
R. F. Helm, elected November, 1886.
J. W. King, elected in 1890.
C. A. Hawkins, elected in 1898, the present incumbent.

ASSESSOR AND TREASURER.

William Hancock, elected April, 1859.
George W. Flynn, elected November, 1861.
V. C. McNeer, elected November, 1863.
Henry B. Evans, elected November, 1865; re-elected November, 1867.

After township organization the office was called collector and treasurer.

COLLECTOR AND TREASURER.

James T. Walker, elected November, 1869; re-elected November, 1871.
James M. Cox, elected November, 1873.
Henry R. Ingraham, elected November, 1875.
Lines L. Parker, elected 1879.
T. S. Wyeth, elected 1886.
L. E. Root, elected 1890.
James Jones, elected 1894.
Henry C. Jones, elected 1898, the present incumbent.

SHERIFF.

Samuel B. Logan, elected April, 1859.
Parmenas Watson, elected November, 1860.

William T. French, elected November, 1862.

Isaac L. Jordon, elected November, 1864.

Henry C. Carico, elected November, 1866.

N. Rice Gruelle, elected November, 1868.

Newton I. Cooper, elected November, 1870.

James H. Shawhan, elected November, 1871.

Francis G. Cunningham, elected November, 1872; re-elected November, 1874; re-elected in 1876, and died in office.

Col. Wesford Taggart, elected 1880.

T. S. Wyeth, elected 1886.

John L. Goff, elected 1890.

J. C. Cutler, elected 1894.

F. D. Bagley, elected 1898, died in office May 20, 1898. F. T. Spies, M. D., then coroner, served out Bagley's time until the next general election.

C. A. Moon, elected 1898, the present incumbent.

SUPERINTENDENT SCHOOLS.

Wm. H. Sipple, elected April, 1859.

S. S. Irwin, elected November, 1861.

J. Frank Lamb, elected November, 1863.

W. W. Monroe, elected November, 1865.

Samuel T. Callaway, elected November, 1869; re-elected November, 1873.

C. W. Woolverton, appointed September, 1875.

J. W. King, elected November, 1875. Mr. King resigned to accept post office appointment at Newman and was succeeded by appointment of F. E. A. Starr.

Joseph R. Burres served from 1882 to 1886.

Nora Smith, 1894.

Mamie Bunch, 1898.

Thomas M. Wells, a most worthy young man, who was elected by an overwhelming vote in 1898, and was killed in a railroad wreck two weeks after being sworn into office.

On March 9, 1899, Blanche Caraway was appointed and is the present incumbent.

COUNTY SURVEYOR.

Henry C. Niles, elected April, 1859, re-elected November, 1861.

Issachar Davis, elected November, 1863.

Enos C. Siler, elected November, 1865.

Issachar Davis, elected November, 1867.

Edmund Fish, elected November, 1869.

Henry C. Niles, elected November, 1871.

Issachar Davis, elected November, 1875.

H. C. Niles, elected 1883.

Wm. E. Price was elected in 1883 and is the present incumbent.

MASTER IN CHANCERY.

Andrew J. Wallace, 1859 to 1880, and was also Circuit Clerk during the time. After his death, in 1880, A. B. Powell served six months, when, in 1881, H. C. Niles was appointed and has since filled that office satisfactorily.

System of surveys.—To one not informed in regard to the principles of the government survey, the map of Douglas county presents a good many difficulties, and it may not be unprofitable to devote a page to this subject. The rectangular system adopted by the United States is peculiar to the public lands of the government, and was devised for the old Northwest. Meridian lines running due north from the mouth of some river are first established. These are intersected at right angles by a base line, running east and west, and arbitrarily located. The meridian lines are known as "principal meridians," the first one being a line running due north from the mouth of the Miami river, and forming the east line of Indiana. The second principal meridian is a line running due north from the Little Blue river, eighty-nine miles west of the former, and near the central part of the state of Indiana. The third principal meridian is a line running due north from the mouth of the Ohio river, and the fourth principal meridian is a line running due north from the mouth of the Illinois river. The base line from which the survey of Indiana was projected, and all of Illinois east of the Illinois river, crosses the state in latitude thirty-eight degrees and thirty minutes. With these principal lines established, the surveyors began at the intersection of the base line and a principal meridian line, and projected meridian lines, at intervals of one mile, parallel with the principal one, working eastwardly and westwardly from a given "principal meridian." Lines at right angles to these were run in similar manner, working northwardly and southwardly from the base line. In running the north and south lines, owing to the shape of the earth, these are found to converge, and sub-base lines were established at intervals of twenty-four miles north of the base line and thirty miles below it, from which the line was begun afresh after accurate measurements east and west were obtained. At each of these "correction lines" a jog in the meridian-parallels will be observed, which shows the error due to convergence of lines. These jogs are known to surveyors as "fallings," i. e., falling to the right or left of the true corner, at the end of the line run. In surveying east and west from the several established principal meridians another "fault" is found in actual practice. The distance between these principal meridians is such as to leave a narrow strip of land between the survey proceeding west (for example) from the third and east from the fourth principal meridian, and the east and west lines from either meridian are not found to exactly coincide at the meeting point.

In actual surveying the first lines were run each way at intervals of six miles, dividing the country into "congressional townships." These townships were subsequently subdivided into sections by lines at an interval of one mile by other surveyors, the law making it illegal for the same surveyor to run both sets of lines, so that one might be a check upon the errors of the other. The land was first offered for sale by sections, but this was found to work disadvantageously to settlers, and these sections, containing six hundred and forty acres, were subdivided into halves of three hundred and twenty acres, and quarters of one hundred and sixty acres each, which last were again subdivided in halves of eighty acres, and quarters of forty acres each. "Fractions" are parts of sections intersected by rivers, or confirmed claims or reservations, and are of various sizes. The sections of a township are designated by numbers, beginning with the northeast corner and following in regular order to the west side, the second tier of sections beginning on the west side of the township and proceeding east, using the numbers from one to thirty-six inclusive.

Townships are designated by numerals increasing north and south from the base line, and are still further defined by ranges numbered east and west from the principal meridian, and both are required together with the further description of north or south, and east or west to accurately locate it.

The survey of Illinois was made from about 1812 to 1824, and presents some exceptions to the above rules. South of the base line both townships and ranges are regular, and north of it, to the southern boundary of township 31, east of the Illinois river. A portion of the state, east of a line running due north from the mouth of the Wabash river to, the southern line of township 31 north, was surveyed west from the second principal meridian, and ranges are numbered westward as high as fourteen; the ranges eastward from the third principal meridian reaching number eleven, the last one consisting of but a single section in width. Above township 30, the ranges extend east from the fourth principal meridian to the eastern line of the state, and reach the number of sixteen. West of the third principal meridian the ranges run regularly to the Mississippi and Illinois rivers so far north as the point where the third principal meridian crosses the Illinois river, where the ranges west cease. The townships are regular, extending south to number 16, and north to number 46. North of township 33 north, the townships on the east side of the third principal meridian only proceed regularly. That part of the state lying west of the Illinois river, and north of the Illinois river and west of the third principal meridian, is surveyed from the fourth principal meridian. The base line for this survey is a line running due west from the point where the third principal meridian crosses the Illinois river and passes just south of Beardstown. The townships extend south from this line to number 14, and north to number 29. The ranges number 9 west and 11 east, the last being fractional. North of the Illinois river the ranges are numbered east from the fourth principal meridian up to the third principal meridian.

In Douglas county the peculiarities of the survey are nearly all exemplified. The jog or "falling" in Newman and Garrett townships shows the presence of the correction line; range 11 east, in Newman and in Sargent townships, shows the result of the independent surveys, eastward from the third principal meridian and westward from the second principal meridian, and in range 11 east, the southern line of township 15 north shows the slight variation in the east and west lines of the two surveys. The long sections in the north tier of township 15, clear through Douglas county, were the result of the arbitrary placing of the correction line; the township surveyor, having found the extra half-mile on closing on his standard or correction line, threw it into lots and so recorded it. Many contradictions between the record and actual measurement are found, but the rule is established that where the original corners can be found they are unalterable, and remain under the law as the true corners they were intended to represent, even though not exactly where strict professional care might have placed them in the first instance. Missing corners must be re-established in the identical localities they originally occupied, and when the spot cannot be determined by existing landmarks in the field, resort must be had to the field notes of the original survey. The history of the first survey of Douglas county is not complete, but township 16, range 8, was surveyed by John Messinger, April, 1821; township 15, range 9, by W. L. May, in May, 1821; townships 14 and 15, in range 8, by C. McK.

Hamtranck, who subdivided township 15, range 9, into sections in June, 1821.

Topography and geology.—Douglas county lies about midway between the north and south limits in eastern Illinois. It is bounded on the north by Champaign, on the east by Edgar, on the south by Coles and on the west by Moultrie and Piatt. It lies on the divide between the hydrographic basins of the Wabash and Kaskaskia rivers, sending its surface drainage through the Embarrass to the one and through the Okaw to the other. The Embarrass, popularly pronounced "Ambraw" through a corruption of the French, takes its rise near Tolono, in Champaign county, and, flowing southeasterly through this county, proceeds in its meanderings some ninety miles before it reaches the Wabash in Lawrence county. It was marked Fox river in the government survey, but the French name seems to have outlived it. It is said that this name had its origin with the original settlers at Vincennes, who found the marshy margins of that river in that region a great embarrassment to early travel. The Okaw is the head waters of the Kaskaskia, and rises in Champaign county. Flowing nearly a direct south course, it passes through Garrett and Bourbon townships, and thence southwesterly to the Mississippi river in Randolph county, after a meandering course of three hundred miles. The regular tributaries to these streams are few, the Embarrass receiving the Brushy Fork from the northeast, a small creek draining the southeast corner of Newman and the northwest corner of Sargent townships; Deer Creek, a prairie creek flowing nearly directly east, and joining the main stream on the line of section 33, in Sargent township; and Scattering Fork, a tributary which divides into three branches, which extend through Tuscola township, about a mile apart, and traverse the township in a southeasterly direction. The tributaries of the Okaw are all on the west side of the river in this county, and all have a southeasterly course. There are three only, Dry Fork, Lake Fork and Big Slough, joining the main stream at points about five miles apart, and are characteristically named.

The whole area of the county is covered so deeply with drift clays that there is no outcrop of the underlying coal measure strata. From the exposures in the adjoining counties, it is known that the underlying beds belong to the upper coal measures, and probably include two or three of the upper coals, but the extent to which they are developed here can only be determined with the drill. It is not probable that any heavy bed of coal will be found short of six hundred or eight hundred feet from the surface, though one of the upper seams, two or three feet thick, might be found at a moderate depth. The drift clays are found here at nearly their maximum thickness, but only the upper part of this deposit is to be seen in the natural outcrops in the bluffs of the streams. Bowlders are rarely found of any great size in the county, and in many parts they are unknown. In other sections, however, there are enough, weighing from one to five hundred pounds, to add some difficulty to the tilling of the soil. The largest specimen of this rock stands in the southeast corner of section 28, township 16, range 7. It protrudes considerably above the ground, showing some one thousand cubic feet. Water is generally obtained of fair quality at a depth of twenty or thirty feet. Upon section 33, township 16, range 9, in Camargo township, is a fine fountain of living water, widely known as "Patterson's Spring;" a similar one near the Okaw on section 14, township 16, range 7, is called the "Sulphur Spring," and another is in Hackett's Grove, section 31, township 16, range 9, the overflow of which finally reaches the Embarrass, through Scattering Fork. The soil is mainly a deep, black, vegetable mold, characteristic of the prairie lands throughout the central portions of the state. On the timber lands the soil is a light grayish clay, rather better adapted to wheat growing than the prairie soil.

The swamp lands.—Douglas county is situated on the Grand Prairie, and is generally a low, level tract of country. This fact greatly retarded its early settlement, as a large proportion of its area was covered with water during certain portions of the year. Cultivation has done much to remedy this evil, but the task of draining so large an area, where but few good natural outlets exist, has been a slow work. In addition to this general character of this region, there was a large area in the county, as well as throughout the central portion of the state, of swamp or overflowed lands. On the 28th of September, 1850, the general government granted to the several states the whole of these lands, "made unfit thereby for cultivation, and remaining unsold" on or after that date. On March 2, 1855, "An act for the relief of purchasers and locators of swamp and overflowed lands," provided upon proof by the authorized agent of the state, before the commissioner of the general land office, that any of the lands purchased by any person from the United States, prior to the passage of this act (March 2, 1855), were swamp lands within the true intent and meaning of the act of September 28, 1850, "the purchase money shall be paid over to the state wherein said land is situated; and when the lands have been located by warrant or scrip, the said state shall be authorized to locate a like quantity of any public lands, subject to entry, at one dollar and twenty-five cents per acre or less, and patents shall issue therefor." By an act approved March 3, 1857, "all lands selected and reported to the general land office," under the above recited laws, were "confirmed to said states respectively so far as the same remained vacant, unappropriated and not interfered with by an actual settlement under any law of the United States."

Under the act of 1855, indemnity for lands disposed of by the United States on scrip or warrant was sought to be secured out of lands outside of the state limits, but the interior department decided (February 5, 1866) that "such indemnity must be limited to the state in which the original selections were situated, and as there are no public lands in Illinois with which to satisfy such awards, if made, this office declines to take cases as the one in question into consideration." On April 12, 1881, the department rendered a decision to the effect that "the right of indemnity under existing laws goes only to sales made prior to March 3, 1857; for sales subsequent to this latter date no indemnity is now provided." Another question arising under these acts, in which Douglas county, with certain others, has a peculiar interest, relates to the original grant to the Illinois Central Railway Company. These lands were granted by the general government by an act approved March 20, 1850, and conveyed every alternate section, designated by even numbers, for six sections in width on each side of the road. Applications for indemnity for certain lands within the six miles limit of this grant were denied by the department in November, 1855, on the ground "that those lands which had been removed by the president under the act of September 20, 1850, did not pass to the state by virtue of the swamp land act." This decision has been repeatedly re-affirmed, and as late as 1881 efforts are being made to set aside the effect of these several decisions by congressional action, and until such remedial legislation is accomplished, Tuscola and Arcola townships will not be able to recover any indemnity for swamp lands.

It will be observed that under existing laws and decisions of the department of the interior, only the cash indemnity is available to Illinois claimants, and that only on lands erroneously disposed of by the United States between September 20, 1850, and March 3, 1857. In most of the counties in Illinois, the original selections of swamp lands were incomplete, for the reason that the county authorities who selected them under instructions of the governor failed in most cases to list any swamp lands which had been entered prior to the actual date of the selection. But few of these selections were made prior to 1852, and most of them not until 1853, so that the new selections are made to include all swamp lands entered after September 20, 1850, and not previously reported. Douglas county has filed its claim and proofs for some six thousand acres, but has only received two thousand, eight hundred and fifty-one dollars and twenty-one cents, which is as yet unappropriated.

Agriculture.—Douglas is a purely agricultural county. The prime essentials of cheap coal, constant water-power and abundance of timber all seem to be lacking in quantities adequate for manufacturing purposes. The different streams of the county are all fringed with a good growth of timber, which includes the usual varieties of this latitude, such as white, black, Spanish and red oaks, shelbark and white hickory, sugar and white maple, white and red (slippery) elm, black and honey locust, white and black walnut, swamp and upland ash, sycamore, cottonwood, mulberry and wild cherry. Since the land has been under cultivation, considerable timber has been added by the cultivation of forest trees on the prairie, to the success of which numerous groves about the county bear witness. Wood is still the principal fuel and is hauled to the various villages in considerable quantities. The varieties generally used are hickory and oak, and bring prices varying from four to five dollars per cord. Since the building of the east and west railroads, coal has come largely into use, not only in the town, but among the farmers also, and will eventually supplant wood as fuel. The coal used is generally the bituminous variety, of Indiana, and is sold at about three dollars and a half per ton. No generally observed system of agriculture is followed by the farmers here. Average success has yielded too liberal returns to make a study of the scientific principles underlying this industry seem a necessity, and many innovations have been introduced in farming methods during the last twenty years. The pioneer farmer had enough to engage his attention and resources in providing a plain subsistence for his family, and did little in the way of improved methods of cultivation, but with the rude, careless method in vogue, the land yielded considerably in excess of the home demand, and in the absence of any profitable market there was no sufficient inducement to increase the annual product by increased care and system. The first settlers began their improvement in the timber, and the scarcity of this in the county greatly delayed its development. It was not until the building of the Illinois Central Railroad that the prairie land began to be taken up for cultivation, and then the great obstacle of its low, wet character retarded the movement. For some years this was borne with as beyond remedy, or at least not to be improved save by years of cultivation. Up to about 1878 the farming interests suffered very much from this cause, many farmers selling their property after several successive annual failures and moving to drier locations in the west. The new purchasers were generally men of some capital, who at once grappled with the evil, and by a system of drainage favored by good seasons revolutionized farming interests and made Douglas county as good an agricultural region as is found in the state. Tiles are most extensively used and the soil is richly productive and does not need enriching by artificial means. Commercial fertilizers are unknown here, and even the accumulations of the barnyard are not preserved with care and seldom used. The lack of demand for its use is the prime reason for this waste, but the large demands upon the prairie farmer's time is also a notable factor in this matter. There is a time in the spring when the hauling and scattering of manure might be done without the neglect of other duties, but in this latitude the soil is generally at this time so soft that it is considered unwise to cut it up with the wagon. The fertility of the soil has led to the practice of cropping the same field for twelve or fifteen years in succession, but this practice has of late years given way to a more or less systematic rotation of crops which is found to be advantageous.

The great staple of the county is corn. This is usually the first crop planted on sod ground, and generally is succeeded by a second crop, and then by wheat. The ground is generally well prepared and the seed put in by a two-horse machine. The rows are laid out regularly both ways, and the crop is generally well cultivated. This is principally done with the double cultivator passing in both directions and continued until the plant is some four feet high or begins to "joint," when the crop is "laid by." The farms are generally large, averaging throughout the county from one hundred and sixty acres to two hundred acres, and the usual amount of help available will not permit further care, even if it was deemed necessary. More care is not, however, considered of any advantage. Corn is husked from the standing stalk, a wagon being driven along one side and two rows taken at a time, the ear being stripped, broken off and thrown in the wagon to be transferred to the crib. This harvesting is generally done in November, but it is often late in the following month before the crop is all housed. Many of the cribs are mere temporary structures designed for the season's yield, and are built at the most convenient point. The present season has been especially unfavorable for housing corn. The warm wet weather has prevented the grain from hardening and drying, and some have been obliged to put lines of tile through the body of the grain to give it air to dry. The different towns about afford good marketing facilities, and it is generally disposed of in the ear, but few steam shellers being found in the county. A large proportion of the yield is fed to stock, but a still larger proportion, perhaps, is shipped away and forms an important source of revenue.

Wheat is an important product of the county. In an early day this was thought to be ill-adapted to the soil and climate and was only found to succeed on the sod ground of the timber lands. Continued cultivation and the careful choice of seed has developed the fact that it can be grown anywhere with fair success, though many still hold that it is more productive on the soil of the timber belt. While it is found to do well on sod ground, is generally sown on corn stubble. In this case it is usually drilled in with a single-horse machine of five hoes between the rows. When sown otherwise, the ground is carefully prepared and the seed put in with a two-horse drill. The grain is threshed in the field, the steam-power and horse-power thresher being in about equal use and favor. The straw was, some years ago, generally burned, but a more economical method has since come in vogue, and the straw stack generally left open to stock, which are found to thrive in an open winter with very little other feeding. The sales of wheat each year reach a high figure and find the general market through the elevators which are found at each of the principal villages of the county. Oats are grown to a considerable extent, and form a considerable part of marketable product of the county.

ILLINOIS CENTRAL RAILROAD.

This road was completed through Douglas county in 1855, the charter having been granted by act of congress in 1850. This was the first public work that received subsidies of land from the United States government. The matter was engineered by Stephen A. Douglas, at that time United States senator, in which enterprise he had the task of reconciling and combining in favor of the measure the influence of both Benton and Clay, who were strongly opposed to each other in everything else. Mr. Clay said in a speech that he "had traveled these prairies for days at a time and never saw a tree as large as a walking stick." Douglas turned to Benton and said, "He never was on a prairie in his life, and on our prairies you are never out of sight of timber a minute."

This road was granted every alternate section of land, designated by even numbers, for six miles on either side of the track, afterward increased by a further grant of the alternate sections within fifteen miles of the track on each side of the road and its branches, all even numbered sections, except section 16, which was reserved for schools and also excepting lands occupied by actual settlers. The United States lands had been selling for one dollar and twenty-five cents per acre and the price of the remaining lands was immediately doubled, and some are said to have sold as high as five and six dollars per acre.

The government reserved the privilege of transportation, free of toll or other charge, of any property or troops of the United States, and a condition was, that the road should be completed in ten years, and the company, by act of assembly, to pay into the state treasury five per cent. of the gross earnings of the road for all future time, and also, three-fourths of one per cent. of stock and assets, or enough to make at least seven per cent. of the gross earnings, a perpetual revenue to the state; and the lands were to be free from taxation until they had been sold and conveyed. By the charter road is free from local and municipal taxation. The number of acres granted to this road in the state was two million, five hundred and ninety-five thousand.

The relative elevations of points along the line of this road in the county are as follows:

The south line of the county	303.0
Arcola station	303.7
Bourbon Switch	279.3
Tuscola station	285.3
North line of county	332.7

This makes Arcola 18.4 feet higher than Tuscola, on the line of the road. The north line of the county is the highest point, but one, between Centralia and Champaign, the highest point being two miles north of Tolono. It is notable, however, in connection with these facts, that Tuscola is conspicuous from the surrounding country, which is not the fact in the case of Arcola, and may be owing to some extent to the elevation of some buildings, as the court house and seminary. These figures apply to this railroad only. It will not do to compare them as they stand with comparative elevations upon other roads in the county.

THE INDIANAPOLIS, DECATUR & WESTERN RAILWAY.

This road traverses the county from east to west, north of the middle, in township 16 and near the middle of Newman, Camargo, Tuscola and Garrett townships, intersecting the Illinois Central at Tuscola, the county seat. It was finished through the county in 1872. The charter of the Indiana & Illinois Central Railroad Company, of Indiana, bears date of December 30, 1852; that of the Decatur & Indianapolis was dated March 21, 1853, and these were consolidated in 1854, forming the I., D. & W. Railway, the road receiving its present name under reorganization in 1876.

In 1868, Douglas county purchased 2,459 shares of the capital stock of the company and there was issued to the county a certificate for the shares. These were at a par value of $122,950 and were purchased of private parties in Indianapolis for $20,000. The transaction was conducted by T. H. Macoughtry, Malden Jones, and Thomas S. Sluss, and reported to April term of county court, 1868. In 1872 the county issued to the company $80,000 in bonds, with interest at ten per cent., payable annually, principal payable in twenty years, reserving the right to pay the principal after eight years; this in accordance with the will of the electors, as expressed at the polls July 15, 1869. There was also subscribed in aid of this road, by a vote of the people in Newman township, $12,000; Camargo township, $15,000; Tuscola township, $20,000; Garrett township, $13,000; making an aggregate of $60,000, payable in fourteen years, with interest at ten per cent. Pending the building of the road large quantities of lands had been acquired by the company, long its line in this and other counties, in subscriptions of private parties for stock.

The relative elevations of points along the line of this road, in the county, are as follows:

East line of county	247
Newman	238
One mile east of Camargo	268
Two miles west of Camargo	268

Tuscola 251
Atwood, west line of county..... 257

THE ILLINOIS MIDLAND RAILWAY.

This line traverses the county from east to west, in the south part, crossing the Illinois Central at Arcola. It was originally an enterprise of citizens of Arcola and the vicinity, and was first called the Paris & Decatur. Upon the extension of the line to Terre Haute, the name of that city was prefixed, and, finally, a further addition was made to Peoria. It is now operated by the Vandalia system. The first train passed over this road October 25, 1872.

THE DANVILLE, TUSCOLA & WESTERN RAILROAD.

This road was instituted by Tuscola people, materially aided by influential parties in Douglas and Vermilion counties. It runs in a northeast direction from Tuscola, leaving Douglas county in the northeast part of Camargo township, thence through parts of Champaign and Vermilion counties to the ancient town of Dallas, and to Danville. The preliminary surveying was done upon this line in January, 1872, and ground broken the following April. It is now the Chicago & Eastern Illinois, running from Chicago to St. Louis.

Other roads have been proposed which were designed to cross the county in some part, as a road from Pana to Tolono, through Garrett township; a Mattoon & Danville, through Bowdre and Newman, and a Charleston & Danville, touching Sargent township, all of which have had preliminary surveys. Another proposed road is

THE TOLEDO & ST. LOUIS,

Which runs in a southwesterly direction from Arcola, has been graded for several miles. In October, 1871, delegations from Arcola and Tuscola met in Shelbyville, in the interests of this road and that of their respective towns; this, of course, was whilst the Illinois Central was the only railroad in the county.

PROPORTION OF INDEBTEDNESS ASSUMED.

In the act creating the county of Douglas, the new county became responsible for one-fourth part of the indebtedness of Coles county to the Terre Haute & Alton Railroad, and accordingly, at a special meeting of the county board, January 8, 1868, the county purchased of John Monroe, of Coles county, bonds numbers 1 to 15 inclusive amounting to $19,070.98, and also paid interest on a remaining $10,000, amounting to $7,800, and since, about $12,500 of interest and principal, making a total cost to the county, in the transaction, of $39,370.98. Coles county had taken $100,000 in the stock of the road, now called the I. & St. L.

THE MILITARY RECORD

OF

DOUGLAS COUNTY.

CHAPTER III.

THE MILITARY RECORD OF DOUGLAS COUNTY.

PUBLIC SENTIMENT AND CIVIL ACTION.

The war of the Rebellion is a great landmark in the history of the nation. It is a no less important one in the history of Douglas county. In its early history the winter of the "great snow" measured the perspective of receding years, but in the maturer age "the war" marked the turning of a new page. In those years of national trial there was scarcely a family in the county that was not called upon to do and suffer for the common weal, and many a heart sorrow or the foundation of a prosperous fortune dates back to those fateful years.

The political events which preceded the war found many anxious watchers here. The senatorial campaign of 1858, with the succeeding presidential contest of 1860, in both of which Lincoln was the exponent of principles then in the ascendancy in Douglas county, served to fix the attention of this section upon the political storm which seemed to be gathering with portentious mutterings over the southern portions of the country. It is doubtful whether hope or fear predominated in the minds of the people as the day approached when Lincoln was to be inaugurated, but the hope and expectation of the great majority was that, in his grasp, the serpent of secession would be strangled, as Jackson had done before in the case of the "Nullifiers." It was in this state of vacillation between hope and fear, that the reverberations of Fort Sumter's guns assailed the ears of the eager North. It was this explosion, echoing round the world, that united the various political elements, and made men Union or non-Union. Niceties of political distinctions were almost entirely lost sight of, and while the change of front was too sudden and radical to secure the adhesion of all to one party, Douglas county, in the main, presented but one sentiment, and that for the support of the Union. Saturday, April 13, 1861, Fort Sumter surrendered. The news spread over the country and Douglas county responded to the call for troops with a patriotic enthusiasm not excelled by any community in the state. Volunteering for the service was spirited, and prominent in the efforts to secure troops for the defense of the Union should be mentioned the names of E. McCarty and J. B. McCown.

It was not until the second year of the war that the county took official action to aid enlistments. In July, 1862, the county court passed an order "for the purpose of aiding in enlistment of volunteers for the United States service to be raised in the county of Douglas; for the support of the families of those who have heretofore enlisted from Douglas county." By this order the sum of $2,000 was appropriated, or as much as necessary for the purpose. At the same time, to carry out the intention of this appropriation, it was further ordered "that the justices of the peace of the county be invited and requested to act in concert with the court in carrying out this laudable intention, by acting promptly in this matter, by ascertaining and reporting to the clerk of this court the names of all volunteers who were or are residents of their respective precincts at the time of entering the service, showing separately the names of all those leaving wives and families or others dependent upon them for a livelihood and support. The said justices shall from time to time keep themselves advised of the condition and wants of all such families as far as the comforts and necessaries of life are concerned, and shall make arrangements with some merchant, or merchants, grocer or grocerymen, to furnish the said families and persons dependent, as aforesaid, with the said necessaries, using due caution and circumspection with an eye to economy, reporting their acts and doings in the premises to this court at each regular meeting of the board, together with the bills made for said support, properly certified to by them, for allowance as other claims by the court; and further to do and perform what other duties may become necessary as time may suggest in the premises." A regular tax was subsequently levied for this purpose, and in December, 1864, it was ordered "that Gilbert Summe be appointed agent, whose duty it shall be to visit all such destitute families and ascertain their exact condition, and supply their wants by giving orders to grocers and merchants for such groceries or clothing as their wants may require, specifying definitely the quantity of each item and article, using all due care and circumspection with an eye to strict economy, and keeping a just and correct account by copy of each order, in whose favor drawn, and to whom the order may be sent. It shall be the duty of said agent further to agree with some merchant or merchants, grocer or grocers, to supply the said volunteers families with such things as they may require at a reduction on their customary rates of sale, if such an arrangement be possible." The tax reached one and a quarter mills upon the dollar for this purpose, and the method of disbursing it was changed so as to pay each wife or mother of volunteers $1 per week, and fifty cents per week for each child under ten years of age. What sum the county expended in this way does not appear in the state reports, and no reliable estimate can be made of it, but it was a very considerable sum, and does honor to the loyal, generous sentiment of the county. No bounties were offered by the county. In fact, there seemed no necessity for this expenditure to stimulate enlistments, the county promptly meeting the demands made upon it and filling its quota without resort to draft. The population of Douglas county in 1860 was 7,109; the enrollment showed, in 1863, 1,491 men subject to military duty, and 1,803 in 1864, and 1,846 in January, 1865. The quota of the county in 1861 was 199 men; in 1862, 136; under the calls of February 1 and March 14, 1864, for an aggregate of 700,000 men, Douglas county's quota was 336, and under the call of July 18, 1864, for 500,000, it was 281, making a total of 952 men as the quota of the county prior to December 31, 1864. Up to this period the enlistment had reached 1,008, making an excess of 56 men. Under the last call, December 31, 1865, the quota was 225, and the enlistments 167, making the grand total of quotas: For the war, 1,177, and the credits, 1,175, a deficit of 2 men. It is probable, however, that instead of a small deficit, Douglas county furnished more than her quota, if all who volunteered from it had found their names placed to its credit.

The first full company—D, Twenty-first Illinois—went out under the command of Capt. James E. Callaway, of Tuscola, who became lieutenant-colonel. President Grant was the first colonel of this regiment. B. Frank Reed, of Bowdre township, was also a captain of this company. He died in September, 1865, of wounds received at Chickamauga. William Brian was the first captain of Company H, Twenty-fifth Regiment. Four companies were made up for the Seventy-ninth, Allen Buckner, of Arcola, being the colonel. A. Van Deren, of Tuscola, was captain of Company B; William A. Low, of Newman, was captain of Company E; Oliver O. Bagley, of Camargo, was captain of Company G, and Dr. H. D. Martin, of Arcola, was captain of Company K. Dr. Martin died of wounds received at Liberty Gap, June 25, 1863. Gilbert Summe, of Tuscola, was captain of Company A, Seventy-ninth Illinois, a three months' regiment. Derrick Lamb, of Tuscola, was captain of Company F, One Hundred and Forty-ninth, and afterward of Company G, One Hundred and Thirty-fifth. J. M. Maris, of Tuscola, was quartermaster in the Sixty-third Regiment. J. B. McCown, of Camargo, was colonel of the Sixty-third, in which regiment J. W. McKinney was surgeon. W. H. Lamb, of Tuscola, was adjutant of the Seventy-ninth. Wesford Taggart, of Tuscola, was lieutenant-colonel of the Twenty-fifth. Dr. J. L. Reat was surgeon of the Twenty-first. Henry Von Trebra, of Arcola, was colonel of the Thirty-second Indiana. He died in Arcola in August, 1863. Simeon Paddleford, of Tuscola, was a quartermaster in the Twenty-first Illinois. Douglas county was represented by a few men in each of the regiments, Twenty-third, Fifty-seventh, One Hundred and Fifty-fourth Illinois Infantry, in the Second, Fifth and Tenth Illinois Cavalry, and the Chicago Light Artillery. In the Twenty-first, Twenty-fifth, Fifty-fourth, Seventy-ninth, One Hundred and Thirty-fifth, One Hundred and Forty-ninth Illinois Infantry and Thirteenth Illinois Cavarly there were larger representations, and a more extended notice of the regiments' career is subjoined from the adjutant general's report.

TWENTY-FIRST ILLINOIS INFANTRY

The first of Douglas county's contributions to the war went out in Company D, of the Twenty-first Regiment. The officers of this company were as follows:

Captains—J. E. Callaway, till September 19, 1862; B. F. Reed, till September 22, 1863; J. T. Kirkman, till June 7, 1864; P. A. Cord, til muster out of regiment.

First Lieutenants—B. F. Reed, till September 19, 1862; Simeon Paddleford, till August 18, 1864; J. W. Pierce, till May 13, 1865; S. H. Ford.

Second Lieutenants—J. T. Kirkman, till September 19, 1862; Lawrence McGrath, not mustered.

Enlisted men from Douglas county were:
First Sergeant—G. P. Barlow.

Sergeants—C. A. Coykendall, died at Tuscola, January 10, 1865; F. T. Westfall, Simeon Paddleford, promoted first lieutenant; Cornelius Hopkins.

Corporals—John Welliver, promoted sergeant; Evan Callentine; S. A. Albin, died January 1, 1863; of wounds; P. A. Cord, W. W. Watson, James Gillogy; Simon Childers, died April 1, 1862; John Pence.

Musicians—J. R. Eldred, William Mitchell.

Wagoner—B. F. Owings.

Privates—S. Ayres; J. C. Ackerman, killed at Stone River, January 1, 1863; W. Avery, died May 4, 1864, prisoner of war; L. P. Bunting, killed at Stone River January 1, 1863; R. B. Bostwick; D. W. Barnett, died January 27, 1864, prisoner of war; W. S. Brasselton, died March 1, 1863; W. W. Bagley; J. E. Bagley, died July 4, 1864, prisoner of war; C. Burns, J. Byers, killed at Stone River, January 1, 1863; J. W. Barrum, J. W. Brinnegar, E. Coffin, S. C. Clubb; I. S. Cross, died September 6, 1864, prisoner of war; J. Condit, J. Coslet, W. C. Coslet, F. M. Daniels, John Daniels, Steven Daniels, G. W. Doyle; L. J. Day, killed at Chickamauga, September 20, 1863; G. Earl, S. H. Ford, William Friddle, G. M. Grace, W. W. Grace; Jacob Good, died January 23, 1863; A. Geer, E. Hollingsworth, D. Haines, Thomas Haines, R. B. Hoofman; G. Helmick, died March 28, 1862; William Hill, A. Hagaman, J. Hornback; Thomas Keaton, died November 21, 1861; William Leston, S. A. Lindsay, John Lyons, N. B. Modissett, Charles Montgomery; L. McDowell, died August 1, 1863; F. Mary, Thomas McGuire, J. D. Maddox, J. N. Neal; E. H. Neal, promoted corporal, died January 9, 1864, prisoner of war; Henry Otten, J. Osborne; A. H. Perry, drowned at Pittman's Ferry, Mary 14, 1862; J. W. Pierce, H. R. Potts, William Polk, J. J. G. Russell, John Robinett, William Riley; Levi Romine, died February 16, 1863; J. Riney, H. Shoap, W. N. Saintford, J. Skinner, G. W. Snyder, B. F. Shook, J. Shireman; W. H. Smallwood, died January 16, 1863, of wounds; J. Tedrow, I. D. Van Meter, R. P. West, John Waters, G. W. White, H. Warren, William Wamsley.

Veterans—S. D. Ayers, C. Burns, R. B. Bostwick; P. A. Cord, promoted captain; J. Condict, promoted corporal; F. M. Daniels, Q. Ellis; S. H. Ford, promoted first lieutenant; William Friddle; G. M. Grace, promoted corporal; E. Hollingsworth, D. Haines, T. W. Haines, William Hill; W. H. Liston, promoted sergeant; A. A. Lindsay, Thomas McGuire, William Mitchell; L. McGrath, promoted first sergeant; A. J. Newport, B. F. Owings; J. W. Pierce, promoted first lieutenant; J. C. Still, John Waters, W. W. Watson.

Recruits—S. C. Bagley, died April 24, 1864, prisoner of war; Q. Ellis, C. C. Lee; W. P. Liston, died October 8, 1863, from wounds; L. McGrath; I. W. Noel, killed at Stone River,

December 30, 1862; J. Nell; Thomas Owens, died May 28, 1862; A. N. Protzman, Gilby Sipple, Thomas Wamsley, J. W. Watson, J. M. Wyckoff.

The regiment was organized in the seventh congressional district, and was rendezvoused at Mattoon, Illinois. On the 15th of May, 1861, it was mustered into the state service for thirty days, by Capt. U. S. Grant. On the 28th of June it was mustered into the United States service, with Capt. U. S. Grant as colonel. A letter from Gen. Grant gives the history of his connection with the regiment as follows: "I was appointed colonel of the Twenty-first Illinois Volunteer Infantry, by Gov. Richard Yates, some time early in the month of June, 1861, and assumed command of the regiment on the 16th of that month. The regiment was mustered into the service of the United States in the latter part of the same month. Being ordered to rendezvous the regiment at Quincy, Illinois, I thought, for the purpose of discipline and speedy efficiency for the field, it would be well to march the regiment across the country, instead of transporting by rail. Accordingly, on the 3rd of July, 1861, the march was commenced from Camp Yates, Springfield, Illinois, and continued until about three miles beyond the Illinois river, when dispatches were received, changing the destination of the regiment to Ironton, Missouri, and directing me to return to the river and take a steamer, which had been sent there for the purpose of transporting the regiment to St. Louis. The steamer failing to reach the point of embarkation, several days were here lost. In the meantime a portion of the Sixteenth Illinois Infantry, under Col. Smith, was reported surrounded by the enemy at a point on the Hannibal & St. Joseph Railroad, west of Palmyra, and the Twenty-first was ordered to their relief. Under these circumstances, expedition was necessary; accordingly the march was abandoned, and the railroad was called into requisition. Before the Twenty-first reached its new destination the Sixteenth had extricated itself. The Twenty-first was then kept on duty on the line of the Hannibal & St. Joseph Railroad for about two weeks, without, however, meeting an enemy or an incident worth relating. We did make one march, however, during that time, from Salt River, Missouri, to Florida, Missouri, and returned in search of Tom Harris, who was reported in that neighborhood with a handful of rebels. It was impossible, however, to get nearer than a day's march of him. From Salt River the regiment went to Mexico, Missouri, where it remained for two weeks; thence to Ironton, Missouri, passing through St. Louis, on the 7th of August, when I was assigned to duty as a brigadier-general, and turned over the command of the regiment to that gallant and Christian officer, Col. Alexander, who afterward yielded up his life, whilst nobly leading it in the battle of Chickamauga."

The regiment remained at Ironton, Missouri, until October 20, 1861, when it marched out from that place, and participated in the battle of Frederickstown on the following day. Returning to Ironton, the Twenty-first remained until January 29, 1862, when it marched with Gen. Steele's expedition to Jacksonport, Arkansas, when it was ordered to Corinth, by way of Cape Girardeau. On May 24, 1862, the regiment reached Hamburg Landing, and took up a position near Corinth subsequently. On the evacuation of this place, the Twenty-first pursued the enemy from Farmington, Mississippi, to Booneville. Returning from the pursuit, it formed a part of an expedition to Holly Springs. On the 14th of August, 1862, the Twenty-first was ordered to join Gen. Buell's army in Tennessee, which it accomplished, marching by way of Eastport, Mississippi, Columbia, Tennessee, Florence, Alabama, Franklin, Murfreesboro and Nashville, Tennessee, arriving at Louisville September 27, 1862. On the counter-march across Kentucky in pursuit of Bragg, the regiment engaged in the battles of Perryville and Chaplin Hill, Company F being the first troops to enter Perryville. From thence the regiment marched to Crab Tree Orchard and Bowling Green, Kentucky, and to Nashville, Tennessee.

When the army marched from Nashville, December 26, 1862, this regiment formed a part of the Second Brigade, First Division, Twentieth Army Corps, and was in the skirmish at Knob Gap. On December 30, in connection with the Fifteenth Wisconsin, Thirty-eighth Illinois and One Hundred and First Ohio, it had a severe engagement with the enemy near Murfreesboro, where it charged the famous Washington (rebel) Light Artillery, twelve Parrott guns, and succeeded in driving every man from the battery, when it was compelled to fall back by a division of rebel infantry. During the battle of Murfreesboro it was fiercely engaged and did gallant duty, losing more men than any other regiment engaged. The Twenty-first was with Gen. Rosecrans' army from Murfreesboro to Chattanooga. On June 25, 1863, the regiment was engaged in a severe skirmish at Liberty Gap. It was subsequently engaged in the battle of Chickamauga, where it lost two hundred and thirty-eight officers and men. Col. Alexander being killed and Lieut. Col. McMackin being wounded, Capt. A. C. Knight took command of the regiment. After the battle of Chickamauga the Twenty-first was attached to the First Brigade, First Division, Fourth Army Corps, and remained at Bridgeport, Alabama, until the close of 1863. February 27, 1864, the regiment re-enlisted, some twenty-five men of Company D veteranizing. The regiment served in the Atlanta campaign, and subsequently was ordered to Texas, where it was mustered out December 16, 1865, at San Antonio.

TWENTY-FIFTH ILLINOIS INFANTRY.

Company H of this regiment was recruited in Douglas county. The commissioned officers were: *Captains*—William Brian, till December 30, 1861; Benjamin F. Ford, till March 2, 1863; J. H. Hastings, till October 2, 1863; John Scott, till mustered out.

First Lieutenants—Allen Buckner, till June 13, 1862; H. C. Paddock, till November 14, 1862; J. H. Hastings, till March 2, 1863; John Scott, till October 2, 1863; Thomas Mallott, till September 1, 1864; James T. Walker, till September 21, 1865.

Second Lieutenants—Archibald Van Deren, till July 15, 1862; J. H. Hastings, till November 14, 1862; John Scott, till March 2, 1863; Thomas Mallott, till October 2, 1863.

The enlisted men from Douglas county were: *First Sergeant*—H. Hopkins died at Jefferson City September 12, 1861.

Sergeants—Daniel O'Root, Henry Cook; G. W. Harris, promoted sergeant; J. H. Hastings, promoted second lieutenant.

Corporals—James Lewis, W. H. Harrison, Daniel Jacobs; J. T. Walker, promoted first lieutenant; John Yaker; John Scott, promoted second lieutenant; G. P. McQuaid, died March 2, 1863, of wounds received at Stone River.

Musicians—G. P. Sargent J. A. Ritter.

Wagoner—William Hogland.

Privates—Charles Allison, promoted corporal, died January 21, 1863; B. F. Allison, J. A. Armstrong, G. W. Anderson, T. Ater; J. R. Biggs, died November 21, 1863, of wounds; S. Bierfeldt, I. Bashalm, A. Banta, Henry Busby, Lewis Cook, Charles Corban, S. Cunningham, William Donley, William Early, B. F. Evans, J. S. Falkner, F. Falster, John Gilmore, Joseph Hammer; Joseph Hamilton, died at St. Louis February 17, 1861; Joseph Harvey; J. W. Hopkins, died at St. Louis December 13, 1861; E. T. Hopkins, died at Iuka, Mississippi, August 30, 1862; George Hopkins, Joseph Hyde, J. Henry, William Hewitt, J. H. Ishum; H. T. James, promoted hospital steward; W. D. Jones; G. Klink, promoted principal musician; William Leyh; Thomas Mallott, promoted corporal, sergeant and second lieutenant; Claus Moner; F. H. Morely, died at Springfield, Missouri, February 19, 1862; J. Moore; William Newcomb, died February 9, 1863, of wounds; J. P. Newell, Elihu Parish, J. C. Perry; W. L. Prose, promoted corporal; John Rierdon; C. D. Randolph, promoted corporal; A. Romine; R. S. Robinson, promoted sergeant; John S. Sargeant, R. W. See, E. H. Slace, W. R. Sackville, H. Stenght, J. M. Siders; W. L. Sowers, died near Ackworth, Georgia, June 13, 1864; Peter Sipple, A. J. Thompson; J. C. Vestal, promoted corporal; M. Whittenborg; John Wilson, died at Chattanooga November 28, 1863; I. S. Wheeler, killed at Pea Ridge, Arkansas, March 8, 1862; A. J. Walston, promoted sergeant.

Recruits—Perry Burnham; J. A. Carthal, died at Rolla, Missouri, January 18, 1862; H. H. Crist; D. Dennis, died at Jefferson City September 12, 1861; I. N. Dickens, S. Epley; William Hehn, died at Nashville November 9, 1862; D. C. Johnson; S. Kingery, died at St. Louis December 25, 1861; William Muir, James Moore, W. R. Medcalf, H. B. Prose, Alexander Perry, William Steyer, J. W. Sleeper, Joseph Vinson, C. Winter.

The Twenty-fifth Regiment was recruited in the spring and summer of 1861, and was organized in August at Mattoon. The regiment was assigned to the Department of Missouri, and proceeded to Jefferson City, which was then threatened by the army of Gen. Price, fresh from its dearly-bought victory at Lexington. Here the Twenty-fifth remained until the latter part of September, when it marched to Sedalia, and was assigned to Sigel's famous division. Here it remained until the middle of October, gaining discipline, foraging, picketing, etc., and then followed the army toward Springfield, remaining here until November, when Gen. Hunter assumed command of the army, and moved it toward Wilson's Creek, the scene of Gen. Lyon's famous fight. This movement of Sigel's division was but a ruse to cover the real destination of the army, and on the 13th it followed the movement of the main army to Rolla, where it remained during the winter. On February 2, 1862, Gen. Curtis having assumed command, the army again took up its line of march toward Springfield, where the rebel Gen. Price had concentrated his forces. The Union forces again took possession of the city on the 13th of February, without serious opposition. Then began an exciting race until the 20th, when the pursuit was abandoned, and the troops allowed a few days' rest, having marched four consecutive days during the most inclement weather, there being six inches of snow on the ground a portion of the time, and skirmishing with the enemy every day during the last week's march. Here the army remained till the 5th of March, when it became evident that the combined forces of Van Dorn, Price and McCullough were marching to give battle, and accordingly, on the 6th, the army moved toward Sugar Creek Valley under the command of Curtis, Sigel, Davis and Ashboth, and in the afternoon of the same day the rear guard was attacked and repulsed by the enemy. Thus began the battle of Pea Ridge, which resulted so disastrously to the rebels, and in which this regiment took a prominent part. The army remained in this vicinity until the 5th of April, when the march was resumed for Forsythe, Missouri, and thence to Batesville, Arkansas. Early in May the march was again resumed, as was supposed for Little Rock, but orders were soon received detaching some ten regiments under orders to proceed to Cape Girardeau, on the Mississippi river, some two hundred miles distant, and from thence to Pittsburg Landing, Tennessee, by water, to re-enforce the troops then besieging Corinth, Mississippi. The regiment reached the Landing on the 26th of May, and the next day marched up to within supporting distance of the main army, arriving two days previous to the evacuation. After the pursuit of the retreating enemy ceased the Twenty-fifth was ordered to Kentucky, where it took part in the memorable campaign against Bragg, reaching Perryville two days after the fight, thence proceeding to Crab Orchard, Bowling Green, and on to Nashville. Here the regiment remained until the latter part of December, when the Chattanooga campaign began, the Twenty-fifth taking part in the bloody engagement at Stone River. Spent the winter at Murfreesboro, and the spring till the latter part of June, 1863, when the movement against Chattanooga was resumed. The regiment took part in the various battles and skirmishes which led up to Chickamauga, in which the Twenty-fifth was engaged. Fell back to Chattanooga, where it remained until the latter part of November. On the 25th of this month the regiment took part in the desperate charge on Mission Ridge. Immediately after this battle the regiment took part in the forced march of one hundred and fifty miles to the relief of Knoxville, arriving three days after the siege had been raised by Gen. Burnside. From this point the regiment moved to Blain's Cross Roads, thence to Dandridge, Tennessee. From this point the army fell back to Knoxville, and from thence to Kingston, and later to Cleveland, Tennessee. From this point in May, 1864, the Twenty-fifth moved out with the army on the Atlanta campaign. The regiment participated in most of the battles of this campaign up to the taking of Atlanta, when it was mustered out September 5, 1864. The veterans and recruits of this regiment were consolidated in one company, designated at Company H of the Twenty-fifth Illinois Infantry, which was mustered out at Victoria, Texas, September 1, 1865.

FIFTY-FOURTH ILLINOIS INFANTRY

In this regiment Douglas county was represented by Company B. The commissioned officers were:

Captains—S. B. Logan, till July 27, 1864; A. B. Balch, till September 18, 1865; Gilman Noyes.

First Lieutenants—Johnson White, till April 21, 1862; A. M. Houston, till March 11, 1863; A. B. Balch, promoted February 16, 1865; Gilman Noyes, promoted, but not mustered.

Second Lieutenants—A. M. Houston, promoted, not mustered; A. B. Balch, July 9, 1863; B. C. Pursell, resigned March 18, 1865; R. B. McComb, promoted, but not mustered.

The enlisted men were:

First Sergeant—James Shrew.

Sergeants—R. B. McComb, E. C. Walton, Alex. Rodgers and John Scott.

Corporals—Levi Jester, G. P. Ross, John Haley, W. A. Griffin, William Moore, H. M. Thompson, J. Bennett.

Musician—I. W. Ross.

Wagoner—William Cosles.

Privates—F. M. Abrams, Isaac Albertz, J. P. Allison; A. B. Balch, promoted second lieutenant; Walter Bailey, E. R. Bagley, John Bear, Simeon Bennett, S. M. Beeman, Cephas Carman, Thomas Denning, George Dehart, David Ford, John Freddle; M. B. Grove, mustered out as corporal; J. D. Henry, died at Memphis November 10, 1863; W. T. Hughes, James Jackson, B. D. Jones, Robert Laughlin, G. W. Lester, G. Loper, J. P. Laughlin, E. Leslie, G. W. Montgomery, R. N. McIntyre, Charles McCaren, G. W. Mussett, John Malone, G. W. Miller, Robert Montgomery, Richard Martin, J. S. Osborne, L. Owen, James Overman; B. C. Pursell, promoted second lieutenant; Robert Perry, N. H. C. Resin, M. Rogers, William Rhinehardt, J. P. Roberts, John Ross, John Shook, Melton Stansbury, Lemuel Semmons, James Stinson, H. Shumefield, D. E. Shull, Elijah Zeigler.

These are the names of those from Douglas county, the balance of the company being drawn from Coles and Cumberland counties. The company was recruited in the summer of 1861, and was assigned as Company B to the Fifty-fourth Regiment, rendezvoused at Camp Dubois, Anna, Illinois. This regiment was organized as a part of the "Kentucky Brigade," in the formation of which E. McCarty, of Douglas county, was so prominent.

The regiment was mustered into the United States service February 18, 1862. On the 24th it was ordered to Cairo, Illinois, and on the 14th of March moved to Columbus, Kentucky. During the fall of 1862 three companies were stationed at Humbolt, Tennessee, but on the 18th of December the regiment was ordered to Jackson, Tennessee. Two days later the Fifty-fourth marched to Lexington, but returned on the 22d; then marched to Britton's Lane and Toone's Station, returning to Lexington. In the meantime Gen. Forrest captured the detached portions of the regiment stationed on the railroad, and destroyed nearly all of the regimental records. The balance were lost by the quartermaster's department in transit from Columbus to Jackson. The balance of the regiment spent the winter and early spring at Jackson, two companies being stationed at Medon Station, and two at Toone's. In April the regiment made a fruitless expedition to Corinth and returned.

May 30, 1863, the Fifty-fourth left Jackson for Vicksburg, as a part of the Third Brigade,

Second Division, Sixteenth Army Corps, under command of Gen. Nathan Kimball as division commander, and arrived at Haines' Bluff, on the Yazoo River, June 2. The regiment was subsequently stationed on the extreme left of Sherman's command on the Big Black, confronting Johnston's army, on the Canton road. After the fall of Vicksburg, the regiment was ordered to Helena, as a part of Gen. Steele's expedition against Little Rock, Arkansas. The expedition reached its destination in September, and the Fifty-fourth was retained until the following January, 1864, when three-fourths of the regiment re-enlisted.

The veterans of Company B were: Isaac Albertz; Henry Barrick, mustered out as first sergeant; Joseph Bennett; Cephas Carman; William Cheeney; G. A. Dehart; Thomas Denning; Duncan Fletcher; William Hughes; Thomas Irwin; B. D. Jones; James Jackson; Levi Jester, mustered out as sergeant; J. P. Laughlin, mustered out as corporal; R. Laughlin; E. Leslie, mustered out as sergeant; G. W. Lester, mustered out as corporal; Charles McCaren; R. B. McComb, mustered out as sergeant; P. Cornelius, mustered out as corporal; William Rhinehart; M. Rogers; I. W. Ross; John Scott; E. C. Walton; John Writner.

Recruits—Michael Fitzgerald, Samuel Montgomery. Re-enlisted as veteran—C. H. Newbanks. The regiment was mustered out February 9, 1864, and left for Mattoon, Illinois, in March, on veteran furlough.

Just before its return to the field, the regiment was involved in a most unfortunate occurrence. There was in Coles county an element which was radically opposed to the war. The regiment had been ordered to move, but, under advice of some radical unionists its departure was delayed a few hours, as the convening circuit court, it was thought, would bring the element opposed to the war out in full force. There is no doubt but that these people acted "with zeal not according to knowledge," and the return of certain portions of the regiment to the county seat made a conflict with the "irreconcilables" inevitable. A conflict followed, the "copperhead" faction led by a county officer, and certain portions of the regiment, unarmed but somewhat excited by liquor, under the semi-official direction of its officers. Riotous action followed, in which Maj. Shubal York, the surgeon of the regiment, was killed, and four privates and Col. G. M. Mitchell were wounded. A number of the citizens were wounded. One hour later the main portion of the regiment arrived from Mattoon and occupied the town, arresting some of the opposing faction, and wounding several citizens. The affair ended with an investigation by the military authorities, without changing results or the punishment of anybody. The affair created great excitement in the country around.

The regiment moved to the front in April; to Cairo on the 12th, to Columbus on the 14th, Paducah on the 16th, and arrived at Little Rock on the 30th. Here the regiment remained until May 18, when it moved out to Brownville, and thence in pursuit of Gen. Shelby, arriving at Little Rock on the 30th of that month. After remaining here until the latter part of June, when the Fifty-fourth again went in pursuit of Shelby, marching to Duvall's Bluff and Clarendon, striking him on the 26th, and after a spirited fight returned to Little Rock. August 5 the regiment was assigned to guard sixteen miles of the Memphis & Little Rock Railroad, having five stations, with two companies at each. On the 24th Shelby made a descent upon these detachments in detail with four thousand men and four pieces of artillery, capturing one station. Six companies were concentrated at one station by Col. Mitchell, and maintained a stubborn resistance for five hours, when, their hay breastworks being fired by the enemy's shells, the garrison was driven out and captured in fragments. The loss of the regiment in this fight was one lieutenant and thirteen men killed and thirty-five wounded. Companies F and H, at a distant station, were not molested. The captured part of the regiment were paroled at Jacksonport, Arkansas, and moved to Benton Barracks, St. Louis, where it arrived September 9, 1864. The regiment was exchanged December 5, 1864, and was moved to Hickory Station, on the Memphis & Little Rock Railroad, January 18, 1865, where it remained as railroad guard until June 6. The Fifty-fourth was then ordered to Pine Bluff, where it remained some two months. It then proceeded to Fort Smith, where it remained until October. It was then ordered to Little Rock, where it was mustered out October 15, 1865; arrived at Camp Butler, Illinois, October 26, and was discharged. During its existence, the Fifty-fourth Regiment had one thousand, three hundred and forty-two enlisted men, and seventy-one commissioned officers.

SEVENTY-NINTH ILLINOIS INFANTRY.

This regiment was more completely identified with Douglas county than any other in the service. Among the field officers were Allen Buckner, major, promoted to colonel March 15, 1863; W. H. Lamb, adjutant; first assistant surgeon, Henry C. McAllister, promoted surgeon of the Ninety-eighth Illinois Infantry; second assistant surgeon, Thomas J. Wheeler, promoted surgeon March 1, 1865; chaplain, C. G. Bradshaw. Four companies of the Seventy-ninth were recruited in Douglas county, Companies B, E, G and K. The commissioned officers of Company B were:

Captains—Archibald Van Deren, promoted major January 1, 1863; H. D. Pitman, till November 6, 1864; Peter Greggers, till muster out of regiment.

First Lieutenants—S. L. Woodworth, till February 2, 1863; H. D. Pitman, till January 1, 1863; Peter Greggers, till November 6, 1864; J. B. Hammer, promoted, but not mustered.

Second Lieutenants—H. W. Rideout, till February 10, 1863; Peter Greggers, till January 1, 1863; J. B. Hammer, promoted, but not mustered. The enlisted men from Douglas were:

First Sergeant—O. L. Woodward, died at Bowling Green, December 27, 1862.

Sergeants—H. D. Pitman, promoted to first lieutenant; J. B. Hammer, commissioned second lieutenant, but not mustered; Edward Dennis, died in Andersonville, July 30, 1864; John Abbott, transferred to Veteran Reserve Corps, August 28, 1863.

Corporals—S. M. Lester, W. M. Beedle, M. L. Westfall, Archibald Linton, Thomas Jester, mustered out as sergeant; L. C. Smith, Peter Greggers, promoted second lieutenant.

Musicians—W. R. Wallace, B. F. Ward.

Wagoner—G. W. Stevenson.

Privates—Lafayette Abbott, died at Louisville, Kentucky, October 8, 1862; W. A. Brown; W. A. Buoy; Henry Banta; Albert

Castor; J. E. Davis; I. N. Doman, died at Liberty Gap, Tennessee, June 25, 1863; John Darjahn; Clinton Davis; Milton Davis, died at Murfreesboro, June 1, 1863; Silas Daggy, promoted to quartermaster sergeant; Jacob Frahm; John Grant; Peter Gulk, died at Andersonville Prison, July 20, 1864; John Goodson; Henry Grimm; J. Hibbs; William Hibbs, died at Murfreesboro, February 9, 1863; Charles Howard; Larkin E. Jones, mustered out as corporal; M. James; C. James, mustered out as corporal; Benjamin Jester; Solomon Johnson, mustered out as corporal; Peter Kruize; George Kruize, mustered out as corporal; A. J. Lyght; H. Loman; Asa Love, died at Nashville, December 8, 1862; Thomas Lester, died at Murfreesboro, March 7, 1863; Virgil Lester; John Lewis, died at Murfreesboro, February 17, 1863; T. J. Lewis; W. D. Martin; C. G. Miller; W. P. Miller; Robert McAllister; William Manus; Cyrus Muire; G. W. Nelson, died at Nashville, December 14, 1862; E. T. Romine; Daniel Romine; H. T. Ring; Jasper Roderick; Perry Roderick and C. W. Rea, died at Nashville; J. R. Rea; C. W. Rose; J. S. Rush, died at Louisville, December 4, 1862; Samuel Randolph, died at Chattanooga, March 6, 1864; David and J. M. Randolph; J. H. Randolph, died at Chattanooga, June 4, 1864; W. T. Rice, killed at Resaca; Allen Rea; G. W. Sharpe; Albert Siler, mustered out as corporal; O. T. Smith; B. F. Shreves; F. Stally, mustered out as corporal; George Stovall; Peter Schnack; Hans Schnack; B. F. Terry; J. Veach, died at Murfreesboro, March 16, 1863; William Vinson; G. C. Wilson; J. C. Wilson; Edward Webb; H. J. Wilkins, died at Jeffersonville, Indiana, December 18, 1864; James Waller; B. F. Wilson; W. B. Watts, died at Murfreesboro, January 6, 1863; Rudolph Yost, killed at Resaca, May 14, 1864.

COMPANY E.—The commissioned officers of this company were:

Captains—William A. Low, promoted major July 14, 1864; H. S. Albin, promoted March 20, 1865, not mustered.

First Lieutenants—H. J. Bassett, till November 20, 1862; H. S. Albin, till March 20, 1865; J. C. Perry.

Second Lieutenants—H. S. Albin, till November 20, 1862; H. W. Peters, killed January 2, 1863; J. C. Perry, till March 20, 1865. Enlisted men:

First Sergeant—H. W. Peters, promoted second lieutenant.

Sergeants—J. C. Perry, promoted second lieutenant; J. G. Hughes, died at Nashville, December 19, 1862; W. R. Laughead, mustered out as first sergeant; D. H. Howard, died in Andersonville prison, August 16, 1864, Grave No. 5812.

Corporals—Anson Skinner, mustered out as sergeant; W. T. Potts, John Skinner, mustered out as sergeants; Samuel Hawkins, captured at Chickamauga; J. Hopkins, died at Nashville; Aaron Britton, died in Andersonville prison; J. P. Ross.

Musicians—I. W. and W. H. Covert.

Wagoner—J. H. Boyce, died at Nashville.

Privates—B. H. Adams; W. H. Allison; William Brockett, killed at Stone River, December 31, 1862; O. Brewer; W. R. Brown; W. T. Bundy, died at Gallatin, Tennessee, January 10, 1863; W. Boyce; Thomas Bull, died at Danville, Kentucky, January 4, 1863; P. Chezem; H. Catler; Alexander Coslett, died at

Bowling Green, November 6, 1862; George Crist; A. A. Craft; J. H. Coslett, died at Nashville, January 5, 1863; P. Coffin, killed at Stone River, December 31, 1862; H. D. Craft; F. Dixon; John Durborow; William Dillon, killed at Stone River, December 31, 1862; E. Drake; H. Entler; John Fairbairn; A. E. Fullerton; Isaac Glass, died at Nashville, December 9, 1862; S. Gillogly, mustered out as corporal; Alexander Hess; E. Howard and Frank Hensely, died at Nashville; G. H. Hess, mustered out as corporal; John Hawkins; J. O. Harvey; John Harris; R. B. Helm; R. W. Harrison; W. H. Jones; B. F. Knipe; W. S. Knipe; Jacob Knipe; J. H. Lyon; Charles Lyon; J. J. Moss; L. Morton; P. Miller; W. P. McWilliams; W. Murphy; W. P. McCool; E. B. Nell; George Pettit, killed near Marietta, Georgia, July 4, 1864; E. S. Root; G. W. Ritter; W. H. Ritter, died in Richmond prison, December 5, 1864; M. Reeves; T. W. Stilwell, died in Andersonville prison, October 28, 1864; L. Shafer; Joseph Shute; John Smith; J. B. Stillwell, died at Chatanooga, June 26, 1864; J. L. Stewart, died at Nashville, July 24, 1863; H. Surber; Henry Stillwell; J. M. Shee; William Skinner, mustered out as sergeant; D. S. Tucker; G. Vanasdel; A .Wylie; G. Wells; J. Whittaker; J. H. Wells, died at Murfreesboro, May 22, 1863; J. P. Worrell; J. B. Yaw.

Recruits—S. T. Bondurant; J. M. Coggshell, mustered out as corporal; R. T. Harvey, mustered out as sergeant; V. T. Norris, wounded at Kenesaw; William Turbyville, mustered out as corporal.

COMPANY G.—The commissioned officers were:

Captains—Oliver O. Bagley, till November 6, 1864; A. J. Jones, till muster out of regiment.

First Lieutenants—M. L. Lininger, till November 19, 1862; T. B. Jacobs, till April 7, 1863; Montraville Reeves, till May 4, 1864; A. J. Jones, till promoted November 6, 1864; Thomas Meeker, who was prisoner of was at the muster out of the regiment.

Second Lieutenants—T. B. Jacobs, till promoted November 19, 1862; Albert J. Jones, till May 4, 1864.

The enlisted men were:

First Sergeant—A. J. Jones, promoted second lieutenant.

Sergeants—Thomas Meeker, promoted while prisoner of war; Harvey Ingrim, John Cummings, John Madder.

Corporals—H. C. Jones,, mustered out as sergeant; B. Jacobs, killed at Stone River, December 31, 1862; E. J. Barnett; S. F. Willis; A. Higgins; John Ball; R. G. McGinnis; J. S. Reeves.

Musicians—W. Woodbury; H. Helton.

Wagoner—Laughlin Stewart.

Privates—James Barnett; Thomas Brandon; David Ball, killed at Stone River; Allen Bryant; John Brockett; H. H. Clark; F. D. Clark; A. C. Clark; James Coslett; Isaac Coslett; Clark Cazard; T. A. Clark; Alexander Dawson, died at Nashville, February 1, 1863; Daniel Dehart; M. C. Drake. mustered out as corporal; W. M. Drake, mustered out as corporal L. W. Easton; Jacob Fry, died at Gallatin, December 15, 1862; J. P. Fry; James Furman; W. H. Froggett; Beers Guire, died at Nashville, April 18, 1864; C. Harlowe; I. Henderson; F. A. Holston; James Harper, Jr., J. A. Hill; John Ingrim; George Ingrim, died at Jeffersonville, Indiana, December 17,

1864; Isaac Ingrim, died at Nashville, December 8, 1862; Herd Ingrim; P. L. Jones; James Jacobs, died at Bowling Green, January 18, 1863; James Kess, died at Galatin, January 12, 1863; Alexander Lana, died at Gallatin, January 15, 1863; J. W. Lett, died at Nashville, January 11, 1863; J. W. Martin; James Munson; James Meek; William McShane; T. W. McDowell; E. Osborn, died in Hart county, Kentucky, November 26, 1862; B. F. Osborn, died at Annapolis, Maryland, February 6, 1863; Thos. Robinson; W. H. Rake; N. Stephen; S. Sears, died at Nashville; William Sites; John Thomason; L. Thomason, died at Chatanooga, July 3, 1864; Elisha Tinker; W. P. Updike; W. D. West, died at Gallatin, Tennessee, February 14, 1863; John Willis; S. S. Weathers; John Whirl.

Recruits—J. S. Osborn, killed at Rocky Face Ridge, May 9, 1864; M. Reeves, promoted first sergeant and then first lieutenant.

COMPANY K.—The commissioned officers of the company were:

Captains—H. D. Martin, till July 3, 1863; W. W. Davis, till March 6, 1864; W. H. Bassett, promoted March 6, 1864, but not mustered.

First Lieutenants— W. W. Davis, till July 3, 1863; W. H. Bassett, till March 6, 1864; W. H. Hutchenson.

Second Lieutenants—Moses Hunter, till October 19, 1862; I. P. C. Taylor, till June 6, 1863; W. H. Bassett, till July 3, 1863; W. H. Hutchenson.

The enlisted men from Douglas county were:

First Sergeant—I. P. C. Taylor, promoted second lieutenant.

Sergeants—W. H. Hutchenson, promoted first sergeant, then first lieutenant; D. C. Hutchinson; J. Douner; G. W. Allen, promoted sergeant major.

Corporals—H. C. Waller, died at Nashville, December 3, 1864; R. Walch; C. Royrk; C. Brawnch, promoted sergeant and died in Andersonville prison, June 1, 1864, number of grave 1619; Lewis Zeller.

Wagoner—A. P. Reeves, died near Stephenson, Alabama, October 21, 1863.

Privates—N. Aldrid, died in Danville, Virginia, January 22, 1864, while prisoner of war; Joseph Brand, died at Nashville, January 4, 1863; W. H. Bassett, promoted first sergeant, then first lieutenant; John Beedle; Samuel Chauney, died at Andersonville prison, October 6, 1864, number of grave, 10459; John Chauney; William Chandler, died at Nashville, December 21, 1862; John Eliss; Stephen Eliss, died at Annapolis, Maryland, February 15, 1863; Philip Eaton, died in Danville, Kentucky, October 20, 1862; Jesse Eavins; Edward Franklin; Barton Fallin, died at Tullahoma, Tennessee, July 5, 1863; James Fallin; Andrew Hayes; Eli How; John Hunter, died near Murfreesboro; Henry C. Jones; Felix Lardenois; James Loyd, died at Murfreesboro, July 1, 1863; J. H. Lett; J. N. Louthan, mustered out as sergeant; G. W. Maxon, mustered out as corporal; Thomas McConley, promoted corporal, died in Jefferson barracks, December 22, 1864; Hugh McKinney, promoted corporal; Thomas Morrison; John Monien; Elihu Monsell; George Near; Israel Price; Lewis Pfifer; Levi Remmel; S. T. Remmel; Jacob Remmel; John Row; James Riley; Jawes Standafer, died at Nashville, March 31, 1863; D. E. Shull; S.

Simmons, died at Nashville, November 30, 1862; W. B. Templeton; G. Waldrof, died at Chattanooga, June 24, 1864; W. H. Wright; E. G. S. Wright; Albert Wood, died at Nashville, December 28, 1862; Henry Wood, died at Danville, Virginia, February 1, 1864, while a prisoner of war; J. F. West, died at Nashville, May 7, 1863; Alexander West; Henry Wolf.

Recruits—Martin Minniet; Leonard C. Taylor, mustered out as sergeant.

The Seventy-ninth Illinois Infantry was organized at Mattoon, Illinois, in August, 1862, by Col. Lyman Guinnip, and was mustered into the United States service August 22, 1862. On September 12, the regiment moved under orders to Louisville, Kentucky, where it was assigned the Third Brigade of Craft's division of the army of Kentucky. On the 29th it was transferred to the Fourth Brigade of the Second Division, October 1, 1862, the Seventy-ninth commenced the march through Kentucky with the army. At Frankfort it was transferred to the Fifth Brigade. The regiment reached Perryville, Kentucky, on October 9, and continued its march thence to Crab Orchard, Lebanon, Bowling Green and Nashville, Tennessee, reaching the latter place on the 7th of November. October 17, Col. Guinnip resigning, Lieut. Col. S. P. Reed was promoted colonel. Here the regiment remained until December, when it moved out with the army toward Murfreesboro, and on the 31st engaged in the battle of Stone River. Col. Reed was killed early in the action, and the command devolved upon Maj. Buckner. The Seventy-ninth was engaged until the 4th of January, 1863, losing one officer killed, three wounded and three missing; twenty-three men killed, sixty-eight wounded, and one hundred and twenty-one missing. During the winter the regiment remained at Murfreesboro, and were assigned to the Second Brigade, Second Division, Twentieth Army Corps. April 25, 1863, Maj. Buckner was promoted to colonel.

June 24, 1863, the regiment move to Liberty Gap, and on the following day engaged the enemy, losing Capt. John Patton, killed; Capt. H. D. Martin, mortally wounded; Capt. Lacey and Lieuts. Foulke, Jones and King, wounded; five men killed and thirty-six wounded. The division then moved to Tullahoma, and on the 16th of August crossed the Cumberland Mountains, the Tennessee river, Sand Mountain, Lookout Mountain, and went into the battle of Chickamauga, in which the regiment was engaged during the 19th and 20th of September. Its loss in this fight was seven officers missing, four men killed, thirteen wounded and ninety-seven missing. On the evening of the 20th the Seventy-ninth fell back to Chattanooga with the army. While here, the regiment was re-assigned, being placed to the Third Brigade (Col. C. G. Harker's), Second Division, Gen. Sheridan, Fourth Army Corps, commanded by Gen. Granger. When the Army of the Cumberland broke from its prison at Chattanooga and assailed Bragg in his mountain fastness, the Seventy-ninth took an active part in the engagements that followed on the 23d, 24th and 25th of November, and on the 25th stormed Mission Ridge, capturing two pieces of artillery. On the 27th, the regiment accompanied the Fourth Corps in that famous march to Knoxville, Tennessee, going, however, to Blain's Cross-roads, and remaining there till January 15, 1864, when it advanced to Dandridge, but fell back two days later to Knoxville. The Second Division being ordered to Loudon, the Seventy-ninth went to Sweetwater, forty-two miles south of Knoxville, on the railroad, where it remained during the larger part of the spring, moving to Cleveland in the latter part of April.

On the opening of the Atlanta campaign, the regiment moved forward with Gen. Newton in command of the division, and Gen. Howard in command of the corps. The movement began May 3, 1864, and on the 9th the regiment took part in its first engagement of the campaign at Rocky Face Ridge; then followed a series of heavy engagements, at Resaca, May 13 and 14; Dallas, Kenesaw Mountain, June 27; Peach Tree Creek, July 20; Atlanta, July 22, 27, and August 3; Jonesboro, September 1, and Lovejoy on the 2d of September. The losses of the regiment in this campaign were four officers wounded, six enlisted men killed and fifty-three wounded. In the latter part of September, the corps was ordered back to Chattanooga under the command of Gen. Stanley. The Seventy-ninth moved to Bridgeport, Alabama, and remained there till October 19, when it returned to Chattanooga. While here it made an expedition to Alpine Pass and returned, and then moved to Pulaski, Tennessee. Held that position until November 22, when it commenced to fall back to Nashville with the army. At Franklin, the Seventy-ninth was engaged four hours, losing three officers and eighty men killed, wounded and captured, out of two hundred and ten veteran troops. That night fell back to Nashville, where, on the 29th, Pat Cleborne's division attacked the brigade and drove it into the city. On the 15th and 16th of December, the battle of Nashville occurred, in which the Seventy-ninth took an active part, and joined in the subsequent pursuit as far as the Tennessee river. The Third Brigade was then sent to Decatur, Alabama, arriving there January 6, 1865. March 30, the brigade moved to Bull's Gap by rail, sixty miles east of Knoxville, Tennessee, where it remained until April 22, and then went to Nashville. Here the Seventy-ninth was stationed until it was musterd out June 12, 1865. It subsequently arrived at Camp Butler, Illinois, June 15, and June 23 received final pay and discharge. In April, 1864, the county court ordered a regimental flag, which was presented to the regiment.

ONE HUNDRED AND THIRTY-FIFTH ILLINOIS INFANTRY.

This regiment was organized at Mattoon, and mustered into the one hundred-days' service June 6, 1864. Of this regiment Company G was recruited in Douglas county. The commissioned officers were: Derrick Lamb, captain; James Easton, first lieutenant; J. T. Switzer, second lieutenant. The enlisted men from Douglas county were:

First Sergeant—J. H. Perrine.

Sergeants—Charles Skinner, died at Jefferson City, Missouri, July 7, 1864; J. Z. Linton; P. Kinder, O. Adams.

Corporals—William Bays, promoted sergeant; I. Watkins, Charles Dickens, A. Fleming, D. Jenkins, B. McAllister, T. J. Bagley, Charles Balen.

Musicians—Austin Bishop; John Crowley.

Wagoner—Thomas Donnelly.

Privates—I. Allison; Erastus Badler; W. H. Bard; A. C. Bragg; F. M. and Alexander Bragg; P. Burton; S. Bye; B. F. Barkley; C.

H. Balch, died at Benton Barracks, June 29, 1864; J. Bogard; B. Bogard; L. Daniel; C. Dragoo; C. M. Donica, promoted corporal; J. Dale; J. R. Erland; W. H. H. Easton; H. M. Franz, died at Benton Barracks June 23, 1864; G. Ford; J. Garrett; William Galls; G. W. Goodson, promoted corporal; J. R. Hull; Thomas Haskell; N. Holden; N. Howard; E. C. Holiday; J. Kennedy; E. Lay; A. Long; J. R. Leslie; A. Moore; J. N. McKinney; J. N. Mosbarger; F. M. Maddox, died in Jefferson City, Missouri, August 4, 1864; C. H. Miller; J. D. McDowell; Newton McAughy; J. B. Peacock; J. Peters; J. S. Prose; F. Puckett; I. S. Reeder; J. A. Richman; J. H. Smith; William Scott; A. H. Sluss; J. W. Tignor; C. H. Wetsell; P. Wildman; Albert Wildman; W. H. Walters; I. N. Wells; S. B. Williams; C. B. Wells; W. H. Wells.

This regiment was assigned to post duty at Jefferson City, Missouri, a point they reached by way of St. Louis, soon after being mustered into the service. Greenbury Wright, of Tuscola, was the first major and afterward lieutenant colonel of the regiment. The regiment was ordered home, and mustered out on September 28, 1864.

ONE HUNDRED AND FIFTY-NINTH ILLINOIS INFANTRY.

Of this regiment Company F was recruited in Douglas county. The commissioned officers were: Derrick Lamb, captain; D. G. Eldridge, first lieutenant; William Bays, second lieutenant. Enlisted men of Douglas county were:

First Sergeant—S. R. Cox.

Sergeants—W. F. Barger, J. P. Hancock, mustered out as first sergeant; T. J. Bagley; Martin Bradford.

Corporals—J. W. Rohrbaugh; I. H. Watkins; E. E. Thompson, mustered out as sergeant; L. Osborn; B. F. Barkley; E. Brewer; A. A. Thomas.

Musicians—A. A. Kertz; S. Brewer.

Wagoner—Richard Davis, killed by railroad accident, near Chattanooga, February 26, 1865.

Privates—William Bays, promoted to second lieutenant; L. H. Brewer; J. Bartlett, mustered out as corporal; R. Bradford; R. M. Brewer; G. W. Busby; Charles Bowlen; J. L. Baugh; D. T. Corbin; F. M. Chambers; G. W. Chase; James Davidson; R. A. Duane; Charles Dragoo; William Ennis; D. Fiddler; J. S. Fiddler, mustered out as corporal; W. J. Fiddler; J. O. Foss, mustered out as sergeant; William Gilkerson; William Hittshew; H. Howell; W. J. P. Hopewell; N. N. Howard; J. T. Hicks; J. H. Henderson; J. R. Leslie; G. L. Linsey; John Lamb; Derrick Lamb, promoted captain; J. N. McKinney; A. Moore; W. T. Miller; James Naphew, died at Cleveland, Tennessee, March 10, 1865; D. B. Overman, died at Nashville, January 27, 1866; J. T. Phillips; William Poor; I. S. Reeder; Alex Ridenour; J. Skinner; William Scott; J. Turryville; M. Wilson; H. H. Wright; W. H. Waters.

The One Hundred and Forty-ninth Regiment was organized at Camp Butler, Illinois, on February 11, 1865, by Col. William C. Kneffner, and mustered in for one years' service. On the 14th, the regiment moved under orders for Nashville and thence to Chattanooga. Here it was assigned by Gen. Steadman to duty, guarding railroads.

On May 1 it was assigned to Col. Felix, Prince Salm's brigade, the Second Separate Division, Army of the Cumberland, and on the following day moved to Dalton, Georgia. Here the regiment remained until July 6, when it was ordered to Atlanta. On the 26th, being assigned to duty in the fourth district of Allatoona, it was put on guard duty in that district. It was subsequently ordered to Dalton, where the regiment was mustered out January 27, 1866, and ordered to Springfield, Illinois, for final payment and discharge.

THIRTEENTH ILLINOIS CAVALRY.

This regiment was composed of only eight companies, one of which, Company G, was recruited principally from Douglas county. The commissioned officers were:

Captain—Charles H. Roland.

First Lieutenants—Albert Erskin, promoted captain of Company E; James G. Kearney, only officer from Douglas county, from August 10, 1862.

Second Lieutenants—William K. Trabue, till August 9, 1862; Forrest D. Spincer, till mustered out of the regiment.

The enlisted men from the county were:

First Sergeant—J. G. Kearney, promoted first lieutenant.

Sergeants—G. F. Green; W. H. Flint.

Corporals—O. E. Vandeventer, W. J. Henry.

Buglers—N. R. Gruelle.

Farrier—Henry Campbell, mustered out as sergeant.

Privates—A. Burton; George Boyer; M. Cavanaugh; Elijah Carr, died at Ironton, Missouri, April 12, 1862; F. Cunningham; W. J. Churls; F. Collum; F. O. Easton; L. Fetters; R. C. Grissom; Gilbert Green; John Keneas; Elizer Lathrop; J. T. Maynor; J. Mosbarger, died at Helena, Arkansas, August 30, 1862; Ezekiel Miller, died at St. Louis, Missouri, March 19, 1862; John Mack; I. McAllister; M. G. Neff, died at Ironton, Missouri, May, 1862; E. Poul; I. S. Reeder; N. Roland; John Shule; J. N. Tannihill; S. Waldrop; L. Wilkins; W. H. Wright; A. H. Wildman; William Woodhall; J. Whitlock; Macey Whitlock, died at Ironton, Missouri, April 30, 1862. There were some from Douglas county transferred to other companies; of these in Company H, were G. W. Austin; John Brighton; Henry Campbell; Robert Davis; C. H. Jones; Henry Littlefield; Ira Magnor; M. Stewart; George Thebedient; William Taylor; S. Walthrop; Samuel Winan.

The Thirteenth Illinois Cavalry Regiment was organized at Camp Douglas, Illinois, in December, 1861, by Col. J. W. Bell. The regiment was moved to Benton Barracks, St. Louis, where it was armed and equipped, and in February, 1862, moved to the field. Until June 1 it was on duty in southeast Missouri, where it joined Gen. Curtis' army, at Jacksonport, Arkansas. With Gen. Curtis, the Thirteenth moved through Arkansas, taking part in the skirmishes of the campaign to Helena, Arkansas. In the fall of 1862 it returned with Gen. Curtis to Missouri, and was engaged with General Davidson, in the campaign of southwest Missouri and northwest Arkansas, driving Marmaduke and his command out of the state. On May 20, 1863, in accordance with orders from headquarters Department of Missouri, the Thirteenth was consolidated; the eight companies being formed into three, Maj.

L. Lippert being retained in command of the battalion. By the same order Col. Bell, Lieut. Col. Hartman and Maj. Charles Bell were mustered out of the service.

In the following July the battalion moved with Gen. Davidson's cavalry division into Arkansas, taking part in the battles of Brownsville, August 24 and 25; Bayou Metre, 27 and 28; Austin, August 31, and again at Bayou Metre, September 4. The Thirteenth was the first organization to enter Little Rock, on its capture, September 10, 1863, and was engaged in the pursuit of Price, to Red River. In the spring of 1864 the battalion accompanied Gen. Steele in the expedition to Camden, taking a prominent part in the actions at Arkadelphia, Okoloma, Little Missouri River, Prairie du Anne, Camden and Jenkin's Ferry, during the month of April. After returning to Little Rock, the battalion was engaged in many raids and scouts, and in skirmishing with the forces of Shelby and Marmaduke, defeating them at Clarendon and Pine Bluff. In the summer of 1864 the battalion was stationed at Pine Bluff, in Col. Clayton's brigade, and engaged in scouting and picketing. On the 25th of January, 1865, the cavalry division having been discontinued, the Thirteenth was assigned to duty at the post of Pine Bluff. In April, detachments were sent to take possession of Monticello, Camden and Washington, leaving the headquarters at Pine Bluff. August 31, 1865, the regiment was mustered out, and received final pay and discharge at Springfield, Illinois, September 13, 1865. The Thirteenth Cavalry Regiment's aggregate strength during its organization was 1,759 men, the battalion having been consolidated with a newly-formed but incomplete regiment in the spring of 1864.

A list of battles and skirmishes in which the regiment was engaged is as follows: Pitman's Ferry, Arkansas, July 20, 1862; Cotton Plant, Arkansas, July 25, 1862; Union City, Missouri, August 22, 1862; Camp Pillow, Missouri, August 29, 1862; Bloomfield, Missouri, September 13, 1862; Van Buren, Missouri, 17, 1863; Eleven Point River, Missouri, March 26, 1863; Jackson, Missouri, April 22, 1863; White River, Missouri, April 23, 1863; Bloomfield (2), Missouri, April 24, 1863; Union City and Chalk Bluff, Missouri, April 25, 1863; Bushy Creek, Missouri, May 31, 1863; near Helena, Arkansas, August 8, 1863; Grand Prairie and White River, Arkansas, August 24 and 25, 1863; Bayou Metre, Arkansas, August 17, 1863; Brownsville, Arkansas, August 16, 1863; Deadman's Lake, Arkansas, August 27 and 28, 1863; Austin, Arkansas, August 31, 1863; Bayou Metre (2d), Arkansas, September 4, 1863; Little Rock, Arkansas, September 10, 1863; Benton, Arkansas, September 11, 1863; Batesville, Arkansas, October 22, 1863; Pine Bluff, Arkanas, November 28, 1863; Arkadelphia, Arkansas, April 2, 1864; Okoloma, Arkansas, April 3, 1864; Little Missouri River, Arkansas, April 4, 1864; Prairie du Anne, Arkansas, April 10, 11 and 12, 1864; Camden, Arkansas, April 15, 1864; Jenkins' Ferry, Arkansas, April 30, 1864; Cross Roads, Arkansas, September 11, 1864; Mount Elba, Arkansas, October 18, 1864; Douglas Landing, Arkansas, February 22, 1865; Monticello, Arkansas, March 28, 1865.

Douglas county was represented in other organizations in the army, but concerning whom there is no reliable information. To notice the especial achievements of the volunteers from this county would be a pleasant but an impossible work. Even to note the individual experiences of companies formed in the county has been found impracticable. A brief sketch of the regiments of which they formed a part is all that can be attempted, and if this shall show that Douglas county was not wanting in patrotism and sacrificing devotion when demanded by the nation's peril, the object of the foregoing pages will have been reached.

HISTORICAL SKETCHES

OF

TOWNSHIPS IN DOUGLAS COUNTY.

CHAPTER IV.

TOWNSHIP HISTORICAL SKETCHES.

CAMARGO TOWNSHIP.

Camargo township enjoys the honor of being the earliest settled portion of Douglas county, the first comers of whom we have any account having arrived in 1829. The township derives its name from the city of Camargo in Mexico, and was suggested by Col. McCown. The first house built in Douglas county is yet standing on section 33, 16, 9, on the Iles land, west of the railroad bridge at Camargo and north of the track. It was raised in 1829 by John A. Richman, the father of John Richman of our day, and well and familiarly known as "Uncle Jack." John A. Richman lived to be over eighty, and even at that age would hardly deign to ride a horse, but would gird himself with knife and tomahawk, and with gun on shoulder would "step over" to the Okaw timber, twelve or fifteen miles back, as coolly as a man of the present day would walk a mile. Mr. Richman came from West Virginia in the year mentioned—some say, however, 1827—and John Richman, then a lad, made a hand at the raising. This house was for a long time the headquarters for elections and military musters.

There was a small tribe of Indians camped at Bridgeport, now Hugo P. O., section 12, 15, 9, which was a trading point with them, and a store or trading post was kept by Godfrey Vesser, a Frenchman, or perhaps Vesser & Bulbory.

John Hammet and his sons, Wm. S. and Jas. R., arrived in November, 1830. The family lived in a tent the first winter and were visited by large numbers of Indians who would call and sit around the fire. Their general conduct was such as to leave the impression that they were honest, and although the family of the Hammets was at their mercy, nothing was stolen, and they had no fears for their personal safety. However one or two battles with Indians from the upper Embarrass are spoken of as having occurred, 1815-1818; one with government surveyors, near the creek in Coles county. John Hammet and Harrison Gill, of Kentucky, were the first land owners in the area of the county, after the government, having entered land on the same day. Mr. Hammet took several hundred acres north of Camargo village, and Mr. Gill entering two hundred and forty acres in section 35, east of Camargo. The patents for these first entered lands were signed by Andrew Jackson, in March, 1830. Samuel Ashmore entered part of section 36, 15, 10, in 1830 also. Mr. Gill came from Kentucky on horseback and in company with his uncle Robert visited the Indians at Hugo.

Jas. R. Hammet was active in the interests of the new county of Douglas and also in those of the east and west railroad, of which he was one of the incorporators and a director for fourteen years. G. W. Henson, Charles Brewer, John Brown, Martin Rice, John D. Murdock, Alexander Bragg and the Watsons were also of the first arrivals. C. Brewer came in 1855. John Brown, who arrived in 1838, was elected associate justice of the county of Douglas in 1865. Mr. Rice came in 1849, and was a resident of what is now Douglas county after 1853. He actively assisted in the movement of the new county, and was a member of the first political convention held in it, in the second year after township organization. John D. Murdock was elected associate justice of Douglas county, was a member of the first county board in 1859, and re-elected in 1861. Coleman Bright, a native of Virginia, came from Indiana to Camargo in August, 1850, and was the senior member of the firm of Bright & Jones, of Camargo and Tuscola. Alexander Bragg came to the state in 1835, and served in the Mexican war, 1846. W. D. Watson, of this township, was in the state senate at the time of forming the county. Geo. W. Henson arrived in 1844. H. L. Thornsbrue, of this township, was born within the area of the county—1830.

The original part of the village of Camargo was laid off in November, 1836, by Isaac Moss, Jos. Fowler, surveyor, and was called New Salem. When Moss' addition was made it was called New Albany, after which it received its present name. It is the most ancient village in the county, and in the long years pending the advent of the I. & I. C. Railway was considered "finished." It was the place of residence of many of the most successful business men of the county. The first county court of Douglas county was held here "under dispensation," pending the selection of a county seat. The town proper composes an area of about eighty acres, lying on the left bank of the Embarrass river and upon the line of the I. D. & W. Railway.

The Methodists and Christians have each a church, the former being a fine brick building costing five thousand dollars.

Camargo Lodge, No. 440, A. F. & A. M., was instituted October 18, 1865. The charter members were: Jas. T. Orr, A. Salisbury, R. E. Carmack, A. K. P. Townsend, Geo. C. Gill, Martin Rice, W. C. Campbell, R. C. Patterson, J. T. Helm, J. R. Henderson, H. G. Russell. The first officers were: Jas. T. Orr, worshipful master; Geo. C. Gill, secretary; R. E. Carmack, treasurer. A commodious lodge room was dedicated October 2, 1875; the Royal Arch Chapter was instituted U. D. November 9, the same year. The institution of the lodge was assisted by Tuscola Masons in 1865, who came out "by land" for the purpose, the railroad having not yet appeared.

The township took stock in the I. D. & W. Railway to the amount of fifteen thousand dollars, payable in fourteen years, with ten per cent. interest. The taxes paid by the road materially reduce the interest.

The area of the township is fifty-six sections of land or about equal to sixty and one-half square miles, some of the sections having over one thousand acres. The township contains thirty-eight thousand, seven hundred and sixty-nine acres.

The notable high-handed and desperate robbery of Wm. S. Hammet and his household occurred on the night of June 8, 1870. The family had retired. Mr. Hammet was aroused by a knock at the door, and upon opening it was instantly seized by two armed and masked men, who demanded silence and money. He was unarmed and partly unclothed, taken by surprise, with a loaded pistol pointing directly at and close to his heart, which might at any instant have been discharged by the trembling hand of his guard, and after carefully weighing the chances concluded to surrender, a prudence that is commended by men of bravery. He was held strictly under guard until the villains had obtained watches and jewelry to the amount of two hundred and fifty dollars and a little money. They had taken care to fasten the door of a room occupied by some work hands, and, having accomplished their purpose with dispatch, released Mr. Hammet and disappeared with great haste in the darkness.

The town of New Boston was laid out by McDowell on section 35, 16, 9, in November, 1837, and vacated February, 1845. Parmenas Watson was made sheriff in November, 1860, and S. S. Irwin was superintendent of schools from the fall of 1861, serving two years. Dr. John C. Parcel was elected county clerk in November, 1869, serving one term of four years.

Timber.—One-third of the area of the township is within the original timber limit, which grew adjacent to the river, as is usual here. Many fine tracts of timber yet remain. Good timber was held as high as seventy-five dollars per acre, and fifty dollars was a common price; it was used, after building with it, and for a long time, almost exclusively for fuel first, and then fencing. As the country grew older saw mills were introduced and native boards appeared; but since the multiplication of railroads leading to the easy transportation of foreign fencing and coal, timber land has depreciated, until good prairie is far more valuable. Some large farmers use foreign planks, or hedges, for fencing, and burn coal exclusively, many of them having not an acre of timber.

Railroads.—The I. D. & W. Railroad crosses this township in an east and west direction, coming in on the west side and near the middle of section 32, township 16, range 9, and runs upon a straight line until shortly after passing the village of Camargo, in section 35, where it deflects to the south about twelve rods, and continues at that distance from the middle line of the section till it leaves the county. It has a substantial bridge, one hundred and thirty feet long, on the west side of the village at the crossing of the Embarrass river, which resisted the ice-flow of the winter of 1882, whilst the wagon bridge, one hundred and fifty feet north of it, gave way.

The township took stock in the railroad under its former name, I. & I. C., to the amount of fifteen thousand dollars, payable in fourteen years, with ten per cent. interest, and the bonds were refunded in June, 1880, being placed with Preston, Kean & Co., of Chicago, at six per cent. interest, which transaction was negotiated by Charles G. Eckhart, Esq., of Tuscola.

CITY OF CAMARGO.

Creation and development.—The original town of Camargo was laid off in November, 1836, by Isaac Moss, being surveyed by Joseph Fowler, and was called New Salem. Mr. Moss made an addition in 1840; the name was then changed to New Albany, the voting precinct being known by the name of Albany, and finally, when, upon the suggestion of J. B. Mc-Cown, the name of the precinct was changed to Camargo, the village accepted the same name. It is the most ancient village in the county, antedating Tuscola, Arcola and Newman, and even the time-honored Bourbon, which was laid off in 1853, Camargo, with her 1836 record, leading Bourbon by seventeen years. This village in the long years preceding the advent of the east and west railroad languished and was long considered finished; the final completion of the road, however, gave it somewhat of an impetus, that may end in some distinction, it being the place of residence of some of the leading men of the county and the starting point of several of its most successful business men.

Struggle for county seat.—The village of Camargo, from its central position, had claims to the honor of being the county seat, which were strongly advocated, and which could not very well be ignored. She had no railroad, but everybody said she would have one at no distant day, the I. & I. C. having been chartered in 1852, and the route through the village selected and staked out, and further encouraged by the almost annual appearance of engineer corps along the line through which, amongst other things, the interest was kept up. Pending the selection of a shiretown, Camargo was made county seat pro tem. The election returns of the county seat contest were stored at the place, and rumor hath it that interested parties, obtaining access to the tickets, procured a set of scales, and upon ascertaining the "weight" of each package of votes, took special care that their favorite point should have superior heft. The first meeting of the county court, presided over by James Ewing, of Arcola, as judge, and John D. Murdock and Robert Hopkins, as associates, John Chandler, clerk, a special term was held April 28, 1859, up-stairs over Coleman Bright's store, and here it was ordered, amongst other things, that a special election be held May 30, 1859, as between Tuscola and Arcola, which rival towns, whose vote had not been considered in the first canvass, were found to embrace the choice of the people, upon which occasion Tuscola won.

Ancient prairie travel.—The new officers all met here to get their commissions. The county was almost covered with water, and the county surveyor, being a small man, was mounted upon a horse about sixteen hands high, and sent from Bourbon to Camargo "by way of Arcola," at which place the owner of the horse had a message to deliver, and told the surveyor it was "on the way," so it was—the way he went; he did not know any better. As there were no prairie fences, or roads, he went straight from Bourbon to Arcola and straight from Arcola to Camargo, across the prairie, with a general direction from his advisors, at Arcola, to keep the northeast wind in his face, which he proceeded to do as far as possible; but as the aforesaid northeast wind came on that occasion from all points of the compass, he accordingly got lost, as was to be expected. The wind was like old Uncle Jack,s compass, which somebody gave him to use in the woods; no matter how he held it, it would diddle-daddle to the southwest every time.

Churches.—The first church built in the village was put up by the Methodists, and we are informed was erected as early as 1850, at a cost of about five hundred dollars. It was eventually sold, and the present brick built.

BOURBON TOWNSHIP.

Bourbon township consists of forty-two sections of land in the southwest part of the county, equal to about the same number of square miles, and twenty-seven thousand, one hundred and seventy-five acres. Among the first settlers were Geo. Dehart and his sons, Samuel and Lucas. He was road-master in Coles county and his district extended from Sadorus' Grove, on the north county line, to a point six miles south of the Springfield road. Allen and William Campbell were also of the first. Allen Campbell was, at the time of his death in 1875, with one exception, the largest land owner in the county. Isaac Gruelle, Malden Jones, Israel Chandler and sons, were among the earliest comers. Dr. Apperson was a large land owner and had an extensive medical practice. He was a nephew of Dr. John Apperson, who was the first physician in Coles county. Malden Jones, who came in 1840, was sheriff of Coles county when Douglas county was parted from it. He was elected in 1858, and was elected to the state legislature in 1864 and again in 1866. Lemuel Chandler was the first supervisor of the township and served four consecutive terms. The Dehart sons were well known active business men. Curtis G. and Campbell McComb were old residents of Coles at the institution of the new county. Thomas Moore entered west half northeast quarter-section 23, 15, 7, in 1831.

John Campbell, called "Uncle Jack," was a brother of Allen and William Campbell, and was probably the last representative or type of the genuine old-fashioned pioneer, scout and hunter, and wonderful stories were told of his endurance and his ability to follow a trail. He was widely known in the early days, passing the greater part of his time in hunting. He was found dead in the woods. His son Hiram, who died in 1864, had the reputation of being one of the best hunters of the time.

Jacob Moore, Sr., was one of the earliest settlers in the township and became an extensive cattle dealer and large land holder. He was also a noted hunter of great endurance. His first land was entered in section 1, 14, 7, in April, 1835. He died July 15, 1860, leaving a large estate to numerous descendants.

Isaac Gruelle, of this township, was county commissioner of Coles county, being elected in 1843, with H. J. Ashmore. The constitution of 1848 provided for a county judge and two associates, and John M. Logan was one of the first two associate justices. Gruelle and Logan have long since passed away, both leaving large estates.

German speaking people occupy a large

area of the north part of the township, the locality being widely known as the "German Settlement." Their farms, compared with western farms generally, are small but exceedingly well cultivated, and the proverbial industry and thrift of this class of citizens it here fully exemplified. The greater part of them arrived with little or no means, and now with hardly an exception they have acquired good and well improved farms. The pioneer of this community is Wessel Blaase, who arrived in 1852. There are several ancient artificial mounds on his place in one of which human bones were found in excavating for a building.

In the southwest part settled the Amish, who were preceded here by M. Yoter, Miller and others in 1864. They much resemble the society of Friends in plainness of attire, integrity and almost total exemption from pauperism. The name is derived from that of the founder of the society who, in the German states of Europe, saw fit to secede from the Menonites, of whom much has been heard lately, with regard to the emigration of large numbers of them from Russia to the West. The proposed marriages are publicly announced and a marriage outside of the Society is "intolerable and not to be endured." They dress plainly, partly to avoid the frivolities of fashion, and partly that there may be no notable distinction between the rich and the poor. They have no churches or meeting houses, but meet at each other's dwellings, as the spirit moves them. The clothing of the men is often confined with hooks and eyes, but the notion that they wear no buttons is erroneous. The heads of the women are always covered with a neat white cap and over the neck and shoulders decorously spreads a plain white handkerchief; this in observance of the hint from the Apostle Paul. Adults only are baptized and that by pouring. Infants are not entitled to this sacrament, they preferring to teach first, for every descendant has a birth-right in the church. Of German extraction and long settled in western Pennsylvania, their speech amongst themselves is an odd mixture of German and English, the "American" part of which can be readily detected by an intelligent observer, and the language is popularly known as "Pennslyvania Dutch." They all speak "American" as well as their neighbors, so that, trusting to the hearing alone, few would suspect the presence of a German speaking person. They are a good class of people in their way, but are bigoted in many ways. They do not teach their children the "American idea," preferring that they become isolated from others who are as true, or truer, in their religious principles than they. They are intensely selfish among themselves and seem to "float in the creed" "we shall be happy in heaven whether we find our God there or not!"

The original village of Bourbon, section 14, 15, 7, was laid out by Malden Jones, in October, 1853, and is the third town in priority, having been preceded by both Camargo and Fillmore. An addition was made in the following January by Benjamin Ellars. At the institution of the county this was a thriving village of some dozen business houses and the most important trading point in the county. L. C. Rust, Dr. J. D. Gardiner, Jos. Foster, Wm. Chandler, Benjamin Ellars, G. W. Flynn and others flourished here at the time. The location of the Illinois Central Railroad some four miles to the east, giving rise to Tuscola and Arcola, interfered with the future prospects of the place to the extent that the merchants, for the most part, not only removed to the new towns on the railroad but took their buildings with them. One of these, a two-story frame, was put upon runners made of large sticks of timber, and with some fifteen yoke of steers, under the conduct of Uncle Daniel Roderick, was hauled in a nearly straight line over the snow to Arcola. "Uncle Daniel" still lives on his farm in section 1, 15, 7. He entered this land on March 13, 1838. Samuel Sharpe, of Bourbon, took Rust's store to Arcola in a similar manner.

The census of 1890 gives Bourbon eighty-three inhabitants. It has a postoffice, two or three stores, two grain buyers, good church and school.

Isaac Gruelle founded the first store near the place in which for some years Malden Jones was a partner. Luther C. Rust was a leading merchant in the early days of Bourbon and was well liked. He died suddenly in Arcola February 14, 1873. H. C. Niles clerked for Mr. Rust and Abram Cosler served in the same capacity for Mr. Fosler, another early merchant of the village.

Fillmore had been laid out by H. Russell in 1848, on section 35, 15, 7, and the firm of Bales & Throwbridge, afterward Bales, Osborn & Co., controlled the trade of a large area; but the business of this house was removed to Arcola, and Fillmore is among the things that were. Mr. Bales was associate justice of the county in 1861, and supervisor of the township in 1872. Bagdad is a point on the Okaw three miles west of Arcola.

Newton I. Cooper, of this township, was elected sheriff of the county in the fall of 1870, up to which time for a period, he had been township collector. In the following March he disappeared suddenly, leaving between five and six thousand dollars of township funds unaccounted for. Cooper, a recent comer in the neighborhood, was a man of pleasing address and appearance, and that, together with his rather notable business qualifications, inspired confidence in all who had dealings with him.

On Thursday afternoon, November 4, 1875, R. P. McWilliams, a well known and highly respected citizen of Bourbon township, was instantly killed at the highway crossing of the Illinois Midland Railway, west of Arcola and near the residence of Jacob Moore. He was driving a mule team attached to a wagon. He approached the crossing and, as he thought, allowed the train to pass and began to resume his way, probably, naturally looking at the train, but he was unfortunately caught by the latter part of the train, which had become uncoupled. The team escaped.

The name of this township is derived from that of Bourbon county, Kentucky, which was represented by several of the first settlers. The people voted bonds in aid of the I. M. Railway to the amount of thirty-five thousand dollars.

The township has contributed liberally of her citizens to the public service. John Chandler, the first clerk of the county, was elected in 1859 and again in 1861. Caleb Bales was associate justice for a term beginning November, 1861, and was also supervisor in 1872. Samuel B. Logan was the first sheriff of the county, 1859. Newton I. Cooper was made sheriff in 1870. Lemauel Chandler served as supervisor in 1868-69-70-71, and had also charge of the interests of the county in realizing from the state the amount due from swamp lands. M. D. Bartholomew was supervisor in 1873, and was succeeded by Andrew Ray in 1874, who was returned in 1875. J. F. Bouck came from Ohio in 1866 to Bourbon township and served with a captain's commission in the One Hundred and Fifty-fourth Regiment of that state in the war of 1861.

Chesterville is a small hamlet with a post-office and store and one church, the United Brethren. The population in 1890 was twenty-eight.

The villages of Fillmore and Bagdad of this township have disappeared from the face of the map.

Arthur, a most progressive village of about seven hundred people, was laid out by the Paris & Decatur Railroad Company on the lands of M. Warren, of Moultrie, and the Murpheys, of Douglas county. The county line divides the village north and south. The Douglas county surveying was done by the railroad engineers, and certified by Mr. Niles, the Douglas county surveyor. This was in July, 1873. Murphy's addition was made January 30, 1875, and Reeves' addition December 30, 1874, both surveyed by Mr. Niles. The first business house was put up by Jacob Sears. William H. Ward brought the first stock of goods to the village and in the spring of 1873 J. W. Barrum founded the first drug store. Arthur was incorporated in the county court of Moultrie county at the April term, A. D. 1877, which was signed by David Crockett, C. G. McComb, William Ellers, M. Hunsaker, M. H. Warren, B. G. Hoover, H. Dehart, J. W. Sears and some forty others. The court found there were three hundred and fifty inhabitants residing in the territory. The petition for the election was granted and the election ordered for May 7, 1877. Under the act approved April 9, 1872, M. H. Warren and James Ellars were appointed judges of the election, the returns to be made to Moultrie county. There were for village organization thirty-three votes, and against it thirty votes. On June 12, 1877, the first election was held for the choice of six trustees and a clerk, in which the persons chosen were C. G. McComb, W. H. H. Reeder, H. C. Jones, J, W, Sears, N. Thompson and M. Hunsaker, and J. W. Barrum was duly elected clerk.

On the farm of Mr. Blaase some mounds have been found from which human remains, apparently ancient, have been exhumed in excavating for a building. The idea that several slight elevations near here were the work of human hands is sustained to an extent by the fact that ancient marks upon trees all facing to one point are noticed. On the same farm, what was supposed to be a large flat rock, some twelve feet square, was found and supposed to cover interesting matter. A relative of Mr. Blaase dug around it on all sides to a depth of about eight feet, but he came to the conclusion that the bottom was in China, and the work was abandoned.

A Hurricane.—May 14, 1858, a hurricane visited this part of the county from the northwest, on its way to Arcola, where it had an engagement, doing considerable damage in and near Bourbon village, the effects of which, however, were more seriously felt in Arcola, where several houses were considerably damaged, and others altogether overthrown. It was a busy day at Bourbon at the time, and it was fun to the perfectly cool fellows who were not at all alarmed to see cursing, swearing, fighting men "hunt their holes." We don't remember just now who the cool fellows were.

BOWDRE TOWNSHIP.

Bowdre township has forty-eight and one-half square miles of territory. When township organization was adopted in 1868, this township was called Deer Creek, after the water course of that name which traverses it, and had been a part of Collins precinct in Coles county. The Embarras river runs through the northeast part and receives Scattering Fork in the north. The township is traversed by the Illinois Midland Railway from the west to the southeast, a considerable deflection having been made in the line of the road that it might pass within a mile of the center of the township, upon which condition and for other reasons, the people of the township voted bonds in ad of the road to the amount of thirty thousand dollars.

Railroads.—This township is intersected by the Illinois Midland Railway, now the Vandalia system, running generally east and west, entering it near the northwest corner of section 4, township 14, range 8, running thence east along the congressional township line for about two miles; thence southeastwardly, leaving the township about the middle of the east line of section 8, township 14, range 10, then making a decided large curve to the north, and back again.

This extra length and curvature was caused by a demand on the part of the citizens that the road should pass within a mile of the center of the township, upon which conditions the township, by a vote of the people, subscribed township bonds in aid of the road to the amount of $30,000. It was shown that the issue was illegal there being no authority whatever for holding the election. The tax was enjoined, and proper steps taken to abrogate the whole proceedings, which obtained. The bonds found their way into the hands of innocent parties, who purchased them as a permanent investment.

Early land entries and early settlers.—As to the first entries of land in this township, the earliest date is found to be the entry of June, 1833, by Samuel C. Gill, who took the east half of northeast quarter of section 2, township 15, range 9, and other lands. John Davis, in October, 1833, entered west half of northeast quarter, same section. In 1836, in February, the northeast quarter of northeast quarter of section 11, township 15, range 9, was entered by the Barnets, and as in other parts of the county, the great bulk of the lands were entered in 1852 and 1853. Isaac Davidson arrived in 1838. James A. Breeden settled, in 1853, upon section 9, township 14, range 9, and built the first house on the prairie, between the old "Wallace Stand," near Hickory Grove, and the Okaw timber, which was eight miles to the west.

The "Wallace Stand" was the residence of A. G. Wallace for some years. Mr. Wallace is noted elsewhere in this book. John Davis, who entered his land in 1833, arrived in the state from Brown county, Ohio, in September, 1834. He died in March, 1865. Shiloah Gill arrived in 1852, and settled on the land entered by his father in 1833. (See sketches elsewhere.)

John Barnet, called "Jack" by everybody, came from Kentucky to the Little Vermillion in 1832, and to Coles county, since Douglas, in 1842. The life partners of several prominent citizens were his daughters.

School lands.—Section 16, township 14, range 9 east, the "school" section, was purchased from the state in the first instance of its occupancy, each section 16 having been set apart by law for the use of schools. The sales were made in 1856. John Cofer took four hundred acres, and W. D. Martin two hundred and forty acres. It was surveyed and lotted as required by law. Lot one is northeast quarter of the northeast quarter, forty and two-thirds acres; Lot two is southeast quarter of the northeast quarter, forty and two-thirds acres; three is west half of northeast quarter, eighty-one acres; the east half of northwest quarter is Lot four, seventy-seven acres; northwest quarter of the northwest quarter; thirty-eight and one-half acres, is five; and southwest quarter of the northwest quarter is six, which also contains thirty-eight and one-half acres.

The south half of the section corresponds in position and area. This lotting was arbitrary, though the surveyor ostensibly preserved the original areas. In this case, the east half of the section is found to contain seventeen acres more than the west half. It is fair, then, to suppose that the quarter section corners on the north line and on the south line must have been found as originally surveyed much too far west.

Section 16, township 15, range 9, another school section in Bowdre bounds, was lotted in forty and eighty acre lots, and found to come out exactly even all around; perhaps it was surveyed in the house. It was aparted into ten lots; east half of northeast quarter was one, and west half was two and three; east half of northwest quarter was four, and west half of northwest quarter was five and six; the south half of the section was made into four lots, of even eighty acres each.

These school lands were sold all too soon, and consequently almost sacrificed, bringing in some instances as low as two dollars per acre. It was not believed in those days that the prairie would be settled. The high grass and weeds, and the absence of roads added to the blank, dreary lookout generally, and forbade the idea that homes would ever have a place there.

As late as 1851, John Davis offered to sell lot two, southwest quarter of section 6, township 15, range 10, eighty-four acres, for the entry money he had paid for it, viz., $1.25 per acre; this was seventeen years after he had entered it. It was in Camargo township.

Old inhabitants.—H. L. Thornsbrue is the oldest living person born in Douglas county; Mrs. Mary West, relict of Thomas West, was the oldest resident. and settled here in 1834. She died March 3, 1884, aged seventy-nine, after a residence of half a century in the county. Issachar Davis is the oldest male inhabitant, his residence here dating from October 3, 1834. Mr. Davis was a farmer and land surveyor. He was elected county surveyor in 1863, 1867 and 1875.

Churches.—In the southeast quarter of section 16, township 15, range 9, is situated Mt. Gilead Methodist church, which offers conveniences to neighboring church-goers. At Hugo is Antioch church. The Methodists have a church in section 14, township 14, range 9, and the Christians and Methodists in Hindsboro.

HINDSBORO VILLAGE.

The town or village of Hindsboro is situated in section 6, 14, 10, and was laid out by the railroad company upon the lands of the Hinds Brothers in 1874, the plat covering about sixty-two acres. The railroad here runs about southeast and the plan of the town is in conformity with it, the principal streets being at right angles and parallel with the line of the road. The place is improving rapidly and has claims as a shipping point which can not be ignored. Here Lodge No. 571, I. O. O. F., was instituted April 12, 1875, the first officers of which were: J. Gerard, N. G.; B. F. Strader, V. G.; J. M. Dwinnell, secretary; and James Stites, treasurer, and J. Gerard, D. G. M.

The town was laid off in 1874, being surveyed by H. C. Niles, from plans furnished by the railroad, which plans, by the way, were changed by the proprietors *before* the town was surveyed, but *after* a map of the town had been engraved and published in an atlas map; this, unfortunately, makes the printed map worse than useless. The lots and blocks were laid off parallel, and at right angles to the railroad, which here runs about southeast, and consequently bad "point" lots occur all around the borders of the plat. In a country where the cardinal points are almost universally used in metes and bounds, a village plan not "square with the world" has many inconveniences for which there is generally no necessity. The village is improving rapidly and has claims as a shipping and trading point, which are rapidly growing in importance.

Hindsboro is a good business center, having two good general stores and two enterprising grain buyers. Its population is about three hundred.

Kemp is a small village in this township.

Hugo has a postoffice and store with a population of about fifty. It is the scene of about the last appearance of Indians in the county, a trading store having been kept there by one Vessar and one Hubbard in 1829-30.

The Indians.—Issachar Davis said that at about the center of southwest quarter of southeast quarter of section 12 township 15, range 9, and on the northeast quarter of the northwest quarter of section 13, near the old trading post, several Indian graves have been discovered and examined. Human bones were found in each, as well as beads and a silver brooch, by William Wiley and John Welliver. A large silver crescent, five or six inches in diameter, and about two and one-half inches wide at its broadest part, was also secured. Samuel Cheney, a former resident, now living near Humbolt, in Coles county, saw the departure of the last band of Indians, in April, 1833. He was a son of James Cheney, who came to the neighborhood in 1830, and the first wife of Issachar Davis was a sister of his. She had a quantity of trinkets, which she had procured from the Indians by trading provisions, etc. At another time, the corpse of an Indian was found against a tree, near the Embarrass, and not far from the mouth of Scattering Fork.

A Christian church.—A Christian church, ycleped "Antioch," is situated here on the southwest quarter of section 12, township 15, range 9, which was built in 1881, at an expense of about twelve hundred dollars.

Murder.—Bowdre is the scene of the second murder committed in the county, Arcola City having the first, third and fourth. At the February term, 1871, of Douglas county circuit court, O. P. Greenwood was indited for the murder of George Mussett. He met him in the woods near Hugo and shot him with a rifle. Greenwood was tried at Charleston, Coles county, on a change of venue, and sentenced to the penitentiary for twenty-one years. Having surrendered himself to the officers, and as there was some probability of self-defense, as well as some supposed justification, domestic difficulty being the cause of the quarrel, and some other extenuating circumstances, a petition was circulated for his pardon, which prevailed after Greenwood had served about seven years. He was defended by Hon. Thomas E. Bundy and Hon. James A. Connolly. Hon. J. G. Cannon was engaged to conduct the prosecution by several citizens who made up a purse for that purpose. Greenwood afterward lived a while in Tuscola and removed South.

GARRETH TOWNSHIP.

Garrett is named in honor of Isam Garrett. Before township organization the area, as an election precinct, was much smaller than at present. It was bounded on the east by the Okaw river, and on the south by the congressional township line, containing only about thirty square miles. There were added about twenty more when the townships were made, and the east line was extended to the range or township line on the east, and to the south part was added two tiers of sections off the north end of the congressional township on the south. As now constituted, it is bounded on the north and on the west by the county line, on the south by the township of Bourbon, and on the east by Tuscola, and consists of all of township 16 north, of range 7 east, of the third principal meridian, and sections 1 to 12 inclusive, of township 15 north, of range 7 east, the total area in square miles being 51.83, the same being according to the United States government survey 33,171.95 acres.

This is the shape it received upon the adoption of township organization in 1868, a particular account of which is given elsewhere in this volume. A section of land is usually estimated to contain six hundred and forty acres, which is indeed the average, the exceptions being the fractional sections, occurring on the north and west sides of all townships surveyed by the government. The north tier of sections in township 15 north, range 7 east, in Garrett, one to six inclusive, are all over one thousand acres in area, and section 6, township 15, range 7, mostly owned by James Drew, was the largest government section of land in the county, containing 1,148.21 acres; it is over one and one-half miles in north and south length, and considerably over one mile in east and west measure.

The government surveyors were instructed to make all townships of thirty-six sections to contain, as near as may be, twenty-three thousand and forty acres, that is to say, to be six miles square and include thirty-six sections. Township 16 north, range 7 east, is the only congressional township in the county which "fills the bill," the area, according to government survey, being exactly the proposed area in gross. It does not follow that each section is exactly six hundred and forty acres.

Topography, drainage, etc.—The Kaskaskia river traverses the east tier of sections in this sub-division of the county, and, being here near the very source of this river, which rises in Champaign county, depends upon the rainfall for its waters. It is therefore about dry in the summer months, while immediately after heavy rains it comes up in a hurry, and becomes a rapid stream of a width of from four to six rods, and in the north part, getting out of the banks, has an indefinite extent. The sudden rise of this and other streams in the county is owing materially to the improved system of farm drainage, which of late years has so much obtained. Every man who ditches his land at all in this region is contributing to the waters of the Okaw, the capacity of which to carry off the accumulated waters is comparatively less than of old, which naturally suggests improvement, and it is only a question of time when the improvement of our main streams will be considered the one thing needful in the proper drainage of the farms of the county. A water course known as Dry Fork runs through the middle of the township in a north and south direction, and, falling into the Okaw at the south line of the township, is an important carrier for the prairie lands to the north. Lake Fork, which is born in Piatt county, comes into Garrett half a mile south of the village of Atwood, and is a contributor to the Okaw in Bourbon township; like all prairie water courses, it is wet and dry by turns and nothing long.

The drainage commissioners of this township have, on petition of interested parties, established a large drainage district, under the statute, which is situated in the southwest part, contains about thirty-two hundred acres of land, and the drains are constructed at an expense of about twenty-eight hundred dollars. These consist of large open ditches, which are by law under the control of the highway commissioners, whose duty it is to keep them in repair from year to year, the same as roads, the expense of which is met by a tax levied upon the land owners in the district, for the benefit of whom the original district was organized. The ditches will average sixteen feet in width, the cost of construction being about one dollar per lineal rod. C. G. Eckert was the attorney for the commissioners, who also employed H. C. Niles as surveyor and engineer. The work was regularly staked out railroad fashion, and the elevations taken. These drains were exceedingly popular in their inception, very much the contrary when the tax is made known and collected, and the pride and boast of the people when completed.

The highest point in Garrett township is, probably, near the southeast corner on the "Gruelle" farm, which place, by actual measure, is thirty feet higher than Tuscola; the bottom of the Okaw, near this point, is thirty-five feet lower than this highest point, which is a "divide" near the line of Tuscola and this township.

The great body of timber in Garrett is on the south side, but the Okaw in its entire length is fringed, as it were, with woods. On the west side, and in the neighborhood of Lake Fork, many small but attractive natural groves occur, notably on the lands of Nathan Garrett and others; and in the heart of the woods, near the south center of the township, a large "glade" occurs; the original surveyors called it a "draught." Goodson's Grove is situated at the northeast corner of section 33, township 16, range 7, and is a nice little piece of woods. All of these glades, cut-offs and groves were duly noted and mapped by the original surveyors, who did their government surveying in this region in 1821.

Bowlders of granite or other rock are rarely found of any great dimensions; in many parts of the county, whether prairie or timber, they are unknown, while in other sections there are enough of small bulk, weighing from one hundred to five hundred pounds, to obstruct to some extent the tilling of the soil; but these are few. The largest granite rock in the county, visible above the soil, is in the southeast corner of section 8, township 16, range 7, upon the farm once owned by Judge Mullen, in this township. It stands above the ground about twelve feet, and is about as much in thickness. All of these surface rocks have been rounded by the action of water, and have evidently been transported by natural agencies from their natural beds. A glacier, for instance, ages ago, was started from the Artics as a frozen river of ice, bearing upon its bed tons of rock, which it deposited as it melted in the summer heat of the then temperate zone. An extensive ledge of limestone, which makes good lime, as proven by actual business, occurs in Sargent township (q. v.).

Railroads.—The St. Louis branch of the I. D. & W. Railway, first called the Indianapolis & Decatur, afterward the Indiana & Illinois Central, and next the Indianapolis, Decatur & Springfield, traverses this township from east to west along the middle line of the south tier of sections, in township 16 north, range 7 east, and is a straight line through this township. It was completed here in 1872.

A bridge burned.—A Howe truss bridge over the Okaw, west side, section 36, township 16, range 7, half a mile west of Howe Station was maliciously burned on the night of July 3, 1873, and as a Fourth of July excursion was on the tapis for next day, it is difficult to imagine the state of mind of the fellow who did it. By withholding his name, he has lost the distinction of being Douglas county's greatest scoundrel.

Land entries.—Among the first entries of land in Garrett township we find that Jacob Lease, in December, 1834, entered the northeast quarter of section 24, township 16, range 7; and in 1835, in June, J. G. Devault took the southeast quarter of section 13, township 16, range 7. I. F. Lewis entered the northeast quarter of section 12, township 16, range 7, in 1836; and June 16, 1849, Benjamin Ellars located and patented the west half of lot 1, northeast quarter of section 2, township 16, range 7, and other lands. Josiah Hoots owned a large body of land in the southeast corner of the township. He was an ancient settler of prominence and influence. He died in October, 1876, in the fifty-eighth year of his age. He was a native of Salem, North Carolina, removed to Indiana at the age of seven, and subsequently to this neighborhood, of which he was a useful citizen for about thirty-eight years. He was buried, Masonically, at Cartright Chapel, three miles west of Tuscola, by Tuscola Lodge, No. 332, of which he was an ancient and honored member.

According to legendary report, Lemuel Randall entered, March 16, 1850, the four forties lying around the center of section 34, township 16, range 7. Thomas Goodson was with Randall, and knowing the numbers of the land, got the patent for him. This entry was made before the railroad had selected its lands, but, under a mistake, the railroad temporarily got these. Meanwhile, Randall had sold to Nathan Drake, who had transferred to D. Maris. Drake had taken the precaution of re-entering the tracts, having had intimation of the error. The books at the office still showed it to be railroad land, and finally the land entry book of the county shows that the land was really and finally entered by J. W. L. Slavens, February 22, 1865. This is, then, the very last entry of government lands in Douglas county. In short, the railroad never had acquired the tracts, and they were left open to have the distinction of being the last entries.

The sixteenth section in township 16 north, range 7 east, reserved for schools, the title to which is derived from the state, was taken up in 1854, having been divided into eight lots by the surveyor, containing seventy-eight to seventy-nine acres each, lot 1 being the east half of the northwest quarter. J. L. Jordan took two, Harvey Otter one, E. T. Romine two, J. C. Wythe two, etc.

Pioneer personals.—Isam Garrett, in compliment to whom the township was named, lived to the advanced age of eighty-two years. He died February 14, 1880. It is the popular opinion that Mr. Garrett never used tobacco or drank spirits, never served on a jury, never was a witness in court, never sued and never was sued, and that he never told a lie in his life. He was an educated free-thinker, and held that life is a terrific problem; that we are placed upon this earth without being consulted, and removed without our consent; and that the golden rule was the only guide; and to "do good and throw it into the sea; if the fishes don't know it, God will."

Dr. Thomas Parsons, of this township, was a noted hunter and marksman, and now, at the advanced age of eighty-three, shows with pride some thirty targets which he has preserved for many years, representing his victories. These are about two inches in diameter, and show the size of a rifle ball repeated to any extent and cutting into each other at all edges. The Doctor was once the preceptor of Caleb Garrett, at Terre Haute, as a carpenter and builder.

Mr. Caleb Garrett, son of Isam, represented the county of Vigo in Indiana in 1842, and was re-elected at the age of twenty-one. He settled in Douglas county in 1847, served on the first grand jury, was justice of the peace in 1854, and for some years after. He was also first supervisor of Garrett township. He first bought land in the west part of the township, subsequently accumulated other and larger tracts, and in May, 1865, sold out and transferred his farming interests to Tuscola township by purchase.

Harvey Otter, James Drew, Jacob Mosbarger, Dr. D. A. Meeker, William Howe and William Ellars were of the early settlers. Howe arrived in the present bounds of Douglas county in 1838. He went to California in 1850, and returned in 1853; he was one of the largest land owners in the township; was elected supervisor of the township in 1876, and again in 1883, and in 1884 William Ellars' family came from Ohio and settled in the Okaw timber near the north line, in 1849, at which time there was not a settler on the prairie to the west.

Joseph Moore, or, to put it more exactly, "Old Joe Moore," arrived in the present bounds of Douglas county in 1832. He was the repository of all the jokes, good, bad and indifferent, illustrative of the manners and customs of the earlier days.

Thomas Goodson entered the north half of the southwest quarter of section 27, township 16, range 7, July 9, 1850, and other lands; he continued a resident until lately, when he died, leaving numerous descendants and a large estate. Goodson was a great hunter; he once killed two deer with a single ball, on what is now the farm of William Brian in the northeast part of the township; he assisted in the extermination of the very last family of wild cats found in the Okaw timber. He relates that he cut a large tree for rail timber in the exact spot where he had cut a similar one thirty-six years before. Notwithstanding the large quantities of timber used for building, fuel and fencing in the early days, the question whether the timber is holding its own or not is an open one. It is a noteworthy fact, in this connection, and without the slightest intention of reflecting upon any old settler, it may be stated that the timber belonging to the lands of actual settlers remained in good condition much longer than that of the government, it being understood that all settlers had a kind of right to use government timber; the timber lands of non-residents, which were called speculator's lands, were included under the same head, and some of the early debating societies had up the question, whether the owners of such lands had any rights which anybody was bound to respect, and being decided in the negative,"bowed the woods beneath their sturdy stroke."

John Lester and his sons, Samuel and Sigler H., were of the first comers. Samuel Lester entered his first land in section 1, township 15, range 7, in 1835, and up to 1838 had entered all the north half of the section, eight hundred acres. Sigler H. entered, in April, 1836, the west half of the northeast quarter of section 25, township 16, range 7, and subsequently other lands. These sons died, Samuel in 1860 and Sigler in 1864, leaving large estates to numerous descendants, which lands, however, by either mischance or choice, have passed out of the hands of the families. The Lesters were men of great natural force and decision of character, and like most other people were great hunters. Goodson related that John Lester once cut a large bee tree, and converting it into a gum, stood it upon end full of honey and covered it with a slab, leaving it for a more convenient season. Goodson had just killed three deer, and finding the gum ready to his hand, filled it up with tallow, and did this to save it from the ravens, for at that time ravens were plenty; they were larger than the common crow, and are since extinct here. Lester, returning and finding tallow in the place of his honey could not understand how anybody would rob him of his honey and leave tallow in exchange, the latter being much more valuable.

F. C. Mullen entered his first land in section 28, township 16, range 7, in 1850. He came from Delaware, and was the second county judge of the new county of Douglas. About these days Judge Mullen was traveling toward his home from Vandalia, where he had been entering land, and upon reaching Sullivan, in Moultrie county, his traveling companion suggested that they should go at once to the tavern and take a drink. Mullen preferred to first take care of the horses, and did so, which made some delay; they then proceeded toward the tavern, and learned that William Campbell, an old resident of this township, had been robbed of one hundred and fifty dollars in gold; that every man in the saloon had been searched and the money not found. It is somewhat interesting to speculate as to what might have been the consequences to the Judge on this occasion, if he had not been fortunately delayed, for he had just arrived a perfect stranger and had on his person in gold precisely the amount they were looking for.

The chase.—Hunting at the proper season occupied the attention of the early settlers considerably, and a principal part of the living was venison; this, with the natural love of the sport born in and with more enterprising and vigorous of the settlers, made the pursuit a favorite. Isaac L. Jordan and his brother "Wash," Caleb and Nathan Garrett, Thomas Goodson and the Lesters were enthusiastic hunters. The Garretts and Jordans had amongst them about twenty-five hounds. In 1853, while on a wolf hunt, Jordan and Garrett had followed the trail from their neighborhood to the present site or Tuscola, eight miles, and the peculiar action of a favorite hound attracting the attention of Jordan, he, with his experience as a hunter, immediately called the dogs off the trail of the wolf, though it had been getting warm, and began cautiously to explore for deer, the nobler game. In a few moments, in the low ground, just about where the Illinois Central Railroad depot now stands in Tuscola, he raised the largest buck ever seen in their experience. The buck started off southwest and was run down and killed by the dogs in the Gruelle farm, four miles southwest.

On another occasion a trained hound compelled the attention of Garrett and conducted him to a place where the dogs had killed a deer, which they had chased of their own notion. The dogs, after running down, would kill a deer and eat till satisfied, and the only trophies secured in the first case was the head, horns and a foot, as the relics of the "biggest buck." In this flat country there was almost no vantage-ground for the deer; he ran till he could run no more, and was too much exhausted to fight. A "stag at bay" was rare, and to be in at the death took rapid riding and good shooting; the horses enjoyed the sport and learned to run by sight.

Many persons remember the reception these hounds gave every visitor to the various farms. He would ride up to the house, and if he passed along, all right, but if he stopped and gave the customary "hello!" ten or a dozen hounds rushed toward him, with an open-mouthed deep baying salute that would make the hair of a timid man "stand on end," but all he had to do to restore perfect peace was to "light." It was only a bay of welcome, and a notice to the family that perhaps a wayfarer wanted his supper and a bed.

A lynching.—Mr. I. L. Jordan, of this township, informed me that in the case of lynching of "Dolph" Monroe, of Coles county, in 1854, the entire jury was selected from the present area of Douglas county. He shot and killed his father-in-law, N. Ellington, the circuit clerk of Coles county, and was hung by a mob in January, 1855, at Charleston. The jury was composed of William and James R. Hammett, Coleman Bright, Henry Lowe and John Frahme, of Camargo township; Amzi Wildman, I. L. Jordan and Israel Harris, of Garrett; S. Meyers, Daniel Martin, Squire Adams and Dan Foster; they brought in a verdict of "murder in the first degree." This mob had no occasion to violate the law, but having come to see the show, and fearing disappointment, concluded to have the show anyway. Mr. Jordan, and others of the jury, think they could have prevented it, if present. It is the blackest blot on Coles county, of which Douglas was then a part.

By the way, is not the fact that burglaries and robberies in the earlier days were rare, owing to something besides the honesty and scarcity of valuables amongst the people. The perception, memory and observation of the residents were sharpened by the want of government, and no man could pass through the country without being especially marked and remembered; not from suspicion—this rarely obtained—but from a habit of observation, born partly of their isolated position, and somewhat of their thirst for news. A man on horseback, or "any other man," who went through the country, could be traced a hundred miles, and if necessary, overtaken.

The "spirit of the times."—The residence of I. L. Jordan, north half of the southwest quarter, and southeast quarter of the southwest quarter of section 29, township 16, range 7 (lands which he entered in 1852), being central in the township, was a point for elections and other public meetings; it was also made a center for the collection of taxes by the sheriff, who was then "sheriff and collector" under the old *regime* (before 1868) and county organization. Upon one occasion, 1859, the first sheriff, Sam Logan, had made his collections at "Jordan's," as it was called, when not only had the people generally met him there to pay taxes according to notice, but Jordan was shelling corn with twelve or fourteen hands. Sam had his saddle-bags with him, containing the results of two or three days' collections, which were augmented at this place. About night, after "Sam" had partaken of the hospitalities of "Ike," which any old settler who knows either will certify were not stinted, he mounted his horse and started for Tuscola, to deposit his money. At about half past ten o'clock—pretty late, in those days, for men who began work at four A. M.—Jordan, in bed, heard the customary "hello," and, as usual, responded promptly, expecting to entertain a belated traveler. It was "Sam;" and the next word was, of course, "light." But Sam said, "No, I can't stop. I hung my saddle-bags on the corner of the stable, forgot them, and went off, and now they are not there." Ike, after joking him a good deal, which he couldn't help, handed him to him, and Sam went on his way rejoicing. The saddle-bags contained about twenty-five hundred dollars. This little incident is related to show the spirit of the times. Sam probably took his "pile," and going on to Tuscola quietly deposited—well, simply woke up some merchant, at a store, and, making up his package, a conglomerate mass of wild-cat money issued by almost every bank in North America, slapped it into such a safe as was used, and calmly went on his way, or more likely went to bed where he struck. The only banks were the safes of merchants—Wyeth, Craddock & Co., J. M. Smith, Davis & Ensey, etc. Every fellow called for his money when he wanted it, and always got it. The depositors would often permit the merchant to use some of the money, and always got it on call. This mutual confidence was never abused, though they never took receipts.

ATWOOD VILLAGE.

The village of Atwood is situated on the

west line of the township, at the county line, lying partly in both the counties of Douglas and Piatt, and on either side of the east and west railroad, its location being in section 30, township 16 north, range 7 east. Harvy Otter contributed the southwest quarter of the northwest quarter, and George Nolind the north half of the southwest quarter; Ritchie and others "put in" land in Piatt county. It was laid off on paper by Patterson, first assistant engineer of the railroad, and surveyed by Mr. Niles, the then county surveyor, in 1873. In those years, the county surveyor was, by law, the only person qualified to survey town lots, the law being changed, so that any competent surveyor can now act.

The streets are named East A street, East B street and East C street, etc., and North Front, North Second, North Third, etc., The Douglas county plat consists of blocks, which are generally forty feet front by one hundred and fifty feet; streets, lanes and alleys are parallel with and at right angles to the railroad, and the whole is compactly and conveniently arranged. The railroad, besides the usual right-of-way reserved of one hundred feet wide, has also reserved a tract north of its line one hundred and fifty feet wide, and extending east from the county line eleven hundred feet, nearly four acres. The dedication of the lots and blocks, in the signing of the plats for record, was made jointly by the original proprietors of the land, and H. C. Moore, the superintendent of the railway, Hammond, the president, and T. H. Macoughtry, the railroad attorney, the owners of the ground having, for certain considerations, agreed to give these gentlemen a half-interest in all the lots and blocks, with some reservations. This led to some confusion, many deeds having been made without the signature of all the parties, but which was finally cured by quit-claiming back to the first owners of the land.

First store.—The first store in the village was a dry goods establishment by Helton & Barrett, at the southwest corner of County street and South Front street.

Churches.—The first church erected in the village is the New-Light Christian church, which was built in 1880 at an expense of about fourteen hundred dollars. It is furnished with a good bell, costing eighty dollars, and commands in its membership many of the best citizens. They are not the same as the Disciples of Christ, which is the Christian church, who added the present edifice subsequently, at a cost of about sixteen hundred dollars. This church has also a good bell. These bells chime in loving unison, and in their sweet accord give no intimation of their preferences.

The Methodist church was removed from Mackville as part of the exodus therefrom in 1883. The building is worth about twelve hundred dollars, and the cost of moving it was about two hundred dollars.

We have in little Douglas the Presbyterians and the Cumberland Presbyterians, the Methodist Episcopal, the Methodist Protestant, the Free Methodist, the Episcopalians, the Christian church and the "Old New-Light" Christian church, and two kinds of Baptists, etc., and are thus able to offer facilities to truthseekers not to be surpassed by any county of our size in the state.

The press.—The first newspaper published in the village was the Atwood Independent, and, under the charge of S. W. and F. E. Lucas, made its salutatory on December 14, 1883. (See sketch of William E. Means.)

Incorporation.—December 14, 1883, a petition was filed with W. H. Bassett, county judge, signed by thirty legal voters residing within certain territory, the greater portion of which lies in Douglas county, setting forth a desire to become incorporated as the "village of Atwood;" that the number of inhabitants in the proposed bounds was three hundred. The county judge accordingly fixed upon January 9, 1884, as the time, and the office of J. W. Merritt, J. P., as the place, when and where the election should be held, and he appointed as judges of election James A. Hawks, M. C. Drake and A. L. Marshall, which gentlemen, in due course, made the following report:

There were cast at such election: For village organization, sixty-six votes; against village organization, forty-two votes; total, one hundred and twenty-eight votes.

The area of the village.—The territory included in the village incorporation is comprised of the west half of the northwest quarter of the northwest quarter, and the southwest quarter of the northwest quarter, and the west half of the southeast quarter of the northwest quarter, and the west half of the northeast quarter of the southwest quarter, and the north half of the southwest quarter of the southwest quarter, and the northwest quarter of the southwest quarter in section 31, in Douglas county; and the east half of the northeast quarter of the northeast quarter, and the southeast quarter of the northeast quarter, and the east half of the southwest quarter of the northeast quarter, and the east quarter of the northwest quarter of the southeast quarter, and the northeast quarter of the southeast quarter, and the north half of the southeast quarter of the southeast quarter in section 36 in Piatt county, all in township 16 north, being in area two hundred and ninety acres, of which one hundred and sixty acres are in Douglas, leaving one hundred and thirty in Piatt county.

The matter was prepared and concluded by C. G. Eckhart, Esq., of Tuscola.

Atwood at present has several first-class stores, a bank, a good hotel, a newspaper, good churches and schools and has a population of about six hundred people.

Garrett has been represented at the county seat by F. C. Mullen, who was elected county judge in 1861. This was under the old style of county organization which stopped in 1868. I. L. Jordan was elected sheriff in 1864. Caleb Garrett was the first supervisor of the township, elected in 1868. He was succeeded by William Ellars in 1869, who was re-elected in 1870-71-72, being followed by J. W. Hackett in 1873, Thomas Owen in 1874, and by Josiah Hoots in 1875. William Howe was in the same position in 1876, 1882 and 1883; Jason Green was elected in 1877, and is the only Democrat placed in that office to date. He was re-elected in 1878-79. Claus Greve, a naturalized German, was sent in in 1880, and Green was returned again in 1881, and returned in 1882.

The village of Garrett has of recent years become quite a trading point; with good school and church. It has a population of about two hundred and fifty.

SARGENT TOWNSHIP.

Derivation of name, bounds, area, etc.—Sargent township takes its name from that of one of its oldest settlers and who was one of the most prominent business and cattle farmers—Snowden Sargent. In the old Coles county days it was a part of "Oakland precinct," set off for election purposes, and that part which remained in Douglas, after the formation of the new county, took the name of Sargent precinct, and was very small, having only about twenty-three square miles. It was bounded on the east and south by the county line, on the north by a line from corner of sections 16, 17, 20 and 21, running east to Edgar county, and it had a southwest boundary at the Embarrass river, which separated it from Deer Creek, since Bowdre township. Sargent at the time of township organization, in 1868, was made into its present shape, and is bounded on the east and south by the county line, on the west by Bowdre and on the north by Murdock and Newman, the north line beginning at the northeast corner of section 9, township 14, range 14 west, and running thence west on the section lines about seven miles to the northwest corner of section 9, township 15, range 9 east, and thence south on the section lines eight miles to the south county line. It contains fifty-two sections of land, which includes, however, only 46.45 square miles, and consequently comprise 29,728.94 acres, and in area ranks No. 5 in the county, the discrepancy between the number of sections and number of square miles being accounted for by the fact that many of the sections are very small—those in what is called township 15 north, of range 11 east, running from two hundred to three hundred and fifty acres, their surveyed width being little over one quarter of a mile. The smallest government section of land in the county is in this township—section 7, township 15, range 11—and has only 198.38 acres.

Surface features.—A large part of the township is prairie, perhaps two-thirds; the balance is the usual proportion of timber land along the borders of the creeks, of which "Brushy Fork," an affluent of the Embarrass river, comes in on the north line, and flows southwesterly toward the west side, when it joins the larger creek, the Embarrass, in section 28, township 15, range 10, and their mingled waters then run southeasterly until they leave the county at the south side of section 1, township 14, range 10, running two or three miles in Coles county and re-entering Douglas on the east side of section 15, township 14, range 10. Deer Creek comes in from the west, and also joins the Embarrass in the north part of section 33, township 15, range 10. Several other natural water-courses of smaller dimensions flow into these creeks at various points, and in the west part provide amply for drainage.

The southeast part being somewhat level, a drainage district is in process of development, under the statute, which, as soon as the advantages are realized, will be followed by others, as is always the case.

The highest point in the township, if not in the county, and at least rivaling in elevation the "Ridge" in Newman township, was upon the farm of Andrew Gwinn, Esq., where the government erected an observatory. This is a wooden structure of a height of about one hundred feet, from which to take instrumental observations for the connection of the triangular survey of the great lakes with that of the Mississippi river and the gulf coasts.

Old Settlers.—Among the most prominent of the earliest settlers was Snowden Sargent, for whom the township was named. He made his first visit to the state in 1830, and entered four hundred acres of land at the office at Palestine, and passed through all the usual vicissitudes and privations of pioneer life, and became eventually one of the largest land owners in the county; dying in 1875, he left a large estate to his descendants.

Andrew Gwinn settled here before 1836, from his last location in Indiana, and visited the Richmans in Camargo (who were the first settlers in the county, 1830). His lands, adjoining Mr. Sargent's and together occupying so much territory, made the establishment of a school district quite a problem. He had the largest farm in Douglas county—three thousand and one hundred acres.

I. W. Burgett lived in this township for more than forty years, and controlled about sixteen hundred acres of land, all of which had been accumulated since his residence there. He represented his township for about six consecutive years as supervisor, and afterward for four years more. Mr. Burgett died of typhoid fever February 13, 1884. He was fifty-five years of age, and had resided in the state forty-five years. He was a man of good appearance and fine business ability.

Other early settlers were the Reddings, Samuel Allison—Casebeer, B. F. Coykendall, William Hancock and W. F. Murphy. Josephus Redding was born in Edgar county in 1829, and came to this region in 1831, when two years of age. Samuel Allison arrived in 1853, since deceased. Coykendall arrived in 1847, and I. W. Burgett in 1839. W. F. Murphy bought his first land here in 1850.

Land entries.—The first entries of land were made in 1830. We find that in this year lands were entered by Eli Sargent, I. Ashmore, Amos Leslie, Joseph Redding, Jr., David Sears, Samuel Moore, Pharmer Leslie and Hez. Rhoades. North half of the northeast quarter of section 1, township 14, range 10, was entered in this year by Sargent, who also took large bodies of other lands in the vicinity. In 1831, June 1, John Laughlin took lot 2, northwest quarter of section 2, township 14, range 10, and other lands. In the same year Stanton Pemberton covered several tracts in section 10, township 14, range 10. Pharmer Leslie, October 29, 1830, entered the west half of the southwest quarter of section 23, township 15, range 10, and east half of the northeast quarter of section 34, township 15, range 10. In 1834 S. and R. S. Williams entered large bodies of land, taking all of section 9, township 14, range 10, and the school section. Joseph P. Winkler, March 11, 1835, took northeast quarter of the northeast quarter of section 7, township 15, range 14. Daniel Landers, 1836, November 30, northwest quarter of the southwest quarter of section 14, township 15, range 10. Snowden Sargent, 1835, November 13, northwest quarter of the northwest quarter of section 1, township 14, range 10, and other lands. Daniel Miller, May 24, 1837, entered east half of the southwest quarter of section 11, township 15, range 10, and Reuben Donalds, 1837, February 22, and May 29, northeast quarter of the southwest quarter of section 1, township 14, range 10, and east half of the northeast quarter of section 6, township 14, range 14. Henry K. Potts settled in this township in 1856. Robert Matson, 1835, April 20, entered northwest quarter of section 22, township 15, range 10; in 1837, the northeast quarter of the northwest quarter of section 27, township 15, range 10, and in 1839, May 27, the east half of the northeast quarter of section 21, township 15, range 10. There is some account of him in Bowdre township (q. v.). In 1837, June 28, Isaac Wells, north half of the southeast quarter of section 7, township 15, range 10. Same year, June 1, John Hopping, southwest quarter of the northeast quarter of sectin 33, township 15, range 10. Jonathan W. Powers entered, in 1849 to 1857, the south half of the northeast quarter of section 5, township 14, range 14, and other lands. Cornelius Hopkins took the northwest quarter of the southeast quarter or section 7, township 15, range 14, and other lands, August 23, 1849; and Robert Albin, on March 4, 1850, entered the northeast quarter of the southeast quarter of section 7, township 15, range 14, and subsequently other lands. There are few if any entries in the years intervening between 1840 and 1849.

The railroad crosses the southwest part of the township, entering at the west side of section 9, township 14, range 10, and leaving at east side of section 15, same township, where it crosses the Embarrass river on a substantial bridge of some six hundred feet in length. This road got no subsidy from the township. The Toledo, Cincinnati & St. Louis Railroad crosses the southeast corner in section 4, township 14, range 14, having been constructed along here in 1881.

Villages, etc.—There is no trading point of comparative importance in the township, the business of the people, with regard to shipping points to railroad villages and post office, going to "Brushy Fork," which is the only post office in the township.

A proposed city called Columbus was regularly laid out in February, 1841, on the land of James H. Hicks, on the west side of the east half of the northeast quarter of section 35, township 15 north, of range 10 east, and contained about forty acres. The land was entered by Eli Sargent October 29, 1830. The town was surveyed by S. Sconce, Coles county surveyor, for Hicks, who does not appear to have had any deed to the land.

County office holders.—Residents, both former and present, of this township have had much to do with the public business. William Hancock was the first assessor and treasurer of the new county, having been elected with the first corps of officers in 1859. James H. Shawhan was elected sheriff in 1871, to fill the unexpired term of Cooper, of Bourbon township, who had disappeared in company with Bourbon township funds. I. W. Burgett was the first supervisor.

MURDOCK TOWNSHIP.

Erection, etc.—In years, area and population, compared with the other political subdivisions of Douglas county, Murdock township ranks number nine and last, having been created at the December meeting of the board of supervisors in 1882.

The petition for the new township was closely followed by a counterpetition in the shape of a remonstrance leading to a warm discussion of the "pros and cons," it being held and strenuously maintained that the board held jurisdiction only of the inhabitants of the proposed new territory, and not of those out of whose area the new township was to be made. This nice distinction evolved from the ingenuity of the attorneys, did not, however, prevail; the matter was taken to the circuit court on appeal, and at the October term, 1883, the action of the board being confirmed, Murdock became an independent township. The name of the township was given in compliment to John D. Murdock, an old resident yet living (see sketch).

Its area.—The area is made up from twenty-two square miles of territory, which were generously donated by the township of Camargo on the west, and about seven from Newman, which lie upon the east side. It includes the west twenty-four sections of township 16 north, of range 10 east, of third principal meridian, and sections 2, 3, 4 and 5 of township 15 north, of range 10 east, comprising twenty-eight regular sections, containing, according to the United States government survey, 30.65 square miles, the same being 19,617.61 acres, being the smallest township in the county.

With regard to the first entries of lands in this township, while there were some very early entries, most of the lands, being all prairie, were taken up along about 1852-53, which years seem to have been at the close of a period in which the government lands were temporarily withdrawn from sale pending the location of the Illinois Central Railroad and its selections of lands within the six-mile limit, which limit was afterward extended to fifteen miles to enable the road to supply the quantity of lands not found in the first limit. The latter extended limit takes in all of Murdock.

On February 23, 1853, William Cline entered the east half of the southeast quarter of section 2, township 15, range 10. This is the extreme southeast eighty acres in the township. The first entry made was by James Brewer June 18, 1847; he entered lot No. 2 of the northwest quarter of section 31, township 16, range 10, and Samuel Roderick took the southeast quarter of section 30, township 16, range 10, in 1849. J. Y. Campbell entered several tracts, as also John Tenbrook and the Baileys, 1852 to 1855.

THE VILLAGE OF MURDOCK.

This village, established and named before the township was made, is situated generally on the north side of the I. D. & W. railroad, and between it and the east and west half-mile line of section 33, township 16 north, range 10 east. It was laid off by the Murdocks in September, 1881. It was shortly afterward followed by an addition made by R. F. Helm on the north side of the east and west public road. The railroad has a reserve on the north side of its track, about eighty rods long and one hundred and twenty-five feet wide, and a right-of-way on the south side of fifty feet; a roomy side track is established which gives ample facilities to shippers in the vicinity.

Mr. S. Baxter purchased a few acres directly east of the village, where he erected several neat tenant houses which assist in giving Murdock the air of quite a busy place; this is further assisted by the elevator erected by the Murdocks in 1878, and later by Fred P. Rush & Co., of Indianapolis.

The Methodists, with their proverbial zeal, erected a substantial church here, and finished it in October, 1882, about as soon as the town was laid out. It has a steeple and a ninety-dollar bell, the cost of the structure being in all about eighteen hundred and fifty dollars.

Fairland is a new and thriving village in the northwest part of the township. It contains several first-class stores, good church and school. The business men are mostly young men and are thoroughly in touch with the advance of the times. It has one bank, the Fairland Exchange Bank, which was recently founded by John Quinn (see sketch).

The first township officers were: Supervisor, David Smith; assessor, W. C. Whallen; collector, R. F. Helm; justice, S. Baxter. And in the distribution of county officers Murdock has had a share. Among those who live within the present bounds, Mr. John D. Murdock, from whom the township was named, was elected in 1859 one of the first two associate justices of the county, and was re-elected in 1861. This was, of course, prior to township organization. The county board consisted of a judge and two associate judges. Mr. Murdock served his first term with James Ewing, of Arcola, as judge, the other associate being Robert Hopkins, of Newman. In his second term, he was with F. C. Mullen, of Garrett, as judge, and Caleb Bales, of Arcola, as the other associate. It was under the care and management of the last named board that the court house was contracted for and begun. A large part of the business of this day, the early days of the county, was the location of new public roads. The board would appoint three commissioners, one always the surveyor, to view the road, and report at next term. There was quite an epidemic of roads these times.

James H. Shawhan, now of the new township, formerly of Sargent, was elected sheriff in 1871, and also served several years with credit as highway commissioner.

The surveyors appointed by the court in October, 1871, were Edmund Fish, of Arcola; H. C. Niles, of Tuscola, and A. H. Guy, of Vermilion county. They worked a week at it and reported to court. The case was tried three times for various reasons, and finally settled down to the lines made by the commissioners. Mr. Issachar Davis, surveyor in the neighborhood, gave the board valuable and willing assistance. The confusion mostly arose originally from a proven mistake of the original government surveyors, they having left two corners on the range line, which they recorded as twenty-two rods apart, while, identified, they proved to be only six rods apart. The writer has seen the original figures made by the government surveyor, and the proof on the ground. The controversy arose from the situation of a thirty-five-acre piece belonging to John Brown, which the surveyors in their report dubbed the "John Brown tract." This whole controversy was conducted by the interested parties with a manly and fair spirit, much superior to the temper usually manifested on such occasions; though Shiloh Gill says that he and Brown had worn out a certain fence four times in trying to conform to the various opinions of its true place. Each moved the fence every time the other fellow got a new wrinkle from anybody, and the surveying business in the close neighborhood was good until the commission surveyors came along and spoiled the job.

TUSCOLA AND TUSCOLA TOWNSHIP.

Origin of the name.—The name of this

township is derived from that of the city, but the origin of it is involved in obscurity, the most diligent inquiry having failed to disclose its source, or to draw out any account of it which promised satisfaction. Tlascala in Mexico, Tusculum, in Italy, and Tuscaloosa, Alabama, etc., have been suggested as possible bases for a guess, but have yielded no conviction. The idea that the name is of Indian origin has been generally fallen back upon as the only hopeful solution, in which the anxious inquirers are joined by a prominent citizen of a county of the same name in Michigan. Township organization was adopted in 1867 and inaugurated in 1868. Joseph B. McCown, of Camargo, H. B. Evans, of Tuscola, and L. McAllister, of Arcola, were appointed by the county court to divide the county into more convenient political subdivisions.

The railroads.—The township is traversed by the Chicago branch of the Illinois Central Railroad, running about north and south, dividing it into nearly equal parts. The road enters at the northeast quarter of section 3, township 16, range 8, and leaves at south line of section 10, township 15, range 8, and is a straight line through the county, varying from true north, however, about seven degrees; that is to say, it bears to the right just about forty rods to the mile.

This road has a right of way two hundred feet wide through the township, which reserve is inclosed for the most part with a substantial fence as required by law, and occupies twenty-four acres of land for every mile it traverses, being in the aggregate two hundred and forty acres in the township; the difference to land tax payers along the line of the road was an item of importance and resisted, until by consent, as it were, the railroad reserve was gradually eliminated from the acres of the adjoining land owner.

The township is also intersected by the St. Louis branch of the Indianapolis, Bloomington & Western Railroad, which runs east and west through it, along, very nearly, the middle line of the south tier of sections in township 16 north, range 8 east, crossing the Illinois Central Railroad at Tuscola. The road was finished through the township in 1872; was chartered under the name of the Indiana & Illinois Central in 1852, and as Decatur & Indianapolis was legalized in 1853; it remained, however, under the name of Indiana & Illinois Central until 1876, when upon re-organization it received the name of Indianapolis, Decatur & Springfield, and finally was known as the St. Louis branch of the Indianapolis, Bloomington & Western, having been leased to that corporation for ninety-nine years. The road is now known as the I. D. & W.

A road was surveyed from Tuscola City northeastward, to be called the Danville, Tuscola & Western, which was instituted by Tuscola people. The preliminary surveying was begun in January, 1872, under the direction of James Davis, Esq., assisted by Thomas E. Bundy, the attorney for the road, the chief engineer being H. C. Niles. A year was consumed in the location and in trying to meet the wishes of everybody, and grading was for the greater part completed nearly to Danville; but the panic of 1872-73 calling a halt, and the railway business generally receiving a sudden check, it was found impossible to build the road with the means at command. It was subsequently completed and is now known as the Chicago & Eastern Illinois Railroad.

Early entries of land and first settlers.—Being all prairie, the township was of the latest settled, the first comers, as a general rule, keeping close to the timber for its seeming protection. The prairie was considered a bleak, barren waste, unfit for habitation or cultivation, the magnificent richness of the soil not being appreciated by men accustomed to hilly woodlands. The timber was convenient for fuel, building and fencing, and men clung to it, for it was considered injudicious to expose one's self and family to the full sweep of the winter storms and the annual and really dangerous prairie fires.

The first entries of land we find are about as follows: Sigler H. Lester, December 5, 1836, entered west half of the northwest quarter of section 30, town 16, range 8; John Hammer, May, 1837, north half of the northwest quarter of section 18, town 16, range 8; 1837, July 22, Jacob Moore took lot 2, southwest quarter of section 30, town 16, range 8; the bulk of the lands entered by him were six miles south; June 19, 1838, Thomas Lewis entered lot 2, southwest quarter of section 18, town 16, range 8; 1837, Samuel Lester, on lots 3 and 4, northeast quarter of section 6, town 15, range 8, and other large lands; 1849, William Brian, north half of the northeast quarter of section 19, town 16, range 8. Mr. Brian distributed his lands among his children, otherwise he would have been the largest land owner in the county. Most of the land entries were made in 1852-53. Up to that time it appears that there was a check upon settlements of lands by entry, or rather the buying of such lands, the district for the most part being withdrawn from sale pending the location of the Illinois Central Railroad, and its selection of the lands granted it by government. In 1853 H. Sandford entered the northeast quarter of section 33, town 16, range 8, which adjoins Tuscola on the west, and in the palmy days was firmly held at one hundred dollars per acre. Amongst the active and prominent of earlier settlers, as farmers and cattle men, were O. C. and M. F. Hackett, Owen J. Jones and Joseph W. Smith in the south part, and in the north B. F. Boggs, Benham Nelson, George P. Phinney and Caleb Garrett. He emigrated from the adjoining township of Garrett in 1874. Ample notes of the career and influence of many of these gentlemen will be found elsewhere in this volume.

The sixteenth section in every congressional township was, by law, set apart for sale for the use of schools, and so sold by the state. It was required to be surveyed into lots, the utility of which is not clear, as the government subdivisions would have answered every purpose of description.

Section 16, town 16 north, range 8 east, in Tuscola township, was divided into sixteen lots, each lot being one of the original forty-acre tracts; the numbering began in the northeast corner and ended in the southeast. The purchases were made in 1857. W. P. Carter took six of them; T. G. Chambers two; J. F. Parcels four; Le Roy Wiley four. There is no record authority in Douglas county for the numbering, the only guide being the various conveyances, which, however, generally give the number of the lot as well as the regular subdivision.

First town meeting.—The first town meeting after township organization was held at Tuscola in 1868. The meeting was called to order by W. H. Lamb; S. D. Stevenson was elected moderator and C. F. Lamb clerk. A committee of five was appointed to divide the township into road districts. It was made up of G. P. Phinney, A. Mc Neill, J. McGinniss, James Jester and Josiah McKee. The place of this meeting is not given, but it was arranged that the next should be held at J. B. Hart's store, northeast corner of Central avenue and Parke street. Here O. C. Hackett was elected the first supervisor, with a majority of only one vote over W. B. Ervin. Thomas E. Bundy exceeded the vote of H. C. Sluss by six votes. C. H. Griffith was elected assessor by getting two votes more than J. H. Purdy, and S. Paddleford was made the first collector, defeating C. F. Lamb by fifty-eight votes. J. M. Ephlin was the first constable and was chosen at this election. W. H. Wood was the first justice of the peace. The first commissioners of highways, and who were elected on this occasion, were Benham Nelson, Noah Ammen and W. Brian.

The original town of Tuscola.—The original town is bounded on the west by the Illinois Central Railroad, and extends eastward to Niles avenue, which is the north and south center line of section 34, and is the street upon which stand the schoolhouse and Methodist church. This avenue was begun by Mr. Cannon in his addition to Tuscola, with the generous width of seventy-five feet, but unfortunately the surveyor or proprietor of subsequent additions saw fit to cut it down to sixty feet. The bound of the original town on the south is the south line of the section at the township line, and it is met on the north by Winston's addition, which is one-quarter of a mile wide.

Winston's addition.—The first addition to Tuscola was made by A. B. Newkirk, of Chicago, and consists of the north half of northwest quarter of section 34, township 16 north, of range 8 east, and was surveyed by H. C. Niles, the county surveyor, in August, 1859, assisted by Henry Beach, who afterward built the first Beach House. The blocks in this addition, nearly four hundred feet square, are divided generally into four lots, which all lay square with the world, except at the railroad. The streets are of the generous width of sixty-six feet, being six feet wider than those of the original town, upon which they join. No street was made between this and the original town.

Wamsley & Cannon's addition.—In the spring of 1860 William Wamsley, with J. G. Cannon as manager, laid off into lots and blocks the southwest quarter of the southeast quarter of section 34, town 16 north, range 8 east, making sixteen blocks, the west tier of which was subdivided into quarters, the surveying of which was done by Niles. Niles avenue, on the west, was named in compliment to the surveyor and is seventy-five feet wide, as also is the next avenue east. Both of these beautiful streets have been spoiled by the mistaken economy, or perhaps want of information, of the proprietors of the subsequent additions on the north, when they suddenly fell to a width of sixty feet, and not only that, but no regard or attention was paid to the abutting streets in the prior addition; the result is the streets, as it were, hit nowhere even, the lot bounds do not "line," and the people find fault with the surveyors when shown the facts.

Kelly's addition.—Kelly's addition (by the way, there is never any "first" addition), November 15, 1861, followed by his second December 30, 1864, consists of the southwest quarter of the northeast quarter and the northwest quarter of the southeast quarter of section

34, town 16, range 8, eighty acres, and was surveyed by E. C. Siler, county surveyor. In the first addition, however, he was the deputy of Niles. The lots were made large, to meet a seeming demand for such, among which streets, lanes and alleys were very scarce. The progress of the times has eventually forced through several highways. Robert Kelly, of Indiana, was the projector of these additions. He was a Quaker of standing and much business ability.

Mathers' addition.—The next addition made was called Mathers' northeast addition, and comprised the east half of the northeast quarter and the northwest quarter of the northeast quarter of section 34, town 16 north, range 8 east, one hundred and twenty acres. It was surveyed July 12, 1864, by E. C. Siler, county surveyor, under the proprietorship of John Mathers, who had previously acquired an interest in the lands of the original Town Company. The greater part of this addition was laid out into lots or blocks, containing in gross about ten acres, and has since been used almost exclusively for farming lands. The streets in this portion of Tuscola do not conform to those in the original town, not only being of different widths, but do not fairly meet the original streets.

Cornelius' addition.—Cornelius' addition consists of about twenty acres of land in the southwest corner of the section, being a reserved portion of the original town plat, and lying east of the Illinois Central Railroad, and north of the south line of the section. The lots are of good average size, with a location not very desirable. It was laid out by P. S. Cornelius and surveyed by Niles August 19, 1870.

Population and condition.—The population of the city in 1870 was placed at fifteen hundred; H. B. Evans was the enumerator. At the tenth census, 1880, the population was about the same; within that decade the city had not progressed much in the way of extending areas or erecting new buildings. While progress in this respect has not been observed, it is notable that Tuscola is one of the neatest and best-kept villages in the central part of the state. Fourteen miles of substantial sidewalk, a large part of which is eight and twelve feet wide, conduct the exploring stranger dry-shod to churches, school houses, etc., in fact, take him anywhere, except to a saloon. Careful and systematic attention has been given to sanitation, and breaches of the public peace are rare. The census of 1890 gives Tuscola eighteen hundred and ninety-seven and it has a present population of about three thousand.

Early events.—The first house which appeared in Tuscola was a part of the present dwelling of Thomas S. Sluss, at the northwest corner of Main and Daggy streets. It was placed there by William Chandler, who hauled it from the close neighborhood of Bourbon. He occupied it awhile and sold it, building subsequently the dwelling now standing directly east.

The first house built was the store at the railroad, on the north side of Sale street, long since gone. Simon G. Bassett, brother of Dr. H. J. Bassett, of Tuscola, was the first postmaster as well as express and freight agent.

The second house built was erected on Parke street, east side, near the present brick, south of Sale street; it was put up by A. L. Otis.

The third house built was the residence of Thomas Woody, erected on the northwest corner of Central avenue and Main street, whence it was removed. Thomas Woody was the father of A. M. Woody, who served as mayor of the city for the four years ending in April, 1883. Thomas Woody was an active Methodist, and before the day of churches he and his wife, with A. G. Wallace and wife, associated with Mrs. Dr. Bassett and Mrs. Kuhn, were the only church people in the place who had any aptitude for conducting religious exercises. Class and prayer meetings were held in Mr. Woody's house for several years after Mr. Woody's arrival. He died in November, 1883, with full honors.

The first child born in the place was Miss May Wallace, daughter of A. G. Wallace. Mrs. Has. Moore, *nee* May Chandler, daughter of William Chandler, moved here from Bourbon at the age of six years.

The first store was a grocery, built on the north side of the court house square by B. F. Lewis, now a farmer northwest of town. The next was probably the drug store of Dr. J. W. Wright, which was located in the present one-and-a-half-story dwelling, now standing directly east of the old court house. These two proprietors were compelled to yield to the logic of events, both eventually pulling up stakes and moving down into town. The Lewis store was removed bodily to State street. The stock was bought by J. M. Ephlin and A. M. Woody, and was the foundation of the large Woody & Russell grocery store. Dr. Wright built a store and dwelling combined on the southwest corner of Main street and Central avenue, where he had sole control of the drug business until 1865. He finally went to California, being succeeded in his business by Dr. J. A. Field, who occupied the old stand for a while, and afterward removed to his brick at the southeast corner of Parke and Sale streets, which he built in 1882. H. C. Niles, who had been bred to the drug trade, opened a new drug store, in 1865 at the southeast corner of Avenue and Main streets in company with E. C. Siler. The latter sold out to Niles, who joined C. A. Davis on the north side of Sale street, in a building which was destroyed in one of the great fires, which occurred in October, 1881. The house stood the second door directly west of Goff's marble works, which is the first establishment of the kind permanently located at this city. Mr. R. Gruelle was in the drug business for a few years; also E. L. Smith, who sold out to Benton, and he to Foster, who is yet in the business. E. L. Smith, after leaving the drug business, began the practice of law, and in 1878 he committed suicide by cutting his throat in his office, up stairs at the southeast corner of Parke and Sale streets. The real causes of his self "taking off" were never known, but were supposed to be business troubles and bodily disease.

William H. Russell and A. M. Woody instituted, in 1859, the first permanent grocery house in the place, succeeding J. M. Ephlin, beginning with scant means, on the north side of Sale street. The house was long and favorably known as "Woody & Russell," and the partnership remained undisturbed until November, 1874, a period of fifteen years, when it was dissolved by mutual consent and mutual good will. Mr. Russell died in June, 1876; he was from North Carolina, whence he removed to Indiana, arriving at Tuscola in 1859. With the exception of serving as school director and a term or two in the city council, Russell had not been in public office. The impress of his character upon the old and new institutions of the city is permanently good, and will not be quickly forgotten.

S. G. Bassett, backed by Alonzo Lyons, began business on the north side of Sale street at the railroad in 1859, and about these days Elijah McCarty built quite a large two-story warehouse on the south side of the same street, also at the railroad. The former building is long since gone; the other remains as part of the large elevator of R. &. J. Ervin. The post office was here then, with W. T. French as postmaster. McCarty in those days was one of the largest farm operators, handling about four thousand acres of railroad land for a wealthy firm in Kentucky. He was large-hearted, liberal and profuse, and controlled a great amount of money for years. The parties, however, disposed of the lands, and McCarty, after becoming involved, went to St. Louis, and died much reduced in financial strength. He was once a candidate for congress in this district.

A. G. Wallace started the first regular real estate office, after leaving the circuit clerk's position. Others had been prominent in the line in connection with their current business. Mr. Wallace was succeeded by P. C. Sloan, also a former clerk and recorder, in which he was joined by A. A. McKee, but they are now dissolved in business.

The insurance business was not taken up as a regular occupation until 1865-66, when W. P. Cannon, who locally represented a large number of companies in connection with other business, sold out to A. P. Helton, who arrived from Bloomington, Indiana, in 1862. Mr. Helton kept a large hardware store on the south side of the avenue for a number of years, and sold to Lodge & Minturn, who kept store for a while in the stand now occupied by the Evans grocery. Mr. Helton's insurance business increased rapidly, and he became, perhaps, the leading insurance man in the central part of the state, representing a large number of companies, and well posted in all that pertains to this branch of the business. He helped to run the first brass band, like the others for amusement only, and was a cornet player of some distinction.

Incorporation.—October 11, 1859, an election by the citizens was held for and against incorporation. The names of all the voters were: William Chandler, I. J. Halstead, Michael Noel, A. L. Otis, F. F. Nesbit, P. Noel, A. J. Gorman, James H. Harrison, James Davis, A. G. Wallace, John Chandler, A. Van Deren, Thomas Woody and Joseph G. Cannon. The vote for incorporation stood twelve; against, two; total fourteen. Mr. Harrison was a prominent stove and hardware man, first on Central avenue, in the store now occupied by Tyler in the same business; afterward in a two-story building which stood on the present site of Bye's shoe store. This building was removed to the north side of the avenue, to a place directly east of the present Opera block, and "went up" in the great fire of 1873. Mr. Harrison was a leading citizen, had much to do with the institutions of the place, and later was president of the National Bank at Farmer City. James Davis was of the firm of Davis & Finney, grain dealers, and served as mayor of the city. John Chandler has a large farm east of town, was the first county clerk, and had an active and useful part in the formation of the new county. Maj. Van Deren is yet a resident and a farmer. Mr.

Cannon removed to Danville. Of the others, Messrs. Halstead, Noels, Otis and Nesbit removed; William Chandler, a carpenter and builder, died here, as also Mr. Wallace and Thomas Woody.

City Charter.—The city charter is dated March 11, 1859. The first mayor was James H. Martin, with a council consisting of I. L. Jordan, E, Price, M. Pugh and W. Taggart. Mr. Jordan, formerly a farmer in Garrett township, was sheriff of the county. Price, though a large land owner in the county, is now a non-resident. Pugh, a wagon-maker, has lately removed, and Col. Taggart, after honorable service in the war of 1861, and serving two terms as sheriff remains a citizen, under the firm name of Taggart & Williams, in the furniture business. In the war record in this volume will be found a more particular notice of those who served as soldiers. Mr. James H. Martin resigned the mayoralty in June, 1870, partly because of ill health, and partly because of ineligibility; he lived outside the corporation, owning land just beyond the northeast corner of the town. With a view of correcting the matter, he had a small addition to the city made and recorded, which was situated in the southwest corner of section twenty-six, township 16, range eight, but no lots were sold, and it was finally dropped. Mr. Martin was from Indiana, resided in Tuscola for about six years in the practice of the law. He died November 15, 1871, and was buried at Camargo, with Masonic honors.

Tuscola is doubtless the first city in the state organized under the general incorporation act, which took effect July 1, 1872. In 1870 Thomas S. Sluss presided as mayor; alderman present, J. C. Walker and James Dilly; A. H. Sluss, city clerk and attorney. August 15, 1870, the city attorney was ordered to dismiss the suit of the city against Niles & Dryer, druggists, defendants paying attorneys' fees. This was a suit for not reporting sales of liquors for the past two months, the ordinance requiring such report, which was to contain the name of the purchaser, quantity sold and purpose used for. The firm was not prosecuted for selling liquor, but for not reporting sales. At this meeting, J. C. Walker moved the remission of the fine, which was promptly seconded by James Davis, and the resolution was carried. In 1865 the board was in session, contemplating serious restrictions upon the druggist liquor sales, and stirring speeches were made *pro* and *con*, the last of which was made by a druggist, who produced as his final argument a large bottle of old London Dock Gin, which, after placing on the table under the noses of the board, he gracefully retired, amid loud and continued applause. The proposed resolution was also laid on the table.

Hotels.—The first boarding house or hotel was kept by A. G. Wallace. This building was a large "story-and-a-half" house, situated just about where the bank now stands on the Avenue. Mr. Wallace had arrived in the county in 1841, and stopped at a place, then widely known as the "Wallace stand," west of Hickory Grove, in the southeast part of the county. He removed to Camargo in 1854, and in 1856 to Tuscola, where he kept hotel as above for about two years. He was deeply interested in and was one of the most active workers for the foundation of the new county. He was the first justice of the peace elected in Tuscola, 1858, and in 1859 was elected the first circuit clerk and recorder. He was continuously re-elected until he had served four consecutive terms of four years each. Upon retiring from the office, he conducted for several years a real estate and loan office, and was always an active and leading member of the Methodist Episcopal church. Mr. Wallace died on the 27th of July, 1879.

The Beach House began an existence as a boarding house on the southeast corner of Ensey and Parke streets. It was then under the conduct of Henry Beach. He built the first Beach House on the site of the present hotel of the same name. Some time after his death, the first hotel was burned to the ground, about 1869, and rebuilt by Mrs. Beach in 1870. She was succeeded by her son-in-law, W. Kissel, who is just completing a very fine and commodious brick hotel.

The Hotel Douglas which was opened to the traveling public April 19, 1899, is by odds the best all around equipped hotel in Douglas county, and in by far the best location. The people of Tuscola and Douglas county owe a debt of gratitude as well as best wishes and their patronage to Mr. and Mrs. John Whittaker for constructing this popular inn, for it is reasonably safe to say had they not built it Tuscola would be without a decent hotel today.

The first hotel was built on the northeast corner of Main and Houghton streets, by the Town company. A large two-story frame, it was for a few years the only hotel and in court season a lively place. It was constructed by M. C. Elkin, who was an old resident. This hotel was burned in 1864, and rebuilt by the insurance company. It was then called the "Tuscola House."

Other early events.—The present court house square had been fenced in with common boards and was the "fair ground" of the first Douglas county fair. The old court house was used for a "floral hall," as it were, and a band and speakers' stand had been erected in the north side of the square. E. McCarty, Caleb Garrett and Ira J. Halstead, secretary, were the managers. The first dance was held in the room over northeast corner of Parke and Sale streets, where Mrs. John Madison danced the first set with Joseph G. Cannon. This old court house was, on its completion, hailed with joy by all who believed in wholesale sociability. Parties, balls and dances were frequent and enjoyable. The first was the celebration of the finishing of the building by a well-attended dance. This was in 1861.

The first session of circuit court was held in the fall of 1859, in the then just finished depot building of the I. C. R. R., and the very first civil case on the docket was Button vs. Johnson,; default of defendant and judgment for $3.20. This was an appeal from Dr. J. T. Johnson, a magistrate in the village of Bourbon. Dr. Johnson was a well-known practicing physician and "Squire" in the west end, at the time of the formation of the new county, and along about 1865 went west. Circuit court was next held in the second story of the building now occupied by George Smith, the same place where J. M. Maris previously held forth as a grocer. This was the largest available room in the place at that time, and was used for all public meetings until the so-called court house was built in 1861. At this time A. G. Wallace, the circuit clerk, had his office in the same building on Sale street, and the county clerk occupied a room in the Tuscola House, the two-story hotel in Houghton street, heretofore mentioned.

The first school house erected in Tuscola was a one-story frame, which cost five hundred dollars, and was built in 1858. Amongst the first school teachers, if not the first, was Ira J. Halstead. This was succeeded by a very substantial two-story brick schoolhouse at a cost of six thousand dollars, erected on the site of the present imposing seminary, which is block No. 3, in Kelly's addition to Tuscola. This was a plain brick building, erected under contract by John X. Miller. He owned and occupied the old one-story schoolhouse after the new one was built. He was a queer old fellow, honest and reliable, but a little sour, and he always "wanted to know, you know," what we thought of a preacher who would "call a man a liar?" and we could only answer, that it depended on whether the preacher told the truth or not. The materials for this two-story seminary were purchased by the contractor when the present fine building was erected on the same site. The contractor and builder of the new and last building was L. Johnson; he married here a daughter of Ross, a carpenter and builder. Johnson was a man of notable integrity and honor in his contracts, and built and finished the structure in the face of failure as to profit.

A corner stone was laid on the 26th of June, 1870, by the Masons and Odd Fellows, with the usual interesting ceremonies. The northeast corner stone contains the organization of Coles county; the partition of Douglas county, 1859; survey of original town of Tuscola, 1857; accounts of the first dwelling; 1857; first store, 1857; and first, second and third bricks built, 1863, etc.; first child born, 1857; burning of first hotel, and incidents; Illinois Central railroad; schoolhouses; first church, 1862; flour mill, 1863; newspaper, 1858; first bank, 1863; first court house, 1861. The names of the first village board were: L. J. Wyeth, W. T. French, James Davis, F. F. Nesbit, M. Vaul, clerk; also date of charter, first election under charter July 1, 1859. J. H. Martin, mayor; council, W. Taggart, M. Pugh, E. Price and J. Williamson.

The school building is a substantial brick, of three stories and basement, a belfry containing a large town clock, which is a most excellent time keeper, and has four dials, facing respectively the four cardinal points. The school building has ample accommodations for about five hundred pupils, is in every possible respect a perfect edifice, and is, as it should be, the pride of Tuscola. The contract price was originally thirty-two thousand dollars, but the amount was subsequently increased, so that the entire cost, when completed, became about forty thousand dollars. The building is heated by an excellent system of basement furnaces, and the board employ an efficient janitor at a fixed salary. The original lot, Block 3, in Kelly's addition, contained about one acre of land; to this has been added, in the last few years, a strip sixty feet in width on the east side, which is Indiana street extended. The board also bought the block next north, block 4, same addition, and was presented by the city with that part of Wilson street extended which lies between said blocks 3 and 4, which also loaned them fifty feet of a street north of block 4.

The first bank was instituted by Wyeth, Cannon & Co., and was in a frame building, which stood at the west end of the present Opera block. This bank was afterward, in 1865, merged into the First National Bank of

Tuscola. The firm also had for a while banking interests in Arcola. In 1870, Mr. Wyeth was merchandising here among the first as a member of the firm of Wyeth, Craddock & Co., occupying the two-story frame directly east of the drug store, now at the southeast corner of Sale and Parke streets. The building was removed to the north side of the avenue to a point east of Opera block, and burnt in the great fire of 1873. The first cashier of the bank was W. P. Cannon, who married a daughter of William Warmsley an old resident.

Whilst the Commercial Block and bank were burning, W. P. Cannon contracted with Coleman Bright for the second story of his brick building on the south side of the avenue, and removed to that location. The bank had a capital of $113,000, and a surplus of $25,000. Mr. H. T. Carraway, president; W. H. Lamb, cashier; A. W. Wallace, teller and bookkeeper at that time. The Douglas county bank was established September, 1870, W. H. Lamb, cashier, on Sale street; and another on the avenue by Champaign parties; both, however, were merged into other banks. The present banks are: The Fist National Bank, A. W. Wallace, president, and F. W. Hammett, cashier. This is one of the best, most substantial and up-to-date banking houses in the state. Baughman, Bragg & Co. is the other banking firm.

The opera house of Tuscola, owned by the Harry Madison estate, is a very creditable affair. It has a seating capacity of about seven hundred and a very well sceneried stage, with mirrors on either side, and is very ornate.

Churches.—The Methodist, a brick church, was finished in 1860, and is situated on Block No. 5, in Kelly's addition, at the southeast corner of Sale street and Niles avenue. It was built through the exertions of Mr. Thomas Woody, A. G. Wallace, O. C. Hackett and others. It was a neat gothic brick about forty feet by one hundred, with a graceful spire one hundred and ten feet high, and a belfry with a standard bell-metal bell of a weight of six hundred pounds. It always commanded the largest congregations, and they, being of the superior class of citizens as to intelligence and standing, have always been able to command the best average talent of the conference. In 1895 the Methodists erected their present church edifice which is the finest church building in the county.

The Presbyterian church, situated on lots 1 and 2, block 32, in the original town, southwest corner of Wilson and Main streets. A Mr. Carnes was the builder. The leaders in the church were Mr. William H. Lamb, Judge Ammen, John J. Jones and others, with their families. This church is second only to the Methodist in point of numbers. The first pastor was George D. Miller, who came to Tuscola in August, 1860, and was in charge up to 1864, when he resigned from ill health.

The Baptist church is the largest in the city with regard to seating capacity; in actual membership it is the smallest. It was erected in 1865, mainly throught the exertions and example of Elijah McCarty and Dr. I. N. Rynerson. Dr. Rynerson was a leading farmer in the northeast corner of Arcola township. He was highly educated and one of the best stump speakers of his day, and was also a former practicing physician; he died in April, 1873.

This church is a substantial brick building about forty by eighty feet, and when built had a very large brick tower about ninety feet high, which had, through the mistake of the builder, been run up nearly square; it was heavy and ungainly, and topped off with four corner spires or ornaments painted white. This was the most conspicuous object in the city, and was the landmark in the country for miles around. The intention had been to make a much lighter tower. Too much weight was put upon it for its foundation, and it began to show cracks in the masonry and settled. It was then rumored unsafe, people getting the idea it would fall of its own weight, and some avoided the church. It was then formally examined by expert builders, and being pronounced good confidence was somewhat restored. Nevertheless, the tower was finally taken down even with the roof. The congregation being quite small, regular pastors have not always been in charge, though this church has commanded some of the best talent the church afforded. The building is situated at the northeast corner of Daggy and Court streets.

The Christian church is situated on the north side of Houghton street, east of Court street, lot 13, block 40, original town, is a good frame building, the second story being the auditorium, with first story reserved for Sunday school and baptistry. It was erected in 1868, mainly through the exertions of Mr. John Chandler, the first county clerk. The present Christian church of Tuscola is a fine brick structure and is next to the Methodist church in cost.

The Roman Catholic church of the Forty Martyrs is a frame building situated on the southeast corner of Van Allen and Center streets. It was erected in the summer of 1882, at a cost of $1,000.

The Episcopal church was erected on the northwest corner of Center and Houghton Houghton streets in 1882; was consecrated in July of that year, by Right Reverend Seymour, Bishop of Springfield, assisted by several clergymen from the surrounding cities. The church was built through the exertions of the Rev. Mr. Peck, then in charge of the mission, and is known as St. Stephen's. Regular services were held for about one year, but the removal of families most interested has so reduced numbers that the services are rare.

The Free Methodists also have a church building. (See sketch of David Cooper.)

Sunday Schools.—The first Sunday school in Tuscola was instituted by Mrs. Archibald Van Deren and others at the old Tuscola House, the erstwhile hotel. The first Sunday school was convened on the second Sabbath of September, in the year 1859. It was started at the instance of Mrs. Van Deren, her coadjutors, among others, being Thomas Woody and his excellent daughters, Mesdames Townsell and Lindsay, who were the first scholars, and who have passed away. Dr. J. L. Reat, with us, Dr. Samuel Daggy and Mrs. Van Deren are the only survivors. Dr. Reat is mentioned elsewhere. Dr. Daggy, a prominent Presbyterian, was an acknowledged leader in religion and indeed in all other matters bearing upon the general elevation of public sentiment from the beginning of Tuscola. After a twenty years' useful residence here, he, with his family, moved to Philadelphia, where he is engaged in real estate business.

Here it may not be out of place to record that the various churches of Tuscola have been remarkable for a cordial co-operation in religious matters, joint meetings and exchange of pulpits being the frequent leading features that go far toward clipping the wings of those smart fellows, who, claiming the difference of creed as a sufficient excuse, would fly to glory unincumbered by a church.

The Press.—Our first newspaper was the Tuscola Press. It was started in 1859. It was short lived, and the proprietor left between two days. M. Vaul conducted it a year or two, but it was not a success. Mr. Vaul was the first city clerk. The Sellers boys instituted the Douglas County Shield, from 1865 to 1867. A little fellow named Gregory established the Union, which was not a success. The newspaper business did not seem to be solid until the present Journal and Douglas County Review were established. The Journal was first instituted by Siler & Lindsay in 1864. They were succeeded by Williams in 1876, with Harry Johnson as paragraphist and general outside manager, and by George Glassco in January, 1881. Afterward by "Tom" Williams and a Mr. Glassco. It is now owned and conducted by A. C. Sluss, the present postmaster of Tuscola. (See sketch.)

Williams was an old Tuscola boy who mastered the printing business and became a "jour," working in various places, and when in Connecticut met and married a lady printer. He returned to Tuscola in 1876, and in connection with Capt. Parks, of the Review, did the typographical work of the centennial history of Douglas county, the only printed book ever issued in the county. Tom died suddenly while in the prime of his usefulness and manhood, at about thirty years of age, on the 29th day of July, 1881. He was a man of wit and humor; was for a time the assistant of "Martin," the assistant engineer of Danville, Tuscola & Western railroad, and while a little "captious" in the view of the younger boys on the work, merited and received on the whole the best respect of his associates.

The Douglas County Review was instituted in 1875 by Converse & Parks, and was Democratic. It was first issued in the two-story wooden building which now stands directly east of the J. M. Smith building, on the south side of Central avenue. The Review passed into the hands of Maj. Asa Miller in December, 1877. (See sketch of Charles W. Wilson, the present proprietor of the Review.)

The Tuscola Republican, now owned and edited by Fred L. Reat, is rapidly coming to the front as a newsy, clean and well printed paper. It has a paid circulation of about one thousand.

Centennial History.—The Congress of the United States, March 13, 1876, passed a resolution recommending that the people of the several states assemble in their several towns on the "centennial anniversary" of our national independence, and have read a historical sketch of said county or town from its formation, and that a copy of said sketch be filed in the office of the Librarian of Congress, as well as in the clerk's office of said county.

April 25, 1876, this is followed by the proclamation of John L. Beveridge, the governor of the state of Illinois, to the same effect, urging a general observance of the recommendation.

In May, 1876, at a special term of the board of supervisors, not, however, specially held for the purpose, the following resolution was adopted, which had been offered by the supervisor from Garrett, Mr. William Howe:

Resolved, That Henry C. Niles be employed to prepare a statistical and biographical history of Douglas county, from its origin to the present time, and to have the same ready by the 4th of July next, provided the said work shall not cost to exceed one hundred dollars.

This work was prepared in manuscript, read to the board of supervisors and approved; an attempt to have it printed at the expense of the county failed, and the author, assisted by D. O. Root, the then county clerk, had it printed in pamphlet form, to save the matter, being eighty pages octavo, in paper covers. This history contained, in a perhaps too much condensed style, a history of the main facts pertaining to the county, with separate histories of townships, and was not much elaborated, the "fixed price" forbidding a thorough detail of the points touched upon. It was dedicated "To the young men of Douglas county.

"In the hope that they may be reminded of the responsibility they are about to assume in taking charge of the destinies of little DOUGLAS, may they emulate the noblest deeds of their fathers, so that the blessings which they secured may descend upon them to posterity. In opening out the resources of the country, converting the rude land into cultivated fields, building cities where none existed before, and making possible the civilizing influences of churches, schools and railroads, their fathers have borne the brunt of the battle, and are now resigning into their hands the result of their labors, for they are passing away."

This pamphlet was printed at the printing office of the Illinois Industrial University, at Urbana. The contract was taken by Converse & Parks, editors of the Review of Tuscola, and the "setting up" done by J. T. Williams, afterward proprietor of the Tuscola Journal.

Mr. Williams took great pride in the matter, and produced a specimen of printing not surpassed by any pamphlet work extant. A copy of the work was duly forwarded to the Illinois state librarian, the congressional library, at Washington, the Historical Society of Chicago, and to various other points, either voluntarily, or on demand, and kindly acknowledgments were received in each case, and in some cases a return was promptly made of similar works.

Photography.—Photography in its advanced artistic evcellence was first instituted here by W. Boyce, who is succeeded by his son David N. Having devoted his entire business time to the perfection of his work, making a study of all the latest improvements, he shows work which is not surpassed by that of the artists in the larger cities. D. N. Boyce is not only a first class artist but he is a gentleman in nature and instinct.

Illinois Light, Water, Heat and Power Company, recently established in Tuscola, is supplied with the very latest type of machinery and renders efficient service. The water power plant operated in connection is so complete, perfect and systematically arranged that the most energetic critic has failed to criticise.

Tuscola Society.—The moral and intellectual standard of the city is far above the average, with plenty of room for improvement. In main the citizens are a peaceable, law abiding and God fearing people. They have good churches, good schools and are lovers of good books. Selfishness and bigotry in many instances are disguised here as true religion, as it is elsewhere throughout the world, and one of the most loved and commendable characteristic of the human heart, love one another, is is asleep in the beautiful little city of Tuscola.

Its retired farmer contingency of its population is wonderfully tired, unprogressive and in many instances is positive and painful hindrance to its future development. Where a citizen with money refuses to assist in needed improvements of the town, to assist in caring for the worthy poor and needy under his nose, he is not only lacking in his religion, taught by the lowly Nazarene, but he is lacking in his good citizenship. Tuscola has nothing worse to fear than to allow the management of its public administration to fall into the hands of the unprogressive, the dollar worshipers and the stingy. There are some so called worshipers of Christ and leading church members in Tuscola who should heed more the teachings of the Master and permit the dead, against whom they might have had a personal grievance without cause, to *Rest, Rest, Rest*!!!

ARCOLA CITY AND TOWNSHIP.

The Name.—Before Douglas county had an existence, the city of Arcola, from which the township derives its name, was called by the railroad company "Okaw," after the river of that name, which traverses the west part of the county. "Okaw" was a local name only, the true name of the river being Kaskaskia, from the French, and it has been claimed by knowing ones that the word "Okaw" is a corruption of Kaskaskia, which, in the vernacular, was "Kawkaw" (Indian: Crow River?) hence, by an easy transition, "Okaw." Col. John Cofer, who had represented the county of Coles in the state Legislature, was postmaster to accommodate the neighborhood at Rural Retreat (in the southeast quarter of section 10, township 14 north, range 9 east, since abolished), from 1854 to 1858, and upon him, as being the nearest postmaser, devolved the duty of certifying the necessity of a new postoffice at Okaw, which had been petitioned for by Judge and Dr. Henry, John Blackwell and others. In due course, Col. Cofer sent the papers to Washington, and they were returned, as is usual in such cases, with the information that there was already in the state of Illinois a postoffice with the same name as the one proposed. This made it necessary that a new name should be selected before the office could, under the law, be established. Mr. E. Hewitt, the first Illinois Central railroad agent at this point, after cudgeling his brains to no effect, observing a knot of citizens near, came out of his office at the depot, and in the presence of Judge James Ewing and others asked for suggestions, whereupon James Kearney said "Arcola." The name took instantly, and was adopted. It appears to have been selected from its euphony rather than from any allusion or reference to a historical reminiscence, though one of Napoleon's greatest battles was fought and gained over the Austrians in Italy at a place by that name. Both of the names terminating alike is food for rumination, but all attempts to connect the two as some relation have failed. John Blackwell was here prominent in all that pertains to good citizenship, and had much to do with the management of affairs. His residence dated from 1857. He was the first magistrate of Arcola. He died in January, 1869. John Blackwell was a grandson of Col. Jacob Blackwell of the Revolution. The Colonel was the owner of Blackwell's Island and nearly all the eastern end of Long Island adjacent to New York, from Astoria to Brooklyn. This tract includes Astoria, Ravenswood, Long Island City, Green Point and Williamsburg. He resided in the old mansion on Webster avenue, where he entertained Gen. Washington and in the grounds attached thereto repose the bones of the Colonel and his wife. Col. Blackwell was prominently identified with the Revolutionary party, and was a member of the Continental Congress. His door, branded with the letter "R" (rebel) because of his opposition to the British Crown, is still kept as a heirloom by some of his descendants.

Arcola Precinct.—At the time of the formation of Douglas county, February, 1859, that portion of its area now known as Arcola township was called Arcola precinct. It was bounded on the north by Tuscola township, but now extends one mile further north. It contained a tier of six sections on the east, which are now included in Bowdre, and it also included eighteen sections of land, all of township 14 north, range 7 east, which were, on regular township organization in 1868, handed over to Bourbon.

This was an election precinct, and contained an area of about seventy-one, which was, in 1868, cut down to fifty-three and eight-tenths square miles, being exactly, according to the government survey, 34,643.26 acres.

Township organization was voted for in 1867, and the apportionment made in 1868, Dr Lucius McAllister being one of the commissioners appointed by the county board to make the partition. Calvin Jones was associate county judge. The township 15 north, of range 8 east, the congressional township laying between Arcola and Tuscola, was surveyed in 1821. The south line was established by John Messinger, deputy surveyor, and finished April 5 of that year. The subdividing of the township into sections was finished by A. McK. Hamtranck, a deputy, June 9, 1821. The surveying was done nine years before the first settler struck the county. In this connection it may be said that no Douglas county surveyor has ever discovered in the interior of this township a single original government corner out of the seventy-eight which the government surveyor certifies he made, and perpetuated with mounds and stakes. Local surveying was done here first in 1850.

Land Entries.—The first of land within the present bounds of this township was made December 24, 1832, by James Shaw. He entered several tracts at about the same time in Bourbon township, and subsequently other lands. His descendants are yet citizens of Bourbon, and one of his sons, W. N. Shaw, represented Bourbon as a supervisor for about six years consecutively, and died in 1882, while in office. Land was also entered in 1853 by the Geres and Malden Jones and O. B. Ficklin.

Many large farms on the prairie were started by men who, coming from a hilly or timbered location, seeing the beautiful rolling prairies for the first time, ready for the plow without stump or stone to hinder, coveted the whole expanse, as far as the eye could reach, and nearly every one purchased too much for his capital. Smaller farms mean more people, more real workers and more real owners. Time and again railroad lands were taken up by the whole section, a house and some fencing built, but, after a few years' experience, the load proved too heavy, and the land was permitted to go back, or perhaps a small portion was paid for, and retained.

The Railroads.—The township is traversed

by the Chicago branch of the Illinois Central railroad, running about north and south, leaving two-thirds of the area to the east side of the road.

Arcola township is also traversed from east to west by the Illinois Midland railway, now the Vandalia. This road was originally an enterprise of prominent citizens of the city and vicinity, and was first called the Paris & Decatur; upon the extension of the road to Terre Haute, the name of that city was prefixed, and finally it received its present name. The first train passed over this road October 25, 1872.

Arcola and other township bonds were issued by a vote of the people, amounting in the aggregate to $165,000, the amount voted by this township being $100,000. These bonds were disposed of by the company, and finally found their way into the hands of innocent parties as an investment. The legality of the procedure was made a question, both as to calling the election and voting the bonds, all of which were finally decided adversely; consequently the bonds have not been paid by the township, though the railroad reaped the benefit of them.

The road enters the township at the northwest corner of section 6, township 14 north, range 8 east, runs in a southeasterly direction to the city of Arcola, thence east along the mid line of the north tier of sections, and leaves the township at about the northeast corner of section 5, township 14 north, range 9 east, occupying a length of about eight miles. The proposed donation of the township bonds to the railroad was in consequence of a petition which suggested that they should draw ten per cent interest, payable semi-annually, the bonds not to be delivered until one mile of track had been graded and ironed in the township, and to be delivered in no greater amount per mile than six thousand dollars, through the county as far as it was practicable, to influence the other townships through which the road should pass, to similar action, the petitioners suggested that a meeting be held for the purpose on June 24, 1869. At this time D. Hitchcock was the supervisor and Thomas Todd, clerk. The petition was signed by C. E. Bosworth, I. G. Bowman, J. W. Douglas, J. B. Ward, H. D. Jenkins, J. R. Smith, John Ray, James Matters, B. H. Burton, P. M. Monahan, J. W. Louthan, James Beggs and L. C. Rust. The election was held accordingly, and resulted for subscription 324 votes, against it one vote. On August 16, 1870, John Ray was authorized to procure the blank bonds; they were made to bear ten per cent interest from May 1, 1871, payable at the Security Bank in New York. John J. Henry was appointed to act as trustee to receive, hold and pay out the bonds, and the signing of them was ratified by the town auditors on the 3d of April, 1871.

This road was projected and put through by three or four residents of Arcola City, who, prior to the beginning of the enterprise, were pursuing the even tenor of their way as quiet and good citizens, not remarkable above their fellows for any more financial ability than the average. They built the road and controlled the franchises until it was consolidated.

CITY OF ARCOLA.

Arcola City occupies all of section 4, west half of southwest quarter of section 3, and the north half of the northeast quarter of section 9, all in township No.

14, north of range 8, east of the third principal meridian. "Okaw," the original town, was laid off by the Illinois Central Railroad Company, upon its own lands in section No. 4, and occupied a tract of land lying on the west side of the southeast quarter of the section, about one-half mile long by about one-quarter mile wide, on either side of the railroad track; it was surveyed by John Meadows, Coles county surveyor, October 22, 1855, so that Arcola antedates the county by about four years. The plat and survey were indorsed by J. N. A. Griswold, president of the company, and they reserved a strip of land one hundred feet wide on either side of the centre line of the track. North and south, across the whole of said plat, they also reserved the right to lay side tracks on both Chestnut and Oak streets, outside the two hundred foot limit, and for warehouses, and it was specially stated, that "no right of crossing that part marked as reserve for Illinois Central railroad, at any point between Second South and Second North streets is granted to the public."

The first town was laid off parallel with and at right angles to the railroad track, and consists of twenty blocks, the lots next to the railroad having a front of forty feet, the back lots being eighty; they all have a uniform depth of one hundred and sixty feet; the east and west streets are of a width of seventy feet; those running parallel with the railroad alternate with widths of seventy and forty feet.

McCann's first addition.—In April, 1858, John McCann made the first addition, consisting of varied sizes of lots and blocks. It was surveyed by Stephen B. Moore, of Coles county. Mr. Moore also surveyed

Henry's addition.—This addition was made by Dr. F. B. Henry, August 2, 1858. It consists of ten blocks of fifty feet front, being one hundred and sixty feet deep. Dr. Henry caused the streets to be continued as first planned by the railroad.

Chandler & Bales' additions.—In July, 1864, Messrs. John Chandler and Caleb Bales laid out their addition on the south, and followed in June, 1865, with the second addition, all surveyed by E. C. Siler. These two additions occupy the north half of the northeast quarter of section 9, township 14 north, range 8 east, eighty acres.

McCann's second addition was made in July, 1877.

Sheldon & Jacque's addition, being the west half of the southwest quarter of section 3, township 14, range 8, was surveyed by Issachar Davis, August 6, 1868.

Council proceedings.—The first city council or board of trustees was convened in May, 1858; Mahlon Barnhardt was the president. The city clerk was I. S. Taylor. W. T. Sylvester and John J. Henry were of the board. City records prior to 1872 do not seem to be available. June 3, 1872, a meeting was held, Mayor D. Tibbott, presiding, and the council consisted of James Matters, P. D. Ray, Byron Willis and J. M. Righter. George Klink was clerk.

October, 1872, a minute appears which recites that "no huckster be allowed to sell produce for less that one dollar or more than five dollars." George Klink, Democrat, was elected mayor in April, 1873, and re-elected April 17, 1877. In 1873 the first council consisted of James Jones, J. H. Magner, James E. Morris and H. M. McCrory. W. J. Calhoun was city clerk.

Incorporation.—A petition for incorporation was circulated in June, 1873, signed by one hundred and twenty citizens. The election was held June 16, same year, and resulted for incorporation under the general law, two hundred and forty-four votes; contra, eleven; total, two hundred and sixty-five, and August 6, 1873, the city was incorporated under the general law for incorporating cities and villages, which was in force July 1, 1872. W. H. Spencer, at or about this time, was made city attorney, the salary being fixed at three hundred and seventy-five dollars per annum. Mr. Spencer was a member of the Douglas county bar, and later removed to Terre Haute. The city clerk's wage was one hundred and fifty dollars a year. Mr. Spencer was authorized to proceed to Springfield to endeavor to procure an amendment to the general incorporation law with reference to minority representation.

The press.—The Arcola Record, the first newspaper to appear in the city, was inaugurated under the auspices of the Sellars Brothers of Tuscola in 1866—the enterprise having been instituted by the subscription of liberal-minded citizens, without regard to political affinities; it was an independent paper until the plant was bought by John M. Gruelle, which occurred soon after it was fairly started. For about seventeen years Mr. Gruelle conducted it as an advocate of Republican principles, during which time, by close attention to the business interests of the office, and a due regard for those of his adopted county and city, he merited and received a fair share of success. He died in Arcola on the 23d of October, 1883, in the prime of life, after nearly a year's illness. The paper is continued under the management of Collins & Son.

The Herald and Arolian are the other two papers of the city.

Early business enterprises.—The first house put up in the city was the Illinois Central station and depot, in the upper part of which E. Hewitt, the first railroad agent, had his residence and the post office; a very short distance northwest Barney Cunningham erected the first dwelling. Mr. Cunningham was the father of Frank Cunningham, who became sheriff of the county in 1872, removing to Tuscola, where he died. The freight house was burned in the great fire of 1881.

John Weber, a little, keen, wiry German, kept store here in 1857, first situated in a little shanty south of the southwest corner of First South street and Chestnut street, and afterward at the corner at Ewald's present location. This corner was twice burned, as a hotel first, and again in the great fire of 1881.

The first dry goods store was instituted by F. B. & J. J. Henry, and was afterward under the name of the latter. The building was located on the south side of First South street, east of the railroad, and was destroyed in the tornado of 1858. Mr. J. J. Henry was associate justice of the county in 1865. He died March 11, 1865, and was the father of Joseph P. Henry.

The drug business was started by W. T. Sylvester and Joseph P. Henry, the latter succeeding to the business at the southeast corner of First South and Oak streets, where he had maintained a profitable trade since 1858. His close attention to the requirements of the case and his popularity resulted eventually in ample means. Mr. Henry died July 19, 1883, in the prime of his life and usefulness.

The drug store of W. P. Boyd was established in 1867. By the way, the first officially recorded survey made in Douglas county was for his father, Mr. W. P. Boyd. It was May 21, 1859—west half of section 5, township 14, range 8, half-mile west of city limits. Wilson B. Boyd came to Douglas in 1859, and resided here until the time of his death, March 10, 1867.

The first banking house was instituted in March, 1868, by Messrs. Beggs & Clark, which bank, December 9, 1875, became merged into the First National Bank of Arcola; *ad interim* Wyeth, Cannon & Co., of Tuscola, bought the business, and in August, 1870, Mr. Wickes, their Tuscola bookkeeper, removed to Arcola, taking charge of their interests until they were relinquished. The bank had a capital of fifty thousand dollars. James Beggs, president; G. L. Wickes, cashier.

The present banks are the First National Bank and the State Bank.

At the first bank of Wyeth, Cannon & Co., at Tuscola, a Pennsylvania Dutchman bought a draft for sixty-nine dollars from Cannon, and taking it home pasted it in with his receipts, and sat down at the stove with the happy consciousness of having done his whole duty. In the course of time he was further pressed by his creditor for a settlement, and pitched into the bank for keeping his money.

The churches.—The Presbyterians built the first church in the city in 1860, the first pastor being Jos. Allison.

The Christian church was instituted July 10, 1863; the first trustees being W. T. Sylvester, Joseph Walling, J. M. Lessinger, J. M. Hollandsworth, John Woodall, L. McAllister, who were elected for five years. The church bought lots 1 and 2, block 7, of Henry's addition to Okaw, October 13, 1864, and built the church the same year.

St. John's Roman Catholic church was built on lot 8, block 7, Henry's addition, in 1874, the deed for the lot being dated January 13, 1871, and first made to the Archbishop of St. Louis, by him to Bishop Alton, and then to St. John's Roman Catholic church. The members of this church, though not generally of the wealthier classes, show a devotion to their lessons and modes well worthy of imitation.

The Methodist church acquired lot 4, block 16, in original town, April 13, 1864. The church was built in 1865. This denomination in Arcola was a little late in building. The Methodists generally build about the time the proposed city is laid out. They are now constructing a fine brick edifice at a cost of several thousand dollars.

The Baptists have also a church building, erected about 1864.

The Lutherans have also a church building.

The Episcopalians. At a cost of about one thousand dollars an Episcopal church was erected on lots 1, 2, 3 and 4, on the northeast corner of block 3, in the original town. Rev. Wells was the first pastor. Among those who are supporters of the church, through natural affinity and education, are the descendants of John Blackwell and the families of J. R. Smith, L. C. Rust, J. C. Justice, Vellum and others. The society has only been able to secure occasional services.

The postmasters.—E. Hewitt, the railroad agent, was the first postmaster (1858), and the office was in the first freight house, where he lived with his family. He afterward removed to Tuscola, and was agent there for many years. Once upon a time a petition was circulated in

Tuscola for his removal, but it failed to get a respectable number of signers; the objection was his manner.

Galton and Filson stations.—Galton is a point on the Illinois Central Railroad, three and a half miles north of the railroad crossing in Arcola, and is situated in the southeast corner of section 16, township 15 north, range 8 east. It had been known as the Bourbon switch, or Tie switch, and was originally located as a point for the reception of cross ties during the construction of the road. It was made a flag station in 1882. Mr. J. P. Woolford is the only merchant and grain buyer here (see sketch).

Filson is a station and postoffice situated in the northwest part of section 5, township 14, range 9 east, on the line of the Illinois Midland Railway. It has a side track, and is a receiving point for considerable agricultural productions.

NEWMAN TOWNSHIP.

Newman township is nearly all prairie. The country rises toward the north and forms a narrow rise of land generally known as the "Ridge." Being all prairie, this township was one of the latest settled, the first comers seeming to prefer the timbered portions as a protection from the bleak winds and also as a means of procuring fuel, building material and fencing. Newman township occupies the northeast portion of Douglas county. In 1882 Murdock township was created out of Newman and Camargo townships.

Forty years ago Newman township was one vast unbroken level and it was not supposed at that time that it could ever be settled. Excepting after a rain, a drink of water could not be had between the Embarrass and the Little Vermillion rivers, for upon these boundless prairies no habitation was seen. Yet a few brave and far seeing pioneers ventured to establish homes here, realizing there was a fortune in the black and loamy soil when they could once get it into proper condition. Some of the land was very low and wet, but they persevered and cut open ditches first, until in course of time a steam dredge was employed which was capable of excavating a ditch ten feet deep and from any width to forty. This afforded an excellent outlet to the lateral tile ditches which the farmers soon had constructed through the low and wet places on their lands, and these farms are among those least affected by drouth. The result of such draining has been to increase the value of land to such an extent that rents within the past five years have increased from three dollars up to as high as seven dollars per acre. What is now the I., D. & W. R. R. was completed through the township in 1872, the first train and engine passing through here July 9, 1873. To this road the township gave twelve thousand dollars. Before this was completed the people, especially in the northern part of the township, hauled their grain to Homer, in Champaign county, taking one entire day for the trip. There being no public highways across the prairies, no bridges were constructed and there were numerous sloughs to be avoided, causing an extra amount of travel. With a light load the sloughs could safely be crossed. With the settling up of the country, farms were fenced off, roads laid out, sloughs and streams bridged and the facilities for travel greatly improved. The development of the United States and especially the great West, can be traced directly to the railroad system. The equipments upon the road going through this township are probably unsurpassed in the west, and when the intended connections are made, it will be one of the largest passenger, freight and mail routes in the west.

Newman township contains some fine farms, among which was that of C. M. Culbertson, lying northwest of Newman, of over two thousand acres, which is the largest contiguous body of land in the eastern end of the county. The view from the rolling prairie known as the "Ridge" in the north part of the township is more extensive than can be obtained in any other part of the county. This is certainly the garden spot of Illinois. Those who first came here half a century ago, hoped to see the desert "blossom like the rose," and the reality has far surpassed their wildest dreams. Struggling settlements have developed into splendid cities and towns, and no one now considers he is in the far west, but right in the heart and center of this great nation. The west of the present day is away towards the setting sun, beyond the Rockies.

One of the earliest settlers in the township was Enoch Howell, who was ont of the associate justices of the county at an early day. The Winklers and Hopkins' were also early settlers. Robt. Hopkins was one of the first judges of Coles county in 1859, at the time of the separation of Douglas and Coles counties. He and his brothers, "Uncle Jimmy" and "Col." Hopkins, located here about 1841. Wm. Hancock came in 1839, and in 1847 was made justice of the peace at Camargo, before the county was divided, an office which he held for over thirty years. He was the first county treasurer and assessor in 1859. In 1867 he was a member of the state board for the equalization of assessments, and in 1868 was elected for four years. In 1872 Governor Palmer appointed him notary public. He was delegate to the state convention that nominated Gov. Oglesby, and was also one of the charter members of the Masonic lodge of this city. Isaac and John Skinner came here in 1839. Isaac Skinner has now three hundred and eighty acres of land, having had nothing when he attained his majority. With one exception he is the oldest living resident in the township. Wm. Shute came here in 1852 and engaged in farming, and was also an extensive contractor and builder. He built the Fairfield Cumberland Presbyterian church, the Pleasant Ridge Methodist Episcopal and the Cumberland Presbyterian church and school building at Fairmount in Vermilion county. He has built in all nine school buildings and many business blocks, among them the large block in this city in which the Newman Bank and other prosperous business firms are located. He was born in 1817, and has been a member of the Methodist church for forty-two years. "Uncle" Andrew Ashmore settled on the prairie south of town in 1826, but moved in 1890 into Newman. His cousin, Major Sam Ashmore, settled on Brushy Fork in 1830, and was one of the leading spirits in getting the slaves of Bob Matterson started off for Liberia. Matterson, in 1840, brought fifteen slaves into the township from Kentucky. The abolitionists in the vicinity determined the "niggers" should be freed, as they had come into a "free" state. Two or three, however, returned to Kentucky with their master, though one old man named Wilmot remained here and was still in 1884 a resident of

Douglas county. Quite a notable trial grew out of the case, in which Abe Lincoln and O. B. Ficklin were opposing counsel. In 1847 or 1848 Jerry Coffey came to Brushy Fork with his parents. D. O. Root came in 1854 from Ohio, and has been prominently identified with the interests of township and county ever since. Wm. Young, of the Ridge, was the earliest settler in that section, coming there in 1853, where he built the first house on these prairies. He died in 1869, leaving three hundred and twenty acres of land to his family. He gave six hundred dollars toward building the Fairfield Cumberland Presbyterian church, and lived long enough to see it erected, and his funeral was the first preached in it. His wife's two brothers, James and John Coolley, came with him and also took up land. When a young man in Indiana James split many a lot of rails at fifty cents per hundred. With a cousin of his he one winter split twenty-five thousand rails. His first vote for president was cast for Gen. Winfield Scott. From 1868 to 1872 he was justice of the peace and has been a life long elder of the Fairfield church. He now owns three hundred and twenty acres of land. John Coolley also started with nothing but has accumulated a fine property. Rev. Jonathan Coolley, father of James and John, came here late in 1854 and organized the Fairfield Cumberland Presbyterian church in 1855, continuing its pastor until 1872, when his mantel fell upon his son, Rev. C. P. Coolley, now the financial agent of Lincoln University. Josiah Daines came from Pennsylvania in 1854. He built a number of houses in the neighborhood. His aged wife, who is a sister of Jas. Gillogly, still survives him. I. N. Covert, James Gillogly, Joseph Dawson, Moses Stickles and a number of others were among the early settlers in the township. David Todd came to the Ridge in an early day. He was supervisor of the township in 1870, finally moving to Newman, where he engaged in the hardware business. His youngest son is now station agent on the I., D. & W. at Tuscola. B. W. Hooe was supervisor of the township from 1868 to 1873. He died in 1875. His wife, who was the sister of Isaac Skinner, died in 1892. She had been a resident of Douglas county since 1839. Isaac Wyckoff came about 1858. He kept hotel in Camargo, finally moving to the Ridge near his son-in-law, Jas. Coolley. He was postmaster for many years of Phoenix post office, which was in 1891 discontinued. Dr. Wm. A. Smith came to Newman in 1860, where he was a successful physician for over a quarter of a century. He was a soldier in the Mexican war, and one of the charter members of the Newman Masonic lodge and its first worshipful master. Jas. McIntyre came from Canada in 1864. He was born in 1805, and died in 1892. Jonathan McCown came to Edgar county in 1852, but his sons are residents of this township, where J. A. owns a fine farm, and was several years highway commissioner. Wm. Heaton, who was born in 1815, came to the Ridge some years before the Civil war. Thos. Hull was born in New York state in 1829, coming to Newman about 1866. James Morrow is another old settler, whose large farm lies just east of town, though he resides in this city. He also belongs to the G. A. R. and is a Mason.

The majority of the early settlers have passed to the great beyond, while a small majority still survive, whose strong hands bore the heat and burden of the day, and who now, in the evening of their life, are resting and enjoying the fruits of their early toil and labors. Many interesting facts relating to the personal history of various prominent men will be found in the biographical department.

THE CITY OF NEWMAN.

The Newman of to-day is not the Newman of twenty or thirty years ago. A person returning here even after an absence of ten years would find but few familiar scenes left. Such a wave of improvement has swept over the town, its boundaries become so extended and the magical wand of enterprise so touched our slothful industries and laggard capital that the progress made through these agencies has so changed the tipographical appearance of the place that old settlers returning on a visit after an absence of some years can scarcely find their bearings. The old home has been replaced by a new Newman which has far outstripped the old one.

The city of Newman, consisting originally of about forty acres, was laid out about 1857 by B. Newman, one of the original proprietors, in honor of whom it was named. Mr. Newman was a son-in-law of Peter Cartwright, the celebrated Methodist itinerant preacher. The progress of the place from the beginning was very slow, the people waiting fifteen years for the railroad to be constructed through it. For very many years it was but a small village consisting of one church, two stores, a school house, Masonic hall, blacksmith shop and a dozen or so small dwelling houses. "Uncle" John Stockton, who is the oldest inhabitant of the city and also the township, kept the first grocery store and was the first white man who slept within the limits of the village. The first dry goods store was kept by John Dicken. First dwelling house was built by Hezekiah Howard, just east of where the Commercial Hotel now stands, no vestige of which remains. His widow, "Grandma" Howard, at the time of her death was the oldest person in the town, living long enough to see the fifth generation of her family in the person of the little daughter of the late Judge Moffit. In 1872 what is now known as the I., D. & W. Railroad, after nearly sixteen years of preparation, was completed, which runs through the city connecting Indianapolis, one hundred miles east, with Decatur, fifty miles west, and the first train run through here in October, 1873. Newman immediately showed the effects of the impetus thus given to business circles. Brick blocks went up like homemade magic. L. J. and S. C. Cash, who for many years had been the sole dry goods firm here, built a fine two-story brick store. Two grain elevators have been erected, a fine flowing well—the equal of any in this part of the state—an elegant two-story brick school building with tower, in which hangs the bell, and a new frame building for the primary department, evidences the fact that the population is rapidly increasing. Two other churches have since been erected, a bank established, lumber yards, canning and electric light company, till mills, marble works, hay press, broom factory, flour mills and various other industries have been located here. A fine Odd Fellows temple has lately been built and last year an elegant K. of P. hall. The Masonic hall at the time it was built, 1875, was the finest in this part of the state. Other orders have also comfortable lodge rooms. Newman has reason to be proud of its public well, as an ever-flowing artesian well for the accommodation of the public is to be found at the corner of the public square.

Newman is beautifully adorned by a lovely park.

The first school house, an ordinary building erected in 1858 at a cost of about five hundred dollars, stood in the center of the park. The upper story was used as a Masonic hall until, in 1875, when they moved to their new hall in the brick block over Finney & Goldman's store. The old school building was then removed and the park set out in shade trees, the pagoda erected and seats constructed beneath the trees for the accommodation of the public.

In 1874 C. V. Walls established the Newman Independent. It has changed hands occasionally, but has come to be, in the hands the present editor, the best local newspaper and the first all-home print established in the county, and Newman owes much of her prosperity to its untiring zeal in promoting the interests and welfare of the city.

The growth of the town was for a time seriously retarded by destructive fires. In 1876 Gillogly's Hotel, occupied by G. A. Fuller, was burned, and in 1881 a large portion of Yates street was consumed, including Gwinn's Hotel and several stores. Another in 1885 destroyed the entire east side of North Broadway, including Gwinn's Hotel again, which he rebuilt, the post office, book store, Ed. Cole's music and jewelry store, groceries, restaurants, lawyer's offices, etc. The population has steadily increased until it now numbers eighteen hundred. A new canning factory has been built. A new Methodist church is now being built. The town has grown so that building lots are at a premium. Geo. White, some few years ago, laid out an addition to the southern part of the city. Thomas Shaw's addition in the north part of the city, and Smith's addition in the southeast part are building up very rapidly. Wealthy farmers are renting their farms and moving into the city. A few years ago I. Streibich established an electric light plant here, patronized only by a few of the merchants, as the terms were exorbitant, and it was finally abandoned. There is to be a plant, however, established in connection with the canning factory that will light the stores, dwellings and streets at more reasonable prices. Newman cemetery lies just west of town, consisting first of ten acres, to which has been added. A good side walk extends from the city to the cemetery.

Some of the leading men of the county and town were former residents of Newman. Newman has given three county clerks and three county superintendents of schools to the county, and has sent forth several ministers who are making their mark in the world. A number of young men, born and raised here, who have graduated from our schools, and later on from medical colleges, are now successful physicians in other fields. The railroad officials say more business is done in Newman with the I., D. & W. than in any other town on the road. This is a great grain center and also a temperance town, there having been no saloons here since 1875. In 1878 a license was granted to druggists to sell liquor for medical purposes. This possibly may have been abused, but there are no legalized licensed establishments for the retailing of spirituous drinks in the city. The first hotel was kept by Mrs. Susan Bell, a house comprising a portion of what is now the Maple Hotel, which is a good house in every respect. The City Hotel was built by Thos. Gwinn, after his being burned out in two fires. Situated close to the depot it is convenient to traveling men, who patronize it largely. R. Thomas has the largest tile factory in the county, its shipments requiring a special railroad switch. The first postmaster of Newman was Frank Wells, who also had a grocery store in an early day. G. W. Smith was his successor. The other "Nasby's" have been Hugh Cook, J. W. King, A. J. Hoover and T. M. Sidenstricker, the present incumbent.

The vast majority of the citizens of Newman own their homes and there is quite a demand here for houses to rent. A number are erecting houses to be rented.

Improvements.—The city of Newman has through the thrift and enterprise of such citizens as Culbertson, Roots and other good people, been placed far in advance of other towns of its size in the state. Mr. Culbertson has taken deep interest in Newman city and Newman township. The interest he took in the building of over six miles of concrete side walk in Newman and the business blocks he has erected attest his public spiritedness and the love he has for Newman and Newman people.

Society.—I shall be easy on Newman people, for, as a rule, I found them warm hearted, hospitable, gentlemanly and womanly people. They seem to well understand that the world was not made entirely for their own special benefit, but for others as well. They are far superior in public improvement and in beautifying their city and homes to any other community in Douglas county. The village is full of first-class business and professional men, whose standing in church and society is, as the world goes, unimpeachable.

BIOGRAPHICAL SKETCHES.

BIOGRAPHICAL SKETCHES.

JAMES P. HEATON.

James P. Heaton, who was a prominent citizen of Newman and a member of its board of education, was born August 16, 1845, and died March 14, 1897, aged fifty-one years, six months and twenty-eight days. He was a native of Greene county, Pennsylvania, where his early youth was passed among the picturesque hills and scenery of that mountainous region. He was a son of William and Mary Heaton. At the age of sixteen years he came to Illinois and located on the Ridge, four miles north of Newman. At that time there was no church building in that section and in 1869 when the Cumberland Presbyterians built their church he contributed liberally toward its construction and helped in the good cause in various ways. In 1872 he joined the Methodist church, and when the M. E. church on the Ridge was built he and his brothers contributed largely toward its erection, upon ground donated by their father, who located on the Ridge sometime during the '50s and entered a tract of land of 1,400 acres. He afterwards lived in Edgar county from 1873 until 1885, when he moved to Newman and lived there until his death in 1897.

James Heaton was not long in becoming one of the most influential and prosperous citizens in his neighborhood. In 1871 he bought a tract of land now known as the Spring Branch Stock Farm, locater just over the line in Edgar county. His principal occupation was stock raising, his farm containing 600 acres. In addition he owned a business block and a residence in Newman, whence he removed in 1885. On March 4, 1873, he was wedded to Miss Lottie

Harris, of Chariton, Iowa, a daughter of John and Lucinda Harris. To their marriage were born five children, three of whom are living: Eva E., who is the wife of Joe Walker, a lawyer of Tuscola; Ada May and Boyd H.

Mr. Heaton held several local offices, was four years supervisor and was collector for the same length of time of his township in Edgar county, and at the time of his death was a member of the board of education, and city alderman of Newman. He was a member of the I. O. O. F., and in the death of Mr. Heaton Newman lost one of her most popular and useful citizens, who was always ready to advance the interests of the community in which he lived for the common good of all.

FRANK E. LOOSE.

Frank E. Loose, one of the leading farmers and business men of the county, residing upon his farm in the north suburb of Tuscola, was born in the city of Springfield, Illinois, in the year 1859. He was reared on the farm and was educated in Springfield, his father's farm lying just south of the city. His father, Jacob G. Loose, was born in Franklin county, Pennsylvania, just across from the Maryland line. He sank the first shaft in the vicinity of Springfield, on his own farm, mortgaging almost everything he had to accomplish this, and his venture was richly rewarded by finding a paying vein of coal. He became quite well to do, and died on his farm in 1874. Mary Elizabeth (Iles) Loose, his mother, was a native of Kentucky, and a daughter of Washington Iles, who was a stock buyer and who was born in Kentucky and emigrated to Springfield, Illinois, where he lived until his death.

Frank E. Loose located in Douglas county in about 1880, and on September 3, 1879, he married Miss Fannie, the only daughter of the late Mr. and Mrs. John M. Madison (see

sketch). She died June 25, 1897. She was born in Tuscola, and was nearly thirty-five years old at her death. At the age of fifteen she united with the Christian church of Tuscola, in which denomination she was an active church worker throughout the rest of her life. When seventeen years of age she was united in marriage to Frank E. Loose, who survives, with their only child, Jennie, who is about fifteen years old and was the constant companion of her mother. In 1898 Mr. Loose married for his second wife Miss M. Estelle, a daughter of Sylvester J. Faris, of Tuscola. Mr. Loose owns two hundred acres of valuable land adjoining the city of Tuscola, and also owns the business block now occupied by Warren & Murphy. About 1892 he joined the Christian church and has been an officer in it ever since. He is the father of one child, a daughter, Jennie Elizabeth Loose, who is now in college at Jacksonville. Mr. Loose and wife reside in their beautiful home in the suburb of Tuscola, where they are ever ready to give a hospitable welcome to their many friends.

REV. W. E. MEANS.

Rev. William E. Means, proprietor of the Atwood Herald, was born at Paris, Edgar county, Ilinois, June 28, 1850. He attended the district school during the winter, working on

prepared to enter Paris high school. In 1874 he matriculated at the Northwestern University, and was graduated from the theological department of this well-known institution in the farm during the summer months, until the class of 1879. After graduation he was admitted to the Minnesota conference of the Methodist Episcopal church, and was appointed pastor of the Rushmore charge, where a handsome four-thousand-dollar church was built, free from debt. In the middle of the second year he was appointed to Lu Verne, where the church was greatly blessed during his labors with a sweeping revival, the church completed, and the way prepared for the paying off of a crushing debt. Finding the Minnesota winters colder than he liked, he found an opportunity, in the spring of 1884, to transfer to South Kansas conference, where during the year he was instrumental in building two places of worship, a temporary building in Fort Scott, Kansas, which afterward became Grace church, and a beautiful village church at Hiattville, Kansas. The two years following were spent at Moran, Kansas, and were very fruitful. More than a hundred were gathered into the church, and the church thoroughly organized. A pastorate of three and a half years on the Caney charge was likewise fruitful in revivals, debt paying and church building. In October, 1891, Mr. Means was invited to become pastor of the Methodist Episcopal church at Sidney, Illinois, and the following year passed a prosperous year on the Atwood charge. Failing health compelled him to retire from the pastorate in the fall of 1893, and he has since held a supernumerary relation to the Illinois conference, often rendering efficient service in the ministry, without assuming the responsibilities of a pastoral charge. In 1895 he leased the Atwood Herald, and purchased it the following year. The paper was established in 1888, and is independent in politics. It has a good circulation and is an excellent advertising medium.

Mr. Means was married in 1884 to Miss Ella M. Chesnut, of Delavan, Minnesota. To them have been born one child, a son, Cyril, aged fifteen years. Mr. Means is a son of Thomas N. and Jane (Quiett) Means, natives of Ohio and Tennessee, respectively. His grandfather, William Means, was of Scotch-Irish descent. In manner Mr. Means is approachable and unassuming, and is highly respected by all who know him.

STEPHEN REDDEN.

Stephen Redden was born in Bracken county, Kentucky, April 14, 1818, and was a son of James Redden, who having a large family of children growing up resolved to give them a better chance by going west. Consequently he made a flat-boat, and, with his family and several of his neighbors and their families, he embarked on the Ohio river for what was then considered the far west. Stephen Redden was at that time four years old. At Louisville they would not trust the flat-boat to carry them over the falls, but were put ashore and either walked or were conveyed in some other manner to Portland, just below the falls, where the boat landed and took them on board. They landed at Evansville, Indiana, sometime in the fall of 1822, and after disposing of the flat-boat and investing in an ox team Mr. Redden and family started for the land of promise, the Prairie state, while the other families cast their lot with the Hoosier state. It was no uncommon thing for them to meet bands of blanketed Indians and see droves of deer, or to be "lulled to sleep" at night by the "music of the wolves," on their journey from the Ohio river to the small village of Terre Haute, Indiana, which at that time consisted of a tavern, a few saloons and stores, and a horse ferry to cross the Wabash river. They located on Big Creek, Edgar

county, where they remained until 1830, when they removed to Coles county, now Douglas county. Here Stephen Redden grew to manhood at the hard labor of making rails and breaking the new prairie soil with ox teams, but occasionally taking a little pastime with his trusty rifle and his faithful dogs, and many noble bucks dropped at the crack of his rifle and many a sheep's life was saved by his dogs getting the wolf before the wolf got the sheep. In his later days, while suffering in his last sickness, he would forget the racking pains while telling of his hunts in his boyhood days. At that time there were no schools that he could attend and all his education was received by reading from the light of hickory bark burned in the old fire place. He never learned to write, but his mark on any note was worth one hundred cents to the dollar.

He was married to Vashti Winkler in March, 1840; he made rails all day and was married in the evening. His wife was born in Warwick county, Indiana, February 2, 1818, and was a little over two months older than him. He bought eighty-four acres of land a short time after he was married, at twenty-two dollars per acre, and by frugality and strict economy he paid for the land and built a house in which he lived until his death. His beloved wife departed this life March 2, 1878, leaving him without any children. His home was desolate, but Providence ruled that it last but a short time, and he was again married, this time to Mrs. Mary A. Tinkle, of Charleston, Illinois, November 3, 1880. She has been to him a loving wife, a faithful companion, and during his last sickness a trusted nurse, prolonging his days by her untiring and constant attention. Uncle Steve, as he was familiarly known, was strictly honest in his dealings. He peacefully fell asleep in the arms of his Saviour at eleven o'clock A. M., April 17, 1897, at the ripe age of seventy-nine years and three days. His widow, Mrs. Mary A. Redden, has two children living by her first husband: Aaron T., in Kansas, and Malissa, wife of H. B. Morgan, of Murdock. Mrs. Redden resides a great deal of her time at South Haven, Michigan. She owns three hundred and four acres of land in Sargent township and forty acres in Bowdre township.

JOHN T. IRWIN.

John T. Irwin, retired farmer, and for many years a highly respected citizen of the county, is a son of George and Jemima (Russell) Irwin, and was born in Lawrence county, Ohio, May 28, 1824. His father was a native of

Montgomery county, Ohio, and his mother of Cabell county, West Virginia. George Irwin was born October 23, 1799, and died May 23, 1871. He followed the occupation of farming principally; emigrated from his native county to Lawrence county, Ohio, in the year 1818. He was a son of Thomas Irwin, who was a native of Ireland, and served in the war of 1812.

John Russell (maternal grandfather) was born in Virginia and was a weaver by trade.

In 1870 Mr. Irwin removed from Ohio to Illinois, and settled on a farm of three hundred and twenty acres, two miles north of Camargo, where he continued the pursuits of the farm until 1894. In that year he retired from active business and removed into the village of Camargo, where he and his wife reside in one of the most beautiful homes in the village. When he retired he divided his property among his children.

On September 11, 1845, he wedded Miss Lettie Wiseman, who was born in Monroe county, Virginia, and was a daughter of Isaac and Sarah (Ramsey) Wiseman. Her grandfather, Isaac Wiseman, was probably a native of Virginia. To John T. Irwin and wife have been born eight children, four of whom are now living: William T., who resides in Chicago; Lewis K., who resides on part of the old homestead; Harriet, wife of Dr. W. H. Burtnette; and Ida May, wife of Charles D. Hammett, of Tuscola. They have four dead: Sarah J., Mary E., Jane and Ella. Mrs. Irwin was born May 6, 1827. They will have been married fifty-five years their next wedding anniversary. John T. Irwin's early advantages for an education were very limited, he having attended only fourteen days in all at school. He has served as supervisor of Camargo township, and he has been superintendent of roads.

On July 4, 1861, he volunteered in an independent company of Ohio cavalry. These were ninety-day men called out to serve until they were superseded by a company of regulars. On July 22, 1863, he joined the Ninety-first Ohio Volunteer Infantry, as first lieutenant of Company D, and in the following October he was wounded in a skirmish near Mt. Pleasant, Maryland, which disabled him for further active service. He was licensed to exhort in the Methodist Episcopal church in 1865.

CHAS. L. McMASTERS.

Chas. L. McMasters, dealer in grain, coal and seeds, and a popular young man of Tuscola, was born on a farm three miles northwest of Tuscola, in Tuscola township, March 26, 1867, and is a son of S. L. and Hannah

(Maris) McMasters, who were natives of Parke county, Indiana. In 1869 his father sold his farm and removed to Sand Springs, Kansas, where he followed farming and stock raising until his death in May, 1870, after which his mother, with three children, two sons and one

daughter—Charles being the younger—removed to Winfield, Cowley county, Kansas, where she resided until the spring of 1877, thence moving to Joplin, Jasper county, Missouri, where she died October 3, of the same year. In March, 1878, Charles, being only in his eleventh year, returned to Tuscola to live with his uncle, James Davis. Here he went to school until February, 1886, when he became a clerk for Davis & Finney, in the grain business, and remained their bookkeeper and confidential clerk up to 1888, when Mr. Davis died. The firm was then succeeded by Finney & McMasters, which business continued up to 1891, when Mr. McMasters bought the interest of his partner and since then has been alone. He is now in the midst of what promises to be a most successful business career. He buys and sells about two hundred and fifty thousand bushels of grain annually, and also deals in coal for the local trade.

Mr. McMasters has thrice been elected to the office of city treasurer, belongs to the Masonic and Red Men fraternities and is deservedly popular in business and social circles.

JOHN LINDSEY.

John Lindsey, owner of the Evergreen farm, two miles west of Tuscola, was born in Fairfield county, Ohio, April 2, 1834, and is a son of Thomas and Mary (Blackburn) Lindsey. They were both natives of Ireland, and after their marriage came to this country in about 1820. They were both descendants of Scotch-Irish ancestry and were members of the Presbyterian church. The father died in 1873, aged about sixty-five years; the mother died when our subject was about twelve years old.

Mr. Lindsey was reared on a farm and received a common-school education, and was engaged in farming in Ohio up to September 14, 1855, when he emigrated to Illinois and located on a farm in Edgar county, which he rent-

ed some three or four years. He then bought forty acres and tilled this until 1874, when he removed to Kansas and remained there for about two years and a half, at the end of which time he returned to Illinois and located near Ficklin, on a farm of one hundred and thirty-four acres, which he bought and still owns. He resided on this farm until 1885, when he came to his Evergreen farm, which contains one hundred and sixty acres.

In 1853 he was united in marriage with Miss Elizabeth Ebert, who was also born in

Fairfield county, Ohio. She is a daughter of Daniel and Mary (Gaul) Ebert. To their marriage have been born ten children. John Lindsey is one of the devout and useful members of the Methodist church. He is a pleasant, affable gentleman, has accumulated a considerable competency, and resides in a beautiful home where he is surrounded by the modern conveniences and comforts of life which fittingly crown an active and successful career.

DAVID COOPER.

David Cooper, an old and universally respected citizen of Tuscola, who has long led an unselfish and benevolent life, was born in

Greenbrier county, West Virginia, in the year 1813. He is a son of Francis and Elizabeth (Miller) Cooper, who were both born in the same county. Simeon Cooper (grandfather) was also a Virginian by birth, and was in the Revolutionary war. Henry Miller, his mother's father, was born in Germany, and was among the old settlers of the Old Dominion. He was also a Revolutionary soldier.

David Cooper grew to manhood in his native county, his early schooling being almost entirely neglected. At the age of twenty-seven years he emigrated to Lawrence county, Ohio, and was there engaged in farming up to 1856, when he removed to Kansas, remaining there but a short time, when he went to Nodaway county, Missouri, and lived there for seven years. In 1862 he returned to Illinois, and settled in Champaign county, and some twenty years ago located on a farm of two hundred acres in Tuscola township, which he still owns. In 1886 he retired from the farm and removed to Tuscola. On April 11, 1839, he was united in marriage to Miss Virginia Asbury, who was a native of Greenbrier county, West Virginia, and was a daughter of William Asbury, also a native of the same county. She is still living and is in the eighty-third year of her age and the sixty-first year of her marriage.

David Cooper, or, as he is familiarly known as "Grandpa Cooper" has been a devout and consistent member of the first Methodist Episcopal church, second, the United Brethren, then joined the Free Methodist church, of which he has been a member about twelve years, making in all about seventy years a member of the church, a most remarkable record of a remarkable man. Without family influence or outside help of any kind Mr. Cooper has not only succeeded in life, but has unselfishly helped others to succeed. In about 1888 he was chiefly instrumental in the building of the Free Methodist church, in the northwest part of the city. It is a frame edifice, 36x46 feet, with a seating capacity of about three hundred. Rev. Jenkins, of Arcola, is the pastor. The membership is composed, in the language of Mr. Cooper, "of the plain, common people." He is the trustee and local elder, and occasionally gives the congregation one of his sermons on "old time religion." The Sabbath school in connection with this church numbers about eighty children. Mrs. Kate Lamb is the class leader of the church. David Cooper has given thousands of dollars toward the building of churches. While living in Champaign county he gave one thousand, five hundred dollars toward the building of the Methodist church located on his farm near Pesotum. It has since been bought by the United Brethren people and moved to the village of Pesotum.

CHARLES W. WOOLVERTON.

Charles W. Woolverton, for many years noted as a lawyer in Douglas county and throughout central Illinois, was born at Belvidere, Illinois, February 27, 1847, and died November 10, 1895, in the forty-ninth year of his age. In June, 1888, he married Mrs. Elizabeth C. Remine, who was at that time the official court reporter of the then judicial district composed of Douglas, Coles and Edgar counties.

Mr. Woolverton was a graduate of McKendree College, and soon after his graduation he began the practice of law at Tuscola, becoming a member of the firm of Bundy & Woolverton. He remained with Mr. Bundy for ten years, until the death of the latter in 1885. From this time up to his death he was alone in the practice. Col. Woolverton was the son of Charles W. and Amanda (Holland) Woolverton, who died when Charles W. was an infant. His father was a millwright by trade, but to his mother much of his success in life was due, she being a woman of fine intelligence and will-

power. In finishing the sketch of Mr. Woolverton, we will substitute the words of the eminent Doctor Hurd, late pastor of the Presbyterian church, instead of our own:

"Charles W. Woolverton was born at Belvidere, Illinois, and at the time of his decease had nearly completed his forty-ninth year. His youth was marked with the most industrious and earnest efforts towards self education, in which he was dependent largely on his own resources, and to which effort was added necessary exertion which he manfully rendered on behalf of his widowed mother and family. He wrought his way through the entire course of prescribed studies, and graduated from McKendree College, at Lebanon, Illinois. While engaged in teaching he pursued the studies preparatory to the legal profession until he was admitted to the bar. His first experience as an attorney was in connection with the office of the well-known lawyer and representative, Thomas E. Bundy, some years since deceased.

"Mr. Woolverton as a lawyer, as a man and as a citizen is well known in Douglas county and beyond. By the same incessant industry, and honorable attention to the fiduciary trusts and duties of his profession, he has won a large success, and a distinction which, with the promise of life preceding his last fatal sickness, would have ripened into eminence among his peers. Even as a young lawyer he was able to execute in two instances the largest bond for the discharge of important financial trusts which had ever been executed in Douglas county, and his fidelity in all commercial and civic relations was so well understood that up to the time of his departure from our midst large trusts were committed to his hands. Of irreproachable character as a man, he leaves large numbers who will deeply feel the loss of his invaluable worth among us. The members of the bar, honoring his memory on this occasion, are sincere mourners with those most nearly and deeply afflicted. The large fraternity who have known him as a member, as a brother and as a man, attend in charge of the interment of his body to-day with regret and with love unfeigned. As his chosen pastor for nearly five years I have been conscious on many Sabbath mornings of an intent and interested listener to such views of truth that I have attempted to present, and the knowledge and expectation of this has been a help and a stimulant such as few perhaps realize. The warm grasp of his hand whenever and wherever I chanced to meet him, with his inquiries and words of sympathy, notwithstanding his habitual reserve, have prepared me to feel that I have lost a friend and to have still deeper sympathy which words cannot express for those most nearly bereaved. Mr. Woolverton was reserved in the expressing of his feelings and sentiments."

The funeral cortege was a lengthy one, and the number of distinguished men in attendance was unusually large, all of which demonstrated the high esteem in which he was held by his fellowmen. The pall bearers were Messrs. P. M. Moore, United States Marshal W. B. Brinton, Rice Ervin, Thomas W. Roberts, James A. Richmond and P. L. Dawson. The remains were laid beside those of the late John J. Jones, both of whom were warm friends in life. The floral offerings were very fine, and some lovely pieces came from those who held him in noble esteem:

The deceased during his twenty years practice of law had built up a large clientage, and his many duties and responsibilities made him a very busy man. At the time of his death he was attorney for the I. D. & W. Railway; also for the Corn Belt Building & Loan Association, the bank of Baughman, Bragg & Co., and was manager of the large estate of John J. Jones, and several other large estates, besides having on hand many important cases in court at all times. He did business on a large scale, and the people sought him because of his integrity and honesty in his dealings with them.

He was a member of the following Masonic bodies, to-wit: Camargo lodge, No. 440, A. F. & A. M., Camargo, Illinois; Tuscola Chapter, No. 66, R. A. M., Tuscola, Illinois; Tuscola Council, No. 21, R. & S. M., Tuscola, Illinois; Melita Commandery, No. 37, Tuscola, Illinois.

EULOGY OF HON. HORACE CLARK TO THE LATE COL. C. W. WOOLVERTON.

The painful duty, at the request of the Douglas county bar, is imposed upon me of officially announcing to this court that one of the members has passed away; one to whom we were bound by strong ties of personal esteem and friendship, and by ties of professional association as a practicing lawyer; one who honored our profession, and was honored by it.

That such a duty should come is painful, yet fate-bound and impossible to escape therefrom. With the dread realities before us, and with power to recognize the same, in our manly strength yielding to the inevitable, it is a pleasing task to speak honest words of eulogy of the dead and words of sympathy to the living. It is always thus with us, when grim death enters our circle and with apparent ruthless hand plucks those who seemingly can least be spared. With the spirit of frankness we say it is always so, for when, perchance, one of less degree is claimed for that bourne of eternity, there comes as a belief, it seems to us, virtue and merits forgotten and unheralded like the still, undisturbed repose of true worth, magnified, it may be, by hidden generosities of our nature, suddenly drawn upon in all of the intensity of deep-seated sorrow, and through the gloom see, as bright lining, the nobler elements of the true man.

This custom is not of mere form, but of deep merit; an opportune time for contemplation of true worth and true manhood, yielding fruitful lessons for the present and enduring thoughts to guide us on into the otherwise obscure and unknown future. So the dark pall of death brings the white-winged dove and proclaims the brightest subjects.

To-day we make no draughts upon our charity in speaking of the subject of the resolutions which I have the great honor on behalf of our living brothers to present to this court. Well we know and realize that to your honor personally our words of praise and commendation will meet with a hearty response. Around the lifeless form of Charles W. Woolverton has been drawn the mantle of death, and we raise the veil with reverence to look upon his life and character with words of truthfulness to speak of him. Knowing the youthful struggle with poverty, and ambition of the American boy of Illinois birth, we see his elastic form and reliant journey up the steps of learning, and while possibly chiding his hard lot, side by side with his more favored companions, with determined mien, nerved by the opposition, he marches alongside his competitors with longing hope of ultimate success. As year quickly follows year we find him with self reliance, without assurance, in the foremost ranks of his profession as a lawyer, and his pathway, among struggles and disappointments, strewn with monuments of professional success. In looking back through those years of untiring labor we see success written upon his every effort. With physical strength and courage the citizen stands with all the embellishment of the practicing lawyer and able jurist. And among those who speak his praise and his worth are many who in every day life received the encouraging word and the helping hand, and joined with these are the expressions of hearty gratitude of his young professional brethren. With sturdy, honest and untiring labor and fidelity came to him remunerating trusts and such a competence as to place the loving ones who mourn his loss beyond the reach of want or dependence. His home has lost a jewel, his wife and daughter a kind husband and father and a genial companion, and his surviving mother a son whose every effort was responsive to her wishes. The community has lost an upright citizen and the Douglas county bar has lost a brother worthy of our profession. With the unbounded confidence of all courts before whom he appeared his professional honor was ever beyond question. He was a close practitioner, eloquent and forcible, seldom indulging in invectives or sarcasm. Yet his power and force of character always inspired the court and jury, as it did himself, with confidence in the justice of his cause, and he was at all times a formidable adversary.

In the forty-ninth year of his age, in the very prime of mental and physical life, with sturdy qualities of honest heart and hand, and in full manhood of usefulness, our brother Charles W. Woolverton, by infinite and unknown Providence, has been cut down. With bowed heads to the inevitable, we must be resigned, and as out of the eternity we today and now seem to hear voices whispering from the "shadowy silence of the grave" we join with reluctance our voices in a long and last farewell to our friend and professional brother.

R. S. FOSTER.

R. S. Foster, one of the oldest citizens of Tuscola, was born in Clermont county, Ohio, March 4, 1818, and is a son of Israel and Mary (Kain) Foster, who were natives respectively of Berkley county, Virginia, and Clermont county, Ohio. His mother was a daughter of Daniel Kain, who was born in Williamsburg,

Ohio, and was a member of one of the early pioneer families of that section. His father, Israel Foster, was born in 1793, and in 1827, with his family, moved to Bracken county, Kentucky, where he engaged in farming on the Ohio river, twelve miles below Augusta, the county

seat of Bracken county. He died in 1878, in the eighty-fifth year of his age, while on a visit to his daughter in Keokuk, Iowa. He was a soldier in the war of 1812.

R. S. Foster received a common-school education and after leaving school he was engaged in farming in Bracken county, residing at Foster, when, in 1878, he removed to Douglas county, where he has since resided. Mr. Foster has been twice married, first, in 1838, to Miss Elizabeth Tuttle, of Maine, whose death occurred in the same year of her removal to this county. His second wife was Mrs. Eliza E. Roberts whose maiden name was Maxwell. She was a native of Bracken county, Kentucky, and at the time of her marriage was a resident of Foster. Mr. Foster owns two hundred and seventy-two acres of land in Arcola township, which is one of the finest farms in the county. He is devoted to the Methodist Episcopal church. In politics he is a stanch Republican. For the past few years Mr. Foster has been confined to his home with rheumatism, getting out only occasionally. He has lived a long and useful life—a man of strictest integrity and fearless in voicing his convictions upon any subject.

W. H. BURTNETT, M. D.

William H. Burtnett, M. D., physician and druggist of Camargo, and a veteran of the war of the Rebellion, was born in Gallia county, Ohio, January 6, 1843, and is a son of John Burtnett, who was a native Virginian. His mother was Mary Gilmore, a daughter of Matthew Gilmore. He was reared and educated in his native county, and at the age of eighteen years he joined Company C, Eighteenth Indiana Infantry, was mustered into the service and was out four years and two months. There are few soldiers who served longer in the Civil war than Dr. Burtnett, although he has never applied for a pension, nor would accept one if it were tendered him. In politics he is the same as he is in all other affairs of life, strictly independent. He is inclined to favor the Republicans of the anti-monopoly type, but in 1896 he voted for Bryan. In 1868 Dr. Burtnett located in Douglas county, in the practice of his profession, and in 1872 he located at Camargo, where he has continued to reside. In 1894 he established his present drug-store, and since that time he has not done so much active practice as formerly.

Dr. William H. Burtnett was graduated from the Miami Medical College, at Cincinnati, in the class of 1867, and subsequently he took a special course at Indianapolis. On January 31, 1879, he was married to Miss Hattie, a daughter of John M. Irwin, of Camargo (see his sketch). She is a native of Lawrence county, Ohio. They have had two children, but both are deceased. Dr. Burtnett is a man of marked individuality; is perfectly frank and outspoken on questions in line with his convictions and which he believes to be honest and right, and is universally popular with all who understand him.

JAMES JONES.

James Jones, ex-county treasurer and present deputy treasurer, and also the present chairman of the Douglas county Republican central committee, was born in Franklin county, Indiana, January 24, 1837. In 1858 he came to Illinois and settled in Whiteside county and engaged in farming. Two years later he removed to this county and bought a farm in Arcola township, where he resided up to the time when he traded his farm for one in Tuscola township; upon the latter place he lived and farmed successfully up to the year 1884. That year he was elected by his party treasurer of Douglas county and most efficiently served in this capacity for one term.

James Jones is one of the most universally popular men in the county. He has been a successful man of business affairs and the same methods used in his own every-day business life he applies in dealing with the public; he is very approachable in manner and of strictest integrity and probity.

WILLIAM H. FRY.

William H. Fry, of West Ridge, who is the grain agent at that place for T. D. Hanson & Co., a position he has filled most acceptably to his employers and the general public for the past eight years, was born in Camargo township, Douglas county, Illinois, February 14, 1869. He is a son of Daniel and Millie Ann (Braughton) Fry, who were born respectively in Pennsylvania and Kentucky. His grandfather, Henry Fry, who was born in Pennsylvania, came west and became one of the pioneer settlers in Camargo township. Daniel Fry, who came at the same time, was born in 1830 and died in 1881; his wife died in 1893 in the forty-first year of her age. To their marriage were born four children: William H.; Mrs. M. Entler, residing near the Mt. Gilead church; James W. and G. W. G. W. Braughton (grandfather) was of English ancestry, a native of Kentucky, and settled in Camargo township at about the same time the Fry family located there.

William H. Fry was reared on the farm, and after attending the graded school of Camargo was one year at the Bloomington normal; leaving there he entered DePauw University, at Greencastle, Indiana, where he continued his studies for three years. After leaving college he taught for three years in Douglas

county, at the end of which time he accepted his present position at West Ridge. On December 1, 1899, he engaged in mercantile business also at West Ridge, and accepted the position of postmaster under the administration of President McKinley.

On February 22, 1892, he married Miss Cora A., daughter of W. H. Dodson, a justice of the peace of Tuscola. Mr. Fry owns twenty acres of land in Camargo township, besides property in the village of West Ridge. He is a Knight of Pythias, and he and his wife are members of the Christian church of Tuscola. Mr. Fry is one of that useful class of young men in every county whose intelligence, sturdy integrity and restless energy add stability and force to its business affairs.

JAMES A. KINCAID.

James A. Kincaid has through his own individual effort and unaided by friends become one of the most successful farmers and stock raisers in Newman township. He was born of humble but honorable parentage in Marion

county, West Virginia, August 22, 1853, and is a son of Alpheus M. and Sarah (Johnson) Kincaid, who in about 1865 emigrated from their West Virginia home and settled on a farm near the village of Chrisman, where they resided on a rented farm for three years, when they removed to Newman township. Alpheus M. Kincaid has been dead for over thirty years, and his wife died March 9, 1900. John Kincaid (grandfather) was born in Rolan county, Ireland, and entered land in West Virginia. Barnett Johnson was born in New England, and also entered land in West Virginia.

James A. Kincaid, by hard work and good management, has achieved a success far above the average farmer. He owns eighty acres of valuable and well improved land and has only recently erected a fine residence at a cost of over three thousand dollars. In 1874 he was united in marriage to Miss Caroline F. Anderson, a daughter of Elijah Anderson, who was one of the pioneers of the Brushy Fork neighborhood, having migrated from Indiana. He was born in Posey county, Indiana, and married in Vermillion county, that state, to Sarah S. James. His death occurred some eight years ago, and he and his wife are buried at Albin cemetery. Mr. and Mrs. Kincaid have four children living: Sarah, Nora V., Rosa Lee, Caroline Elizabeth and James A. A son, Moses Ewen, died September 12, 1876. Mr. Kincaid is a member of the Modern Woodmen, and is well and favorably known as an intelligent and up-to-date farmer.

DANIEL ATTO.

Daniel Atto, an honest and hard working farmer of Newman township, was born near

Bedford, Lawrence county, Indiana, July 15, 1844. He came to Newman township in 1861 and was for three years a tenant farmer before

he purchased his farm of forty-seven acres, which he yet owns. While our subject was yet small, his parents removed from Lawrence to Greene county, Indiana, where he remained until he was eighteen years of age, when he migrated to Illinois with his mother and her family. His father, Joseph Atto, a native of Natchez, Mississippi, was left an orphan at an early age. At the age of five years by some means he was sent north stopping at Evansville, Indiana, and was taken by Isaac Mitchell, who raised and educated him. In 1841 he wedded Fannie, a daughter of Isaac Mitchell, who was a native of Virginia, and who lived and died near Bloomfield, Indiana. Daniel Atto has been a busy man all his life, had few school advantages, but knew well the advantages of an education and has seen that his children have amply received what he lacked. For many years he has taken an active interest in school matters and for eighteen years past has served as president of the school board.

In 1866 he was united in marriage to Miss Phebe Ogdon, who was born in Illinois, a daughter of Alexander and Adaline Ogdon, who were born in Virginia. Five children have blessed their union: Ira; Ora, who is in his twenty-third year and is one of the bright young school teachers of the county; Barney, Alma and Lucy. Mr. Atto is a stanch Republican in his political opinion, and occupies a high place in the respect and esteem of the people among whom he has dwelt for so many years.

M. D. BARTHOLOMEW.

Michael D. Bartholomew, a reputable and highly intelligent farmer of Bourbon township, has been numbered among the residents of

Douglas county since 1861. He and his estimable wife are among the pioneer settlers who have lived to witness the phenomenal growth and development which has placed Douglas county in the front rank as one of the most prosperous and highly cultivated portions of the great state of Illinois.

Mr. Bartholomew is a native of the state of New York. He was born in St. Lawrence county, August 21, 1825. His parents were Luman B. and Lydia (Daniels) Bartholomew. The family was well and favorably known where they resided. In 1843 they emigrated to the West. Soon after reaching their new home in McHenry county, Illinois, the father died and the family were thrown upon their own resources. The subject of this sketch was then eighteen years of age. He continued to reside in McHenry county, sharing the hard toil and privations incident upon the life in a new and unsettled region, until 1847. For the next nine years Vigo county, Indiana, became his home. Here, in 1854, he was united in marriage to Sarah Durham, a native of Vigo county, and a daughter of Daniel Durham. Their marriage proved a happy and congenial one. Both Mr. and Mrs. Bartholomew are of English ancestry. The grandfathers of the subject of this sketch rendered honorable and distinguished service in the Revolutionary war; the genealogy of the family is traced back to the earliest settlers of America. Mr. and Mrs. Bartholomew have been greatly prospered in their Douglas county home. They now own over five hundred acres of fertile and well cultivated land, situated in Bourbon and Arcola townships. They are both members of the United Brethren church at Chesterville. Mr. Bartholomew has well and acceptably performed the duties of township treasurer for a period of twenty-eight years. He has been supervisor and held minor offices of trust. Of the five children, two, Luman and Isaac Bartholomew, are well known and prosperous farmers of Bourbon township. One of the daughters, Miss Eliza, is a successful teacher. Two beautiful and interesting little grandchildren complete the family circle.

ANSON H. GREENMAN.

Anson H. Greenman is probably as well known in Tuscola and its environment as any other citizen in the county. With the exception

of four years he has continuously held the office of township assessor since the year 1881, and is now a candidate for re-election without opposition.

Anson H. Greenman was born in Noble county, Indiana, November 11, 1841, and is a son of Anson and Olive (Cunningham) Greenman. The former was born in Canada, and the latter in Ohio. Mr. Greenman, at an early age, at the death of his parents, was bound out, and went through the hardships that generally befall an orphan under similar circumstances. At the time of his country's peril he volunteered his services in the Civil war, and joining Company B, Eighty-fourth Indiana, as a private, August 1, 1862, under Captain Ellis, of Muncie, and Colonel Trussler, of Connersville, Indiana. He was four times wounded and of late has suffered from one wound received at the battle of Franklin. He also participated in the battles of Resaca, Nashville, Tennessee, and Atlanta, Georgia. The Eighty-fourth Indiana participated in twenty-six battles and skirmishes. In 1865, after being mustered out, Mr. Greenman settled on a farm in Tuscola township, and moved into Tuscola city in February, 1891, and never cast a vote any where else; he is a member of the Grand Army of the Republic.

In 1866 he was wedded to Miss Mary E. Gish, a lady of fine intelligence, who has borne him four children: John L., employe of the Illinois Central Railroad Company; Ollie, employee of the Mt. Pleasant (Iowa) Hospital for the Insane; Dora, wife of James Highland, of Champaign, Illinois, and Emma, who is at home. Mr. Greenman is a pleasant, genial gentleman, an ardent Republican and an active worker for the success of his party.

W. S. MARTIN, M. D.

William S. Martin, M. D., a well-known physician of Tuscola, was born in Putnam county, Indiana, August 2, 1837. After leaving the common schools he taught school for eight years. During the last three years while teaching school he studied medicine under Doctor Price, of Westfield, Illinois. He then went to New York and entered the Bellevue Medical

College, the recognized leading school of the United States, taking two full courses, the first in 1871 and the last in 1877, in which year he was graduated.

His father was William H. Martin, who was born in Bath county, Kentucky, in 1806, and died in 1897. At the age of twenty-one he located in Putnam county, Indiana, where he resided until 1860, when he removed to DeWitt county, Illinois, and there remained eight years, then removing to Tuscola. His life was marked by deep religious sentiment and by the highest sense of Christian duty. When twelve years of age he united with the Methodist church, whose discipline he took at all times as his standard and rule of faith. In about 1827 he was married to Elizabeth Walton Dills. William Martin (grandfather) was a Virginian by birth, removed to Kentucky, and thence to Putnam county, Indiana, where he died. He was a minister in the Methodist church for many years. His wife was Mary Cook, of English parentage, and a relative of Captain Cook. Dr. Martin's maternal grandfather, John Dills, who was a descendant of Holland ancestry, and of a prominent and early settled family in the vicinity of Cynthiana, Kentucky.

Dr. Martin in 1887 took a post-graduate course at the Chicago Medical College, and in 1895 took a post-graduate course in the New York Post Graduate Medical College, giving more particular attention to diseases of the nose and throat. He is a member of the State and the American Medical Associations, and keeps himself thoroughly in touch with the progress and advancement of his profession. Dr. Martin ranks high as a physician and surgeon. His office is the best supplied with instruments for surgical operations of any town in central Illinois, as well as bath rooms and electrical appliances for the successful treatment of chronic diseases, of which for the past few years he has made a specialty.

In 1861 he was united in marriage to Miss Katherine Thompson, of Manhattan, Indiana. To their marriage were born five children, three daughters and two sons, the latter dying early in life. The daughters are: Margaret, single, who resides at home with her father; Catherine, who is the wife of E. A. Link, a piano manufacturer of Chicago, and Nellie, wife of Horace Wortham, who resides in Tuscola. Dr. Martin's first wife died in 1894, and in 1896 he was married to Miss Laura E. Smith, a very estimable lady of Tuscola.

Dr. Martin owns one of the most elegant homes in Tuscola, and has a splendid office; and also owns two farms, one of one hundred and ten acres adjoining Tuscola, and a fruit farm in Marion county. He has served as mayor of the city and is a member of the Presbyterian church. Dr. Martin's splendid intellectual gifts, deeply rooted in his character, shine forth without any effort on his part to display them, and he is a man of fine personal appearance who favorably impresses all who come in contact with him.

JOHN E. ROGERS.

John E. Rogers, of Tuscola, was born near Jacksonville, Morgan county, Illinois, October 5, 1838, and is a son of John and Anna Beasley Rogers, who were natives of Kentucky. John Rogers, his grandfather, born in Kentucky, was one of the early pioneer Baptist preachers in the neighborhood of Jacksonville. His maternal grandfather, Joseph Beasley, was probably a native of Virginia.

John E. Rogers, with his remarkable energy and foresight, has attained a prominence in his calling few men reach, and in the commercial growth and development of Douglas county, as to its lands, he stands uniquely alone. His enterprises have been great and have involved a stupendous amount of money in accomplishing them; but time has proven his good judgment and the great good he has done

the county since he begun his work of dredging and draining. For eight years he has been a resident of Tuscola, and for twice that number of years has been extensively engaged in draining the county. In dredging, draining and regaining swamp lands his contracts extend as far south as New Orleans, where he has performed several contracts with the state of Louisiana and is still engaged in that section.

In 1859 Mr. Rogers married Angeline A. Brooker, of Sangamon county, Illinois, who is of English parentage. They have never had any children of their own, but have three adopted ones. Mr. Rogers is a Knight Templar in Masonry and bears an enviable reputation as a neighbor and friend, a courteous gentleman and a public-spirited citizen in the community in which he lives. In all his relations of life he has been honorable and just, scrupulously prompt in meeting his engagements and in performing his contracts.

WILLIAM EDGAR RICE, M. D.

Among the leading physicians of Tuscola and Douglas county there have been none more active and aggressive in accomplishing good results in the practice of their profession than Dr. Rice. He was born in Clermont county, Ohio, January 23, 1865. He was reared on a farm and attended the country schools, after which he attended Wesleyan University at Delaware, Ohio, and subsequently entered the State University at Columbus, Ohio, in both colleges pursuing scientific studies. After leaving college he took up the study of medicine, matriculating at the Miami Medical College at Cincinnati, from which well-known institution he was graduated in the class of 1891. In the same year he opened an office at Greenville, Ohio, but remained there but a short time, coming to Tuscola that year. With his well-known

ability and energy for hard work, it is useless to state that he was not long in getting into a successful and lucrative practice. He remained alone in the work of his profession up to October, 1898, when, his practice having become very extensive, he formed a partnership with Dr. Walter C. Blain. (See sketch of Dr. Blain.)

Dr. Rice is a member of the Ohio State Medical, Miami County (Ohio) Medical, and the Douglas County (Illinois) Medical Societies. He is also a member in good standing of the Knights of Pythias and the Uniformed Rank, Knights of Pythias, and has been a representative to the grand lodge of that order for the past six years; is also a member of the I. O. O. F.; a member of Tuscola lodge, No. 332, A. F. & A. M.; Tuscola Chapter, No. 66, Royal Arch Masons, and Melita Commandery, No. 37, K. T., and a Woodman; also a member of the city board of health of Tuscola, and a member of the Methodist church. Dr. Rice is surgeon for the I. D. & W. Railroad Company and local surgeon for the Illinois Central.

His father, George W. Rice, was by occupation a farmer, stock raiser and tobacco grower, and a native of Kentucky, but reared in Ohio. His mother before her marriage was Miss Kate G. Frazier, born in Ohio. In 1890 Dr. Rice wedded Miss Sarah P. Rust, of Ohio. To them has been born one child, Mary Katherine, aged seven years.

S. H. BAKER.

S. H. Baker is classed among the successful and enterprising young business men of Arthur. He is a member of the well-known grain firm of Baker & Cahill (see sketch of latter on another page), which partnership was formed February 1, 1895.

Mr. Baker was born on a farm in Juniata county, Pennsylvania, April 12, 1862, and remained on the farm, receiving the advantages of the common schools until he had arrived at the age of fifteen years, when he entered the employ of the Pennsylvania Railroad Company and filled the positions of telegraph operator and ticket clerk at different points on the middle division, on the main line between

Harrisburg and Altoona. In 1880 he came west and located in Illinois, remaining one year, when he returned to Pennsylvania and re-entered the service of the Pennsylvania Railroad Company in the capacity of telegraph operator and ticket clerk on the Schuylkill division at Pottstown, Montgomery county. In 1888 he came back to this state and located in Piatt county, and was station agent at Milmine, on the Wabash system, continuing there up till 1892. In that year he changed to the employ of the C. & E. I. Railroad Company and was their station agent at Arthur up to his going into the grain business in 1895.

In 1885 Mr. Baker was united in marriage to Miss Alice Dobson, a daughter of Robinson Dobson, of Milmine. To their marriage have been born three children: Florence and S. H. Baker, Jr., living, and Jesse, dead.

S. H. Baker comes of sturdy Pennsylvania Dutch ancestry, and is a son of Jesse and Susan (Zeiders) Baker. The father was born in Montgomery county, near Philadelphia; the mother in Perry county, near Liverpool, Pennsylvania. His grandfathers were Peter Baker and Henry Zeiders, who were members of old and respectable families of the Keystone state.

The firm of Baker & Cahill, who carry on business for themselves as dealers in grain, coal, seeds and mill feed, do an annual business of about fifty-one thousand dollars. Mr. Baker is a member and secretary of Arthur lodge, No. 825, Free and Accepted Masons, and is also an active member and one of the oldest trustees of the Methodist Episcopal church, which was organized in 1894. He has attained his present position in the business world by industry and close attention to the details of his every day's work; is public spirited and in favor of all improvements calculated to benefit the community in which he resides.

ELI F. CAHILL.

Eli Foster Cahill, member of the well-known grain firm of Baker & Cahill, of Arthur, was born in Mercer county, Kentucky, October 2, 1851, and is a son of Granson and Ellen (Goff) Cahill. He was reared on a farm in central Kentucky and came from that state to Moultrie county in 1874. In 1894 he and his partner succeeded C. A. Davis in the grain buying business, and the firm of Baker & Cahill is rapidly becoming one of the most important in the county. Mr. Cahill owns one hundred and sixty acres of land northwest of Arthur, in Moultrie county, and while residing on the farm he served three years as highway commissioner, was clerk of the school board

for nine years and for eleven years served as school director.

In 1878 our subject was united in marriage with Mrs. Emily Robertson, of Moultrie county, Illinois, and they have one child, Nellie. Mr. Cahill is a member of the Masonic fraternity and of the Christian church, and is a pleasant and courteous gentleman, well known, wide-awake and progressive, and is in the vigor of manhood, with prospects of many years of usefulness in store for him.

D. N. MAGNER.

D. N. Magner is classed among the reliable and successful business men of the county. He located at Arthur in 1873, and has since been identified with the best interests of the village,

and is the pioneer of Arthur in the lumber, coal and cement business.

Our subject was born in Rush county, Indiana, October 30, 1843, and is a son of Z. H. and Margaret (McCorkle) Magner. His father is a native of Berks county, Pennsylvania, and his mother of Bourbon county, Kentucky. His father, who was born in 1803, and died in August, 1868, was formerly a merchant at Paris, Illinois. His mother died in 1855, aged fifty years. James Magner (grandfather) was a native of Maryland and a son of a Revolutionary soldier. The Magner family, which came from Ireland, has resided in America since about the year 1650. James McCorkle was a Virginian by birth, emigrated to Kentucky as a pioneer and died there. In 1853 D. N. Magner, then nine years old, came to Paris, Illinois, and upon the first call for troops in 1861 he volunteered in Company H, Ninth Illinois Infantry, and served for three years and four months. He was wounded at the battle of Shiloh or Pittsburg Landing, was taken prisoner at the battle of Corinth, and participated in sixty-six engagements during the war. For fourteen years he was in the railway mail service, on the Chicago & Eastern Illinois Railroad and Vandalia line. In 1873 he started in his present business, but in 1880 he sold out to C. A. Reeves. He bought the business back in 1894, and since that time has been carrying on a most successful business. Mr. Magner has been president and trustee of the village board, and is a member of the G. A. R., I. O. O. F. and Masonic fraternities.

In 1862 he was wedded to Miss Mary Thom, of Hillsboro, Illinois. They have three children living: Margaret, Mary and Ruth. He and wife are members of the Christian church of Arthur.

COL. WESFORD TAGGART.

Col. Wesford Taggart, a resident of Tuscola, who for many years has been well and favorably known throughout Douglas county, was born on a farm near the village of Nashville, Brown county, Indiana, November 17, 1833. His father was Capt. James Taggart, who served in the Mexican war as captain of Company E, of Senator James H. Lane's regiment, of Indiana, and was killed in the battle of Buena Vista in the year 1847. Col. Taggart's mother was Jane Weddell, who was born near Bristol, Tennessee, and whose father, Thomas Weddell, was a lieutenant in command against the Indians in the battle of Horseshoe Bend, Florida, where he was killed. The Colonel's grandfather, James Taggart, was a native of North Ireland, of Scotch-Irish ancestry, who, while yet a boy, emigrated to Rockingham county, Virginia, where he married a Miss Petterson, and soon thereafter removed to In-

diana territory. He first located at Leesville, Lawrence county, thence to the vicinity of Nashville, where, in the year 1852, he died, aged ninety-two years. All his life he was engaged in farming, and was a member of the United Brethren church.

Col. Wesford Taggart remained on the old Brown county homestead until he arrived at the age of seventeen years, when he went to Bloomington, in the same state, where he engaged in blacksmithing, and from there removed to Edinsburg, where he remained until 1860. He then removed to Charleston, Illinois, there continuing at his trade until the breaking out of the Civil war, when he was among the first to volunteer his services, but was rejected from the First Illinois Regiment on account of it being so quickly equipped with the required number of men. He at once commenced to raise a company himself, which he soon completed, and was mustered into the service June 1, 1861, at St. Louis, in Gen. Seigel's division, under the command of Gen. Fremont. He campaigned through Missouri and Arkansas; was in the battle of Pea Ridge; transferred to the Army of the Mississippi, and was in the siege of Corinth. After the capture of Corinth he was transferred to the Army of the Cumberland, and was in the march to Louisville, Kentucky. On his return he was in the attack on Bragg at Perryville, thence went to Nashville, Tennessee, and was in the fight against Bragg at Stone River; also in the attack at Tullahoma, where Bragg was driven across the Cumberland mountains, the Union forces still pursuing until the hard fought battle of Chickamauga, September 19 and 20. At Stone River Col. Taggart was promoted to the command of his regiment, and after the battle of Chickamauga, for meritorious conduct, he was promoted to lieutenant-colonel of his regiment. He was also in command at Missionary Ridge, where the Confederate lines were broken and Bragg's army routed. Immediately after this he was in the forced march to Knoxville to relieve Gen. Burnsides. He was also in the battle of Dandridge, Tennessee, where the rebels under Longstreet were routed; then he returned to Knoxville, where he remained some time, when he joined Sherman at Ringgold, Georgia, and participated in the capture of Atlanta. Immediately thereafter he came north and was mustered out of the service at Springfield, Illinois, September 5, 1864. He returned to Charleston, and in January of the following year removed to Tuscola, where he has since resided. From 1865 to 1868 he was successfully engaged in the grocery business at this place, but in the latter year sold his stock of goods and engaged in the manufacture of buggies and light wagons, being engaged in this up to 1876, when he was elected sheriff of Douglas county on the Democratic ticket. The county was strongly Republican, but it did not prevent his re-election in 1878. In 1886 he was elected to the house of representatives from the district composed of Douglas, Coles and Cumberland counties. He served on the military, penal, elections, soldiers and orphans' home committees. In 1881 Col. Taggart engaged in the furniture and undertaking business with A. L. Elkins, who has since died, his present partner being Silas R. Williams. Their house is the largest of the kind in the county.

On January 20, 1859, he was married to Miss Julia Skinner, of Hamilton, Ohio. To them have been born seven children, of whom three are living: Lizzie, wife of Andrew Ingram, of Tuscola; Susan, wife of H. C. Morris, of the same place, and Margaret, single and at home. Col. Taggart was a member of the city council several times and takes a deep interest in the welfare of the city, where he resides in one of the most pleasant homes in the county.

JUDGE J. D. MURDOCK.

Judge John D. Murdock, of Murdock, is a descendant of Scotch-Irish ancestry. His grandfather, William Murdock, left the north of Ireland and came to this country previous to the war of the Revolution, in which he took an active part. As far as is known, he was the first of the name in direct line who came to the new world. He settled in Monmouth county, New Jersey. (Charles Uhlera, nephew of Judge Murdock, has a complete genealogy of the Murdocks in America.) John Murdock's father was born in Monmouth county, New Jersey, about the year 1775, and followed farming, as did his father. At the age of about twenty-one he emigrated to Butler county, Ohio. This was in the early part of the

last century, and he was among the earliest settlers of that section. Here he married Rebecca Little, who was also descended from an old New Jersey family. She was the mother of John D. Murdock, of Murdock, who was born on June 15, 1816. Three years after his birth she was drowned. The sad incident occurred in fording a small stream swollen by recent rains, while returning in a wagon to her home from Cincinnati.

John D. Murdock received his education in a subscription school, the first taught by a Dr. Johnson, in the little town of Washington, Wayne county, Indiana. It was here by close attention to his studies he laid the foundation for the education which afterward served as a means of raising him to a position of influence in the community. After a residence of about six years in Wayne county he, with his father, in 1827, removed to Tippecanoe county, then a wild and unsettled region. He was eleven years old at this time and grew to manhood in this county. The life of the family was that of pioneers. Here he developed those qualities of self-reliance which subsequently entered into his success in life. In March succeeding his twenty-first birthday, he wedded Miss Martha Morgan, whose ancestors were of the early settlers of Tennessee. Her father, Venzant Morgan, removed from Tennessee to Ohio, and from Ohio to Tippecanoe county. Mr. Murdock after his marriage removed to a rented farm, his cash capital at this time consisting of $12, he owning one horse and buying his farming implements on time. A good crop crowned his labors of the first year and he was put on a better footing for the second year. In four years he had accumulated money enough to purchase eighty acres of land, which he did in Fountain county, Indiana, where he removed with his wife. He gained a prominent position in the county and was chosen county commissioner.

In January, 1854, he visited Illinois in search of land. He first came to Georgetown, Vermilion county, thence by the way of Hickory Grove to Camargo. He bought three hundred and thirty acres of land at eleven dollars an acre, and removed his family from Indiana the following April. A split-log house, too small for the accommodation of his family, stood on the tract at the time of the purchase, so he prepared a frame house in Indiana, hauled it to Douglas county and put it upon the premises ready for the reception of his family. He has owned over one thousand five hundred acres of land since his residence in Douglas county. Among his neighbors in the Murdock settlement were James Brewer, Denis Daniels, Ephraim Drago, Anderson Campbell, and Isaac and Robert Carmack, John Jordon, and Uncle Billy Timbrook, who came later. On the organization of Douglas county Judge Murdock took an active interest in the project, devoting both time and money. He was associate judge of the county for six years, and has held various township offices. He is at present trustee and steward of the Methodist Episcopal church. In 1837 he married Martha Morgan, of Indiana. She died February 8, 1891. Their children living are: Watson, a farmer and grain buyer; Nancy Jane, the widow of Sinclair Helm; Wilbur, residing on a farm adjoining Murdock; Mrs. Martha Helm, of Tuscola, and Mrs. Lida Dewees, of Terre Haute. In 1892 he married for his second wife Mrs. Sarah M. Bentley, *nee* Campbell, the former wife of Dr. Morgan A. Bentley, who died in Kankakee, May 3, 1890. He was a graduate of Jefferson Medical College, of Philadelphia. Mrs. Murdock has two children, now living, by her first husband: Nellie, wife of Mr. Van Morgan, and Rev. L. C. Bentley, who was born in 1864, and was graduated from the DePauw University, at Greencastle, Indiana, in 1894, and from the Theological Seminary of Boston, in 1895, and is now pastor of the First M. E. church in Brazil, Indiana.

JOHN H. CHADWICK.

John H. Chadwick, state's attorney of Douglas county, is a native of Washington county, Pennsylvania. He was reared on a farm seven miles south of Washington, the county seat. He attended the country schools

until about fourteen years of age, and then attended school at Washington for a short time. He also attended college at Waynesburg, and the State Normal school at Edinboro, Pennsylvania. He graduated from the latter institution in the class of '86 and came west in the summer of 1887. Mr. Chadwick taught school for ten years, was one year principal at Miles Grove, two years at Dempseytown, one year at Spartansburg, all in Pennsylvania, and one year at Camargo, Illinois. After coming west he read law with the law firm of Eckhart & Moore at Tuscola, Illinois, afterward entering the law department of the Wesleyan University, located at Bloomington, Illinois, and was graduated in the class of '91. He returned to Tuscola in 1892, and was elected to the office of state's attorney, which position he has held ever since. The first law suit he ever tried was as attorney for the state.

He was united in marriage to Miss Ella Russell, of Chrisman, Illinois, in July, 1894. They have two children, Perry Moreland and John Russell.

Mr. Chadwick is entirely self educated, having earned the money to obtain his education by working on a farm, selling books and maps and teaching school. He has been a hard student all his life, and has obtained success by hard work and devotion to duty. As a public prosecutor he has been very successful. In addition to his official duties he has a good civil practice.

ISRAEL A. DRAKE.

Israel A. Drake, one of Tuscola's retired farmers, was born in Butler county, Ohio, January 23, 1834, and is a son of Nathan Drake, also a native of the same county. His mother was Sarah Gardner, a native of New Jersey. Nathan Drake emigrated from Ohio to Vigo county, Indiana, in about 1831, and in 1849 located in Coles (now Douglas) county, in Garrett township, where he took up about three hundred acres of land at a dollar and twenty-five cents an acre. He resided here for about twenty years, becoming wealthy, prominent and highly respected. He only recently returned to Vigo county, and died in Terre Haute, March 29, 1899, in the eighty-seventh year of his life. He was a member of the Baptist church, and the first Baptist meeting held in the county was held at his house. After the death of his first wife, by whom he had five children, he was married to Rhoda La Forgee.

Israel A. Drake remained on his father's Butler county farm until the age of sixteen, since which time he has resided in what is now known as Tuscola, with the exception of twenty years in Decatur, Douglas county. While in Decatur he ran the Drake Hotel, which he owned. At present he owns one hundred and fifty acres of highly improved land in Garrett township and a beautiful home in Tuscola.

In 1854 he was united in marriage to Miss Nancy Garrett, sister of Caleb and daughter of Isom Garrett. The latter was among the very first white settlers in the township which bears his name and he it was for whom it was named. A full and complete sketch and portrait of him will be found elsewhere. To Mr. and Mrs. Drake have been born three children: Jasper, who resides in Lincoln, and is a member of the Masonic and Knights of Pythias fraternities; William, who lives at Milwaukee, and Mrs. Minnie Drake Tyler, who is one of Tuscola's leading milliners. Mrs. Drake is a member of the Tuscola Presbyterian church. Mr. Drake is a member of the Masonic fraternity, and his son William is one of the highest and brightest Masons in the state of Wisconsin, and is also a Knight of Pythias.

WILLIAM ILES

Wiliam Iles, a member of an old and early settled family of Kentucky, and at present one of the most successful farmers in Douglas county, was born at Iles Mills, Bath county, Kentucky, December 31, 1844. He is the son of William Iles, a native of the same county, who was a son of Thomas Iles, born in Chester county, Pennsylvania. His grandfather Iles was a member of the old Kentucky militia and fought in many battles against the Indians in the vicinity of Bryant's Fort. The Iles have been tillers of the soil back to William Iles' great-grandfather, who was a native of England. His wife was Mary Iles. Mr. Iles' mother was Miss Jane H., a daughter of William F. George, of Montgomery (now Bath) county, and was a native of Greenbrier county, Virginia.

William Iles was reared in Bath county, and at his father's death, February 22, 1846,

he was left an orphan at the early age of a little over one year. On account of the war, his educational advantages were limited and all the property belonging to the family was swept away. His mother died in 1884. In 1865 he came to Camargo township and bought a tract of land and resided in a log cabin on the farm on which he now lives. At the present time he owns three hundred and sixty-three acres in one tract and three hundred and forty in another.

In 1892 he was married to Miss May Hammett, a daughter of the late James R. Hammett, whose sketch is found on another page of this work. William Iles is a worthy example of a self-made man. Commencing with nothing except his own indomitable energy and courage, he has succeeded in the business world far above the average man. He is one of the most extensive stock raisers in the county, as well as one of the most public-spirited of its citizens. For the past thirteen years he has been president of the Douglas County Fair Association, filling this place with rare executive ability, and has been connected with it in one way or another ever since its organization. He has held the office of supervisor of Camargo township several terms and was recently defeated for the same office by manipulations unworthy of the opposition. In politics he is a stanch Democrat, that kind of Democracy which Jefferson taught and which is being revived to-day by William J. Bryan.

LEONARD J. WYETH.

Leonard J. Wyeth was one of the pioneers of Douglas county, and a man of varied business interests, amassing a fortune of about

three hundred thousand dollars while a resident of Douglas county. He was of Welsh ancestry, and was born in Wendell, Franklin county, Massachusetts, January 13, 1827, and died at his home at Tuscola, January 24, 1898. He was a son of Nathan and Hannah (Kellog) Wyeth, natives of Massachusetts, and his grandfather was Gad Wyeth. In 1839 Mr. Wyeth's parents moved to Licking county, Ohio, and eight years later our subject was united in marriage to Miss Melinda Northway, a native of the town of Sherman, Chautauqua county, New York, and a daughter of Samuel Hiram and Charlotte (Seagers) Northway, natives of Connecticut and Massachusetts, respectively. Seven children were the result of this marriage, three of whom attained the age of maturity: Mrs. George Callaway; Mary, and Clarence L., whose death preceded his father's only a few months.

The prosperity and growth of the west attracted Mr. Wyeth, and in 1851 he came to Illinois and settled in Coles county. Here he resided until 1858 and then moved to Douglas county, where he afterward resided. Building a small store room on Houghton street, just opposite the court house, he engaged in merchandising with Merrill and Oliver Hackett. That was the beginning of Mr. Wyeth's business career, a career which has scarcely a counterpart in the history of the county. The partnership with Merrill and Oliver Hackett was dissolved in 1859, and a new firm was formed with Thomas D. Craddock, of Charleston, which was continued until 1864. In 1859 the firm erected a business room on the site now occupied by Field's pharmacy. This building was sold, and another and more commodious structure was built on the site now occupied by the Conover building. In 1865 Mr. Wyeth disposed of his dry-goods store to W. H. Lamb and J. M. Maris. He then formed a partnership in the banking business with Jos. G. and William P. Cannon under the firm name of Wyeth, Cannon & Co. This firm remained in business until 1870, when the First National Bank was organized, Mr. Wyeth being one of the promoters of the institution. He was a director from the organization of the bank until within a few weeks of his death. In October, 1872, when W. P. Cannon retired from the presidency of the First National, Mr. Wyeth was elected to fill the vacancy, which he did until January, 1873, when H. T. Caraway was elected. In 1875 Mr. Wyeth bought the Garrett farm of eight hundred acres in Garrett township. He moved on that farm in 1875, but returned to the city in the fall of 1878, taking up his residence in the house on East Scott street which was afterward his home. At one time he lived in a house that was erected on the site of the Wamsley grocery store. Later he built a residence just east of the M. E. church, which he sold to the late Thomas E. Macoughtry. Mr. Wyeth also built the house now occupied by Farmer Cox.

Mr. Wyeth was the largest property holder in Douglas county. He amassed a fortune of $300,000, represented by three thousand acres of land located in this county, $50,000 in bank stock, $7,000 to $8,000 in government bonds, besides personal property. In 1893, during a severe attack of illness, Mr. Wyeth made a division of his wealth, disposing of the greater part of his property. The will that was executed at that time was revoked. The latter part of December, 1897, Mr. Wyeth made a new division of his property. The division was about equal between his daughter, Mrs. George Callaway, and daughter-in-law, Mrs. Lizzie Wyeth. He executed deeds to them conveying what property he had allotted to each one. To Dr. Callaway he transferred his one hundred and ninety shares of stock in the First National Bank. This will which was executed at this time bequeaths only the property which his wife was to have, consisting of the homestead, seven or eight thousand dollars in government bonds, and his bank account and other personal property. All this property was given to her absolutely without any restriction whatever. Mr. Wyeth has four brothers and one sister living, Samuel, Albert and Thomas, of Coles county, Joseph S., of Garrett, and Mrs. Cofer, of Arcola. This town at that time welcomed every newcomer. Mr. Wyeth, at the very start of his business life, was as bold in his purpose as in form were the hills on his father's farm in the state of Massachusetts. Success in honorable business was the end he sought, and that end was attained by wise foresight, just means, unflagging endeavor and unimpeachable character. Out of respect to Mr. Wyeth, all of the business houses were closed during the hour of his funeral.

JAMES MORROW.

James Morrow, one of the well-known citizens of Newman, and who has led an active and successful business life, was born in Brown county, Ohio, November 3, 1832, and is descended from English and Irish progenitors. He is a son of James and Levina (Drake) Morrow, who were natives of Brown county, Ohio. His grandfather and grandmother on his father's side were born in Ireland, and married in Brown county, Ohio. His maternal grandfather and grandmother (the latter Miss Weatherspoon) were respectively born in England and America. James Morrow remained on a farm in Brown county until he had arrived at the age of twenty years, during which time he attended schools three months free and three

months paid for. In 1852 he migrated to Montgomery county, Indiana, and here for some time worked as a common day laborer. In 1854 he came to Illinois, locating in Champaign county, where he bought and located on eighty acres of land two miles south of Urbana, where he remained for about four years. He then removed to Edgar county, and bought and located on a farm four miles east of Newman, where he resided up to 1862. In that year he enlisted in Company E, Twelfth Illinois Infantry, and lacked but a few days of being in active service three years. He served as a private and first belonged to the left wing of the Sixteenth Army Corps until after the Atlanta campaign, when he was transferred to the Fifteenth Army Corps under Gen. Logan. Mr. Morrow was never wounded or sick in all of his active service during the war. After the final surrender he returned to the farm and in 1875 came to Newman, since which time he has been numbered among her best citizens. In 1894 he rented out his farms and since that time has been practically retired from business cares. Mr. Marrow owns two hundred and forty acres of land in Edgar county and six acres within the corporation of Newman. Mrs. Marrow, his wife, owns four hundred and ninety-six acres of land in Illinois, one hundred and twenty-six acres one and a half miles east of Newman, fifty acres near the corporation line of Newman, and one half-section in Edgar county.

Mr. Marrow has been twice married, the first time to Miss Lawhead, in 1860. After her death he married his present wife, Rachel Fisher, who was born in Indiana, a daughter of Daniel Fisher, who followed farming, and died in Champaign county. To his first marriage he has three children living, and by his second wife he has one child, George, who resides in Burlington, Vermont, and is superintendent of the anti-liquor league of Vermont, The other children are: H. L., W. B. and Edgar D. Mr. and Mrs. Marrow are consistent members of the Cumberland Presbyterian church. He is a public-spirited citizen, is plain and unassuming, yet dignified in appearance, and has won a competency and an honorable position by honesty, correct business methods, and a due reard for his fellowmen.

WILLIAM F. MURPHY.

William F. Murphy, one of the wealthy retired citizens of Tuscola, was born in Ohio, January 9, 1821. His great-great-grandfather came from Ireland and settled in Maryland, in which state his father, Wilson Murphy, was born in 1787; he served as a soldier in the war of 1812. In 1815, with his wife, who was Nancy Slaughter, he removed to Ross county, Ohio.

William F. Murphy was reared on the farm and attended school about two months in

the year, remaining on his father's farm until he had arrived at age, when he worked on the farm at six dollars and twenty-five cents to fifteen dollars per month, and in 1839 came to Illinois, subsequently visiting in Douglas county, then a part of Coles. He was favorably impressed with the country and determined to settle here. Therefore he returned in 1847 and began life here with two hundred dollars in money, a wagon and three horses.

He seized the first favorable opportunity to get possession of land and in July, 1850, bought one hundred and sixty acres of school land and about eighty acres of timber in Sargent township, paying for it six hundred and forty dollars. Since that time he has been dealing extensively in real estate and is at present one of the wealthiest men in this county. For many years he was engaged in banking at Newman, succeeding Z. S. Pratt. He now owns about one thousand four hundred acres of valuable land in the county, and three hundred and thirty-five acres in Jasper county, Indiana.

He has been three times married: First to Miss Adelia H. Smith, a native of Kentucky, this marriage occurring January 15, 1845. His second wife was Miss Rebecca J. Maddox, of Ohio. After her death he married Miss Julia Page, of New York, who is a lady of fine literary accomplishments and prominent in church work. In 1891 he removed to Tuscola, where he and his wife reside in one of the city's most beautiful residences, surrounded by all the comforts of life. The only offices Mr. Murphy has ever held were township supervisor, and trustee appointed by the governor to build the asylum for the insane at Kankakee.

William F. Murphy has throughout his life been a shrewd business man, and his success has been the result of his own efforts. During the Civil war he largely assisted in filling the quota of his township under President Lincoln's different calls for troops. His life has been one of action and his accumulations of this world's goods have been the result of economy and close attention to business.

JAMES R. HAMMETT.

James Richard Hammett was descended from Irish ancestry, his grandfather, Richard Hammett, having been a native of County Cork, Ireland. Here the Hammetts resided for a long period of time. Richard Hammett, as far as known, had five children, four sons and one daughter, all of whom at different periods emigrated to America.

John, the father of James R. Hammett, was the first to come. He came to this country

when a young man and settled in Montgomery county, Virginia, and there married Diana Gardner, a native of the Old Dominion and of Irish descent. The three younger brothers came to America at a later period and likewise settled in Virginia. One of them, William Hammett, became a Methodist preacher and about 1835 he returned to his old home in Ireland, where his labors as an evangelist attracted large crowds of people. He resumed preaching on his return to America and settled in Mississippi. Subsequently he was elected to congress from the Vicksburg district and after leaving congress he continued to preach. As an orator he was of a high order. Of the other brothers, Richard Hammett was a man of great energy and versatile talents. The greater part of his life after his arrival in America was spent in Mississippi, where he was a prominent politician and for a time editor of the Vicksburg Whig.

Douglas county had perhaps few men who have lived on its prairie soil for three score and four years, and whose labors have contributed so largely to the development of its resources and whose life has been more upright and exemplary than the late James R. Hammett, who was born in Montgomery county, Virginia, January 1, 1826, and who died August 11, 1896, in the seventy-first year of his age. His parents removed from Virginia to Bourbon county, Kentucky, and in the fall of 1830 came to Illinois, halting at sunset one evening almost on the spot where he spent sixty-four years of his life. The farm consisted of eight hundred acres lying just north of Camargo, which was then in Park county, the northern limits of which at that time extended to Wisconsin. The hardships of the early pioneer only served to call forth all the energy and enterprise of Mr. Hammett, and his success was due to his untiring industry and financial ability, which placed him among the leading financiers of this county.

In 1854 Mr. Hammett was married to Miss Sarah C. Watson, who was born in Fountain county, Indiana, July 4, 1836, a daughter of William D. and Mary (Low) Watson. Her father was born in the neighborhood of Vincennes and her mother in Madison. To James R. Hammett and wife were born ten children, four of whom are now living: Mrs. William Iles, of Carmargo; F. W., cashier of the First National Bank of Tuscola; Richard and Roy, both farmers of Carmargo. Politically, Mr. Hammett early attached himself to the Whig party, and upon the birth of the Republican party, inheriting his father's dislike of slavery, he became connected with that party and very generally supported its candidates, as he gave an enthusiastic adherence to its principles.

Mr. Hammett was connected with the development of the railroads in this county and took an active part in the building of the Illinois Central Railway. He visited Springfield and was influential in obtaining the charter from the Legislature. In the original bill granting charter rights he was named as one of the incorporators and subsequently became a member of the board of directors. He was re-elected several times and filled the office for twelve years. When the First National Bank was organized, in 1870, he became a stockholder and in 1873 was elected director, filling this place until the time of his death. He was one of the ablest financiers of the county and was worth about one hundred and fifty thousand dollars, owning about two thousand acres of land. Mr. Hammett was not a member of any church, but practiced Christianity in his every-day life. It is not to be wondered that the people revered him, because his sympathetic and generous heart was always responsive to every touch of distress and he was ever ready to extend a helping hand to his fellow man. It may well be said of him that he has made the world better by having lived, and his life is

WILLIAM T. SUMMERS.

William Thomas Summers, of Newman, came from Sangamon county, Illinois, to Newman township in 1877, and located on a farm seven miles northwest of the village. He was born near Augusta, Bracken county, Kentucky,

May 15, 1845, and is a son of Lewis and Elizabeth (Threlkeld) Summers, who were natives of the same county, both being members of pioneer families of that section. His grandfather, Thomas Summers, was a native of Virginia, and was a soldier in the Mexican war.

W. T. Summers was reared in Kentucky and came to Sangamon county, Illinois, when a small boy. With the exception of two years, during which time he was associated in business with James Barr, of Newman, he has always been engaged in farming.

In 1865 our subject was wedded to Miss Virginia C. Woltz, a daughter of John and Sydney (Halbert) Woltz, natives of Virginia. Mr. Summers and wife have no children. He is a member and one of the organizers of the Christian Scientist church of Newman, and is a firm believer in its principles. Mr. Summers has just completed a fine residence in Newman at a cost of over five thousand dollars, and it ranks with the most elegant homes in the county. He owns three hundred and twenty-six acres of land, two hundred and six acres lying southwest of Newman and one hundred and twenty acres one mile and a half northwest. He is a member of the I. O. O. F. and Masonic fraternities. Mr. Summers has, ever since his residence in Douglas county, been identified with the county's best interests, progress and development, and ranks among its best and most progressive men.

MOSES S. SMITH.

Moses S. Smith, the genial and talented editor of the Newman Independent, was born July 19, 1869, a son of George W. Smith, and was raised at Newman, the place of his birth. In 1887 he and his brother, A. B., who had been connected with the mechanical department of the Independent, purchased the paper, succeeding C. V. Walls, who removed to Arcola, where he edited the Arcola Record for a time. It has now been twenty-six years since the first copy of the Newman Independent was issued.

During all these years the Independent has tried to chronicle all the events of interest transpiring in the town and vicinity, as well as a synopsis of those occurrences in adjoining

towns, the state and nation. It has striven to represent the best interests of the community and assist as much as possible towards building up the town. The efforts of Mr. Smith have not been in vain, proof of which is the large and increasing circulation of the paper. The paper has grown from a puny infant to strong and well developed manhood, owing largely to the generous patronage given it by the progressive business men of the town and county. The Newman Independent was first instituted in April, 1873, by Cicero V. Walls. He experimentally conducted it for six months and then suspended it for a year, when he resumed its publication. In 1882-83 the paper was leased to Carl H. Uhler for about a year, during Mr. Wall's absence from Newman. On his return he again assumed control with John W. King, who was postmaster at the time, as assistant editor. In 1884 he again leased it to A. B. Smith, his foreman, while he went to Paris and took charge of the Paris Beacon. M. S. Smith, since he has succeeded to the entire control of the paper, has added materially to its mechanical completeness by the purchase of two new job presses, also a new four-horse power gasoline engine, and on April 1, 1900, the paper came out in an entire new dress, and is now one of the cleanest and newsiest local newspapers in Illinois.

Mr. Smith was united in marriage to Miss Isabelle Root, a daughter of D. O. Root, of Newman. They have two children, Hughes Blake and Harriet Elizabeth. Mose Smith, as he is generally known by his friends, is one of the most accommodating and agreeable gentlemen found in the county, and in business is an all-round hustler.

WINFIELD S. REED.

Winfield Scott Reed, a prominent and intelligent farmer of Arcola township, was born in Union county, Indiana, May 13, 1851, and is a son of John T. Reed. The latter was a native of Butler county, Ohio, and emigrated to Douglas county and settled in Tuscola township in 1862. He moved to Arcola township in 1867 and there resided up to his death, which occurred in March, 1891, in the seventy-first year of his age. His wife was Ann Walters, who was born in Lancaster county, Pennsylvania, in 1826, and moved with her parents to Butler county, Ohio, in 1836; she is now in the seventy-fourth year of her age. John T.

Reed was a renter when he first came to the county, but in 1867 he bought the farm where his son, W. S. Reed, now resides. He was a

tailor by trade, but quit that and went to farming. W. S. Reed owns one-half of the old homestead farm, which contains one hundred and twenty-two and a half acres. He has been a successful farmer, progressive in his ideas, and owns a beautiful home.

February 24, 1875, he was married to Miss Nellie Watson, a daughter of Thomas Watson, of Clark county. They have three children: Ollie, wife of A. Wright; Dora M. and John G. Thomas Watson was a native of Frederick county, Virginia, where he was born in October, 1794, and was married to Susanna Thomas, in 1824. To them were born two sons and one daughter. His wife died in 1832, and he was married the second time, in 1834, and removed to Ohio in 1837, residing in Fairfield county until October, 1854, when he came to Illinois. Mrs. Reed's mother was Nancy Franklin, who was born near Greencastle, Pennsylvania. Her father died in 1872, aged seventy-eight years. He was in the war of 1812. His father, Henry Watson, came from England. Mr. Reed is a member of the Masonic fraternity, Court of Honor and the Woodmen.

LEMUEL CHANDLER.

Lemuel Chandler, of Bourbon, is one of the oldest and most universally respected citizens in the county. He was born within three miles of Cynthiana, Harrison county, Kentucky, August 30, 1824, a son of Israel and Lydia (Grewell) Chandler, who were born in the "Blue Grass" regions of Kentucky. Israel Chandler emigrated from Kentucky to Cler-

mont county in 1831 and remained there seven years, when he came to Douglas county and located in Bourbon township, settling on what is now known as the old Chandler homestead, upon which William Chandler now resides (see his sketch). John Chandler (grandfather), a Quaker in his religious belief, emigrated from Chester county, Pennsylvania, to Kentucky and settled in Harrison county in about the year 1791, the year preceding Kentucky's admission into the union. John Grewell (maternal grandfather) married a Miss Temple, a native of Delaware, and settled near the Chandlers in Kentucky.

Lemuel Chandler was reared to manhood in the neighborhood in which he has always resided. For that day he received a very good education, attended the Paris Academy and later taught school in the Bourbon neighborhood. He has never been an aspirant for office, in the usual acceptation of that term, but he has held the office of supervisor of his township.

In 1849 he was united in marriage to Mrs. Prudence W. Bacon, a native of Hampshire county, Virginia, and a daughter of Robert and Elizabeth Beavers, the former born in the state of New Jersey, and the latter in Baltimore, Maryland. To Mr. and Mrs. Chandler have been born six children: John, who is a farmer and resides in Bourbon township; William, whose sketch is found elsewhere; Beatrice, wife of Dell Henry, of Hastings, Nebraska; Lydia Belle; Gertrude, wife of Clifford Jones, who resides in the edge of the village of Bourbon; and Ernest M. Chandler, in the live stock commission business at Peoria, Illinois. Mr. Chandler is a member and deacon of the Baptist church, of which church his wife is also a member. Mr. Chandler owns two hundred and sixty acres of land in Arcola township and five hundred and forty in Bourbon township.

O. V. MYERS.

O. V. Myers, a grain buyer at McCown's Station, and one of the wheel horses of the Douglas county Democracy, was born in Edgar county, Illinois, March 13, 1863. He is a son of William Myers, who was a native of Kentucky and who became an early settler of Edgar county. His mother was Eliza Sizemore, a daughter of Martin Sizemore, who was also born in Edgar county.

Mr. Myers grew up on the farm and received the advantages of a good common school education, and also attended the high school at Paris. For the past ten years he has lived on his farm of one hundred and twenty acres, about one mile and a half east of Newman. His firm handles about one hundred and fifty thousand bushels of grain annually. In the recent Democratic primary of Douglas county he received the endorsement for state senator of the district composed of Douglas, Coles and Shelby counties. In 1898 he was the Democratic nominee for the office of county treasurer of Douglas county. On March 4, 1885, he was wedded to Miss Alice Estes, of Edgar county. They have seven children: Edna, Harry, Don, Charlie, Laura, Edwin and Nellie.

David Meyers (grandfather) was a native of Kentucky. Our subject's maternal grandfather, Martin Sizemore, was a North Carolinian by birth and served in the Black Hawk and Mexican wars.

O. V. Myers is a young man of good ability, and there is little doubt should he be elected to represent this senatorial district that the best interests of the people will be carefully and ably looked after.

JOHN LOWRY.

John Lowry, one of the promising young business men of Fairland, where he has been extensively engaged in buying grain since 1896, was born in the county of Tipperary, Ireland, in 1858, a son of John and Margaret (Nolan) Lowry, who were born in the same county. His father settled in Champaign county on a farm in the vicinity of Fairland in 1871, and was engaged in farming up to the time of his death, in 1874.

John Lowry was reared and educated in the country and was engaged in farming up to the time he became engaged in his present business, then becoming a member of the firm of Lowry & Hanson. They buy on an average about five hundred thousand bushels of corn and oats annually. He is now building a new elevator and making other improvements in connection with his business.

In 1887 our subject was married to Miss Nelly Ryan, a native of Will county, Illinois. They have five children: Maggie, George, Kittie, Maud and Paul. Mr. Lowry's business interests at Fairland are gradually extending, and he is becoming to be recognized as one of

the village's most successful business men. He owns one hundred and sixty acres of land two miles and a quarter north of town, one hundred and sixty acres in Edwards county, Kansas, and several houses in the village. He is public spirited and generally lends a helping hand to any cause or enterprise which is intended to add to the material, moral and social interests of Fairland.

JAMES W. HANCOCK.

James W. Hancock, editor and founder of the Newman Record, was born in Champaign county, Ohio, August 18, 1839. The family from which he is descended is of English origin and for many years resided in Patrick county, Virginia. His grandfather, Major Hancock, was born in this county in March, 1792. He married Mrs. Elizabeth Adams, whose maiden name was Fuson, also a native of Patrick county. Directly after their marriage, in 1812, they emigrated to Ohio and settled in Champaign county. Their journey from Virginia was made on horseback, and when they arrived they found themselves pioneers in the wilderness.

Our subject's father, William Hancock, was born in Ohio, February 10, 1819, and spent the early part of his life in that state. He grew to manhood on the farm, attending school part of the time, and at the age of nineteen years and seven months he was married to Susanna Stier, who was born in Ohio, but belonged to a Virginia family. His marriage occurred September 16, 1838, and soon afterward he emigrated to Illinois, coming to the neighborhood of Brushy Fork, where he rented land of a Mr. Coffey. In 1843 he entered forty acres of land near the Pleasant Grove church, and a short time afterward bought an additional forty acres. He remained on this land until 1845 and then rented a farm a mile west of Newman, where he resided for two years. After occupying Col. Hopkins' farm, southwest of Newman, he, in 1849, bought of the government eighty acres and removed onto the land in December, 1850. Tracts he added later comprised several hundred acres. He died in 1892. He was in politics a Whig and later a Republican, and was a delegate to the convention which nominated Gov. Oglesby. He was first elected justice of the peace at Camargo in 1847. He was a member of the first board of county officers for Douglas county, and filled the offices of treasurer and assessor. On the establishment of the state board for the equalization of assessments, in 1867, he was appointed a member from the ninth congressional district, composed of the counties of Coles, Douglas, Champaign, Vermilion, Iroquois and Ford. In 1868 he was elected by the people in the same district to the same office for a term of four years. Cornelius Stier, father of Susanna Stier, was a soldier in the war of 1812 and was for five years in the regular army. He was reared near Baltimore. Major Hancock, above mentioned, was a minister in the New Light Christian church.

James W. Hancock attended the ordinary schools in the neighborhood of Brushy Fork, residing with his father on the farm. He followed farming and teaching school up to the time he located in Newman in 1861, and from 1874 to 1879 was cashier of the Newman Bank. He was married April 9, 1860, to Miss Amy Shute, and to their marriage have been born six children: William L., Lulu F., Isaac L.,

James P., Howard L. and Everett H. Mr. Hancock, in 1896, founded the Newman Record, an independent newspaper, which has a circulation of about six hundred. From 1893 to 1896 he served as police magistrate of Newman. He owns two hundred acres of land in Newman township, besides town property. On December 4, 1898, he, in conjunction with W. T. Summers, W. D. Goldman, S. C. Hicks and Mesdames Goldman, Moffitt and Vance, organized the First church of Christ, Scientist, of Newman, Illinois.

JOHN HAWKINS.

John Hawkins, another of the Hawkins brothers, and an ex-soldier of the Civil war, residing in the town of Newman, is a native of

Pickaway county, Ohio, where he was born November 30, 1828 (for ancestry see sketches of Samuel and J. M. Hawkins).

In 1859 he was united in marriage to Miss Iva, a daughter of Cornelius Hopkins, who was one of the earliest settlers of Newman township. To their marriage were born twelve children, of whom but seven survive, viz.: Marion; Cora Ann, who is the wife of Samuel Johnson, of West Ridge; Emma Alice; Rosetta Estella; Ida Lucretia; Wiley Sherman and Harrison Sylvester. In 1862 Mr. Hawkins volunteered in the same company in Newman as his brother, Samuel, but he did not meet the same fate at the first day's battle as did his brother Samuel at Chickamauga. In all he was out three years and has scarcely seen a well day since. Mr. Hawkins' wife died December 30, 1899, in the fifty-seventh year of her age, and in the fall of 1894 he removed from the farm to Newman. His wife was a daughter of Cornelius Hopkins, who was born May 10, 1818, and who wedded Rachel F. Albin; both are buried at the Wesley Chapel. Two of his sons, Jeremiah and George, were soldiers in the war of the Rebellion.

CLARENCE L. WYETH.

Clarence L. Wyeth, the only son of Mr. and Mrs. L. J. Wyeth, was born in Tuscola July 27, 1860, and died September 7, 1893. His boyhood days were passed in this city and on his father's farm he developed into manhood. In 1882 he was united in marriage to Miss Lizzie Atwell, of Atwood. Seven children were the result of this union, who together with the wife have suffered such an irreparable loss.

Mr. Wyeth was one of the best financial

managers in the county. He possessed remarkable business sagacity and his great brain force would have been felt in commercial centers had

he been thrown among the foremost financiers of the country. At the time of his death he was probably worth one hundred thousand dollars, and the future with all of its possibilities and opportunities was before him.

MARTIN RICE.

Martin Rice, who was, up to the time of his death, in 1883, prominently identified with the interests and growth of the county, came to Illinois in 1849, and to what is now Camargo township in 1853. He was descended from old Virginia and Kentucky families, and his grandfather, Charles Rice, was a pioneer in the wilderness of Kentucky, a companion of Daniel Boone, and a participant in the romantic incidents which marked the early frontier life, when the present Commonwealth of Kentucky formed a county of Virginia. He was born in Virginia, and about the breaking out of the Revolutionary war resided in Kentucky. The maiden name of his second wife was Sarah Bryant, she being a member of the family which gave the name to the fort known as Bryant's Station, celebrated in the annals of the early history of Kentucky. Charles Rice took part with Daniel Boone in the adventures which have made historic the home of the early pioneers. He bought of Boone a tract of land in what is now Fayette county, and settled there. Boone subsequently lost nearly all of his estates in Kentucky through his carelessness in neglecting to record and prove his title, and among the tracts which changed ownership in consequence was the one occupied by Charles Rice. One thousand and six hundred acres

were subsequently confirmed to Boone, and of this, in compensation for his loss, he gave Rice a portion lying within the presents limits of

Madison county, and here Charles Rice lived to the close of his eventful life. He had borne the hardships and dangers of frontier life, had been through the memorable siege of Bryant's Station, and taken part in many other conflicts with the Indians of that day.

Martin Rice was born in Madison county, Kentucky, July 28, 1822. He was brought up on his father's farm, where he remained until after reaching his majority. He attended subscription school, which was of the rudest character, but he diligently improved his time and formed the foundation for a sound, practical business education. In the summer he spent the time working on the farm, and on November 16, 1843, he married Mary Ann Adams, who was a native of the same town in Kentucky. After his marriage Mr. Rice took up his residence on a farm belonging to his father, where he lived for about four years, when he removed to Illinois. This was in November, 1849. He settled in Coles county, nine miles east of Charleston. He purchased one hundred and sixty acres of land, upon which he lived for four years. He found this tract too small to suit the plans according to which he proposed to carry on agricultural operations, so in the fall of 1853 he disposed of his land in Coles county and removed farther north. The place in which he settled is now the home of his son, Eugene. Land here was cheaper, the location better and the soil richer than on his former farm. The neighborhood had but few residences. There were some settlements in the neighborhood of Camargo, but with one exception no improvement had been made for eight miles west until the timber bordering on the Okaw was reached. As the country settled up Mr. Rice became recognized as one of the leaders in the community. He was deeply interested in the formation of Douglas county, and did all in his power to make the measure a success, there being considerable opposition at the time in some sections in Coles county, from which the territory was taken. After the new county was organized he was a member of the first political convention ever held in it. The convention, which placed in nomination the candidates chosen as the first board of county officers, was held in a temporary board shanty on the farm of Col. McCarty, two and a half miles east of Tuscola. The men composing the ticket were nominated and elected irrespective of party. In 1869, the second year after the township organizations were effected, Mr. Rice was elected the first supervisor of Camargo township, and re-elected in 1873, 1874 and 1875. He also took a deep interest in the cause of the common schools. In the early day he was a Whig in politics, and cast his first vote for Henry Clay, and later became a Republican. His first wife died in 1869. His second marriage occurred October 25, 1871, to Mary Jane Caraway, a native of Virginia, and whose father's family came to Vermilion county from that state in 1834. Of his six children, three are living: Eugene, Josephine (now Mrs. Goff, of Tuscola), and Martin, who resides on part of the old homestead in Camargo township.

R. R. THOMPSON.

R. R. Thompson, one of the most hospitable and clever gentlemen in the county, was born in Edgar county, Illinois, May 22, 1837, and is a son of Andrew E. Thompson, who was a native of Scotland. His mother was Elizabeth Simpson, before her marriage, and was

born in England, and married in Fredericksburg, Virginia. To them eight children were born, of whom only three are living, one in Kansas and the others in Oklahoma.

Mr. Thompson was reared on the farm and has always been engaged in that occupation. In 1858 he was united in marriage to Miss Lucy Hardwick. To this marriage were born three children: George D.; H. V.; and Lenie, who died when ten months old. Mrs. Thompson died in 1863. She was born in Kentucky. In 1864 Mr. Thompson married for his second wife Miss Sallie A. Lain, who was born in Lincoln county, in the same state. Mr. Thompson has been a consistent member of the Methodist Episcopal church at Murdock and other places for forty years. In 1898 he was the Democratic nominee for the office of sheriff, but the Republican majority was too strong for him, and he was defeated by a majority of five hundred and forty-one votes.

John Simpson, his maternal grandfather, was a native of England and emigrated to Virginia, thence to Illinois, and died in Edgar county.

E. C. FINNEY.

E. C. Finney, a retired grain merchant and one of the supervisors of Tuscola township, was born near the village of Annapolis, Park county, Indiana, April 4, 1836. From 1869 to 1891 he was extensively engaged in the grain business at Tuscola, but in the latter year he sold his interest to his partner, Charles L. McMasters. His father was Robert Finney, who was a native of North Carolina, and who

emigrated to Indiana in the year 1844. Robert was a son of Joseph Finney, who came to this country in its early history and participated in many of the conflicts for liberty. His mother, whose maiden name was Malinda Hunt, was a daughter of Nathan Hunt; she was born in North Carolina and moved to Indiana when but a child. Robert Finney died in Indiana in 1861, in the fifty-fourth year of his age, and his mother in Tuscola, Illinois, October 16, 1897, at the ripe old age of eighty-one years.

Mr. Finney has been identified with the business interests of Tuscola since 1868 and is an upright and universally respected citizen. He belongs to the Methodist Episcopal church and is a member of the Masonic fraternity.

D. F. COYKENDALL.

D. F. Coykendall, whose death occurred in Chicago, December 16, 1892, was born near Brushy Fork September 8, 1850, at a time when the county was in its primitive state, and was there reared to manhood. He was a son of Benjamin F. Coykendall, whose ancestors were in all probability among the emigrants from Holland who in an early day settled in New Jersey, the descendants of whom now comprise some of the best families of that state. William, the father of Benjamin F. Coykendall, was born in that state and married Mary Van Ziekiel, whose family had sprung from the same stock. Benjamin F. Coykendall was born in Tompkins county, New York, near the town of Ithaca. On reaching his majority he came west and located in Wisconsin, and in 1847 sold out his property in Wisconsin and located in what is now Douglas county, where he lived for the remainder of his life. Two of his sons, Cyrus A. and Marvin A. were in the war, both having enlisted before they were twenty-one. The death of Benjamin F. Coykendall occurred in the spring of 1889

On November 14, 1878, D. F. Coykendall was married to Miss Francis E. Cash, a daughter of Mr. and Mrs. L. J. Cash, of Newman. To this marriage was born one child, a daughter. Lenoria. For two years before Mr. Coy-

kendall removed to Chicago he resided in Newman, while his life previous had been spent on the farm near Brushy Fork. After his removal to Chicago he became associated in business with two firms, the Columbia Manufacturing & Supply Company and John Hosbury & Company, live stock commission merchants. He was possessed of more than ordinary business ability, combined with genuine integrity and uprightness, and was very highly respected by all with whom he had dealings. He was devoted to his family and his death was a great loss to both wife and daughter. He was buried in the Newman cemetery. He was a member of the Masonic fraternity, but was not a member of any church. He always did his part willingly in supporting the church and attended the same.

W. P. BOYD.

W. P. Boyd, who was for many years a prominent druggist and chemist of Arcola, was born in Flemingsburg, Kentucky, January 6, 1847, and was a son of Wilson P. and Susan

E. Boyd. His father was a prominent lawyer and served in both branches of the Kentucky Legislature.

W. P. Boyd received his early education at the old Bethel school in Kentucky, and subsequently attended the university at Bloomington, Illinois. In 1875 he was married to Miss Emma Wyatt Hamilton, of Lexington, Kentucky, a step-daughter of Alexander Hamilton (her real parents being Edward and Annie (Smith) Wyatt, natives of England). To Mr. and Mrs. Boyd were born four children, namely: William H., deceased, Wyatt, Anna M. and Wilson P.

In 1867 Mr. Boyd commenced the drug business for himself in Arcola and until 1884 had the only exclusive drug store in the county. He was a successful business man and remained in charge of the store until a few weeks before his death, November 17, 1899, when he disposed of it to A. Magnusson. He was one of the first movers in the state for the organization of suitable legislation for the elevation of the drug trade in the state. He was an active worker in the Illinois Pharmaceutial Society, and was president of that body one year and a delegate to the national convention in 1884. Never in all her history has Arcola known a more public spirited man, a better leader in every progressive movement, or a truer sympathizer in every just and noble cause. He held many positions of trust and honor, such as member of the school board, alderman, chief of the fire department, and chairman of the board of supervisors. In offices he regarded the trust and the duties devolving upon him as sacred, and acted accordingly. In politics he was a Democrat, and he served his party faithfully and conscientiously.

He was a member of several lodges, but allied his interests more closely with the Masons that any other order. The poor and needy have lost a true friend, and one from whom they had learned to expect sympathy and aid. Never a Christmas passed by but that every poor family received something from him, and his charity was not confined to Arcola alone, but reached for miles around. He was a lover of children, and the child learned to expect some token of remembrance from him, nor was it ever disappointed. His life furnishes us many expressions of good which show the real character of the man. His life was made up of little things well and faithfully performed. But after all it is the little things that give us the true index to the real character of the man. His home relations were the most pleasant, and he remained true and devoted to his home fireside and altar until the close of his career. The town has lost a foremost man, the lodges a faithful member, the home a true head, the poor a sure and helping hand, and the world one of her noblest men.

J. P. WOOLFORD.

J. P. Woolford, merchant and grain buyer at Galton and one of the most successful business men in the county, was born in Butler county, Ohio, February 18, 1855. His parents were Daniel and Elizabeth (Echert) Woolford, who were natives of the same county. His grandfather Echert was born in West Virginia, and in about 1812 removed to Butler county, Ohio. His paternal grandfather, Jacob Woolford, was born at Lancaster, Pennsylvania, and moved from there to Butler county, Ohio. Daniel Woolford came to this county in March, 1869, and located on a farm two miles from Arcola.

Since 1893 J. P. Woolford has resided at Galton, and was first engaged in grain buying for R. & J. Irvin, of Tuscola, succeeding M. S. Filson at this place. In 1894 he built an elevator of twenty thousand bushels capacity and has since become one of the most successful grain dealers in the county.

In 1879 Mr. Woolford was united in marriage to Miss Carrie Kelso, who resided one mile south of Arcola, and is a daughter of William Kelso, who is now living in Tazewell

county, this state. They have three children: Roscoe M., Alfred J. and Samuel M., all at home with their parents. For the past four years Mr. Woolford has been buying grain for himself, and in connection does a general merchandising business. He buys about one hundred thousands bushels of grain annually. In political opinion he is a stanch Republican, but his wife is a Democrat and is the postmistress of the village.

RICHARD C. HAMMETT.

Richard Clyde Hammett, the second son of James R. Hammett, whose sketch and portrait are found on another page, was born on the old

Hammett homestead in Camargo township, September 9, 1871, and was principally educated at the State University and a business college at Indianapolis. He has always been engaged in farming and owns four hundred and twenty acres of finely improved land, a part of which is the old Hammett homestead.

In 1895 he was married to Miss Ginerva Barnett, of the village of Camargo, and has two children: Ruth and Bessie. Mr. Hammett is a member of the Camargo Blue Lodge and Tuscola Chapter and Commandery of Masonry. Mr. Hammett is an intelligent young man and conducts his farming on business principles. He is at present remodeling his farm residence, three miles north of the village of Camargo, and when finished it will rank with the most commodious and beautiful homes of the county.

JASPER S. RECORDS.

Jasper S. Records, who is one of the most prominent tenant farmers in the county and who was born two miles north of the village of Bourbon, January 31, 1856, is a son of John Records, who settled in that neighborhood in about the year 1850. The latter was a native of Kentucky, where he was born August 18, 1800, and died in July, 1863. His wife was Hanora O'Roark, who was born near Staunton, Virginia, and whose parents were both born in Ireland. J. S. Records' paternal great-grandfather, with five brothers, came from Scotland and settled in Kentucky, and were contemporaries of Boone and Kenton. He was killed by the Indians. John Records was a carpenter in early life and later turned his attention to farming, at which he continued up until the time of his death. While working at his trade he built the first frame church in Indianapolis.

Mr. Records has for the past thirteen years successfully superintended the cultivation of the

farm he now resides on (owned by William Iles), on which place he plowed the first furrow and laid the first tile. He has been twice married; first to Miss Elnora O'Brian, in 1879, the latter's death occurring in November, 1895. Her home was at Parkville, Champaign county. They had two children, both of whom are living: Bessie and Lloyd. His second wife was Miss Rachael Froman, of Switzerland county, Indiana. They have one child, Louise Iles. Mr. Records is a member of the Odd Fellows, Home Forum, the Court of Honor and the Modern Woodmen, and is an independent Republican. He is well informed on the topics of the day, is public spirited and is a man of marked individuality.

LINES L. PARKER.

Lines L. Parker, the subject of this sketch, was born in Brown county, Ohio, September 1, 1832. At the age of five years he removed with his parents to Vermilion county, Illinois. His father, John W. Parker, and his mother, Hannah Parker (*nee* Pangburn), were both born in Brown county, Ohio, and after October, 1837, lived in Vermilion county, Illinois, where they died. John W. Parker was sheriff of Vermilion county just preceding the Civil war, and after the war he was county superintendent of schools for two terms. Lines L. Parker went into the war in 1861 as a member of Company D, Twenty-fifth Illinois Infantry. He was soon commissioned a second lieutenant and after the battle of Pea Ridge was promoted to first lieutenant, and afterward commissioned captain of Company E, One Hundred and Fiftieth Illinois Infantry. His final muster out of the service was at Atlanta, Georgia, January 16, 1866. At the next November election he was elected sheriff of Vermilion county, Illinois, and after the expiration of his office, in November, 1868, he removed to Douglas county, Illinois, and lived upon his farm for eleven years, when he was elected county treasurer of Douglas county, and was afterward re-elected for a two years'

term. At the expiration of his term of office he retired to his farm, where he and his faithful wife have lived for the last thirteen years. His wife, Mary A. Parker (*nee* West), was united to him in marriage on the 12th of April, 1855. She was born in Fountain county, Indiana, August 28, 1837, and as the fruits of this marriage there were born to them five children, all living and settled in life near home: Alice is the widow of Alexander E. Fullerton, and now lives near Hugo, Illinois; John W. is a farmer in Bowdre township, near Hugo;

Oliver Lincoln is a grain dealer in Tuscola, Illinois; Hannah O. lives with her husband one mile west of her parents' home, and Hattie lives with her husband within hailing distance of her father and mother.

Mr. Parker is a member of the Grand Army of the Republic, also of the Masonic fraternity. He owns three hundred and thirty acres of land, which he has divided among his children, who live upon or manage the part they expect to get at their father's death. Mr. Parker and his wife are members of the Christian church at Hugo, Illinois, and are liberal contributors to its support.

JAMES M. GOODSPEED.

James M. Goodspeed, a resident of Tuscola, Illinois, and who has for many years been a preacher in the Methodist Episcopal church, was born in the city of Wooster, Wayne county, Ohio, June 22, 1845. His parents were S. S. and Anna (Fish) Goodspeed. The former was born in Essex county, New York, and his mother in Vermont. His grandfather Goodspeed was a soldier in the war of 1812 and for his services drew a pension from the government up to the time of his death.

During the Civil war the subject of this sketch enlisted in the services of his country four times. On June 4, 1862, he enlisted in the Sixty-ninth Regiment Illinois Volunteers and served four months. After being honorably discharged he enlisted in the Twenty-sixth Illinois Volunteers, but was rejected.

On March 4, 1864, he enlisted in the One Hundred and Thirty-fifth Illinois Regiment and became sergeant in Company A. After serving four months and twenty-four days he was honorably discharged. When the government called for men to serve for one year, he enlisted again, but was rejected on account of a disabled arm. He is now a member of the Grand Army of the Republic.

Rev. Goodspeed was reared and educated at Urbana, Illinois, and after leaving the schools of that city he entered the University of Illinois, where he attended as a student for two years. He taught school near Urbana in 1869 and 1870, and then entered Garrett Bibical Institute, at Evanston, Illinois, where he prepared himself for the duties of the ministry. He joined the Illinois conference of the Methodist Episcopal church September 30, 1873, and served the following charges: Tuscola circuit, two years; Ludlow, two years; Catlin, two years; Camargo, three years; Fairmount, two years; Georgetown, three years; Homer, three years, and was sent from Homer to Arcola. After serving the church here for one year, on account of ill health in his family, he, in 1892, located at Tuscola. From that date until the present he has continued in the active ministry, serving such charges as he could and live at Tuscola.

April 14, 1875, he was united in marriage to Miss Rebecca, a daughter of D. H. Jessee, who is an enterprising stock raiser and shipper residing near Villa Grove. They have two children: Wilbur F., who is a graduate of the Tuscola High School, and Edith, ten years of age. Rev. Goodspeed owns a valuable farm of two hundred acres in Douglas county and other property. He has preached twenty-six years in this state, is an earnest and able speaker and is highly respected by his neighbors and friends.

JOHN SKINNER.

John Skinner, a retired and highly respected citizen of Newman, was born in Vermillion county, Indiana, April 4, 1831, and is a son of Joseph and Mary (Gaston) Skinner. His father came to the county in 1839 as a renter, but afterward owned a tract of land of eight hundred acres. The city of Newman is located on part of this land. He took stock to the value of four hundred acres of land and one thousand dollars cash in the construction of the I. D. & W. R. R., from which he realized nothing. He was an enlisted soldier in the Black Hawk war, and died in 1857 (for further ancestry see sketch of his brother, Isaac Skinner).

John Skinner grew up on the farm and has always been identified with farming interests. He has held the office of township commissioner, and has always identified himself with the best interests of Newman and Newman township. He owns three hundred and seventy acres of valuable and well-tiled land, which comes almost to the corporation line of Newman.

In 1859 our subject was married to Miss Hannah J., a daughter of Dr. Ringland, one of the first physicians of Newman, who emigrated from Pennsylvania to the neighborhood of Kansas, Edgar county, later removed to Newman in 1857, and thence back to Kansas, where he died. The death of the wife of our subject occurred within six weeks after her marriage to Mr. Skinner; he has remained unmarried ever since.

In 1862 he volunteered in the Seventy-ninth Illinois Infantry, and participated in the battles of Stone River, Liberty Gap and Chickamauga. He and his brother Anson were captured at the latter place on September 19, 1863, and were placed in Libby prison for three days. They were placed in the Pemberton building, just across the street from Libby, and kept there for six weeks. They were afterward taken to Danville, Virginia, and kept in an old tobacco factory through the winter of 1863 and 1864 with sixteen hundred other prisoners, and were made to sleep on the bare floor without bedding or lights in the building. They were taken from this place in April, 1864, and sent to Andersonville, Georgia. This prison contained about twenty-three acres, being enclosed with logs standing on end, making a wall around about fourteen feet high. This prison had about thirty-five thousand men in it. In September, 1864, they were taken to Charleston, South Carolina, and remained there four weeks, thence to Florence Stockade, in February, 1865. They were kept prisoners here for about four months, when they were removed to Goldsboro, South Carolina, and back to Wilmington, where they were mustered out after enduring a prison life of seventeen months and nine days. In these prisons they were reduced in flesh by starvation to less than half their natural weight. Mr. Skinner was with his regiment all the time after being mustered in until he was captured, excepting two weeks sickness at Stone River. After being captured he was ten days on his way to Libby, where general starvation began. He issued rations to a squad of twenty men about one year. There were seventeen members of his company captured at the same time and he had charge of them in prison and kept them all in his squad except Lieutenant Albin, who was wounded and taken from this place. Joseph Harvey and William Ritter were left sick at Richmond, Virginia; Ritter died and Harvey was paroled. D. N. Howard, Aaron Briton and Wm. Stillwell, of his company, died in Andersonville. These were all that died of the seventeen who were captured.

After they left Danville, Virginia, there was never a vessel of any kind issued for them with which to eat, drink or cook. All they had was old cans that they could pick up that had been thrown away.

Our subject got hold of an old iron hoop and made a saw and a pocket knife, these being the only edge tools he had. With these he began making buckets out of cordwood. He could make one bucket a day and sold them for from one dollar to one dollar and a half. This was his occupation while in Andersonville. While he was in the Florence stockades he mended shoes and made from two dollars to two dollars and fifty cents per day. At Danville he got a job of keeping the back yard clean, for which he received four rations per day; he divided these rations with his company and by so doing saved the lives of six or eight men. In November, 1864, he went out to the commissary, where he had plenty to eat, taking his squad along, besides several members of other companies. While he was in Andersonville prison he was starved down to the weight of eighty-five pounds, but when he left the commissary at Florence, in February, 1865, he had goten back to his natural weight, one hundred and ninety-seven and one-half pounds, so it can be seen how starvation had reduced him. He was mustered out of service June 5, 1865, at the city of Springfield, Illinois.

Anson Skinner's death occurred in February, 1896. William, another brother, now residing in Newman, was a member of the same regiment; they were all sergeants. John Skinner's friends are legion in the community in which he resides. He lives a quiet, contented life, and enjoys the highest confidence of all who know him.

JOHN V. JORDAN.

John V. Jordan, one of the old and well known of the early settlers now living and residing in Murdock township, settled in what is now the confines of Douglas county in the fall of 1854. He is a son of Edward Jordan, who was born in Virginia and reared in Ken-

tucky, a son of Samuel Jordan, who was one of the pioneer settlers of that state. Edward Jordan wedded Christina Van Duyn, who was born in New Jersey and was a daughter of Mr. Jordan's parents emigrated to Vermillion county, Indiana, where he was born in the year 1830. Here he was reared and received John and Rebecca Van Duyn. In about 1823 the meagre education obtainable in the early pioneer schools of that day. After arriving in Douglas county, he entered first an eighty-acre tract of land, and soon after bought another eighty-acre tract, which was second hand. For that which he entered he paid one dollar and twenty-five cents per acre, and the other at three dollars and seventy-five cents per acre. He now owns in all three hundred and fifty acres. He has only recently donated one acre to the Fairland Cemetery Company. He has always taken an active interest in common school education and was school trustee and treasurer before he became a voter in Douglas county.

In January, 1855, he was united in marriage to Miss Lydia C. Lemon, who was a native of Lawrence county, Indiana, and a daughter of M. B. and Eliza Lemon. To their marriage were born six children: Lemon, Ella, Edward, John, Lucy and Dell. Lucy died in 1888, at the age of twenty-one years.

John V. Jordan, before the formation of the Republican party, was a Whig, and since the latter party went down he has been a Republican. When he first came to the locality in which he now resides, among those who had come previously were Robert E. Carmack, who was born in Tennessee and located here in 1852; Samuel and James Wishard and Jacob Caufman; also Samuel A. Brown, all coming from Vermillion county, Indiana; Rev. Jones and Arthur Bradshaw were the early preachers.

N. C. LYRLA.

N. C. Lyrla, of Tuscola, a young lawyer of brilliant prospects in the future, was admitted to practice in the Douglas county courts, in 1896, having previously prepared himself for the law under the tutelage of the late Hon.

Charles W. Woolverton. He was born October 4, 1875, in Champaign county, Illinois and is the son of H. J. and Rose (Christy) Lyrla, who were natives respectively of South Carolina and Ohio. His father is a tubular well driller by trade and resides in Tuscola. His grandfather Christy was born in Ohio and served in the war of the Rebellion.

N. C. Lyrla was graduated from the Tuscola high school in the class of 1894. He takes an active interest in the success of the Democratic party and was the party's nominee for county judge in 1898, but withdrew before the election. In the legal profession he is rapidly fighting his way to the front; he is a young man of excellent good judgment, is a good judge of law and is engaged in some of the most important cases that come before the Douglas county courts.

HENRY C. NILES.

Henry Clay Niles, master in chancery, local historian and an old and well known resident of Tuscola, is a native of Baltimore, Maryland, and a son of Hezikiah and Sally Ann (Warner) Niles, the former was born near Wilmington, Delaware, and the latter being of Quaker extraction and the daughter of John Warner, one of the leading Quakers of that state. Hezikiah Niles was an intimate friend of Henry Clay, and prominent in Whig politics of his day; in 1811 he was editor and proprietor of the Niles Register, which was a strong Whig and pro-slavery paper and always supported the candidacy of Clay. It was one of the most influential newspapers in the eastern country, being one of the acknowledged organs of the Whig party. The International Cyclopedia says of him that he was born in

1777, in Pennsylvania, received an ordinary education and became a member of Bonsal & Niles in the newspaper business at Wilmington, Delaware, which was not a success. He then became a newspaper correspondent and in 1811 founded Niles Register at Baltimore, and died in 1839.

H. C. Niles was reared to manhood in the city of Baltimore where he attended school up to the age of fourteen years. He then became a clerk in a wholesale drug store and later was a clerk in the Baltimore postoffice for seven years. He was then engaged in the drug business up to 1856, when he came to what is now Douglas county and located at Bourbon, where he became a salesman for his brother-in-law, L. C. Rust, who was one of the early merchants of the county, and with whom he remained for two years. After Douglas county was formed in 1859, he was elected to the office of county surveyor, since which time he has served several terms in this office, and is one of the best known surveyors in central Illinois. He is still actively engaged in the business. Various acts of the legislature making any correct survey by a competent surveyor perfectly legal (thus destroying all inducements to hold the office), he, like many other experienced surveyors in the state, has since refused the position. In 1881, he was appointed master in chancery of the Douglas county circuit court, which position he has continuously held, thus attesting his popularity witth all classes of people who have business in his court.

In 1858 he married Miss Rebecca Brown, of DeWitt county, Illinois. They have five children, four of whom are living. Mr. Niles was made a Mason, in Baltimore, in 1854, and is one of the oldest members of that craft in the county. He has materially assisted in the making of both county atlases and is the author of the old Douglas county history, published in 1884, and in this compilation of this volume I am under permanent obligations to Mr. Niles for his unselfish help.

JOSEPH H. FINNEY.

Joseph H. Finney, late of Newman, was born in Parke county, Indiana, January 10, 1849, and died September 9, 1897. In 1873 he was married to Miss Kate Porter and after her death married Miss Agnes Valodin. For twenty-three years Mr. Finney was in business at Newman at which he successfully continued up to the time of his death. He left a wife

and two sons: Porter and Everett; also two sisters, Mrs. W. P. Miller and Mrs. W. D. Goldman, and four brothers; E. C., Daniel, David W., and Robert. For several years Mr. Finney was an active and influential member of the M. E. church at Newman, and at his funeral in speaking of the deceased, the pastor spoke in substance as follows: "Joseph Finney did not lack in noble habits. He was a true friend. Friendship to him was not an ideal something, but a living reality. He had no enemies, for he let his life cast true friendship on every other life. No envy or malice could grow in his nature. He was benevolent to a fault, if it is ever a fault to be benevolent. Some man who knew him well, said, 'If Joseph Finney only had twenty dollars in the world and someone in need were to ask him for aid, he would give nineteen of the twenty to the destitute.' Such was his nature.

"Gentleness was a marked characteristic of his nature. No unkind words would Mr. Finney say of those who may deserve them.

"He understood human nature well and because he knew the need of sympathy he understood now to look with charity on the failings of others.

"No man was ever discouraged or weakened by associating with Joseph Finney. On the other hand, all who knew him felt the influence of an honest, gentle, manly spirit. Probably none have felt natural weakness more, but none have shown more truly than the deceased a strong heart and an irreproachable character. If ever a man was worthy of charity, that man was Mr. Finney.

"In his home, in social life, and in business relations he was ever the same. No harshness, no sharp criticism, no fault finding marred his intercourse with others.

"He was ever a man of noble aspirations. He was never satisfied with present experience or achievements. His testimonies in class meeting and prayer meeting always spoke humility and resolution and noble desire.

"He knew how to struggle. And though like every other man he may sometimes have erred, yet, like David, he knew how to rise above difficulty and even defeat. His frankness was striking. He was never afraid to do the manly thing.

"To his pastor he spoke with Christian confidence during his illness of his trust in God, and conscious peace at heart. He was the kind of man that God loves,—humble, sincere, trustful, penitent.

"The words of Shakespeare may be truly said of him: 'His life was gentle, and the elements so mixed in him, that nature might stand up and say to all the world, This was a man.'"

He was buried at Tuscola, the funeral ceremonies being conducted by Rev. J. M. Oakwood, assisted by Revs. Calhoun and Piper. Mr. Finney was a Mason and was a member of Melita Commandery at Tuscola, the members of which had charge of his remains; he was also a member of the Knights of Pythias and Modern Woodmen. His widow, Mrs. Finney, resides at Newman and before her marriage was a Miss Valodin, of Oakland. She was a daughter of M. B. and Sarah Ann (Redden) Valodin. Her father was born in Ohio and her mother in Illinois. Mrs. Finney is a member of the Methodist Episcopal church at Newman and highly interests herself in church work, being one of the class leaders.

SAMUEL HAWKINS.

Samuel Hawkins, a member of one of the earliest settled in Douglas county families and a soldier in the Civil war, was born in Pickaway county, Ohio, October 12, 1836, and is a son of John Hawkins who was born in Loudoun county, Virginia. His mother, who was Margaret Cassady, was also born in Virginia. In October, 1851, Samuel's father, with a family of several sons, came and settled in what is now Douglas county, two miles and a half southwest of Newman. After he had located his children urged him to enter a large body of land which he could have done at one dollar and twenty-five cents an acre, but it was his opinion at that time that the prairie land would never be settled, and consequently he

did not do so. But later on he bought a farm of seventy-two acres along the Brushy Fork timber, where he resided until his death, November 10, 1880.

Samuel Hawkins remained on a farm in Ohio until he arrived in Douglas county with his father. He has been twice married, the first time on October 23, 1858, to Miss Elizabeth, a daughter of Robert Hopkins, who emigrated from Pickaway county, Ohio, and settled in Newman township before the Hawkins family, and by this marriage he has two children living: W. S. and Mrs. Mary E. Busby. His first wife died August 12, 1866. In 1870 he wedded Miss Elizabeth, daughter of William Hopkins, who was a brother of Robert, and was among the pioneer settlers in what is now known as the Hopkins and Hawkins neighborhood. Mrs. Hawkins is a granddaughter of Joseph and Elizabeth Winkler, who came to this county in a very early day. Both died in 1836, and were among the very earliest buried in the Albin cemetery. Mr. Hawkins by his second wife has two children: Eva B., wife of Harrison Hawkins, and Luther B., unmarried.

On July 30, 1862, our subject volunteered in the Seventy-ninth Illinois, and became a corporal in Company E, W. A. Lowe's company. Mr. Lowe was an old and prominent early settler in Newman township, and for him the Newman Grand Army post was named; before the end of the war he became lieutenant-colonel. Mr. Hawkins was at the battle of Chickamauga, but was captured the first day of the fight and was sent to Richmond and later to Danville. He is a member of the Grand Army of the Republic, of the Masonic fraternity, and the Wesley Chapel Methodist church. He owns eighty acres of land and is one of the substantial and highly respected citizens of Newman township.

FRANK C. DEVER.

Frank C. Dever, present principal of the Hindsboro public schools, and the editor and proprietor of the Hindsboro News, was born in Clark county, Illinois, January 26, 1860, and is a son of F. C. and Eliza (English) Dever, natives of Ohio. The parents removed to Camargo township in 1868, thence to Bowdre township in 1870, and the father at present resides in Missouri, the mother having died May 31, 1900. Frank C. Dever attended Lee's academy at Loxie, Coles county, and later at the Danville normal. He has

been teaching since 1880, and was superintendent of the public schools at Anna, Illinois, for four years, and of Barry, Illinois, for two years. Since 1897 he has held his present position in the Hindsboro public schools. In 1892 he was married to Miss Eva Worley, of Anna. They have two children: Lena and Wesley Collins.

In 1898 our subject was the Democratic nominee for superintendent of the Douglas county schools, but was defeated. The Democratic side of the board of supervisors in the contest to fill the vacancy in that office caused by the death of Thomas M. Wells, in 1899, gave their united support to Mr. Dever for twenty-three ballots, the board being a tie politically. The deadlock, which had held the board of supervisors for several weeks, was broken by both parties meeting on neutral ground and giving their united support to Miss Blanche Caraway, the present incumbent.

The Hindsboro News, which is in the line politically with the Chicago platform, was founded by Sisson & Miller in 1896. Mr. Sisson soon withdrew, and the paper was managed by Charles B. Miller until the summer of 1897, when he was succeeded by Monroe McIntyre, known as the "fighting editor" of the News, and who sold the paper to Mr. Dever in March, 1898. The paper has a circulation of about five hundred, comes out on Fridays and is a six-column folio. Since October, 1899, C. L. Watson, the present supervisor of Bowdre township, has been associated with Mr. Dever in business, under the following names: Dever & Watson, publishers; and C. L. Watson & Co., real estate. Mr. Dever is president of the village board of trustees of Hindsboro, and is identified with all movements which aim toward the advancement of the best interests of Hindsboro and its vicinity.

GEORGE W. SIDERS.

George W. Siders is one of the early and prominent settlers of Camargo township still living. He settled in the northeast part of Camargo township in 1852. He is a son of Jacob and Susan (Clark) Siders, who were natives respectively of Virginia and Maryland. After their marriage they emigrated from Virginia to Fairfield county, Ohio, thence to Pickaway county, Ohio, and from there to Douglas county, Illinois. In the year above mentioned Jacob Siders was a renter and never owned but twenty acres of land. He died in this county in the sixty-third year of his age, and was buried at Camargo. His wife, who was born in 1811 near Harper's Ferry, Virginia, is still living. Jacob Siders was a son of Solomon Siders, who was a sol-

dier in the war of 1812 and the Horse-shoe war against the Indians. The father of Solomon Siders was also named Solomon; he was in the war of the Revolution and according to the traditions of the family lived to be one hundred and fifteen years old. James Clark, the maternal grandfather, was born in Dublin, Ireland, was a weaver by trade, and when he came to Ohio was one of the pioneer school teachers.

George W. Siders was born February 10, 1836, in Pickaway county, Ohio, and was sixteen years old when his father came to Douglas county. In 1869 he settled on his present farm, which contains one hundred and twenty acres. In 1862 he was united in marriage to Eliza Ann Hughes, who was born and reared in Logan county, Ohio. Her death occurred on Sunday, April 27, 1900. To this marriage were born five children, four of whom are now living: Mary, who is the wife of Charles Reynolds; Ella, wife of John Huls; Alice, wife of Thomas Huls; and Milo, who is at home; he married Miss Maud Grimes, of Indianola. Robert Eldon, who died in April, 1900, aged thirty-seven years and five days, was much attached to his family. Mr. Siders has been school director for three years, a member of the Grange and F. M. B. A. order. Among Mr. Siders' neighbors when he first came to the county were Jack Richman and his brother Jim, and George Ritter, now postmaster at Villa Grove, and among the early ministers were Arthur Bradshaw, Peter Wallace, who was the presiding elder of the district, and Rev. Saulsbury.

WILLIAM H. BUSH.

William H. Bush, a well-known auctioneer and respected citizen of Hindsboro, was born in Bowdre township, Douglas county, Illinois, April 1, 1859. He is a son of E. B. and Margaret Ann (Moyer) Bush. His father was one of the earliest settlers in Bowdre township. He was a native of Hardin county, Kentucky, and came to the county when seventeen years of age. At present he resides at Galesburg, Illinois, in the sixty-second year of his age. He is a son of John Bush, who was born in Elizabethtown, Hardin county, Kentucky, April 1, 1802, and died July 5, 1852. Our subject's mother, Margaret Ann Moyer, was born in Rockingham county, Virginia, and was the daughter of John Phillip Moyer, who was of German ex-

traction, and who came to the county a year previous to the coming of the Bush family.

William H. Bush was reared on the farm and educated at the country schools of Bowdre township, Douglas county, Illinois. In 1882 he was united in marriage to Miss Lola E. Mulliken, of Champaign county, a granddaughter of Samuel F. Miller, who has ever since he was a young man been a prominent light in the ministry of the Christian church. Mr. Miller is still living, in the eighty-fifth year of his age. He was born in Kentucky, April 26, 1815. His wife, Bertha M. Jean, was born in Illinois, May 7, 1817, and died July 8, 1838. (See sketch of I. M. Mulliken, of Newman.) To Mr. and Mrs. Bush have been born eight children, whose names and dates of birth are as follows: Zella M., September 3, 1882; Clarence E., December 7, 1883; Stella F., September 12, 1887; Gertie B., June 22, 1889 (died September 14, 1898); Waldo H., August 17, 1890; Vieva M., February 26, 1893; one which died at birth unnamed, May 19, 1895; Frederick E., November 23, 1899. Mr. Bush has in addition to his work as auctioneer dealt in broomcorn with Duncan & Tarbox, of Arcola, since 1888. He has also been in the undertaking business in Hindsboro since June 10, 1897. He was one of the principal organizers of the Court of Honor at that place on March 1, 1899, of which order he has been the worthy chancellor since its organization. This order is in a flourishing condition, having initiated about one hundred members. He was elected delegate to the county convention of the Court of Honor January 9, 1900; from there he was elected delegate to the State meeting at Springfield for February 14, 1900; and at the state convention he was elected delegate to the supreme session, which was held in Peoria on May 22-25, 1900. William H. Bush is also a member of the Masonic and I. O. O. F. fraternities and of the Modern Woodmen of America. He stands high in his community, and is recognized as a man of good business ability; he has filled all the principal offices in the Odd Fellows lodge of Hindsboro, as well as deputy of the lodge for several terms. He also represented his lodge in the Grand Lodge at Springfield in 1893 and 1894. At present he is senior deacon in the A. F. & A.

M. lodge at Hindsboro; has also been the venerable consul of Hindsboro Camp No. 968, M. W. of A., and served as worthy banker of this camp for four successive years. He has interested himself in politics, having been elected constable of Bowdre township three times; has also served as trustee of the village. Mr. Bush has the management of the Douglas County Telephone Exchange, located in his residence at Hindsboro, which is operated by his eldest daughter, Zella M. Bush.

JAMES BARR.

Among the many successful men noted for their fair dealing with the public and their uprightness in character, who have made the city of Newman famous, none deserve more credit than James Barr. Our subject was born in Clermont county, Ohio, April 7, 1839, and in 1852 moved with his parents to Charleston, Coles county, Illinois, where he was reared and schooled. At the age of sixteen he began the trade of a tinner, which he mastered and has continued to follow through life. When he was but a boy his father died, leaving him to do for himself. His educational advantages were, as was the case with many of the pioneers, very limited, although he received a fair business education. Being of a mechanical turn of mind, he soon became an expert workman. During the first call of the Civil war he enlisted in the Eighth Illinois Volunteer Infantry, and remained out until the end of his term of service, after which he returned to Charleston.

In 1864 Mr. Barr married Miss Eliza E. Harmon, of Clermont county, Ohio. In 1865 he started in business at Oakland and continued until 1887, when he moved to Kansas and entered into partnership with his brother, W. W. Barr, under the firm name of W. W. Barr & Brother.

His wife passed away April 2, 1878, leaving two children, Stella and George H.

In 1879 he started in business in Newman and one year later sold his interest in the store at Kansas to his brother and bought the latter's interest in Newman.

In 1881 he married Miss May W. Curd,

of Newman, and to this union one son, Clayton C., was born.

In 1890 he sold a half interest in his business to W. F. Summers. They conducted the business under the name of Barr & Summers until 1893, when Mr. Barr bought Mr. Summers' interest. On the 8th of October, 1895, our subject's son, George H. Barr, died at the age of twenty-one years, four months and fourteen days.

In 1896 he sold a half interest to I. M. Mulliken, of Charleston. The firm runs under the head of Barr & Mulliken. They own two of the largest stores in the city, one, hardware, stoves and tinware, and the other, furniture and undertaking, where a full line of each can always be found on hand. James Barr is a stanch Republican and has been elected mayor of Newman three times, always making a good executive officer. He is a great believer in secret orders and is ever ready to further their interests. He is a prominent Odd Fellow and Mason; is a Knight Templar, being a member of the Melita Commandery No. 37, at Tuscola. He is Eminent High Priest in Newman Chapter, No. 72, and is the president of the Odd Fellows Benefit Association of Douglas county. He is the son of Samuel and Sarah (Wise) Barr. The former was born in Steubenville, Ohio, in 1800, and died in 1856. The latter was born in Pennsylvania in 1803 and died in 1880. Mr. Barr's present wife is the daughter of Daniel and Evaline Curd, of near Frankfort, Kentucky. Daniel Curd was born in 1808 and Evaline in 1801.

Mr. Barr is a member of the M. E. church and his wife is a member and worker in the O. E. S. and Rebekah lodges of Newman, and is a leading worker in the Christian church.

ADOLPH HAPKE.

Adolph Hapke, the leading jeweler and optician and one of the rising and successful young business men of Newman, was born in the province of West Prussia, Germany, May 30, 1869, and is a son of Christ and Christian (Schlack) Hapke, who were natives of the same province. His father was a blacksmith by trade, who emigrated to this country in 1871 and located in Michigan City, Laporte county, Indiana, where he followed his trade and also engaged in farming. He resides at present four and one-half miles east of Michigan City. He served in the war of Germany against Austria in 1866.

Adolph Hapke received a common school education and at the age of seventeen went to Michigan City, where he served an apprenticeship of four years at his trade. In 1898 he located at Newman, having previously taken a course in optics at the Chicago Ophthalmology College.

On October 11, 1899, he was married to Miss Josephine, a daughter of Enoch Gordon, of Newman. After his marriage he purchased the residence of C. E. Eagler, and it is one of the elegantly furnished homes of Newman. After his marriage the Newman Independent spoke of him as follows: "Mr. Hapke came to Newman about two years ago, and since then his dealings with our people have been honorable, and he has formed ties of friendship that will always last. The bride is one of Newman's most deserving young ladies, who was graduated in the spring of 1899 from the high school of Newman with honors."

Mr. Hapke carries a large stock of jewelry, and by his honest and upright mode of doing business has put himself on the road to building up a most prosperous business.

J. M. HAWKINS.

J. M. Hawkins, an intelligent farmer, who saw three years of service in the war of the Rebellion, is a son of John Hawkins, who was born near Harper's Ferry, Virginia, and who came to Douglas county in 1851, and settled on a farm three miles south of Newman, where he resided and was prominent in his neighborhood up until his death, which occurred in the year 1880. Among some more of the earlier settlers are mentioned Cornelius, Robert and James Hopkins, Robert Albin and Enoch Newell, who are all early settlers from Indiana. John Hawkins wedded Margaret Cassady, of Ohio, but a native of Virginia.

J. M. Hawkins was born in Pickaway county, Ohio, February 5, 1839, and came to Douglas county in the fall of the year above mentioned. In February, 1862, he volunteered in the First Missouri Regiment of Infantry and participated in many of the principal battles of the war, remaining out until its close. He afterward returned home and engaged in farming, and succeeded in making an honest living and securing the good opinion of his neighbors. His farm contains only forty-four acres, but he is satisfied with it.

In 1867 our subject was united in marriage to Miss Sarah Johnson, a daughter of J. T.

Johnson, who practiced medicine at Bourbon up to 1871, when he removed to Barton county, Missouri, where he died some sixteen years ago at the age of sixty-four years. He was a native of Ohio. Mr. Hawkins is a member of the Grand Army of the Republic, Masonic fraternity and Knights of Pythias. He is unassuming in his manner and gentle in his conduct toward his fellow men.

ABRAM H. MOORE.

Abram H. Moore, deceased, father of Edward M. and Morris L. Moore, was born in Bourbon township, Douglas county, Illinois,

December 7, 1838, and was of old Virginia ancestry. He died May 11, 1883, at the age of forty-four years. His father was Jacob Rice Moore and his mother Amanda Moore (see sketches of Wm. F., Jacob R., Jr., and others.) Abram H. Moore was married to Mary E. Miller, of Mattoon, Illinois, January 31, 1865. To their union were born three children: Edward McClellan, Morris Logan, and Mary Catherine, Morris and Kate being twins. Mary Catherine died September 18, 1890, and Mary E. died October 20, 1894. Abram H. at his death owned a farm of three hundred and twenty acres in Bourbon township, adjoining the old Moore homestead. He was of a sober, industrious disposition and was highly respected by his large circle of friends and neighbors. He was an invalid for five years prior to his death.

EDW. McC. MOORE.

Edw. McC. Moore, the oldest son of Abram H. and Mary E. Moore was born at the home of his father, three miles west of Arcola, Bourbon township, Douglas county, Illinois, October 20, 1865. He secured his education in the neighborhood schools. At the age of sixteen years Mr. Moore left school on account of the death of his father and took charge of the farm, and he has been successful as a farmer, stock raiser and feeder. In 1893 he was married to Miss Lena Kelley, a daughter of Mr. Benjamin Kelley, who was an early settler in Moultrie county, from Kentucky. At present he spends most of his time among his children, in Florida, California, Kansas, Washington, Nebraska and Illinois. To Mr. and Mrs. Moore two very interesting children have been born: Albert Henry and Mary Vivian. Mr. Moore owns two hundred and sixty acres of

well improved land, and has had some experience in office. He is of good moral character and his friends are many.

MORRIS L. MOORE.

Morris Logan Moore, son of Abram H. and Mary E. Moore, was born April 28, 1869, at the home of his father, three miles west of Arcola, Illinois, in Bourbon township, and

owns and lives on the old home, consisting of two hundred and ten acres of well improved land. He received his early training at the common country schools and attended Lee's Academy at Loxa, Illinois, one year, Prof. Lee being one of the eminent educators of his time. Later he attended the normal at Valparaiso, Indiana, for a period of two years, where he pursued the scientific and teacher's course. After leaving college he taught school for one year and then traveled extensively throughout the west and southwest. He is unmarried, has served his township as collector for two years, and is a Royal Arch Mason in high standing. Courteous, quiet, well informed and enterprising, he stands as one of the representative and successful young business men of the county.

J. PARK McGEE, M. D.

J. Park McGee, M. D., a prominent and well known citizen of Brushy Fork, and closely identified with the material interests of the county, was born January 5, 1847, in Clark county, Indiana, and is a son of William Park McGee, a native of Washington county, Pennsylvania, of Scotch-Irish extraction. He was a saddler by trade, and a son of Robert McGee, who was an early settler in Pennsylvania. The Park family are a very prominent family of Washington county, Pennsylvania, and the old homestead still belongs to John Park, of the third generation from Isabella Park. Our subject's mother, whose maiden name was Tamar Tom, was born in the oil regions, on the Allegheny river in Allegheny county, Pennsylvania. His father was born on the Monongahela river, in Washington county, the same state. The

Doctor's grandmother, Isabella Park McGee, was a daughter of John Park and sister of Hugh Park. William Park McGee

(father) learned his trade in Pittsburg, emigrated about the year 1820, on a flat-boat to Louisville, Kentucky, but settled across the river in New Charlestown, Clark county, Indiana, where he farmed and followed his trade. He died April 27, 1862, and is buried in Owen Creek cemetery.

J. Park McGee was reared in Clark county, and was principally educated in Wabash College, taking an irregular course with the object in view of preparing himself for his profession, remaining in this college three years. He subsequently read medicine with Dr. Work, of Charlestown, entered the Eclectic College of Cincinnati and was graduated in 1872. He afterward took one course of lectures in the Rush Medical College of Chicago, and had a complimentary degree conferred upon him by the faculty of this well-known institution in 1887. He was elected to the Legislature from the Republican district composed of Douglas, Coles and Cumberland counties, in 1884, 1888 and 1892. He was elected as a Democrat and at each re-election carried the district by increased majorities. He assisted in passing the bill to legalize dissecting, and for so doing Rush Medical College conferred upon him a complimentary degree. During the first term he was chairman of the sanitary committee, and member of appropriation, education, insurance, revenue and railroads committees. Dr. McGee is one of the pioneer silver men of the state, as proclaimed in the Chicago platform of 1896, and was a delegate who took a prominent part in the state convention at Springfield in 1895, the first silver state convention ever held. The Doctor located at Brushy Fork in 1874, and has practiced his profession there ever since. In 1864 he joined Company K, One Hundred Thirty-seventh Illinois Infantry, and served to the expiration of his term of enlistment, and he has a certificate of thanks from President Lincoln for services rendered his country. He owns two hundred and fifty acres of land; is a Knight Templar in Masonry, and has never been married. He will visit the Paris Fair this year and make a tour of Europe. Dr. McGee's life has been a busy one and during all the years of his residence in the township the time has been fully taken up in what he conceived to be his public and private duty. He is a man of unquestionable integrity, honesty in his business transactions, and generous in his disposition, with a wide charity for mankind.

CHARLES F. JENNE.

Charles F. Jenne is one of the most successful merchants and enterprising business men of Douglas county, residing at Arthur, where he and his partner, Fred B. Beckman,

own and conduct two large stores, one a general hardware establishment and the other furniture and undertaking. He has resided at Arthur since 1885, and was in business alone until three years ago when he took in his present partner. Since his residence in Arthur he has always given his support to all worthy enterprises calculated to promote the welfare of his town and county, and is valued as a citizen by the entire community.

Charles F. Jenne was born in Ross county, Ohio, in 1855 and is a son of Henry W. and Mary (Smith) Jenne, who were natives of Germany. He was reared and educated in the common schools of Ross county, Ohio. In 1880 he was united in marriage to Miss Sallie J. Warren, a daughter of T. T. Warren, a native of Douglas county. Mr. Jenne is a Mason and takes deep interest in Masonic affairs, having served as master of Arthur Lodge, No. 825, for three years.

THOMAS H. RUTHERFORD.

Thomas H. Rutherford, the present supervisor of Newman township, and one of the acknowledged leaders in farming as well as in political affairs of Douglas county, was born at Oakland, Coles county, Illinois, January 16, 1853. He is a son of Dr. Hiram Rutherford, settling there in the year 1840, one of the pioneers, and at the time of his death he was one of the oldest physicians in eastern Illinois, and one of the largest land owners as well. He has written much of the early settlers, especially of the eccentric ones of this region. He has a remarkable memory, and probably knew more of the early history of Douglas and Coles counties than any other man within their bounds.

He was born in Cumberland Valley, near Harrisburg, Pennsylvania, December 27, 1815. (For further facts pertaining to ancestry, see work of Dr. Eagle, state librarian of Pennsylvania, on early families of the Cumberland valley.) Dr. Hiram Rutherford, after attending Jefferson University, commenced the practice of medicine at the age of twenty-five years, at Millersburg, Pennsylvania.

Thomas H. Rutherford received his education in the schools of Oakland, and on October 15, 1874, he was united in marriage to Miss Sarah R. Zimmerman, a daughter of John B. Zimmerman, who settled in Oakland township in 1837. To them have been born four children: Cyrus W., Bessie (deceased), Hiram B., and Katie. Mr. Rutherford resides on his beautiful farm of two hundred and forty acres, just north of Newman, and is one of the most influential leaders of the Republican party in the county. He has been school treasurer of township No. 16, range 11, since the spring of 1876. In 1885 he was elected commissioner of highways and he'd that office until December, 1890, when he resigned to be appointed supervisor to fill the vacancy of L. E. Root, who was elected county treasurer. He was re-elected supervisor in 1892, also in 1894, and was elected chairman of the board in 1893 and 1894. He is now a member of the committee on finance, refunding of tax and public buildings and grounds. Socially he belongs to the Newman Blue Lodge and is past high priest of the Royal Arch Masons, Newman Chapter, No. 172, and is also a member of Melita Commandery, No. 37, Knights Templar; is a Knight of Pythias and a member of the Modern Woodmen.

Mr. Rutherford is a man of action and business capacity, and whatever cause he espouses he generally carries through successfully, with a vim and earnestness which are in a high degree characteristic qualities of his makeup.

JOSEPH S. WYETH.

Joseph S. Wyeth was for many years previous to his death prominently identified with the affairs of Douglas county. He, with his brother, L. J., and their wives, came to Coles county in 1850 and settled on farms four miles south of Hindsboro, where they remained until 1860, when they removed to Tuscola and engaged in mercantile business. The partnership lasted four years, when it was dissolved, L. J. remaining in the business and Joseph S. locating on a farm in Garrett township where his widow now resides. This was in 1864. (For a very full and complete ancestry of the Wyeth family see sketch of L. J. Wyeth on another page).

From the Tuscola Review: "Tuesday morning, at his home in Garrett township,

Joseph S. Wyeth, a pioneer resident and farmer of Douglas county, departed this life. He was seventy years and two months old.

"Deceased was born in Franklin county, Massachusetts, April 15, 1828. In 1850 he was united in marriage to Miss Joanna Hunt in Licking county, Ohio. Mrs. Wyeth and six children survive him, and two children long since preceded their father to the grave. Mr. Wyeth had been in poor health for many years, and the last few years of his life seldom left the home place."

"At one time he was quite a wealthy man and was a large dealer in live stock, but owing to failing health he was obliged to retire from active life a number of years ago. He leaves his family well provided for. Those who best know him speak of Mr. Wyeth in the highest praise as a citizen, neighbor and Christian man. During his life he followed the bible injunction to 'do unto others as you would have them do unto you,' and he went to the grave honored and respected by all who knew him.

"Funeral services were held at 2 o'clock yesterday afternoon at Cartwright church, Rev. Geo. Rippey officiating, and it was one of the largest funerals ever held in Garrett township."

Mrs. Wyeth, his widow, is a daughter of Elijah Hunt and Rhoda (Hillyer) Hunt, who were born respectively in Vermont and Connecticut and were engaged in agriculture pursuits. Elijah Hunt, her father, was in the war of 1812. His death occurred February 12, 1873, in the seventy-seventh year of his age. Her grandfather, Justin Hillyer, was a Revolutionary soldier. Her grandfather Hunt was a native of Vermont. To Mr. and Mrs. Wyeth were born the following children: Rhoda, wife of W. B. Brenton, of La Salle, Illinois; Franklin L., farmer in Garrett township; Harry L., also a farmer in the same township; Susan, wife of Joseph Gregory, of Garrett township; Luella, wife of William Romine, of Garrett, and Daisy, who is the wife of John Burk, a merchant of Garrett. The farm upon which Mrs. Wyeth resides is owned by her and two of her sons and contains three hundred and thirty-seven acres.

WILLIAM T. MOORE.

William T. Moore, generally known as Squire Moore, is a leading citizen and farmer of Arcola township, and is a member of one of the earliest and most prominent families in Douglas county. He was born in Parke county, Indiana, September 5, 1830, and is a son of Jacob Moore, the pioneer of the family in the county, who was a native of Kentucky.

'Squire Moore's grandfather, Abraham Moore, and his wife, natives of Virginia, were early settlers in Shelby county, Kentucky, where they spent the remainder of their lives. 'Squire Moore removed with his parents from Parke county to what is now known as the Moore neighborhood when he was but four years old. Here he grew to manhood and obtained the advantages of an ordinary school education. In 1856 he was united in marriage to Margaret E. Louthan, who is a daughter of John and Margaret (Carter)

Louthan, both of whom were born in Frederick county, Virginia, she being the youngest of twelve children. John Louthan was born December 11, 1779, and died May 7, 1864. He first removed to Edgar county, and in 1844 settled on the Okaw in Bourbon township, where he bought about one thousand acres of land. He was a son of Henry Louthan, who was a native Scotchman. His wife was a daughter of Arthur Carter, who was born in Ireland, and who later emigrated and lived in Virginia.

To Mr. and Mrs. W. T. Moore have been born six children: Sarah M., living at home; Charles A. and Ferdinand, who are prominent farmers in Coles county; Laura, who is the widow of Robert Black (see sketch), and resides in Arcola; Alice B. and Henry. Mr. Moore has for eighteen years filled the office of justice of the peace, has served three terms as township collector, and two terms as assessor. He owns one hundred and ninety acres, and the old homestead and one hundred and twenty acres in Coles county. He has been twenty-five years a Mason and a member of the Arcola lodge and chapter, and is also an Odd Fellow. He is well known and popular with all classes of people and is one of the stanch Democrats of the county.

BENJAMIN W. GERE.

Benjamin W. Gere, a talented young lawyer of Arcola, with brilliant prospects in the legal profession, was admitted to practice in the courts of Illinois in February, 1897, after having read law in the office of Barrick & Cofer, of Arcola.

Mr. Gere was born January 23, 1871, at Bourbon, and is a son of Warren B. and Jennie (Thompson) Gere. His father has been engaged in the grain business all his life and is one of Arcola's highly respected citizens.

Mr. Gere, in partnership with Mr. Albert Snyder, act as agents for fifteen of the leading

fire insurance companies of the country. He has served Arcola most efficiently as city attorney. In the recent race for county attorney Mr. Gere was a candidate and had many friends throughout the county, but the conditions were such that would force the nomination of Mr. Chadwick, so Mr. Gere withdrew; by doing so it will no doubt increase his chances four years hence. He owns probably the second largest law library in the county, and is rapidly forging to the front in his profession. In political opinion he is a stanch Republican and takes an active interest in his party's success.

JOHN A. REEDER, JR.

John A. Reeder, Jr., who is one of the leading farmers in Bourbon township, was born in Darke county, Ohio, October 3, 1854, and is a son of John A. and Mary B. (Harter) Reeder, natives of the same county in Ohio. John A. Reeder removed to Douglas county and located where his son John A. now resides. After coming to the county he rented for eight years and then purchased two hundred and fifty acres of land and later became one of the influential citizens of Bourbon township. His death occurred in 1892 in the seventy-seventh year of his age. He was also a very successful trader in both real estate and buying and selling live stock. (For further facts of the family see sketch of brother at Garrett.)

John A. Reeder was united in marriage to Miss Mary A. Corbett in 1881. She is a daughter of Michael Corbett, of Arthur, who was born in Ireland in 1827, emigrated to this country in 1846 and was for five years employed on Mississippi river steamboats, after which he located in Sangamon county and purchased fifty acres of land, paying ten dollars per acre. After working and improving it for two years he sold it for fifty dollars per acre. He then came to Douglas county, where he purchased land for nine dollars per acre, part of which he afterward sold for one hundred and twenty-five dollars per acre. In 1858 he married Miss Elizabeth York, of Sangamon county. Mr. Corbett is living a retired life at Arthur.

To Mr. and Mrs. Reeder have been born five children: Harry, aged sixteen years; Bertha, fifteen; George, thirteen; Fred, eleven, and Katie. He owns ninety acres of land, which is a part of the old homestead, and deservedly ranks as one of the reputable citizens of the county.

DANIEL W. REED.

Daniel W. Reed, the popular and accommodating deputy county clerk, was born in Tuscola, March 11, 1864. He is a son of John T. and Annie (Walters) Reed, who were natives of Pennsylvania. John T. Reed was reared to manhood in Pennsylvania, where he learned the tailor's trade, at which he worked in his younger days, and in 1862 came to Illinois and settled on a farm in Tuscola township.

Daniel W. Reed grew to maturity on the farm and was engaged in school teaching for seven years, having been principally educated at the Danville, Indiana, Normal School. For two years Mr. Reed served efficiently and acceptably to the citizens of Tuscola on the city police force. In 1887 he was united in marriage to Miss Alice Price, and to their marriage have been born two lovely children: Lucile and Louise. Mr. Reed is a member of the Masonic fraternity and also of the Woodmen. In political opinion he has always been a consistent Republican and an effective worker in the ranks of his party. As an officer he is almost universally liked by the people throughout Douglas county.

ROBERT E. MILLIGAN.

Robert E. Milligan, the accommodating and gentlemanly liveryman of Tuscola, who succeeded Dr. Ramsey to his business in 1897, was born in Lawrence county, Illinois, November 24, 1856. He was reared to manhood on a farm in his native county and is a son of

David Milligan, who was also born in Lawrence county and who was a son of John Milligan, who emigrated from Scotland in the early days and later became an early settler in Lawrence county. Robert E. Milligan's mother, Elvira Grout, was a daughter of Nayham Grout, a native of Vermont.

Robert E. Milligan, like many other successful men, has made his own way through life unaided. His rule of life has ever been one of strict integrity, and whatever he does he does well. In manner he is pleasant and genial, easily making friends and holding them.

In 1879 our subject was united in marriage to Miss Mary Butler, of Lawrence county, Illinois. They have one child, a daughter, Gertrude. Mr. Milligan and wife are consistent members of the Methodist Episcopal church.

JAMES A. RICHMAN.

James A. Richman is one of the best known farmers in Douglas county, and owns one of the finest and best improved farms and most beautiful homes in the county. His farm is situated in the northern part of Camargo township, and his residence is three-quarters of a mile west of Villa Grove.

Mr. Richman was born near Camargo, Illinois, September 13, 1844, and is the third son of David Richman. He grew to manhood on his father's farm near Camargo, and in 1864 volunteered in the Civil war and was a member of Company G, One Hundred and Thirty-fifth Regiment. In 1865 Mr. Richman was mustered out of the service and returned to his former home, and in November of the same year was married to Miss Sarah Williams, who is a daughter of John Williams, a native of Kentucky. The latter was a volunteer in the

Union army, and died while in the service in 1862. To Mr. and Mrs. Richman have been born six children, five of whom are living:

Franklin and Charlie, both engaged in farming; Hattie, wife of Dr. Gilmore, of Villa Grove; Guy, a telegraph operator in Tuscola, and John, at home. An infant daughter died in January, 1875.

In 1869 Mr. Richman bought one hundred and sixty acres of land upon which the homestead now stands, and in April of the same year he moved upon it. By hard labor and shrewd management Mr. Richman was enabled from time to time to buy more land, and now he has equipped one of the largest and best stock farms in the county, he having devoted much of his time to the raising of cattle and hogs. Mr. and Mrs. Richman are members of the M. E. church at Villa Grove, and are always among the first to give for the aid of the poor and needy. Mr. Richman has always been a strong supporter of the Democratic party.

James A. Richman is a member of the old and prominent Richman family which enjoys the distinction of being the oldest settled family in the county, his grandfather, John A. Richman, having been the oldest resident in the county at the time of his death. He located here over three-quarters of a century ago, the first permanent white settler in the district now embraced in Douglas county, The Richmans are of English and German descent. David Richman was born in Greenbrier county, West Virginia, October 25, 1816. When in his eleventh year his family left Virginia. John A. Richman, his father, had a large family of children and wanted more land, hence his removal from Virginia to Illinois. The cattle, sheep and horses could not be sold at home, and so were driven to their western destination. Arriving in Vermilion county, Illinois, they settled on the head of the Little Vermilion river. Here they lived on rented land, and raised two crops. In company with one Moses Bradshow, Mr. Richman's father visited the Embarrass timber on a bee hunt. In eight or ten days they got three or four barrels of honey. Mr. Richman was so well pleased with the land in the neighborhood of where they encamped that he resolved to remove to that country and take up some of the wild land there. The family left Vermilion county in May following and settled on the Embarrass timber one-half mile west of Camargo. There was not another family of whites living in the present limits of the county at the time. There were no settlers north of Charleston. For a year they remained the only family in the county. In about eighteen months after their arrival they had a neighbor in Isaac Moss, who settled about a mile east of the present town of Camargo. The Indians were in the neighborhood for about three years after their arrival. Bridgeport now occupies the site of their old village. They came in the fall and remained over winter, and in the spring journeyed further north, where they spent the summer. The first summer the Richmans lived in a rough camp built of logs split in two. They commenced farming by trying to break the prairie, but found their teams too weak for this, and so began work in the timber. They kept at work, clearing, breaking and planting, till the 10th of July, when they succeeded in putting fourteen acres in with corn. They then began work at building a house. The logs were hewn out, and part on the ground, when several members of the family were taken down with the ague, seven out of eleven, and for several months were able to do nothing whatever. Their house was not put up in consequence till the succeeding summer. This house may still be seen in a good state of preservation, just north of the railroad and half a mile west of Camargo. For many years the family endured the hardships and inconveniences of pioneer life. Their pork was sold for one dollar and a half to two dollars a hundred, but they saved a little money even at these prices and invested it in land, till finally the amount reached seven hundred acres.

At the age of twenty-three David Richman was married to Ruth Haines, a native of Ohio. To them were born seven children: John, George, James, Samuel, William, Taylor and David, of whom John, George and David are deceased. Mr. Richman's life was full of hardships and exposure. In 1832 he contracted a severe cold, which settled upon his lungs and soon resulted in his death.

OLIVER T. HUNT.

First Lieutenant Oliver T. Hunt (known as Captain), a retired farmer of Tuscola, Illinois, and a well known and highly respected citizen of the county, is a native of Randolph county, Indiana, and was born within eight miles to Winchester, the county seat, June 13, 1832. He is a son of Miles Hunt, who married Mary L. Botkin; they were natives respectively of Fleming county, Kentucky, and Knox county, Tennessee. Bazil Hunt (grandfather) was born in England. Four brothers of the Hunt family came from England in about the year 1779 or 1780. One was killed in the Revolutionary war; one settled in Maryland; one in Virginia, and Bazil, the grandfather of the subject, settled in Fleming county, Kentucky, and moved in an early day to Indiana, where he died, leaving a family and widow. Miles Hunt, his youngest son, laid out and platted the village of Huntsville, expecting at some future time it would become the county seat. His family were eleven in number, seven boys and four girls. All the

children married when of age and settled as follows: Three of the girls, Malinda Keever, Rachel Stevenson and Caroline Okerson, were all married in Randolph county, Indiana, and moved to Nodaway county, Missouri, with their husbands. Also John C. Hunt, who married Emma Lane in Atchison county, Missouri, and is an attorney of no mean standing in Rockport, the county seat of Atchison county. William Tipton Hunt was married on the same date as was our subject, to Celestine Baum, daughter of Charles Baum, of Vermilion county, Illinois. He died at Oklahoma City while a juryman of the United States court in the Indian Territory, April 15, 1891. His wife returned to Vermilion county, Illinois, and died July 3, 1893.

Miles Hunt, the father, departed this life in Logan county at the home of his youngest son, Alonzo, in Oklahoma Territory, on December 14, 1893. James D. Hunt, his son, now resides in Oklahoma county, that Territory. Miles Hunt's wife died April 10, 1895, in Logan county, Indian Territory, and is at rest by the side of her husband. Bezelleel and Henry C. Hunt both enlisted in the Sixty-ninth Indiana Regiment in 1862. Henry C. was wounded at the battle of Richmond, Kentucky, and Bezelleel, remaining with him, was taken prisoner, but was paroled. Both were afterward married, but first studied medicine and became M. D.'s. Henry lives in Montpelier, Blackford county, Indiana, and has a lucrative practice. Bezelleel died in Douglas county, Illinois, in August, 1869, leaving a widow, whose maiden name was Branham. Sarah J. married Leander McMillen, of Pennsylvania, who was also a physician. He died leaving one son, Bennett H. The widow afterward married a man of Vermilion county, Illinois, Benjamin Dickson by name. There were seven of Miles Hunt's children who taught school, VIZ.: O. P., William T., Henry C., B. T., J. C., A. L. and Sarah Jane. (See new history of Indiana by the Hon. W. H. English.)

Our subject, O. T. Hunt, received a common-school education, unlike the common schools of the present day, as in his early boyhood schools were secured by subscription. His father would pay the tuition of five scholars and send but one or two in order to secure a teacher. Often men with no children to send to school would pay the tuition of a scholar to induce some one who could read and write to teach. The old elementary spelling book was the text book, with some reading in it, with the stories of "the man's ox that had been gored by his neighbor's" and the "boy in the apple tree." The primary class constituted the A B C divisions (with the alphabet torn from the spelling book and pasted on a paddle to protect and preserve it). When one had mastered the old elementary spelling book, grammar and arithmetic, writing and geography were studies the parents could choose from, any or all of them. The old English reader was indispensible, and all who had thoroughly mastered the spelling book must read in it, which was not suitable to the condition of the children. As well had them enter the Latin class of to-day, as there was not half of the words the children knew the meaning of, while the facilities of to-day are much improved as the child climbs step by step and is expected to master every study. Yet we are pained to see the graduate who, parrot-like, can only repeat what he has thoroughly committed—"Polly wants her breakfast." The greatest trouble, we think, especially in the common schools, is with the teachers. A child recites well when it recites by rote or has committed the language of the author. This is no test, only of memory; it does not show that the student has any thought of his own, or that he understands the recitation he recites. Hence, while life at best is short, the main object should be in teaching anything to stimulate and draw out of the child all the reasoning powers, and you have laid a foundation that is everlasting when the child has learned that the first and great step in an education is for one to think for himself.

Now as to the subject. O. T. Hunt's mother was a daughter of Hugh M. Botkin, of Scotch descent, a native of Tennessee, who settled near Winchester, Indiana, in an early day, with his family, where many of his descendants are now living. William Botkin, one of his sons, owns and lives on the farm his father first settled on in Indiana. When O. T. Hunt arrived at manhood he taught his first school in Huntsville, Randolph county, his own brothers and sisters attending the school, and he says they gave him more trouble than all the rest of the scholars, and if it had not been for his father he expects he would have had to give up the school; but between them they settled down to business. He commenced the study of law when only twenty years old, read Blackstone's Commentaries, and in 1855 he bought Kent's Commentaries, Parson on Contracts, Greenleaf on Evidence and Gould's Pleading. In 1856 he went to Vermilion county, Illinois, and taught school, studied at his spare times his text-books, and taught school in that State over two years. He returned to Randolph county in 1858 and on motion of Judge Jeremiah Smith he was admitted to the Randolph county bar to practice law. He then went back to Illinois and married Eliza J. McDowell on September 1, 1859, and returned to Randolph county, Indiana, where he and his wife both taught a winter term of school. In the spring they went to Illinois, where he rented a farm near Indianola, in Vermilion county, and in 1862, when Lincoln revoked the order of Gens. Hunter and Fremont, saying he did not have the constitutional right to free the slaves of the south, Hunt concluded to raise a company. He called two or three meetings and secured quite a number of names near Indianola, in Vermilion county, Illinois, and went to Danville and reported to Governor Yates. At this time George W. Cook, of Catlin, Illinois, learning of the matter, went to see Hunt, as he had quite a number of men enlisted, and they consolidated and were made Company K, of the One Hundred and Twenty-fifth Regiment of Illinois Volunteers. Cook was made captain of the company, O. T. Hunt, first lieutenant, and Franklin Crosby, second lieutenant, and O. T. Harmon, colonel of the regiment. The latter lost his life at the charge of Kenesaw Mountain, after which Hunt commanded the company (hence the appellation "Captain"), and the Captain played major. The regiment was mustered in at Danville, Illinois, on the 3d day of September, 1862, and served during the war. The regiment went with Sherman to the sea (Savannah, Georgia), thence to Richmond, and the muster-out rolls were made out at Washington City, D. C. They were dated June 9, 1865, but were not delivered to the men until the latter part of June, when the regiment was paid off at Chicago and disbanded. Hunt bought a Peter Schutler lumber wagon in Chicago and returned to his family in Vermilion county. His wife, a daughter of John B. McDowell, a native of Kentucky, inherited of her grandfather, David Yarnell, one hundred acres of land in Douglas county, Illinois, and Hunt improved the same, and through their economy and industry added thereto three hundred and fifteen acres of land, making a total of four hundred and fifteen acres of land in Douglas county. After Oklahoma Territory was opened up he went to that country and bought two claims of George Grant and his brother, or one half-section, within ten or twelve miles of Oklahoma City. But he claims his environments and the war spoiled a good lawyer. He was commander of the McCowan Post, of Camargo, Grand Army of the Republic. That order growing weak, he surrendered the charter and joined the Frank Reed Post, of Tuscola, and is also or has been a member of the Grange. But he is opposed to secret political organization, as he says the Knownothing party of 1852-1854 killed the old Whig party, and any party that will not bear the light of day and free discussion is dangerous to a free and independent government. He is a Stephen A. Douglas Democrat, as are the rest of his father's family, while all his near relatives are Republicans, or have been. He takes a lively interest in politics and the success of his party, making the race twice for state's attorney and once for county judge with credit to himself.

WILLIAM HEATON.

William Heaton is one of the old landmarks of the county. For over half a century he has been an active and successful man of affairs, and at the age of eighty-three is still attending to business. He was born in Greene county, Pennsylvania, July 24, 1817, and is a son of Samuel and Margaret (Rose) Heaton, who were also born in Greene county, Pennsylvania. His grandfather, John Rose, and President McKinley's grandmother were cousins. William Heaton (grandfather) was a native of New Jersey, born September 16, 1764, and fought under Andrew Jackson at the battle of New Orleans. His wife, Abigail, was born August 28, 1767. John Rose, his maternal grandfather, was an early settler near Clarksville, Greene county, Pennsylvania, and owned a distillery, and in the words of Mr. Heaton was a great inventor, as he could draw five kinds of liquor out of the same barrel, and neither he nor any of his sons were ever known to be drunk either. He and his five sons were also opposed to drinking; in that early day there were no organization known as the Prohibition party, but principally Democrats and Whigs. William Hea-

ton's father grew quite wealthy for that day, but lost it by going on other people's bonds. He removed to New Washington, Ohio, where he died. His mother died in Greene county.

William Heaton received a moderate education in his younger days and worked hard on the farm. In 1838 he married Mary Hedge, a daughter of Jacob Hedge, of Greene county. Jacob Hedge was a good citizen, a good farmer, but never had opportunities to sit in the state Legislature. William Heaton's wife died in 1886. To them were born seven children. His second and present wife is a most agreeable companion for him in his old age. She is a cousin of his first wife. Mr. Heaton has been a very successful trader and has probably bought and sold more land than any man in the county. For several years he kept a land office at Des Moines, Iowa, and paid twelve thousand dollars out of his own pocket toward the removal of the state capital from Iowa City to Des Moines. He laid the foundation for the Adair County Bank at Greenfield, Iowa, which is now owned and managed by his son, D. D. Heaton. He is now passing the sunset of life near the Pleasant Ridge church, in North Newman township, where he still enjoys life, and appreciates a good story as well as he ever did. While in Iowa he was a political disciple of James B. Weaver and E. H. Gelette, serving as delegate to conventions and in other ways adding strength to the cause. He hopes to live to vote for William J. Bryan this fall. In the neighborhood in which he resides he is something of a political freak, as nearly everybody around him believes most devotedly in an honest dollar and the constitution.

STRODER M. LONG.

Stroder McNeal Long, who was the second president of the Bank of Newman, Illinois, was born in Fayette county, Ohio, October 6, 1840, emigrated with his parents to the state of Illinois in 1848 and located on a farm nine miles north of Paris, in Edgar county. He is a son of Andrew and Margaret (Mark) Long, who were natives of Ohio. He worked on his father's farm in the summer and attended school in the winter until 1860, when he commenced an academic course at Paris, Illinois. In the year following the Civil war broke out, and he enlisted in Company E, Twelfth Illinois Infantry. After three

months' service, on account of a severe spell of sickness, he was honorably discharged and returned home. He engaged in farming and school teaching until the spring of 1867, when he moved to Douglas county, where he purchased eighty acres of land on South Prairie, three miles south of Newman. He remained here until 1880, making farming and stock raising a specialty. He represented Sargent two terms on the county board of supervisors, 1878-79. In 1884 he was elected a member of the Thirty-fourth General Assembly of the state by a large majority in the district. His fidelity to party as well as to the people's interest, his sterling integrity and rectitude of purpose, won for him the appointment by the Republican caucas a member of the advisory committee that directed the party on all political questions. He was a member of the committees on education, farm drainage, house contingent expense, state and municipal indebtedness and canals and rivers. When he retired from the house of representatives at the close of the session he had made a host of friends and few enemies. In 1898 he was again nominated by his party of the fortieth senatorial district, but his death occurred before the election. In the spring of 1888 he succeeded I. N. Covert as president of the Newman Bank, which position he held most acceptably to all parties concerned up to 1898, the time of his death. He was one of the promoters of the organization of the Newman Building & Loan Association, and was one of its prominent and ruling directors. He was also a charter member of Templestone lodge, No. 76, Knights of Pythias, and an enthusiastic worker in that order. Mr. Long was a shrewd business man, straightforward, upright and capable. During the World's Fair he was a member of the board of congress from Illinois.

In 1872 our subject married Mary E. Pound, of Newman, Illinois. She is a daughter of John M. and Rosalinda (Kester) Pound, the former born in Clark county, Indiana, and the latter in Shelby county, Kentucky. To Mr. and Mrs. Long were born five children: Mabel M., wife of Henry A. Wine, of Indianapolis, Indiana; Potter P., married and residing on his farm south of Newman; Garnet A., wife of William McGee, of Mattoon, Illinois; Cecile R. and Fay E. reside with their mother. Mrs. Long and children own seven hundred acres of land, one hundred and twenty acres of which lies in Edgar county, also other valuable city property. She has recently completed one of the most imposing and beautiful residences in Newman.

JOSEPH S. WILLIAMSON.

Joseph S. Williamson, one of the leading farmers and most favorably known citizens of Douglas county, was born August 22, 1840, near Muncie, Indiana. He is a son of Peter

Williamson and Rosana, his wife. His father was born in Portsmouth, Ohio, and his mother in Germany. His paternal grandfather, Joseph Williamson, was a native of New Jersey, and his maternal grandfather, John Adams Shaffer, came from Germany.

Joseph S. Williamson was reared and educated in Muncie. In early life he taught school during the winters and worked upon the farm in crop time, after which he spent three years with a New York dry-goods firm. In 1865 he came to this state and located in Tuscola, where he was successfully engaged in the mercantile business in partnership with the late C. W. Calvert for six years. In 1870 he returned to Indiana and located at Mount Summit, where he was engaged in mercantile business. In 1876 he returned to Douglas county, where he has been engaged in agriculture and stock raising on the present farm, containing one hundred and sixty acres, and which is one of the best improved farms in the county. He has been twice married. His first wife, Miss Rebecca Ice, who died in 1875, was a daughter of Colonel Jesse Ice, of the war of 1812, and Sarah Ice, whose maiden name was Hickman. There were born to their marriage five children. The living are: Jesse Peter, Francis Eugene and Joseph Alva. Deceased: James and Andrew. His second wife, Miss Frances R. L. Kinsey, is a daughter of the late Joseph Kinsey and Josina, his wife, who was also a daughter of the above Col. Jesse Ice. To their marriage were born six children. The living are: Pearl May, Harry K., Earle W., William L. and Mira Marie. Deceased, George L.

Mr. Williamson, while a resident of Tuscola, was identified with the board of education, a member of the board of aldermen, and, though never an office seeker, has filled many other positions of honor and trust. In all these public capacities he has been faithful, and by his careful study of the political principles of our country and his deep interest in education has proved his devotion and interest in the common welfare of the people. For some time his health has not been good and the past winter he and Mrs. Williamson spent in Florida in search of health. Socially Mr. Williamson is agreeable and companionable and has many friends who appreciate his worth as a neighbor and Christian gentleman.

CALEB GARRETT.

Caleb Garrett, son of Isam and Mary (Puckett) Garrett, was born in Clinton county, Ohio, on the 6th of July, 1816. In 1819 the family moved to Randolph county, Indiana, and, in 1823, to Vigo county, in the same state,

where they remained until the final removal to Illinois. Whilst in the former state, the residence of the family was generally on the

Fort Harrison prairie and about four miles south of Terre Haute. Caleb was about seven years old when the family resided near the latter place. He was educated at a subscription school; his father being a man of education, he progressed under home instruction and learned rapidly. In 1830 his mother died in Vigo county, Indiana, and for several years thereafter Mr. Isam Garrett and his two sons, Caleb and Nathan, kept house for themselves. In these days Caleb drove an ox team for L. H. Scott; he worked in the corn field for twenty-five cents a day, and made fence rails at from twenty to thirty cents per hundred, averaging one hundred and fifty for a day's work. He went into the printing business at the office of the Western Register in Terre Haute under Judge Amery Kinney and John W. Osborn, the proprietors of the office. Mr. Garrett returned to farming for awhile, and also worked as a carpenter and builder under Dr. Thomas Parsons, and having finally resolved to think and act for himself he returned to his favorite pursuits, farming and stock-raising, making success in them the object of his future life. He was for several years a tenant of Chauncey Rose, the well-known millionaire, for whom at the outset he worked at the ordinary occupation of a farm hand, during which time he made thousands of rails at the then usual very small compensation; and here began between the two men a warm personal regard, which was only terminated by the death of Mr. Rose. In 1833, in the company of George Jordan, the father of I. L. Jordan, of Tuscola, and of Levi Westfall, an uncle of R. E. H. Westfall, of Garrett township, and also with a Kentucky friend, Mr. Garrett passed through this portion of Illinois, partly to indulge his love of adventure and partly to look up a location for a future home. The trip began at Terre Haute, by Baldwin's store, in Edgar county, Sadorus Grove, and into Springfield, Beardstown and Quincy, then a wild, sparsely settled country. Mr. Garrett returned to Terre Haute by way of Meredosia, on the Illinois river, to Springfield and Decatur. From 1833 to 1839, pursuing his natural bent for exploration and adventure, he followed flat-boating down the Wabash, the Ohio and the Mississippi to New Orleans. The boats, made generally by the owner, were from eighty to one hundred and twenty feet long, and were laden to the gunwale with corn, pork and other produce. In 1840 he started from Terre Haute bound for New Orleans per steamer, and upon reaching the Wabash rapids they were run upon the rocks by a drunken pilot. Garrett and two others hired a skiff, and, crossing the river to Mt. Carmel, Illinois, they chartered a hack and repaired to Evansville, at which point they took the large river steamer Louisiana with two companions, one bound for the mouth of the Cumberland, the other for the Tennessee. After a tedious voyage he arrived at New Orleans, took a steamship and passed out to the gulf, and after a very stormy passage arrived safely at Galveston. He went thence to Houston, and there failing to get a conveyance, started on foot through Texas. He arrived at a house where he was offered and accepted the use of a pony. The next day he was presented with a horse by a Dr. Heard, and proceeding got into the vicinity of hostile Indians. He became for the nonce a Texas ranger, in which capacity he experienced considerable fighting with the Indians. In Travis county, Texas, Mr. Garrett married Miss Irene Puckett, a daughter of Thomas Puckett. With her he left Texas in an ox wagon loaded with pecans and dry hides. They arrived at Houston and took a steamer to Galveston, and thence to New Orleans, and by the Mississippi to Evansville, Indiana, landing March 5, 1841; they shortly after arrived in Vigo county, that being the county in which his wife was born. Mrs. Irene Garrett has always been remarkable for an open-handed liberality toward her less fortunate neighbors, which dispensed generally from her own private means earned her the blessings of the poor. In Vigo county Mr. Garrett returned to farming and stock-raising, during which time, about 1842, he was elected to the Indiana state legislature, and at the succeeding term was re-elected. In 1845 he made his second trip to Illinois, and in 1846 bought land in the west part of Tuscola township, near the present farm of William Brian. He finally sold this land and located in the forks of the creek on section 3, township 15, range 7. He also selected one hundred and sixty acres of land, being lots 2 and 3 in the northeast quarter of section 3, township 15, range 7, and hewed a set of walnut logs for a home. In 1856 Mr. and Mrs. Garrett revisited Texas, including a long trip in a carriage by Price's Springs and Brazos Falls in Cherokee county, where he examined lands; thence to Palestine and Marshall, from which place they went forty miles to Shreveport, Louisiana, thence by steamer to the mouth of Red river, and by a similar conveyance to Evansville, Indiana, reaching home November 8, 1856, which was then Coles county. He then began improving his lands with orchards, barns and dwellings. Mr. Garrett's lands in Garrett township at one time covered nineteen hundred acres. In 1875 he sold these lands and reinvested in Tuscola township, having concluded to settle in Tuscola City. He was the first supervisor of Garrett township, which had been instituted with the other townships in 1868, and he was also a member of the first grand jury in Douglas county. Mr. Garrett always took a deep interest in all the public affairs of Douglas county.

WILLIAM HOWE.

History first relates of William Howe grandfather of the late William Howe, as a native of Virginia. Whether this is correct, we are not able to say. But he afterward emi-

grated to Kentucky when it was yet a wilderness. He formed a member of Daniel Boone's first colony and participated in the dangers incident to "the dark and bloody ground." His son, George W. Howe, was born in Kentucky and there married Angeline Hildreth, a native of that state, but of English descent also, and in Bourbon county, Kentucky, William Howe, Jr., was born on November 23, 1829.

In 1832 George Howe and family emigrated to the southeastern part of Missouri. On the breaking out of the Black Hawk war he joined the forces sent against the Indians, and was supposed to have been killed by them near Galena, Illinois, for no word came from him afterward. The mother then moved with her children, five in number, back to her old home in Kentucky in 1835. Here she stayed for three years, when she and her family moved to Vermilion county, Illinois, arriving there on the 6th of April, 1838. Mr. Howe was at this time nine years old. He continued with his mother for almost two years, when he was indentured to the service of William J. West, who resided on a farm in Sargent township. It was in the spring of 1840 when he first came to West's and he remained with him nine years, till in his twentieth year, in the spring of 1849. During this time his board was the only compensation he received for his service. He was signed to school about thirteen months, but out of this he only received about nine months' regular schooling, and this was scattered over a long period of years so as to be of but little service. The good general education he possessed was principally picked up by his own ingenious industry. After his term of service with Mr. West had expired he worked a year by the month, still having his headquarters at West's. At this time the excitement consequent upon the discovery of gold in California was spreading over the country. Mr. Howe, as we have seen, comes from an adventurous race of men, his earlier ancestors having fought gallantly for King George, while his later ones had many a skirmish with the Indians, his father dying by their hands, and led by the same spirit of adventure and hardihood he determined to try his fortunes in the new El Dorado. In March, 1850, in company with West and others, eleven in all, he started overland for California. Before starting all promised that unless in case of illness none should be allowed to ride, and on all that long and rough journey Mr. Howe kept his place by the side of the oxen. The spring of 1850 was one of deep mud and high water, so their journey was made doubly difficult. The party passed through Quincy and across the state of Missouri, following very nearly the same route now traversed by the Hannibal & St. Jo railroad. The Missouri river in the southwest corner of the state of Iowa was crossed; the northern route was taken, through the South Pass of the Rocky Mountains; north of Salt Lake; by the Oregon trail to the Soda Springs; then over to the St. Mary's river, down which they traveled to the Sink. The Sierra Nevadas were crossed by the Carson trail, and the party arrived August 27, 1850, at Nebberville, only losing, in accomplishing the journey, one man, who died of disease and whom they buried by the way. The men went to mining gold in this region. Mr. Howe remained nine months, during which time he got together a considerable quantity of gold dust. The Klamath excitement then came up and he joined a party to go to Oregon. His experience here was very adventurous, but there were no flattering results. In company with two others, he was robbed by a party of Modoc Indians. He lost about twelve hundred dollars, including everything he had, even to a greater part of his clothing. He returned to the mines on the Yuba river in destitute condition, without clothes or money. Here prospects brightened, the gold panning out sometimes to the amount of eighty dollars a day. But he could only remain two weeks. High water came and Mr. Howe went to California, where he followed "teaming" from Stockton out to the mines and during his eighteen months sojourn here he accumulated some money. In 1853 he decided to return to Illinois, and in February of the same year he left California, taking a vessel from San Francisco, crossing the Isthmus of Panama, sailing from there to New Orleans, then up the Mississippi to his old home in Coles county, as it then was. During his three years stay in California he learned the Spanish language and could converse fluently in it.

Mr. Howe now turned his attention to the peaceful pursuit of agriculture, hoping in that 1853, he married Harriett Anne Lester, a na- 1853, he married Harriett Anne Lister, a native of Douglas, whose ancestors, like those of Mr. Howe, were of English and Kentucky blood and birth. In December he started his long and prosperous career as a farmer, and at the time of his death he was in the possession of almost eighteen hundred acres of land in the neighborhood of his residence. Hunting was his favorite amusement, and every year he made a trip to Kansas, Colorado and Arkansas, where he indulged in the exciting sport. He was celebrated for his skill as a marksman and seldom failed to bring down his game.

He was the father of eight children: James M., who now resides on a large farm in Nebraska; John S., living now on the old homestead; Perry N., who lives, also, on part of his father's farm; Mary E., wife of James Drennen, living on an Iowa farm; Charles R., residing on the first farm that Mr. Howe owned; Effie A., wife of James C. Reed, a lawyer in Kansas City; Leona M., wife of William Joseph, assistant manager in the firm of Bradley Manufacturing Company; and Lora A., who lives with her mother in Tuscola. William Howe died January 27, 1892, at his country home near Ficklin.

JAMES DREW.

James Drew one of the earliest pioneers in the western part of Douglas county, and also one of the largest land owners, is a native of the state, having been born in Hamilton county, Illinois, on the 14th of June, 1819. He came to

the territory now embraced in Douglas county in 1839, and continued to reside on the place of his first location until his death in 1894.

The Drew family, from which Mr. Drew has his descent, formerly resided in South Carolina, where John Drew, the father of James Drew, was born. The maiden name of his mother was Tempy Farmer, and she was also a resident of South Carolina. The family afterward removed to Indiana, and then to Illinois, settling in Hamilton county. Here James Drew was born on the date given above. When about four years old the family moved north to Shelby county. The children were nine in number, five boys and four girls, only two of whom are now dead. After the family had lived in Shelby county about eight years, then moved to Coles county, south of Charleston. The principal part of his education Mr. Drew received in this county. He attended a common country school, held in an old shanty, with a fire-place occupying nearly all of one end. The most of the children were without hats and went barefoot in winter. Mr. Drew's father was a farmer, and kept the boys at home a great deal of the time to work on the farm. After a residence in Coles county of some years the family moved back to Shelby, this time making their home in the territory afterward embraced in Moultrie county on its formation. Mr. Drew was now about eighteen years of age. He stayed at home part of two years, one summer going to Galena, and working in the lead mines there. No money could be obtained at this period for farm labor, and the lead mines offered the only opportunity for obtaining ready cash. While employed here he received twenty dollars a month and board. In the year 1839 his father took a job of making rails for one Jacob Taylor, probably the first settler in what is now Garrett township, and James agreed to give his assistance. He was now old enough to do for himself, and with the same foresight and business tact which has marked his subsequent career, he was on the lookout to secure land for himself. Land could be obtained in that part of Coles county where Taylor lived, and young Drew embraced the first opportunity of settling. He entered eighty acres of land at the government price of one dollar and twenty-five cents an acre, borrowing one hundred dollars of Taylor to make the purchase, and agreeing to discharge the debt partly in day's labor. Mr. Drew's present house stands on the original land entered. His brother and brother-in-law each entered eighty acres at the same time, and the whole amount came into the possession of Mr. Drew. It was the close of the year 1839 when Mr. Drew first came into the county, and the next spring he bought his land. He put up a split log cabin on the premises and lived with his brother-in-law. All the time he could spare for improving the property he devoted in paying off the debt of one hundred dollars, which was finally accomplished in three years. A good portion was worked out by labor, at fifty cents a day. There were only four families in the neighborhood at the time of Mr. Drew's settlement. For thirty miles to the west, in the direction of Decatur, there was not a single house. The prairies were all unoccupied, covered with tall grass and resin weeds, over which roamed deer and prairie wolves.

After living with his brother-in-law for a couple of years, Mr. Drew concluded to go to keeping house for himself, and married Angeline Waller, a native of Hamilton county, but who at the time of the marriage lived in Shelby. Mr. Drew was then twenty-three and his wife about twenty. Mr. Drew had early learned industrious habits, and from his childhood knew the meaning of hard work. By his industry and frugality he won success, investing his surplus capital in land and adding from time to time as opportunity offered. Farming was the pursuit to which he directed his whole energies and ever since his residence in the county he has given considerable attention to raising and feeding stock.

Mr. Drew's first wife died in 1855, and he subsequently married, on the 13th of October, 1857, Miss Martha L. Baker.

EUGENE RICE.

Eugene Rice, ex-member of the Legislature and a man of considerable prominence throughout the county, was born in Madison county,

Kentucky, March 22, 1848. He is a son of Martin Rice, who was one of the most widely and favorably known of the early settlers of Camargo, and whose sketch with ancestry of the family is printed in full on another page. Mr. Rice came to the township with his parents in 1854 and resides at present on the old homestead. He is extensively engaged in farming and stock raising and is known as one of the most successful farmers in Douglas county. In 1887 and 1889 he was elected to the Legislature from the district composed of Coles, Cumberland and Douglas counties, as a Republican. He served on several committees—federal relations, agriculture, penitentiaries, fish and game, contingent expenses, drainage, live stock and dairy, printing and others—and during the extra session helped to pass the World's Fair bill.

Mr. Rice has never married, and resides on his beautiful farm within a half hour's ride from the village of Camargo, where he entertains his friends and enjoys life. As a member of the Legislature he was conscientious and a hard worker in the interest especially of the farmer, who it has, it seems, been sadly neglected as to legislation in both state and nation.

D. O. ROOT.

D. O. Root, second son and third child of Levi and Polly Root, was born in Decatur township, Washington county, Ohio, September 24, 1834. His father was a native of Livingston county, New York, and was born April 9, 1809. He came with his mother and stepfather to Washington county, Ohio, soon after the close of the second war with the mother country, in which war his own father had been a soldier, and died just at its close. The mother of the subject of this sketch, whose maiden name was Stewart, was born upon the farm upon which now stands the village of Stewart, in Athens county, Ohio, March 7, 1809, and her mortal remains are sleeping in a cemetery near that village, upon the old Stewart farm, less than one-fourth of a mile from the place where she was born. She died in May, 1857. Her father, Daniel Stewart, born in November, 1762, in Litchfield, Connecticut, was a soldier in the continental army in the war of the Revolution. He came to Ohio in 1802, and died upon the farm he then settled upon, in 1859, of an accident, and not of disease or old age, though he was in his ninety-

eighth year. The parents of our subject removed from Washington county to Athens county, same state, when he was a mere infant, and settled on the Big Hockhocking (now abbreviated into simply Hocking) river, just below the village of Stewart. Here he spent the first twenty years of his life, except two years—1852-53—during which he was a student in the Ohio Wesleyan University at Delaware, Ohio. Failing health caused him to quit school before graduation.

After arriving at sufficient age, when not in school—the common and select—he was engaged in the ordinary farm work, in a woolen factory and as clerk in a country store of general merchandise. At the age of twenty he left the parental home for good and struck out for himself and for the west as well. He landed in what is now Douglas county—then Coles—October 17, 1854. It may be of some interest to the younger generation, at least, as showing the difference in the mode of travel then and now, to state that the first thirteen miles of Mr. Root's westward journey—from the home he was just leaving to old Athens—was made in a common road wagon; from Athens to Lancaster, forty-five miles, in a canal boat, towed by horses, and twenty-three consecutive hours were consumed in making this distance. From Lancaster to Terre Haute, Indiana, via Cincinnati and Indianapolis, by rail. And, by the way, it was the only route by which it could, at that time, have been made by rail. From Terre Haute to Paris, Illinois, was on a construction train, on the old I. & St. L. R. R., its track having just been completed as far west as that point. From Paris to Oakland the trip was made in an old time "hack" or "stage coach," which was then run from Terre Haute westward, on the old Springfield "trace," passing through Oakland, then locally known as Pinhook. During the winter of 1854-5 Mr. Root taught a term of school at "Catfish Point," near where the village of Isabel, in Edgar county, now stands. For this he received the sum of twenty-five dollars per month, an amount considered rather extraordinary for the times.

In the spring of 1855—April 5—he was united in marriage with Mrs. Sarah Winkler, the widow of Charles V. Winkler, who had been a prosperous farmer and an old settler on the Brushy Fork timber. He died in June, 1854, leaving, besides his widow, two children, Vashti, who became the wife of L. E. Root, a brother of our subject, and who is now deceased, and Luther, who is one of Newman's enterprising farmers and stock raisers The latter occupies the old farm entered and improved by his grandfather and father, to which he has made various and substantial additions and improvements. After his marriage Mr. Root settled upon this same farm and remained on it until the fall of 1873, after his election to the office of county clerk. To Mr. and Mrs. Root there were born nine children, five sons and four daughters: Harriet E., January 10, 1855; Edward T., November 6, 1857; Ornon L., July 3, 1860; Rosecrans, November 2, 1862; Leula, October 9, 1864; Pitner, November 26, 1866, and died September 25, 1867; Isabelle, January 12, 1868; Mary, April 13, 1869; a son, unnamed, September 30, 1873, died October 3, 1873. Edward T., oldest son died December 23, 1892, unmarried, in the thirty-seventh year of his age. Hattie F. has been mistress of her father's house and, as nearly as it is possible for any but a real mother to be, a mother to the other children ever since the death of her mother, in October, 1881, while the family resided in Tuscola.

In July, 1861, Mr. Root entered the service of his country, in the war of the Rebellion, and became a member of Company H, Twenty-Fifth Regiment Illinois Volunteer Infantry, and served until October, 1862, when, his health failing, he was discharged for disability From 1868 to 1873 he was four times elected the assessor of his (Newman) township. In November, 1873, he was elected to the office of county clerk, re-elected in 1877, and, by reason of a change in the constitution of the state, an extra year was added to this term, which expired in 1882, making in all nine years. Shortly after his retirement from office, and while on the lookout for some permanent business, he entered the store of F. M. Friend & Son, of Tuscola, as a clerk, remaining until February, 1884, at which time he bought a half interest in the large general store of James Gillogly, of Newman, forming the firm of Gillogly & Root. Four years thereafter L. E. Root, a brother of D. O. Root, bought Mr. G.'s interest in the firm and it was changed to Root Bros. The firm is still in business, occupying a large two-story brick on the north side of the square, fronting on Yates street and extending north to Mathers street, with a rear entrance on same. It is the leading firm in the city. Mr. Root is a member of the M. E. church of long standing, having entered its fold in January, 1851. He is a Freemason and a Knight Templar; has also taken all the degrees in Odd Fellowship except the uniform rank, and is a member of the K. of H. and of H. & L. of H. orders.

The family to which Mr. Root belongs is in some respects remarkable. To his parents there were born twelve children, eight boys and four girls, of whom eleven are living, one son having been killed fighting for the flag in the war of 1861-5, at Perryville, Ky., in October, 1862. These children were all born between 1831 and 1852. His mother, as has before been noted herein, died in 1857, and in 1862 his father remarried. From this union one son was born, making the family to-day consist of the original number, eight boys and four girls, the youngest thirty-seven years of age, the eldest near seventy. Six of the boys were in the Union army during the Rebellion, five returning. All served three full years except the subject of this sketch. Few families can show such a record.

JOHN QUINN.

John Quinn, private banker, grain dealer, and one of the most successful young business men of the county, located in Fairland in 1884 as a grain agent for the firm of Barnett, Kuhn & Company, of Terre Haute, Indiana. He is

still associated with this firm, handling in the neighborhood of one hundred thousand bushels per year.

Mr. Quinn was born in Union county, Ohio, February 15, 1863, and there he remained until he was six years of age, when his parents removed to Champaign county. He is a son of Patrick and Bridget Quinn, who were natives of Ireland. His father is retired from active business and resides at Philo, Illinois. John Quinn was reared on the farm and received the advantages only of the neighboring schools. In 1899 he founded the Fairland Exchange Bank, which is his own private institution. As a business man he is known to be careful, safe, and possessed of sterling integrity. In 1890 he was united in marriage to Miss Sarah F. Suddeth, a native of Edgar county and a member of a Kentucky family. They have three children: Otis, Anna and Cecil. Mr. Quinn owns eighty acres of land northeast of Fairland, five miles distant. He is a charter member of the Woodmen, and is also a member of the Court of Honor.

SCOTT BURGETT.

Scott Burgett, the proprietor of the Newman Bank and one of the successful financiers and business men of Illinois, was born in Brushy Fork, this county, September 14, 1857, and is a son of the late I. W. Burgett, whose sketch is found upon another page of this book. During the summer months Scott Burgett worked upon his father's farm and in winter attended the district school. When about seventeen years of age he entered Lee's Academy at Loxa, Illinois, and after leaving that institution went to the state normal at

Normal, Illinois, where he completed his education. After returning home he taught three terms of school in the Coffey district, in Sargent township, and much of his success as a teacher he claims he owes to his life-long friend, W. H. Coffey. In March, 1879, he entered the large dry-goods house of James Gillogly in Newman as bookkeeper and head salesman, with whom he remained until 1884, when he, with I. N. Covert, established the Newman Bank. Mr. Covert retired from

active business in 1888 and was succeeded to the presidency by S. M. Long, who remained president until his death. From that time, August 20, 1898, to the present, it has been the private property of Mr. Burgett. In the bank's management he is assisted by J. W. King and George Moore.

September 2, 1879, he was married to Miss Alice V. Hopkins, daughter of the late James Hopkins, who was one of the prominent pioneers of Douglas county. They have had six children, five of whom are living: Jay T., Bessie M., Eva O., Paul H. and Charles C., and James is deceased.

Scott Burgett's business ventures have been thoroughly successful and he has the absolute confidence of the entire public. He owns some of the fine lands in both Newman and Sargent townships, and his real estate holdings in Newman are large. He is treasurer of the Newman Building & Loan Association, is a member of the Methodist Episcopal church, is a Royal Arch Mason and is a member of the order of Knights of Pythias. At present he is erecting what will be the finest residence in Newman, costing some six or eight thousand dollars. Quiet and unassuming in his manners, he treats all alike, the poor man as he does his rich neighbors, and counts his acquaintances as his friends. In all the relations of life he has been true to his duty as he has seen it, and in business and in society a well-deserved success has come to him as a reward of earnest industry and his upright dealings with his fellow men.

A. HAYWARD.

A. Hayward, who has been the railroad station and ticket agent at Camargo for twenty-three years, was born near Belfast, Ireland, November 23, 1849, and was reared to manhood in the neighborhood of Cranbrook, county Kent, England, where he attended the ordinary school of that day. He is a son of Benjamin Hayward, who was a member and organist of the Church of England at Inch, near Belfast, Ireland. He was a fine musician, playing both organ and violin with great proficiency. His father died in 1855. His mother, who was, before she was married, Margaret Carr, was a native of county Down, Ireland, and was reared near Belfast. His great-grandfather, John Hayward, was an exceedingly wealthy man, and because his sons were of dissolute habits he bequeathed his

wealth to charity, and it is known to this day as the Hayward charity fund, so much of which is given out each year by the parish of Cranbrook to the poor of the parish. His maternal grandfather, Edward Carr, was born in Scotland.

A. Hayward came to this country in 1870, and after spending three months in Syracuse came direct to Tuscola, where he followed the painter's trade and remained here six years. He soon afterward learned the telegraph business and located in Camargo.

In 1880 our subject was wedded to Miss Julia O'Connor, a step-daughter of Martin Cogley. They have one daughter, Mary Elizabeth, who is nineteen years of age. He is a member of the Court of Honor and at present holds the office of chancellor. Mr. Hayward owns a pleasant home in Camargo, besides eighty acres of land in Murdock township. He has been town clerk of Camargo for six years and was secretary of the Douglas county fair for ten years. He was also assistant general superintendent of the state fair in 1897-98, and served as a delegate to the Court of Honor for Douglas county, which met in Springfield in 1899. He has made his own way in the business world and at present occupies an enviable position in the affairs of Douglas county.

CHARLES S. SANFORD.

Charles S. Sandford, of Tuscola, Illinois, is the son of Isaac and Belinda (Foster) Sandford. The father was born at Bridgehamton, Long Island, in 1796, and married Belinda Foster, who was born in Hamilton county, Ohio, in 1798. The progenitor of the Sandfords on Long Island first settled near Boston, Massachusetts, in the year 1640. This branch of the family tree has had numerous descendants, identified with important movements at an early day in the history of Long Island. Many of them participated in the battle of Long Island, and some of them were minute men. Isaac Sandford emigrated to Edgar county, Illinois, in 1820. He served as captain in the Black Hawk war and was later commissioned as brigadier-general of the state militia by Governor Reynolds in 1833. He held that position for fifteen years, after which time he resigned. General Sandford was a man of great financial ability and remarkable

energy. At the time of his death, in 1853, he was one of the wealthiest men in Edgar county.

Charles S. Sandford's maternal grandfather, Luke Foster, was one of the associate judges of Hamilton county, Ohio. He was born at Riverhead, Long Island. The Fosters settled on Long Island as early as the Sandfords.

C. S. Sandford grew to manhood on the farm; attended school at Edgar Academy, at Paris, Illinois, and afterward for a time at Greencastle (Indiana) Asbury University—now known as the DePauw University. In 1855 he was married to Susan J. Judson, a native of Connecticut. Her girlhood home was in Vicksburg, Mississippi, but her later education was received at Steubenville, Ohio. Mrs. Sandford hails from a family of decided literary tastes, her own inclinations and practice in the several communities where residing being to promote and forward intellectual advancement. To their marriage have been born six children: Walter Alexander died in infancy; Janet J. is the wife of Capt. Wm. T. Wood, who was graduated from West Point in the class of 1877, and at present is serving as treasurer at Manila, in the Phillipine Islands, under General Otis. They have sons: Halsey W., Sheridan C. and Isaac Russell. Sheridan C. has had an extensive experience as a commercial traveler. Grace Foster is the wife of Dr. W. E. Purviance, assistant surgeon in the United States army, with the rank of captain, now stationed at Fort Egbert, Alaska. Isaac Russell, the youngest of the family, is partner with his father in dry-goods and general merchandise at Villa Grove. Illinois.

Mr. Sandford's business career has been one of unusual diversity. In 1850 he made the overland route to California and engaged in mining for two years; afterward handled cattle in Edgar county and Douglas county, Illinois; made and improved two farms from the virgin soil—one in each of the above counties. He was a partner in the wholesale and retail house of C. C. Smith & Co., Terre Haute, Ind., in 1893. Came to Tuscola and followed merchandising, in which, since 1863, he has been actively engaged.

JOHN T. TODD.

John Thomas Todd, who is one of the most active and successful business men of Tuscola and who has been with the exception of two years, agent for the I. D. & W. Railway Company from the time the road was built to the present, having first entered its service as agent at Marshall, Indiana, on August 1, 1879, was born in Edgar county, Illinois, June 8, 1862. He was reared in Edgar and Champaign counties and received his education in the public schools at Newman. In 1866 his parents removed to Douglas county and settled on a farm near Newman. He is a son of David and Mariah (Wilson) Todd, who were natives of Ireland, and who were both Episcopalians in their religious belief. David Todd was a bookbinder by trade and in about 1844 emigrated to this country, first settling in New York City, where he worked at his trade until 1855, when he emigrated west and located on a farm in Edgar county. The grandfathers of Mr. Todd were James Todd and William Wilson, both born in Ireland.

In 1883 Mr. Todd was united in marriage to Miss Laura, a daughter of L. J. Cash, of Newman. He is the founder of the Douglas County Telephone Company, now a sub-licensee of the American Bell Telephone Company, the change being made in order to get the use of the instruments and the long-distance connections of the Bell Company. Mr. Todd is still the president and business manager of the company, with J. W. Hamilton as secretary. In 1892 he removed to Chicago, where he was engaged for two years in perfecting and developing an invention known as the "thermograph," of which Mr. Todd is the patentee and inventor. This instrument is for automatically recording the variations of temperature of refrigerator cars while in transit, also of the several rooms of cold storage plants, hot houses, etc., where it is desirable that a uniform temperature be maintained With Mr. Todd's invention it is possible to have a printed record made on a narrow strip of paper ribbon, showing the variations of temperature at such intervals of time as may be desired, from the time a car of meat leaves Chicago until it arrives in San Francisco, from which record any neglect in re-icing car en route may be located, and as the record shows the time of day and date of every variation, it is an easy matter to place the responsibility for any neglect by the several railway companies handlig the car.

John T. Todd is a member of the Masonic fraternity, and his standing as a man, especially in railroad circles, is second to none. During his residence in Tuscola he has borne an important part in the progress of the city, and his courteous manner and his integrity and ability have won him a high place in the esteem of his fellow citizens.

CARL S. BURGETT.

Carl S. Burgett was born in Sargent township, Douglas county, Illinois, July 2, 1867, and is a son of I. W. Burgett, whose death occurred in 1884 and whose sketch is found elsewhere. After leaving the common schools Mr. Burgett attended high school at Green-

field, Iowa, and the Commercial College at Terre Haute, Indiana. In 1891 he located in Newman and has been engaged in buying and selling broom corn and the manufacturing of brooms; he is also engaged in the fire insurance business and buying and shipping stock.

In 1894 Mr. Burgett was wedded to Miss Emma Gillogly, a daughter of James Gillogly, of Newman. To them have been born three children: Lois V., Carl Stanton and Gladys. Besides his business interests in Newman Mr. Burgett owns one hundred and twenty acres of land in Sargent township. He is a Mason and belongs to the Melita Commandery of Knights Templar of Tuscola. Mr. Burgett has for several years past taken an active and influential part in the councils of his party and was elected as a Republican to the lower house of the General Assembly of Illinois in the fall of 1898. While a member of this body he was conscientious in his work and was seldom absent at roll-call. He served on the committees on agriculture, appropriations, banks and banking, labor and industrial affairs, penal and reformatories and railroads. It was largely due to his efficiency as a law maker that his party in the recent primaries gave him the renomination without opposition for re-election to the same office. Socially Carl S. Burgett is one of the most companionable of fellows and thoroughly appreciates the confidence and esteem placed in him by the general public.

ALBERT B. SAWYER.

Albert B. Sawyer was born in the town of Milton, Chittenden county, Vermont, January 3, 1837. Since 1885 he has been a resident of Tuscola, Illinois, having from that time until 1899 been a member of the dry-goods firm of Wardall & Sawyer.

In Mr. Sawyer's childhood his parents came to Illinois, living near and finally in Joliet. His boyhood and youth were spent in that part of the state, on the farm, going to school or assisting his father, Jed Sawyer, in filling the extensive railroad contracts which he took when the railroads around Joliet were being built. Having gone to Texas in 1860, he lived near Houston until after the Civil war broke out, when, being unable to return to the north except as a Confederate soldier, he turned to the west, finally entering the Republic of Mexico. There he turned his attention to the great business of northern Mexico—

silver mining—in which he was engaged from 1862 to 1884, when he sold out his mining interests there and returned to Illinois. Two years previously he had married Miss Fanny M. Wardall, of Tolono, Illinois. To their union five children have been born: Harriet, Albert B., Jr., Margaret, Gertrude and John W. Since 1885 their home has been in Tuscola.

I. N. COVERT.

I. N. Covert, one of the retired men from active business and a most worthy citizen of Newman, Illinois, was born in Butler county, Pennsylvania, December 2, 1832. Mr. Covert descended from ancestors who came from Holland in about the year 1685 and settled in eastern Pennsylvania, near Philadelphia. In about 1790 Morris Covert, his grandfather, came to western Pennsylvania and settled in Butler county. He became a large land owner, being able to give each of his twelve children a farm. John Covert, the father of the subject of this sketch, was one of the steady, substantial farmers of that section. I. N. Covert grew to manhood on his father's farm. After attending the common schools he completed what school education he received at North Sedgwick Academy, in Beaver county, Pennsylvania. In the fall of 1859 he came west and located at Newman, Illinois, and taught the Hopkins school, one mile south of Newman, three successive winters before the Civil war and one year after its close. He was married, September 2, 1860, by the Rev. Peter Wallace, of the Methodist church of this place,

to Miss S. L. Webster, of Athens, Ohio, having been the first couple who were married in the church. Mrs. Covert, who was a very worthy woman, was a niece of Mother Stewart, who was known in Ohio as the pioneer temperance crusader. Mr. Covert, in 1862, enlisted in the Seventy-ninth Regiment of Illinois Volunteers, and served honorably in that regiment throughout the war, receiving his discharge in June, 1865. He bought and improved a farm in Edgar county, three and one-half miles south of the city, where he resided from the year 1866 to 1882, when he rented his farm and moved to Newman. In the spring of 1884 he formed a partnership with Scott Burgett and engaged in the banking business, having been the first president of the Newman Bank. Mrs. Covert died August 17, 1887, and in 1888 he found the close confinement of his business injurious to his health and sold his interest in the bank to S. M. Long, deceased, whose sketch is found on another page. Mr. Covert has recently completed one of the most beautiful cottages in Newman. He has been an elder in the Presbyterian church since its organization and is one of the church's most devoted leaders; he is also a Knight Templar in the Masonic fraternity.

LAWRENCE E. ROOT.

Lawrence E. Root, member of the well-known dry-goods firm of Root Brothers, of Newman, was born in Rome township, Athens county, Ohio, November 16, 1848, and was the ninth child born to Mr. and Mrs. Levi Root, pioneer settlers of Athens county (see sketch of brother, D. O. Root, for ancestry). He remained on the farm with his parents until 1863, when, in the spring of that year, he enlisted in Company K, Third West Virginia Cavalry. At the time of his enlistment he was only a little past fourteen years of age, being the youngest private soldier there has been any record found of so far. Going out in the winter of 1862-63, he served with Sheridan in the Shenandoah valley, Custer's division, and

served up to the surrender of Lee, at Appomattox Court House. At the close of the war Mr. Root returned to Athens, and in 1867 came west and settled in Douglas county, locating on a farm south of Newman, where he was successfully engaged in farming up to 1888. In that year he formed a partnership with his brother, D. O. Root, in the general dry-goods business, which has continued most successfully up to the present time. While on the farm he served four years as supervisor of Sargent township, in which township he resided from 1871 to 1888. He also served as supervisor of Newman township two years, and from 1890 to 1894 he served most efficiently as treasurer of the county. Mr. Root since his residence in Newman has served in the city council, and has been thoroughly identified with the best interests of the city. He is a large stockholder in the Newman Electric Light & Canning Company. He is a member of Newman Lodge, No. 369, of Masons; a Knight Templar, belonging to Melita Commandery, No. 37, of Tuscola; a Knight of Pythias, and a member of the G. A. R. and Knights of Honor.

The store room occupied by Root Brothers is one hundred and twenty feet by twenty, two stories; the upper story is filled with clothing, boots, etc. The firm employs five clerks, and carries from fifteen to twenty thousand dollars worth of stock.

In 1870 our subject wedded Miss Vashti Winkler, of Newman, a daughter of Charles and Sarah (Lane) Winkler, natives of Kentucky and Ohio respectively. To the union have been born nine children, whose names, with dates of birth, are as follows: Melvin L., January 27, 1871; Wallace E., January 11, 1873; Blanche, March 28, 1875; Ina, March 22, 1877; Grace, July 22, 1879; Paul A., September 8, 1881; Hattie Lane, December 28, 1883; Madge, December 11, 1887; Lois, August 9, 1890. Only Melvin and Wallace are married. The members of the family are identified with the M. E. church of Newman.

CLARENCE H. CARNAHAN.

Clarence H. Carnahan, one of the leading merchants of Hindsboro, and a promising business man of the county, was born in Douglas county, Illinois, March 1, 1876. He was reared on a farm and received his principal education at Tuscola and Terre Haute. His first business venture was in partnership with A. J. Parke, in the restaurant business in Hindsboro, at which they continued successfully for a short time. In 1898 Mr. Carnahan engaged in his present business, and his success has been remarkable. He carries a full line

of dry-goods, notions and groceries and has the entire confidence of the people in Hindsboro and Bowdre township. In addition to his mercantile interests he owns forty acres of valuable land near the village.

Mr. Carnahan is a son of Robert A. Carnahan, who was born September 22, 1839, in Fleming county, Kentucky, and is a son of Jackson and Margaret (Sousley) Carnahan, with whom he removed from Kentucky to Indiana in 1847. In 1857 the family moved to Coles county, where, in 1860, Jackson Carnahan died, which threw the support of the widowed mother and younger children upon Robert, who was the eldest child. His business in life was farming, cattle dealing and trading, in all of which he was very prosperous; havng no capital to start on, he accumulated a good property by industry and good management. In 1869 he bought eighty acres of the present homestead and later added eighty acres more. It was unimproved, but later became one of the fine farms of Bowdre township.

Our subject was twice married. His first wife was Miss Sarah E. Herbert, daughter of William J. and Martha G. (Arasmith) Herbert, of Coles county. His second wife was Miss Mahala Herbert, sister of his first wife. By the last marriage there was born one child, a son, Clarence H. Jackson Carnahan's death occurred March 8, 1879. Clarence H. Carnahan is one of the youngest men in successful business in the county, and displays a remarkable tact and aptitude in handling details. Socially he is popular with his friends.

V. C. McNEER.

"Probably no death that has ever occurred in Tuscola came more suddenly or caused more expressions of regret and genuine sorrow to be heard among our people than that of V. C. McNeer, which occurred at Arcola at about 8:30 o'clock on Friday morning last. It came like a shock to his innumerable friends in this city, and many could hardly realize that he had passed to the beyond and that he would mingle no more among us.

"Mr. McNeer, who has bought stock in this county for many years, had occasion to go to Arcola that morning to receive some hogs from John Jones. The fast mail leaves here at an early hour, and in order to make the train he was compelled to run from the First National Bank to the depot. It is supposed that this over-exertion had the effect of bringing on the attack of cerebral apoplexy which carried him off soon after his arrival in Arcola.

"After arriving in that city he went to the scale office of W. S. Jocelyn, where he met his agent, Israel Travener, and soon afterward he sat down to write a check in payment for the animals. He arose, and a moment later was

seen to have a peculiar look, as though in agony. He passed his hand to the back of his head and said that he felt a severe pain. He had scarcely made the remark when he seized the arm of Travener and reeled as if about to fall. The latter eased him to the floor and sent for a physician at once, but it was too late. The stricken man never breathed a word after receiving the fatal stroke, and died in fifteen minutes. Dr. McKinney attended him, but no assistance could be given. He was carried to the Arcola hotel, near by, and expired in a room adjoining the office. W. H. Hancock and John Walling were in the city at the time, but arrived a few minutes after he passed away.

"On receipt of the painful news here, the Odd Fellows appointed a committee to go at once and take charge of the remains, he being an honored member of that order. His remains arrived here on the afternoon train, and were met at the depot by several hundred people.

"The funeral occurred at his home near the southern limits of the city on Monday afternoon at two o'clock, when, notwithstanding the intense cold at the time, a large number of friends gathered to pay their last respects to the one who they had known so well in life, and mourned so sincerely in death. The services were brief, and were conducted by Revs. Calhoun and Wyatt, after which the remains were placed in charge of the Odd Fellows, who conducted the services according to their rites.

"The deceased was born near Anderson, Indiana, December 31, 1839, and was consequently fifty-seven years of age at the time of his death. He leaves a wife and four children to mourn his loss, besides one brother and one sister. The sister, Mrs. Catherine Jones, of Alexandria, Indiana, was in attendance at the funeral. The brother, Dan, is a resident of Omaha, and it was impossible to reach him by telegraph, as he was absent from home. Mr. Castle, a brother-in-law, from Alexandria, was also present, and on Monday Mr. and Mrs. John Renner, parents of Mrs. McNeer, arrived from Kansas. Also Mrs. Coffey, of Newman. The funeral was a sad one, and universal sympathy is expressed for the bereaved wife and children, who have suffered the loss of one who was near and dear to them, and whose every thought was to make them comfortable and happy.

"For a quarter of a century Mr. McNeer has made his home in this community, and during that time he has had business relations with hundreds of people throughout the county. His business took him to every town within a radius of twenty miles, and his circle of acquaintances was perhaps larger than that of any other citizen among us. In his business relations covering these many years he was found to be honorable and upright with his fellow men, and it might be said that he has aided more men in a financial way than almost any citizen in the community. He had a large and sympathetic heart, and no friend ever went to him in trouble and was turned away. Many who have been aided by him in the past will remember his kindly acts through life and bless him for it. All feel that an honored and respected citizen has been called, and that his place will be hard to fill.

"It is more than probable that the deceased was aware that he would be taken suddenly, as he had had previous warning of his trouble. Last summer he was stricken while at home, and a few years previous he suffered a light attack."—[Copied.]

JAMES G. TODD.

James G. Todd was born in New York City, July 16, 1846; removed to Illinois with his parents, David and Mariah Todd, in the year 1855, settling in Edgar county. In 1864 he moved with his parents to Champaign county, but two years afterward his father purchased a farm in Douglas county, six miles northeast of Newman, and he remained on the

farm with his parents until January 29, 1873. He was there united in marriage to Miss Jennie Coolley, daughter of Mr. and Mrs. J A. Coolley, of the Ridge. Three children were born to this union, Minnie, Lena C. and Albert D. Mrs. Todd died February 26, 1891. Mr. Todd was afterward united in marriage to Mrs. Jennie McClure and occupies a neat and comfortable home in this city. Mr. Todd is a Republican, as was his father, and has been a prominent factor in the success of the party in Newman township the past few years, filling offices of trust and honor. He is now serving as township clerk and so well does he attend to the business affairs of the township that no one has reason for complaint. Socially he is a member of the K. of P. lodge and takes quite an active part in the work. He is also a member of the M. E. church and teacher in the Sunday school. Mr. Todd is kind and generous at all times and is one of the men that it is safe to "tie to." He numbers his friends in this city by the score.

Very recently he has mourned the death of his most estimable wife.

CHARLES M. CULBERTSON.

The biographies of Newman township would be incomplete without an extended notice of Mr. Culbertson, who has done more than any other one man toward developing the eastern part of the county and the improvement and beautifying of the town of Newman. The family from which he is descended is of Scotch

origin. One of his great-grandfathers emigrated from the north of Ireland in an early day, and settled in Lancaster county, Pennsylvania.

Another great-grandfather, William McClay, who was born in Pennsylvani, and who, with Robert Morris, were the first United States senators from Pennsylvania. The descendants of the Culbertsons became quite numerous in Lancaster county, and the settlement was known as Culbertson's row. Here his father, Charles M. Culbertson, was born, and after his marriage of Elizabeth McPamma emigrated in 1818 to Indiana, and settled in Jefferson county. In this county Charles M. Culbertson was born August 5, 1819, and received only the meagre school advantages common in that day, consequently he had to rely on his own industry and perceptions for the elements of knowledge which he acquired. At fourteen years of age he left home and went to Newport, Indiana, where he commenced clerking in a store, which position he held for about eight years. At first he received a salary of eighty dollars a year, out of which he clothed himself. His salary for the year 1841 was two hundred dollars. He soon exhibited business qualifications of a high order and it was not long until he entered into a partnership with Daniel A. Jones, who carried on a general merchandising and pork packing business at Newport, which lasted up until 1865. Up to 1854 the business was carried on at the latter place and after that date in Chicago (Mr. Culbertson removed to Chicago in 1857). In 1843 he was married to Miss Rhoda Williams, of Newport, whose parents were from Pennsylvania. In 1852 he entered a section of land in Newman township and kept on increasing it until at one time he owned two thousand, three hundred and forty acres, and his farms, which he recently divided among his heirs, are the finest and best improved in the county. The home farm of five hundred and sixty acres, that he gave his grandson, E. C. Remick, is situated four miles north of Newman and is decidedly the most beautiful and attractive country home in this vicinity. Mr. Culbertson has erected a beautiful brick business block and it was principally due to his efforts that the town of Newman has over six miles of fine concrete sidewalks. He is still hale and hearty, active and straight, and would easily be taken for a man not more than past sixty.

DANIEL A. CONOVER.

D. A. Conover, ex-circuit clerk and recorder, was born in Adams county, Pennsylvania, on one of the farms where the battle of Gettys-

burg was afterward fought. About 1840 our subject with his parents moved to Owen county, Indiana; he was given a thorough schooling at the Bloomington, Indiana, state university and at twenty years of age he engaged with his brother in the drug business at Bowling Green, Clay county, Indiana. After a year he bought his brother's interest and owned the store until 1864. In 1862 he organized Company D. Seventy-First Indiana Volunteer Infantry. At the battle of Richmond, Kentucky, he was wounded and taken prisoner, but at night with some others escaped. The Seventy-first sustained such loss that the reorganization was abandoned. The remaining members returned to Terre Haute and there organized the Sixth Indiana Cavalry and Mr. Conover was commissioned major. Owing to disabilities sustained at Richmond he was mustered out at Knoxville, Tennessee, and on returning home he was appointed provost marshal of the seventh Indiana district with headquarters at Terre Haute; he was appointed inspector of interpublican ticket for mayor of Terre Haute. In 1869 he came to Tuscola where he afterward resided. He traveled for eleven years in the interests of a Cincinnati hat house until 1880, when he was elected to an office on the Republican ticket. On January 24, 1854, he married Miss Bradshaw N. Elkin, of Bowling Green, Indiana. Major Conover belonged to the Masonic lodge from the age of twenty-one years; was a Knight Templar of Melita Commandery and was circuit clerk and recorder. Mr. Conover was respected in Tuscola up until his death.

DR. C. RUTHERFORD, M. D.

Natural ability, thorough study and long experience have placed Dr. C. Rutherford in the very front rank of successful professional men of Douglas county. He is a native of Illinois and the son of Dr. and Mrs. H. Rutherford, of Oakland, Illinois, being born in the present family residence in Oakland, August 14, 1850. After the completion of a common school education he taught school in and near Oakland for three years, during which time he was engaged in the study of medicine. After this he attended lectures and graduated at the University of Pennsylvania, at Philadelphia, Pennsylvania, the 12th of March, 1877. He returned to Oakland and began the practice of medicine, which he continued until

he came to Newman, September 27, 1877, and has ever since been actively engaged in his chosen profession, building up as he has a large and lucrative practice.

Dr. Rutherford was united in marriage to Miss Mary E. McIntyre on the 22nd of September, 1885, and together with his family occupies a very neat residence in the south part of the city. To Mr. and Mrs. Rutherford have been born two children, Eugenie, born June 29, 1892, and Florence, born July 8, 1894. He has served on the school board twelve years and was elected the first president under the new organization of seven members, having been re-elected each year since, which is conclusive evidence that he serves the people honorably in that capacity.

When the people of Newman desired to convert Newman into a city, he was chosen as the proper man for the mayoralty and was elected. He is a prominent member of the Masonic and K. of P. lodges of this city. His medical skill has been the means of him being selected as a member of the board of pension examiners and also elected county coroner for four years, although his extensive practice kept him for serving as coroner. Dr. Rutherford has always been a great promoter of Newman's interests and in 1890 in partnership with R. Thomas was the designer of the beautiful Newman cemetery. A city full and running over with such men as Dr. Rutherford could not help but advance. "God made the country and man makes the town" as the old saying goes; and it is a true one. Every town is just what its inhabitants make it, is dead or alive according to the composition of its men. Of course all can not be leaders; some have not the talent, others have not the time. But when the leader arises, then the duty of the ordinary citizen is to follow in the wake of his advancing footsteps. Dr. Rutherford possesses honest qualifications and so varied are his gifts that many men naturally seek his companionship for consultation. Noble models make noble minds.

W. W. PEPPER.

W. W. Pepper, a popular lawyer and a successful young business man, was born on a farm seven miles south of Newman May 24, 1866, and is the eldest of seven children born to Dudley H. and Nancy Liston Pepper. His father was a native of Kentucky and resides at Oakland. Mr. Pepper received his early edu-

cation in the public schools of Oakland and afterward took a three-years' course in the University of Illinois in Champaign. After leaving the university he took a two-years' law course at the Northwestern University at Evanston and was graduated with honor in 1893, shortly afterward being admitted to the bar.

On June 28, 1890, Mr. Pepper married Miss Nora Hinds, of Hindsboro. In March, 1894, Mr. Pepper located in Newman and commenced the practice of law. He became at once deservedly popular and in May, 1895, was chosen city attorney, which office he filled with due honor until the expiration of his time. He was re-elected to the same office, but resigned to look after his other business. It can be truly said of him that he is a man peculiarly after his own style. He has no model and seeks after none, save that which is the creation of his own mind. Starting out in life as he did, without means, perseverance and energy constituted his only capital. He entered his profession with a determination to fully acquaint himself with the law and the rules of practice. This he has done. He has built up and now enjoys an extensive practice in all the courts of Douglas county. His splendid success is due to the fact that he is a ceaseless worker and when once employed he pursues his case until he has thoroughly mastered it in all its details.

OLIVER O. HOCKETT.

Oliver O. Hockett, one of the younger members of the medical fraternity of Douglas county, and one of the leading men in the social, professional and educational life of Newman, was born in Paris, Edgar county, Illinois, March 2, 1866. He was graduated from the high school of Paris in 1882 and subsequently entered the state university at Champaign, where he remained for three years. He then took up the study of medicine with Dr. M. P. Smith, with whom he remained until he entered Chicago Hahnemann College, from which well known institution he was graduated in the class of 1889, and the following year he spent in the Hahnemann hospital. In March, 1890, he came to Newman and opened out in the general practice of medicine, and has succeeded far beyond his expectations. He is skilled and successful, and although having been in Newman but a few years, he enjoys one of the most extensive and lucrative practices in the county. He is a member of the Hahnemann Medical Society, contributes to the medical journals and keeps himself thoroughly in touch with the advancements being made in his profession. As a diagnostician in his profession, as well as in his judgment of human nature, he would pass muster in any community.

Dr. Hockett is a son of Mahlon and Mary

(Kimble) Hockett, natives of Vermilion and Edgar counties respectively. His father was a well-to-do carriage manufacturer, who has recently retired. During the war of the Rebellion he was first lieutenant of the First Missouri Volunteers. His grandfather Kimble walked from Ohio to Edgar county, and died in 1877 worth ninety thousand dollars. In 1895 our subject married Miss Luella Gillespie, and has by this marriage one child, named J. Maxwell. Dr. Hockett has a suite of rooms in the Swaggert building, which is his office, elegantly fitted up, and where he takes care of a large and growing practice, built up by close application to his work. While in medical college special honors were conferred upon him, and on his entering the great school of active life his thorough education and medical training did him great service in beginning his practice. He is thoroughly equipped with the finest outfits for use in his specialties that can be had. Socially he belongs to the Knights of Pythias, and in 1881 was a member of Company H, Eighth Regiment, Illinois State Militia, retiring in 1887.

J. W. PHILLIPS.

Of the many leading and successful business men of Tuscola who have fought their way successfully through life and who have been the architect of their own fortune in the true sense of that term is the subject of this sketch. He is a dealer in poultry, produce, fish, etc., and is also interested in the ice business. He founded his present business in Tuscola in 1896, constructing a building 80x20 feet, and one and one-half stories high. This building burned in August of the following year, and he immediately erected on the same site a more commodious one, 120x30 feet. It is safe to say that Mr. Phillips' poultry business is one of the very largest in the state outside of Chicago. He has about twenty-five men traveling and buying poultry and produce throughout the year. For fifteen years previous to his coming to Tuscola he was engaged in the same line at Arthur.

Mr. Phillips was born in Clay county, Tennessee, April 18, 1861, his parents removing when he was quite young to Hawkins county, some fifty-five miles east of Knoxville, in the same state. He is a son of William Phillips,

who was a native of Hawkins county, Tennessee. William married Miss Emily Phillips (no relation, though bearing the same name). The father died in 1863, and his mother in 1898, aged seventy-seven years. In February, 1881, Mr. Phillips wedded Miss Nellie M. Fitch, of Coles county, Illinois. They have four children: Vena, Dona, E. W. and Herald. Mr. Phillips is a member of the Woodmen and Redmen.

MALDEN JONES.

In touching upon the history of Douglas county for the past sixty years, none have been more prominently connected with its growth and industrial expansion than the Hon. Malden Jones. He endured all the hardships incident to the rough pioneer life and has passed through a most honorable and enviable career. He is a native of Lee county, Virginia, and was born February 8, 1818. When a child he went with his parents to Kentucky, where he was reared and where, at about the age of seventeen, he entered a store as clerk and remained

three years. In 1840 he came west, making the trip on horseback, settled with his brother, Alfred, five miles southwest of Arcola, and there engaged in farming and the live stock business. In 1848 he removed to his present locality and, in company with Mr. Gruelle, opened a general store about half a mile north of Bourbon, his store being the only one west of Charleston. He was engaged extensively in buying and selling cattle and horses, and drove them from his home to Wisconsin, which at that time was the only market worthy of the name in the west. They continued at this point about one year. Mr. Jones then built a store in Bourbon and laid out the town. He continued merchandising here about six years. In 1858 he was elected sheriff of the county of Coles, and removed to Charleston. There he resided for three years, returning to Bourbon in 1861. He was elected to the Legislature in 1864 and re-elected in 1866, and was the first member elected from the new county of Douglas. In 1876 he was elected state senator and served four years. He was also a candidate for the senate in 1880, but was defeated by a few votes.

On coming to Coles, now Douglas county, he had but forty dollars and a pony. He now owns fifteen hundred acres of land and the finest residence in the township, which cost over six thousand dollars. He was married in 1880 to Mary, daughter of Isaac Gruelle, who was one of the earliest settlers of this county. Eleven children have blessed this union, nine now living, four sons and five daughters. His wife died June 23, 1895, in her sixty-first year. Amongst Mr. Jones' neighbors, when he first settled in the vicinity of Bourbon, might be mentioned the Abbots, Stovals, Ellises and the Chandlers. Mr. Jones and Lemuel Chandler, in the 1860 days of old, were the leading stump speakers and authorities of the day, and being on opposite sides of the important political questions, made the old brick school house in Bourbon fairly ring with the eloquent pros and cons of political debate, the condiments of which were not a little personal feeling, which, to the knowing ones, lent an added zest to their enjoyment; but, happy to say, old time fixed them with his glittering eye at last and the foolishness of political animosity gracefully gave way to the sober philosophy of increasing years. In a public career of about forty-five years, Mr. Jones, while occupying positions of trust and responsibility, such as sheriff, representative and state senator, has retained his integrity and, consequently, the respect of his fellow citizens. His character has never been assailed and he stands before the world to-day retaining the reputation of an honest and influential man. Mr. Jones is universally respected. He has seen many changes in the county and at the sunset of life still takes an active and influential part in the political, social and industrial life of the day.

ALLAN CAMPBELL.

Allan Campbell, son of John Campbell, died October 13, 1875. Without a sketch and portrait of Allan Campbell this book would be very incomplete, as the Campbell family was among the earliest and most prominent pioneers in Bourbon township. Allan came before his father, and soon after his arrival bought five acres of land just south of Lesterville, at the Bagdad bridge, and ran a ferry here for three years. Allan Campbell was born in Knox county, Kentucky, in 1809. His grandfather, Allan Campbell, was born in Virginia, and was among the early settlers in Kentucky. His father, John Campbell, removed to Bourbon township soon after his brother. His mother was Lucinda Sullivan, also a native of Kentucky.

Allan Campbell first married Miss Mary Ann Hoots, who was a daughter of David Hoots, of a German family. Of this marriage there are three children living, all residing in Bourbon township: Hiram, John H. and ———, the wife of William Warmsley. His first wife died, and on February 13, 1851, he wedded Miss Mary Fleming, who still survives him. She was born in Parke county, Indiana, and was a daughter of Stephen and Jane (Kerr) Fleming. Her father was born in Fleming county, Kentucky, and her mother in Pennsylvania. Her grandfather, Stephen Fleming, was a native of Scotland, and her grandfather, Thomas Kerr, was a native of Ireland. To Allan Campbell and Mary Fleming Campbell were born three sons and one daughter, now living: Joseph A., James H., Annette, who is the wife of Albert Ellers, of Garrett township, and Stephen S. At the time of Mr. Allan's death he owned about thirty-five hundred acres of land. At that time it was divided up between the widow and the children Mrs. Campbell receiving nine hundred and twenty acres, all in Bourbon township, which she still owns. She resides on the old

Campbell homestead, two miles south of Lesterville. She is in her seventy-fourth year, and is a devout member of the Presbyterain church.

T. W. SWIGART.

T. W. Swigart, the leading harness dealer and one of the most successful business men in Newman and Douglas county, was born in Carroll county, Maryland, in sight of Westminister, July 3, 1831, and was a son of Joseph Swigart. When nine years of age T. W. Swigart removed with his parents to Seneca county, Ohio, where he spent a large portion of his life on a farm. From the years 1848 to 1851 he devoted his time to learning the trade of har-

nessmaker at Bellfontaine, Ohio. He was a young man of good habits and of splendid mechanical turn of mind; he learned the trade thoroughly and soon became a first-class workman. In the year 1852 he removed to Attica, Indiana, where he resided and worked at his trade successfully up to the year 1870, when he went to Princeton, Illinois. There he met Miss Sarah Jane Martin, who, in 1871, became his wife. In the same year he came to Danville, Illinois, where he followed his trade until the month of February, 1873, when he came to Newman and succeeded Speelman & Ogden in the harness business. During his residence in Newman he has become one of the most successful business men in the city and has accumulated quite a lot of property. In politics he is thoroughly independent and there is very little of hypocrisy in his nature. He is thoroughly candid and outspoken in his convictions. He has served three terms as president of the town board. He has also been a member of the board of health and director of the Building & Loan Association. He is a Mason and member of the Knights of Honor. In his business relations with the public he is unimpeachable and supplies the people for miles around with the most improved style of harness. He is a clever gentleman and respected by most every body.

EDWARD W. CALVIN.

Edward W. Calvin, the leading druggist and owner of both livery stables of Newman, was born in Wayne county, Illinois, December 21, 1860. He is a son of Dr. J. W. Calvin, who was born in Kentucky in 1829, and he the son of Hiram Calvin, who was a native of Virginia. His father was a graduate of Rush Medical College. He married Sarah Brown, of New Buffalo, Michigan, whose death occurred some twenty years ago. He has practiced at various places, was at Newman one year and is at present in active and successful practice at Toledo, Ohio.

E. W. Calvin has for several years extensively engaged in buying and selling horses and has been remarkably successful in all business enterprises in which he has been interested. In June, 1897, he opened out in the drug business and keeps on hands one of the most complete assortments of drugs found in a first-class drug store.

In 1889 he was united in marriage to Miss Emma Smith, of Vermilion county. They have one child, Okal McCrea. Mrs. Calvin is a daughter of Michael Smith, who was born in Vermilion county, Illinois. Her mother was Mary Ann Snapp. She was a daughter of George Snapp, a native of Richmond, Virginia. He was a carriagemaker by trade and after working some time at his trade in Richmond he removed to Georgetown, Vermilion county. He was in the war of 1812. Mrs. Calvin's grandfather, Joseph Smith, was a native of Nashville, Tennessee, and later removed to Vermilion county, where he resided until his death. In about 1890 Mrs. Calvin started her present millinery store in Newman and carries a stock as large and varied as can be found in many towns of from ten thousand to fifteen thousand people. Edward W. Calvin has made a success of every business venture he has ever undertaken. He takes an active interest in political and social affairs and is public spirited and interests himself in everything that helps Newman and Douglas county.

JACOB R. MOORE.

Jacob Rice Moore, who recently died, was one of the best known and most generally respected farmers in the county. His illness lingered and lasted for two long years before death relieved him. There were probably but few people in the neighborhood of Arcola and its surroundings who were aware that Mr. Moore at the time of his death was one of the oldest residents of the county. He was born within sight of the place on which he died and the same section of rich Illinois soil which claims the honor of his birth witnessed his rise to manhood and his gradual advancement to comparative old age. For sixty-two years he lived and thrived on the same farm where his birth occurred, when Douglas county was unheard of and the old prairie state was a wilderness of a few scattering hamlets. Before Arcola was a dot on the map he was living on the farm where he died and he witnessed the swamp lands of the county mature into the richest and one of the most fertile counties on the continent. He was one of those quiet, unassuming men who let the great world fight its battles while he built a beautiful home for his wife and interesting children. He was careful and economical and what he earned he saved. Through this method of economy, his land interests broadened out and

he became one of the successful men in the business affairs of the community. It is said of Mr. Moore that during his entire life he was never absent from his home more than a period of thirty days at the most.

Jacob R. Moore was born September 18, 1836, and died June 2, 1899, aged sixty-two years, eight months and fourteen days. He was married to Mary W. Bacon, of Bourbon, December 31, 1862. To them were born seven children, whose names are as follows: Richard, George B., Rice J., Anna M., Wade H., Emma B. S., and Leonore Moore. As a neighbor, Mr. Moore was always ready to lend a helping hand and passed through the trials incident to the life of early settlers in what was then the far west. For years he was one of the directors of the First National Bank of Arcola. He helped to build Bethel church, and lent valuable aid in organizing the congregation during the fall of 1883, although not an active member; he and his wife became members October 4, 1884, and in June, 1890, he was raised to the dignity of elder. Mr. Moore was a man of strong, positive character and unswerving dignity, and in his death the community in which he had so long resided lost a kind neighbor and a good citizen, and the church with which he had been so closely identified, one of its strongest stays and most helpful members.

Capt. Rice J. Moore, a son, volunteered in the Illinois National Guard, March 31, 1894; saw field service in Chicago, in July, 1894; appointed corporal July 10, 1895; appointed quartermaster sergeant March 15, 1897; commissioned second lieutenant Fourth Infantry, Illinois Volunteers, May 20, 1898; detached from Fourth Regiment July 25, 1898, and assigned to Engineer Corps of the Seventh Army Corps in 1898. He resigned his commission in the army November 9, 1898, and returned to the farm.

GEORGE W. BROCK.

George W. Brock, one of the reliable and representative farmers of Newman township, residing within the corporate limits of the city of Newman, was born twelve miles southwest of Crawfordsville, Indiana, September 8, 1846. His father, Seth Brock, was a native of Warren county, Ohio. He was a carpenter by trade and farmed also, owning farms in

Wayne and Montgomery counties; he later removed to Mason county, Illinois. He was a strong pro-slavery man, and a member of the Methodist Episcopal church; was born in 1813 and died in 1873. He wedded Mary A. Palmer, who was a daughter of Jesse Palmer, a native of North Carolina, but who became one of the early settlers of Indiana. Elijah Brock (grandfather) was born in Ohio.

George W. Brock was reared on a farm and educated in the common schools. At the age of sixteen years, on account of a severe spell of sickness, he lost the use of his right side. He married at Camp Butler, Miss Malinda Vanhook, daughter of Thomas and Matilda (Mann) Vanhook, and the result of this union was one child living, Ada Lucy, aged fifteen years, and three dead: Phillip L., Harry C. and Ethel Ellen. Mrs. Brock, who was a most estimable woman, died February 16, 1899. She was a devoted member of the Christian church at Newman and her loss was deeply felt in church circles.

Mr. Brock owns one hundred and sixty acres of land in Newman township, and three acres inside the corporate limits of Newman. He is one of the useful citizens of Newman township, careful and prompt in business, and at his home courteous and hospitable.

FRANCIS A. McCARTY.

Francis A. McCarty was one of the most remarkably successful business men who ever resided in Douglas county. He was born in Schuyler county, New York, April 23, 1837,

and died at his home in Filson, May 14, 1899. He was a son of John and Laura (Frost) McCarty, natives of New England.

Charles McCarty, brother of Joseph McCarty, was born at Morristown, New Jersey, in 1776, and died in Montour, Schuyler county, New York, November 15, 1858, in his eighty-third year. Joseph McCarty (grandfather) was the father of John, Charles, William and David, was born January 9, 1778, and died July 25, 1845. His wife, Mary Harnerd McCarty, was born August 15, 1774, and died January 20, 1846. John McCarty (father), son of Joseph, was born May 15, 1805, and died January 14, 1875. Joseph Frost (grandfather) was born June 4, 1797, married Sallie McCarty, and died October 27, 1847. He was a son of Joseph Frost, a soldier of the Revolution, who was born May 22, 1754, and died May 28, 1844, at Catherine, New York. He married Lucy Couch, a daughter of Jonathan Couch, who was married September 19, 1781, died April 8, 1843, and was buried at Catherine, New York. Appended herewith is a certificate from the Adjutant General's office of the state of Connecticut: "Hartford, September 11, 1895. This is to certify that Joseph Frost (grandfather of Francis A. McCarty) served in the war of the Revolution, and the following is his service according to the records of this office; Private in Colonel Benjamin Hinman's regiment. Discharged in northern department September 11, 1775. Private in Captain Elijah Able's company, Colonel Philip Burr. Bradley's regiment. Enlisted June 16, 1776. Dicharged November 16, 1777. Prisoner at Fort Washington." He was a resident until 1803 of Redding, Fairfield county, Connecticut, when with his family he removed to Schuyler county, New York, where he resided until his death. He and two of his brothers were made prisoners when Lord Howe captured Fort Washington, in November, 1776. They suffered great hardship in a British prison hulk in New York bay, and the two brothers died while prisoners. Joseph Frost was wounded in battle and received a pension up until the time of his death.

Francis A. McCarty was reared and educated at Catherine, New York, and also attended Lima (New York) Seminary. February 12, 1879, he married Miss Emma Young, of Binghamton, New York, who was a daughter of William and Caroline B. (Munder) Young. They were both natives of Germany. Mrs. McCarty has in her possession a medal given her grandfather, Jacob Munder, by the King of Wurtemberg for faithful services in the field. To Mr. and Mrs. McCarty were born five children, all living: John William Fred, Laura Frost, Carrie Louise and Frances E.

In 1879 Mr. McCarty came to Douglas county and settled in Arcola township, where he bought a tract of land where he resided on the farm until 1894, when he located in Tuscola. He had great energy and talent for organizing and conducting business affairs, and by his great natural ability and indomitable perseverance attained a high prominence in the industrial and financial affairs of Douglas county. At the time of his death he owned two thousand acres of land in Douglas county, five hundred acres in Marion county, Illinois, and eight hundred acres in Missouri. These large estates are looked after by his widow, Mrs. McCarty, who possesses in a large degree great business tact, fine intelligence, and is a highly educated lady.

GEORGE WHITE.

George White, the well known implement dealer and auctioneer of Newman, was born near Glasgow, Barren county, Kentucky, August 18, 1842, and is a son of M. L. and Mary (Biby) White. Middleton White was born in Barren county, Kentucky, and moved to Edgar county, Illinois, where he was married. His wife was also from near Glasgow, Kentucky. They are both dead and buried in the Paris cemetery.

George White came to Newman and located in business in about 1874, since which

time his business has steadily grown until he is known as one of the most successful and extensive implement dealers in the entire county. He also handles the Mitchell wagon and several makes of buggies and carriages. His sales run from $25,000 to $35,000 annually.

In 1844 Mr. White was united in marriage to Miss Della Clark, who is a native of Kentucky. They have two children: Henry W., who will graduate from the Chicago Homeopathic School of Medicine in March, 1901, and Fred, who is in business with his father. George White has here held the office of township supervisor and while he resided in Edgar county held the same office. In 1861 he volunteered in Company E, Twelfth Illinois Infantry, and served through the entire Civil war. During the month of February especially his services are in great demand as a public auctioneer. He is a member of the Knights of Pythias and also the Grand Army of the Republic. He has a pleasant home in Newman and is classed among that town's best business men.

JUDGE JOHN BROWN.

Judge John Brown has been for over sixty years identified with the best interests of Douglas county. He was born in Ross county, Ohio, May 7, 1822, on a farm, where he remained until the age of seventeen. This farm was located on Paint creek, two miles from Chillicothe, the county seat of Ross county. Our subject is a son of Nimrod Brown, who was a native of Augusta county, Virginia, and who served in the war of 1812. His mother was, before her marriage, Elizabeth Eigelbright, and was born in Monroe county, Virginia. When our subject was but seven years old his father died, and his mother, with three sons and four daughters, emigrated to what is now Douglas county, in about 1838, and settled in what is now Sargent township. The

Judge's paternal grandfather, Washington Brown, was a Virginian by birth. At the time his mother located in Sargent township she was very poor, the oldest son, Washington, managing the business. Land at that time sold for from four to six dollars an acre, but money was very scarce. This was in September, 1838, the date of his mother's settlement in Sargent township.

Judge Brown married, in 1844, Sally Ann Barnett, who was a daughter of William and Mary Barnett, natives of Kentucky and early

settlers in Vermilion county. Mrs. Brown died in 1853, leaving one child, William R. Brown, who is a farmer residing in Jasper county, Indiana. Judge Brown subsequently married Mary Barnett, a double cousin to his first wife and a daughter of John M. and Ana Barnett, of Vermilion county, Mary having been born, however, in Bowdre township. Their family consisted of six children, four of whom are living: Bright resides in Bowdre township; Charles F., in Camargo township; Ella, who is at home; and Kate is the wife of W. S. Burgett.

Mr. Brown was elected county judge during the war of the Rebellion and served in that office for four years. He is a stanch Republican, and the owner of about nine hundred acres of fine land. He is the oldest living settler in the five eastern townships. Among some of the early settlers whom he intimately knew were Andy Guinn, Henry and Snowden Sargent, James and Stephen Redden, Ambrose and John Martin and their father John, Washington Boyce, Rev. William Watson, a Methodist preacher, and his brother, Parmenus.

I. W. BURGETT.

I. W. Burgett, deceased, was, during his residence in Douglas county, one of its leading and most successful farmers. From the time he was ten years old he spent the whole of his eventful life in Sargent township. He is a descendant of English and German ancestors, who were among the early residents of Ohio. His grandfather was in the war of 1812. His father, Abraham Burgett, lived in Pickaway county and there married Eliza Wells, a native of Ohio. He and his wife continued to live in that county, and there Isaac W. Burgett was born. The family shortly afterward removed to Indiana and settled in Vermillion county, near Perrysville, on the Wabash river. Here Abraham Burgett followed the occupations of cooper and farmer. He died in 1840, leaving five children.

Isaac W. Burgett was born June 18, 1829,

When the family removed to Douglas county they settled near the mouth of Brushy Fork. He went to school in the Sargent neighborhood and in the vicinity of Newman. On coming

to Douglas county his mother rented land, and when a mere boy he had charge of the farm and with a younger brother performed nearly all the labor. This continued until his mother's second marriage. In the summer he worked at home and in the winter went to school. When about eighteen years of age he started out for himself and worked on a farm for from eight to ten dollars a month. Two or three years were spent in this way.

December 28, 1848, he was married to Telitha Howard, a native of Jackson, Ohio, whose parents had emigrated to Vermillion county, Indiana, and then to Douglas county, Illinois. At this time his capital consisted of twenty-five dollars in money and one horse, and on this he rented land on Brushy Fork and began farming, renting land for two years. He afterward bought, on credit, twenty acres of timber and entered eighty acres on which he moved in the spring of 1853, and at the time of his death owned over one thousand and six hundred acres of land. He became not only prominent in farming, but also an extensive dealer in live stock. Mr. and Mrs. Burgett had eleven children: William B., Margery A., John Wesley, Hezekiah W., Eliza Ellen, Sarah Elizabeth, Scott, Wilson S., Maud L., Carl S. and Thomas P.

WILLIAM H. NEWPORT.

William H. Newport, of the neighborhood of West Ridge, and one of the most successful farmers in Douglas county, was born in Tuscarawas county, Ohio, February 9, 1840, a son

of John and Susanna (Rensberger) Newport, natives of Ohio. He has resided on his farm of several hundred acres for thirteen years, and while he has always been a tenant he has been most successful.

In 1862 he was married to Miss Fannie Mishler, who was born in Tuscarawas county, Ohio. To their marriage have been born five children, Charley, Israel, Eli, Otis and Grover Newport. Mr. Newport is a member of the I. O. O. F. fraternity, and is now serving as one of the road commissioners of his township. He is liberal and benevolent toward all enterprises for the betterment of the community in which he lives.

ROBERT M. BLACK.

Robert M. Black, the subject of this memoir, came from an ancestry of more than ordinary importance and prominence.

His great-grandfather, with his family, removed from Scotland and settled in Virginia some years before the Revolutionary war, passed through the terrors and excitement caused by the traitor Arnold in portions of Virginia, volunteered, though far past the age of liability, for military service, and was one of the soldiers, who, under Lafayette and Gen. Wayne, turned and drove back Lord Cornwallis. He was intimately acquainted with Lafayette, Gen. Wayne and Gen. Lord Sterling, who were frequent guests at his house. His youngest son, George Black, the grandfather of our subject, was born on the 8th of July, 1767. He was nine years old when the Declaration of Independence was issued. He was a son of the Revolution and saw and caught the spirit of most of the stirring scenes of that eventful period. George Black, with his family, removed from Virginia and settled in Kentucky, some time before the war of 1812. He became a soldier of this war in a regiment of mounted rifleman and rendered important service under the command of Gen. Harrison.

With such an ancestry, whose character and qualities he reproduced and reflected, together

with his own individual traits, we may understand the life of Robert M. Black, who was the ninth in a family of thirteen children born to Andrew and Margaret (Lockridge) Black. Andrew Black and his family left their home in Mt. Sterling, Kentucky, and went to Greencastle, Indiana, in 1850. The life of Robert M. Black dates from December 13, 1845, to June 11, 1899, a period of fifty-three years of great activity and success. His Scotch blood, fired with the spirit of the Revolution, produced a fine type of American patriot and citizen. In his boyhood days the future man already appeared. Obedient to parents, kind in disposition, solicitous about the welfare and happiness of his brothers and sisters, and loyal and unselfish toward his playmates, he early developed into a true man, who was willing and anxious to contribute his part to the world's progress as a man and citizen. At the age of sixteen he enlisted in the Seventy-eighth Indiana Regiment and in his first battle, at Union City, Kentucky, was wounded in the knee in the midst of a display of uncommon bravery. Yet his bravery probably saved his life, since, while he was facing the enemy alone, his company being in full retreat, the rebel commander ordered his men "not to shoot so brave a boy." Thus early in life, under the most trying circumstances, appeared those sterling qualities which made him prominent throughout his entire life and endeared him with peculiar strength to his comrades, friends and acquaintances. The wound received shortly after his enlistment greatly hindered him the rest of his days, but was borne with the same cheerful bravery with which it was received.

In 1873 he was married to Miss Mary Hutchings, who lived but two years afterward. In 1889 he married Miss Laura Moore, whom, with their four children, he left at his death well provided for. He was engaged in farming and stock business, which took him out over the country and into the neighboring states and caused him to handle a vast amount of money. His business brought him in contact with men, and, on account of his fair dealings and sturdy sociability, he made many friends and exerted a great influence. He was interested in politics and was a stanch Republican. In religion he was a Presbyterian, was for many years a member of the church, and as a father carefully brought up his children. His religion was not too sacred to be used in every-day affairs and it was the real foundation of his many excellent qualities shown in touch with his fellow men. His loyalty to his friends knew no bounds. Every true man found in him a worthy and constant companion, and friendships, formed upon manly qualities, were never broken. His large heart found pleasure in responding, in a substantial way, to the poor or those in temporary distress. To help others was a real pleasure to him, and being interested in those battling with adversity he was interested in all. He was progressive and public spirited, and in no sense lived for himself alone. Cheerfulness was his constant companion and it never forsook him, although all others were gloomy. He had a source of radiance and sunshine that seemed denied to many of his fellows. Some four years before his demise he moved to this county on a large farm four miles north of Oakland City, and being a careful business man he made money and friends in his new home, and he and his family were soon holding a large place in the affections and good-will of the entire community. A community may with pardonable pride record the name of so true and noble-hearted a citizen in its county history.

C. D. GREVE.

C. D. Greve, one of the successful young business men of the county and the leading grain buyer at Garrett, was born one mile west of the village September 27, 1868, and is a son of Thomas Greve, who emigrated to this country from Germany at the age of twenty-one and settled in Garrett township. His wife was Catherine Ritz. Thomas Greve has lived in Garrett township for forty years, engaged in farming, and at present owns four hundred

and fifty acres of land. Both he and his wife are members of the Evangelical church.

C. D. Greve was reared on a farm, and after leaving the common schools spent two years in the Valparaiso (Indiana) Normal. After leaving school he engaged in the hardware and implement business and continued in the same for seven years. In 1898 and 1899 he was elected assessor.

In March, 1894, Mr. Greve was married to Miss Katie Frahm, a daughter of Jacob Frahm. They have four children: Victor, Hilda, Roy and Paulina. Mr. Greve is one of the charter members of the Knights of Pythias lodge that was recently organized at Garrett. He owns nine acres of land in the corporate limits of Garrett, and also a very fine home in the village, besides some other town property. He is a thorough business man, enterprising, and promises to become one of Garrett's most useful citizens.

ISAAC SKINNER.

Isaac Skinner was born in Vermillion county, Indiana, January 5, 1829, and is a son of Joseph Skinner, who was among the earliest settlers in the neighborhood of Newman, coming, in 1839, from Vermillion county, Indiana, and settling along the timber a mile and a half southwest of where Newman now is. There were no schools in the vicinity when he first came to the county. He worked for his father until of age and then engaged in farming on rented land. In about 1853 he had saved money enough to enter one hundred and sixty acres of land. His mother, whose maiden

name was Polly Gaston, was a daughter of Thomas Gaston, who lived in Meigs county, Ohio, and probably was a native of Canada.

His father, Joseph, was born in Maine. His grandmother, Sarah Gaston, was born on the St. Lawrence river, while her parents were held captives by the Indians.

Isaac Skinner was reared on a farm and received the limited school advantages that were common in that day. He was first a Whig and since the birth of the Republican party has been identified with that organization. He has been three times married. First, in February, 1859, he married Miss Mahala Drake, who died in 1865. His second wife was Mrs. Mary Hill, whose maiden name was Lewis; her death occurred in 1869. His third wife was Mrs. Catherine Barnes, whose maiden name was Bell. He has five children, one, Robert, born of the first union, and four, Katie, Margaret, Elvin and Arthur, by the last marriage. Mr. Skinner owns three hundred and twenty acres of land adjoining the city of Newman, and has about retired from active business pursuits. He joined the Methodist church in 1858. As a christian gentleman and public-spirited citizen, Mr. Skinner has an enviable record, one upon which he and his friends can look with pride and satisfaction

ALEXANDER HANCE.

Alexander Hance, who is one of the ideal farmers of Douglas county, came to Newman township in 1871 and engaged as an ordinary farm hand, at which he continued for some seven or eight years. His career is a fine example of what a man can do with a determined purpose in life. From the ordinary walks of life he has gradually risen to the front rank as a farmer, stock-raiser and a business man.

Mr. Hance was born in Washington county, Tennessee, February 19, 1850, and there he remained until he came to Douglas county. He purchased his first land of three hundred and twenty acres in 1889, paying thirty dollars per acre for it, and has since added one hundred and sixty acres. He is a son of Mordecai and

Millie (Lackey) Hance, who were born respectively in North Carolina and east Tennessee. His father, who resided at Tompkinsville, Kentucky, volunteered in 1861 in the Ninth Kentucky Cavalry, and remained out until the close of the war. He was with Sherman mostly, and was with him from Atlanta to the sea. He was a son of Samuel Hance, who was born in England. Alexander Lackey was Mr. Hance's maternal grandfather. Alexander Hance carries on farming on a very extensive scale and feeds regularly about one or two hundred head of cattle.

In 1874 our subject was united in marriage

to Miss Nancy, a daughter of John H. Biggs, who came to north Newman township from Edgar county in about 1855. His wife died in 1895. To them were born seven children: Burnette, Robert, Myrtle, Jay and Joseph, living; and Glenn and an infant, deceased. His second and present wife was Miss Generva, a daughter of W. H. Holton, of near Jeffersonville, Indiana. Two children have blessed this union: Leon and Leonard. Mr. Hance has served as commissioner of highways and has been a ruling elder of the Cumberland Presbyterian church, at Fairfield, since 1872.

JOSEPH ASHURST.

Joseph Ashurst, principal and superintendent of the Camargo public schools and present nominee of the Democratic party for the office of county superintendent of schools, has been a leading educator in the county for several years. He was born in Somerset, Pulaski county, Kentucky, April 16, 1872, and is a son of Henry Clay and Elizabeth (Thurman) Ashurst, who were both born in Pulaski county, Kentucky. His grandfathers, Henry Ashurst and Joseph Thurman, were natives of Virginia and early settlers in Pulaski county, where they were engaged in agricultural pursuits. His father, Henry C. Ashurst, was one time sheriff of his native county.

Joseph Ashurst attended the common school and afterward the high school, and is largely self educated. In Douglas county he stands at the very front rank as a successful educator and teaches in his schools at Camargo, beside the common branches, botany, philosophy, zoology and algebra. Prior to his coming to Camargo, which was in September, 1899, he resided at Arthur, where he located in 1890 and taught school in the country and subsequently was grammar teacher in the Arthur schools which position he resigned to accept his present one. In 1894 he was united in marriage to Miss Lucy B., a daughter of Henry C. Wood

a retired farmer, of Arthur, but formerly of Moultrie county. Mr. Wood was born near Vincennes, Indiana, in 1845, and is a son of Eli Wood, who was an early settler in Knox county, migrating from North Carolina. He was a soldier in Company F, Eighteenth Infantry, and served until the close of the war. His wife was Miss Ann Shultz, of Piatt county.

Joseph Ashurst, because of his high merit as an educator and general popularity as a gentleman, was chosen by the Democratic party to make the race for county superintendent in the next election, and it is conceded that he has most excellent chances of being elected. He owns eighty-five acres of land just south of Arcola; is a member of the Masonic and Odd Fellows fraternities and of the Woodmen. He has been retained in the Camargo schools for another year at quite a good increase in salary, thereby showing to the people of Camargo and Douglas county that his work is appreciated. Although the majority in the fall election is against him he has a better show for election than any other candidate that the Democratic party has put out in several years.

GEORGE H. MOSER.

George H. Moser, a well known and successful homeopathic physician of Arcola, was born in Auburn, Schuylkill county, Pennsylvania, December 19, 1859, and is the son of John Moser, a native of the same state. His mother was Alvinia Hellig, who was a descendant of Quaker ancestry. The Moser family are descendants of the Dutch, whose lineage is traced back by some of the members to Daniel Moser, who made his settlement in Pennsylvania in the year 1799.

Doctor Moser came west and early in life turned his attention to the study of medicine. After a thorough preparation he entered the Homeopathic Medical College of Missouri, at St. Louis, which is one of the leading medical institutions of the west, and was graduated with distinguished honors in the class of 1889-90. He immediately entered upon the practice of his profession at Belleville, Illinois, where he remained in active practice for two years. Then he removed to Bond county, where he was located until 1895, when, on the 12th of October, in the same year, he came to Arcola. He came here with a fixed purpose of making Arcola and vicinity his field of work, and time has proven that he has made no mistake in his location. He almost immediately got into a paying practice, and within the last year he has all the business that he could possibly attend to.

Dr. Moser is a splendid judge of human nature, a close observer and skilled in the diagnosis of his patients. Affable and approachable, he has within a very short time made a host of substantial friends. On December 10, 1881, he was united in marriage and has three children: Lola, Viola and Hattie.

J. A. McGOWN.

J. A. McGown, a most successful business man and a typical farmer residing in Newman township, was born in Edgar county, Illinois, March 30, 1832, and is a son of John and Olive Blackman, who were natives of Kentucky and New York respectively. His father emigrated to Edgar county, where he resided up to his death, which occurred April 18, 1882. His mother died in 1892.

J. A. McGown was reared to manhood on a farm in his native county and in about 1875 located in Newman township, where he now resides. He owns four hundred and seventy-two acres of highly cultivated land and one of the most magnificent residences in the county. He farms on business principles and has made himself independent in a financial way by his careful and methodical way of doing things. On November 22, 1881, he was united in marriage to Miss Martha C. Todd, and to their marriage have been born five children: Florence, Olive, Grace, Arthur and Anne.

Our subject has held the office of road commissioner for nine years, and twenty-one years out of the twenty-five he has resided in Newman township he has been school director and is greatly interested in the success of education. In 1898 he built his new house. He is a member of the Knights of Pythias and the Order of Woodmen.

JOHN M. MADISON.

Within the past two years Tuscola has lost many of its oldest and most prominent citizens by death, but in the list none have been more sadly missed or sincerely mourned than our subject, John M. Madison, whose death occurred Monday, July 13, 1896. He was born in Harrison county, Kentucky, May 6, 1823, and was at the time of his death in the seventy-fourth year of his age. He belonged to a family of ten children; one brother and two sisters are still living: H. B. Madison, Tuscola; Mrs. Harriet Parrish, of Cynthiana, Kentucky; and Mrs. Parmelia Carter, of Washington.

On September 22, 1851, our subject married Miss Jennie Rankin, at Cynthiana, a good and noble woman, who preceded him to the grave only a few years. To them were born Harry, Robert and Fannie, all of whom reside in Tuscola, the two former composing the large clothing house of Harry Madison & Company. In 1854 Mr. and Mrs. Madison came to Charleston, Illinois, where he opened up a store, and in 1860 they removed to Tuscola, where Mr. Madison engaged in the mercantile business, which he continued up to within two years of his death. For many years he conducted the leading general store in Tuscola and by his honesty and straightforward dealing with his fellow men prospered in a gratifying manner. He was a man of unquestioned character and possessed the fullest confidence of all of our people. He and his wife spent the later years of their lives with their daughter, Mrs. Fannie Loose, who made it the purpose of her life to care for them and make their last days pleasant, granting their every wish.

OWEN E. JONES.

Owen E. Jones, one of the leading merchants of Murdock since 1893, and the second son of Abram Jones, was born in Murdock township, January 31, 1862. After leaving the common schools, he took a course at the commercial college at Terre Haute in 1897. In 1899 Mr. Jones took in as a partner Percy Welliver, and the firm is doing a thriving business.

In 1894 our subject was married to Miss Nora B. Dever, of Murdock, Illinois. Mr.

Jones is a member of the Modern Woodmen; he and his wife are members of the Methodist church; he is classed as one of the progressive and successful business men of the county.

William Jones, eldest son of Abram, and a well-known grain buyer and hotel keeper of Murdock, was born in Newman township, this county, April 4, 1858, and was reared on the farm one and one-half miles from Murdock. His education was received in the neighborhood schools, and at the age of twenty-one started in merchandising at Hume, where he continued to do business for three years. In 1882 he engaged in the same line of business at Murdock, and remained there until 1889. In the latter year he, with John W. Burgett, of Sargent township, formed a partnership in buying grain at Murdock. They continued to do business for two years, when the firm was succeeded by Fred I. Rush & Co., of Indianapolis, Mr. Jones acting as the buyer. He buys about three hundred thousand bushels of grain annually, which is purchased principally from Murdock township farmers. In October, 1899, he took charge of the Jones House, which was previously managed by his father, Abram Jones.

In 1880 Mr. Jones was wedded to Miss Victoria Dever, of Clark county, Illinois. They have two children, Asher C. and Nellie B. From 1893 to 1898 he served as postmaster at Murdock, and is now serving his twelfth year as justice of the peace. He is a member of the Modern Woodmen, and himself and wife are members of the Methodist church. He is one of the substantial citizens who has done well his part to add stability to the business and social life of Murdock.

Abram Jones, father of William W. and Owen E., was one of the early settlers of what is now Douglas county. He came in the fall of 1853 and located on a farm southeast of Tuscola, where he resided with his cousin, Owen Jones, until his marriage in 1855. He married Miss Elizabeth Eagler, of Macksburg, Ohio. In 1857 he became a tenant farmer in what was then called Coles county, and in

1863 moved to what is now known as Murdock township, Douglas county, where he has lived since and become the owner of one hundred and twenty acres of land, which he has only recently sold and retired from active business. He was born October 16, 1826, in Monroe county, Ohio, and is a son of Samuel Jones. His grandfather, Ephraim Jones, was born in Wales, and his maternal grandfather, Patrick Hamilton, was born in Ireland.

To Mr. and Mrs. Abram Jones were also born four daughters. (1) Anna Belle was born September 5, 1856, and became the wife of Hugh M. Wilson. To them were born two children, one of whom died in infancy; and Marvin A. Mrs. Wilson died June 26, 1898. (2) Mary Frances was born November 4, 1860, and died January 2, 1861. (3) Carrie was born November 6, 1864, and on March 19, 1885, became the wife of Samuel Baxter. Their children were Samuel H. and Gertrude. (4) Lulie Iowen was born September 25, 1867, and on September 4, 1895, married John Horne. The death of Mrs. Abram Jones occurred July 8, 1893.

CAPTAIN DAVID BAILEY.

Captain David Bailey, of Tuscola, one of the best and most favorably known citizens of the county, was born in Edgar county, December 24, 1845, and was reared on the farm and received his education in the Westfield College. For some years he resided on his farm of 320 acres in Murdock township. In May, 1887, with his family, he removed from his farm to Tuscola, where he resides in one of the beautiful homes for which this place is noted.

In 1870 he married Miss Elizabeth Calhoun, who is a most estimable woman. They have two children, Gertrude and Edward. Captain Bailey is a Knight Templar in Masonry, and is of easy and pleasing address, very approachable and a genial companion. He is a son of David Bailey, who was born in Salem, Rockingham county, New Hampshire, August 2, 1814, of poor but honest parents, his father being a farmer and shoemaker, to which business most of the boys in that section of the country were brought up. There were nine children in this New England home, three boys and six girls, and the story of their early life is only that which has been written of so many others, of hard work and of a few months only at the district school during the winter season. David Bailey had no further opportunity for scholastic training. Indeed, while yet under twelve years of age he was put out to work. After spending a number of years on the farm Mr. Bailey found an opportunity to enter a clerkship at Haverhill, Massachusetts, but did not long remain there on account of poor health. He soon drifted into Boston, or rather to Charlestown, where he for a time held a clerkship in the state penitentiary. Late in the '30s he decided to follow the star of empire, and came west as far as Danville, Illinois, entering a general store, and it was while there that he first met Miss Hannah A. Finley, to whom he was married February 9, 1841. Of this union were born five children: three sons, Edward, president of the Champaign National Bank, of that city; David, of Tuscola, and Ozias, of Texas, who survive their father; and two daughters, Abiah, who died in childhood, and Sue Bailey Slayden, who died some years ago in Waco, Texas.

After spending some time working in Danville, Mr. Bailey went to Bloomfield, Edgar county, walking all the way because he had not the means to pay coach fare, that being the only mode of travel in those days. There he took a position on a salary. Later, with his brother Ozias, who had recently come west with a few dollars saved, he formed a partnership, under the firm name of O. & D. Bailey, and the Bailey peddler wagons became well known all over the country between the Wabash and Sangamon rivers. The brothers also operated a pork packing establishment at Clinton, Indiana, on the Wabash, shipping their product by flat-boat to New Orleans.

About 1855 Mr. Bailey moved to Monticello, thence, after a short sojourn, to Urbana, and in March, 1856, he removed to Champaign, where for a number of years he successfully conducted a dry goods business in the location where now stands the Metropolitan block, occupied by F. K. Robeson & Brother.

Aside from this Mr. Bailey was one of the original shareholders and directors of the First National Bank, and it was largely through his efforts that the charter was secured. The names appearing with his in the original articles of incorporation were James S. Wright, John F. Thomas, William M. Way, Hamilton Jefferson, B. F. Harris, John S. Beasley, Daniel Gardner, William C. Barrett, Simon H. Busey, S. P. Percival, John G. Clark and A. E. Harmon. Mr. Bailey disposed of his holdings in this institution some time during the '70s. In 1882 he became one of the charter members of the Champaign National Bank, in which his holdings were always considerable and in which he had been a director continuously since its organization. During Mr. Bailey's residence in this city he was several times elected to the board of supervisors, and also served one term as school trustee. He was a public-spirited citizen, contributing liberally, yet wisely, to every worthy enterprise, whether secular or religious. His givings were never ostentatious, but it may be said in passing that among his gifts are numbered the lot occupied by the Baptist parsonage, he being a member of that society, and the valuable ground now occupied by the city building.

Mr. Bailey gave up his residence in Champaign about 1877, traveling for a season, and finally locating in St. Joseph, Missouri, where he remained until after the death of his wife, in 1879. He then lived for a time in New York City, and finally returned to his boyhood home in New Hampshire where he resided most of the time until his death, visiting his old home and friends in Champaign frequently. March 22, 1882, he married Miss Harriet Haseltine, of Methune, Massachusetts, and only two weeks afterward followed her remains to the cemetery. He was again married, on November 1, 1886, at Salem, New Hampshire, to Mrs. Mary B. Ewins, who survives him. She has often visited here with him and has made many warm friends, whose sincere sympathy attends her in this bereavement.

Mr. Bailey's new home in Champaign, built on the site of the old family residence, had just been completed and occupied by him, and it was his intention had he lived to spend the closing days of his life amid the scenes of his greatest successful activity. Mr. Bailey was a man of magnificent physical presence and it may be truly said that he carried within his breast a soul worthy so splendid a habitation. He sought no man's praise, satisfied to have the approval of his own conscience, and he was unmovable in his adherence to justice and right. Once his duty was made plain nothing could swerve him from it. Yet under a stern exterior beat a great, big, kind heart, as those who knew him can best testify. He was a manly man, and that means much. His character, developed in the pioneer days, may not have take on the esthetic finish of these later times, but what it lacked in polish it made up in strength and integrity. The life and labors of such as he have made possible the greater comfort and beauty in the world of the present.

During the war of the Rebellion David Bailey, Jr., enlisted as a member of the Sixty-seventh Illinois Infantry, and at the close of his three months' term of enlistment returned home and in 1864 enlisted in the One Hundred and Thirty-fifth Illinois Infantry, serving until the close of the war.

ALBERT F. FIDLER.

Albert F. Fidler is one of the self-made and highly successful young farmers and business men of the county, and is a son of Levi

Fidler, who was born April 28, 1819, in Berks county, Pennsylvania. Albert F.'s grandfather, Samuel, was a native of Lancaster, Pennsylvania, and was of Dutch ancestry. Adam Fidler (great-grandfather), who came originally from Germany, was the founder of this branch of the Fidler family in America.

Our subject's grandfather, Samuel Fidler, fought in the war of 1812, and his great-grandfather, Adam, in the war of the Revolution. Samuel Fidler was a brick plasterer and contractor by trade, and was married to a daughter of Valentine Showalter, who was born in Pennsylvania and was descended from German ancestry.

Levi Fidler was reared to manhood in Lebanon county, Pennsylvania, until he became of age, when, in 1840, he emigrated west and settled in Union county, Indiana, and in 1861 located in what is now Newman township, Douglas county. He learned the carpentering business, at which he was engaged up to 1861, when he bought what is now known as the Thomas H. Smith farm, one of the finest in the county. He kept this farm until 1885, when he sold it. In 1842 Levi Fidler wedded Mary Ann Hessler, a native of Bourbon township and a daughter of John and Mary (Thomas) Hessler, who were formerly of Kentucky. To Mr. and Mrs. Fidler were born the following children: John, Matilda, William J., Joseph S., Dan G., George W., Smith T., LaFayette, Sarah C., Levy Eddy and Albert F., the subject of this sketch. John S., William J. and Daniel G. served in the Civil war

Albert F. Fidler has made it a rule in his life to do what he does well. Commencing life with comparatively nothing, but with a willing mind and heart he has attained a degree of success in life far above the average. He is yet a comparatively young man, and his farm of two hundred and forty acres is one of the most productive and successfully managed in Douglas county. In 1883 he was united in marriage to Miss Anna Lewis, of Newman, Illinois, to whom he is much devoted and who has been a true and devoted wife to him. They have the following children: Mona and Wayne.

JAMES H. WRIGHT.

James H. Wright, one of the oldest grain buyers in the county, residing at Arthur, was born near the town of Poland, Trumbull (now Mahoning) county, Ohio, February 6, 1827, and is a son of James and Mary (Kidd) Wright, who were born near Poland, Trumbull (now Mahoning) county, Ohio, of Scotch-Irish origin.

Rev. James Wright (father) received his education for the Presbyterian ministry at the Canonsburg College, and spent most of his life in preaching the gospel, first at Poland, and later at Westfield, Pennsylvania. He died in 1843 at the age of fifty-nine years. His father was Alexander Wright, who was an early settler from the north of Ireland, to Washington county. He married a Scotch girl by the name of Esther Silcox. Robert Kidd (grandfather) was also a native of Ireland, was an early settler in Trumbull county, Ohio, and in religious affairs he was known as a Seceder in that day, now known as a United Presbyterian.

James H. Wright was reared in his native county, and in Pennsylvania, receiving the advantages of an ordinary education. In 1857 he came west and located at Arcola, which at that time contained but three houses, and was for several years engaged in farming in that vicinity. In 1873 he commenced buying grain at Hindsboro, where he continued successfully in business until 1886, when he removed to Arthur, where he has since resided, engaged in buying grain for the firm of Bartlett, Kuhn & Co.

In 1848 Mr. Wright was united in marriage to Miss Sarah E. Rogers, who was a daughter of Samuel and Sarah Waugh Rogers. She was born in New Bedford, Pennsylvania. They have seven children: William, who resides in Cairo; Sadie; Frank E., who lives in Arthur, engaged in the lumber business; Samuel R., a farmer in South Dakota; John M., engineer of his father's grain elevator; Nettie, wife of G. H. Damron, of Arcola; and A. K. resides in Springfield, Illinois. Mr. Wright has been an Odd Fellow since 1852, and has served as president of the town board of Arthur. James H. Wright has passed the allotted three-score and ten years of man, but, owing to his abstemious habits and good constitution, he still enjoys good health, and it is hoped that he will live for many years to continue the good which has been characteristic of his life.

CHARLES W. WILSON

Charles W. Wilson, editor and proprietor of the Tuscola Review, was born fourteen miles west of Plainfield, Indiana, February 15, 1856, and in 1865 located in Tuscola. He attended school more or less up until fourteen years of age. In 1872 he entered the office of the Tuscola True Republican as office boy. The paper was owned by Charles Smith and was Democratic in politics. Later he entered the office of the Tuscola Gazette, which was edited by Hon. Leander B. Lester, now of Washington. Mr. Wilson remained here about one year when he went to the Review, then owned and edited by Converse & Park, who founded the paper July 23, 1875. In 1876 he went on the printing force where he remained for some years. Converse & Park were succeeded by the well-known writer, Col. Phecian, who was the editor for six months; the latter was known as one of the wittiest writers the newspaper fraternity afforded. During this time he wrote a great deal for the Inter-Ocean, which kept him away a great deal, and this forced Mr. Wilson to take charge of the editorial tripod. Howard was succeeded by Major Asa Miller, who managed the paper up to December, 1892, when he sold out to Charles W. Wilson, who reconstructed the plant throughout, buying new machinery, and to-day issues every Friday one of the newsiest, wittiest and cleanest county newspapers published east, west, north or south. Mr. Wilson has a paid circulation of three thousand and there is little doubt but what his paper is read by twelve thousand people every week. His career as a newspaper man has been remarkable; commencing as the "editor's devil," he has become recognized as an able writer and all-round newspaper man. Within a year after he became proprietor the circulation of the paper became double. As to the newspaper history of Tuscola, college bred men have come and gone, who were writers on different papers of the city, but Mr. Wilson, who has educated himself, remains, and it is a fact that might be mentioned, that his paper, while Democratic, is popular among the Republicans.

Mr. Wilson was united in marriage to Miss Christina Cosler, a daughter of the late Isaac Cosler, who was for twenty years president of the Douglas County Fair

EMMOR W. JEFFERS.

Emmor W. Jeffers, the present circuit clerk of Douglas county, who has occupied that office since February 3, 1899, was born in Pike county, Illinois, November 19, 1861. He is a son of John C. and Elizabeth (McKinney) Jeffers, both natives of Ohio, who removed to Douglas county and settled in Camargo township about 1864. His mother died in December, 1893, while his father resides in Bloomington, Illinois. (For further ancestry of the Jeffers family see sketch of George C. Jeffers, of Camargo). James McKinney, our subject's maternal grandfather, was a native of Ohio.

In 1889 E. W. Jeffers was married to Miss Carrie F. Hill, a daughter of Thomas W. and Rebecca (Underwood) Hill, and as a result of this union they have two children: Villa and Beulah.

Since 1890 Mr. Jeffers has been secretary and keeper of records and seal of the Knights of Pythias lodge of Tuscola, and is also promi-

nent in several other fraternal orders. He was nominated without opposition at the Republican primaries held March 24, 1900, for the same office he now occupies.

The Tuscola Journal of March 11, 1899, says of Mr. Jeffers: "In selecting Emmor W. Jeffers as their candidate for the office of circuit clerk the Republican representatives in convention have voiced the sentiment of the people. Mr. Jeffers is of that class of young Republicans who are enthusiastic in their support of their party, and while in the office with the late Major Daniel A. Conover as deputy, he became thoroughly familiar with every detail of the work and is in every way particularly qualified to fill the position with credit to himself and party besides giving the people entire satisfaction.

"He is a native of this grand state, having been born in Pike county on the 19th day of November, 1861, and about 1864 he came to this county with his parents and was employed on his father's farm until he reached his majority when he started out for himself, working by the month for two years for Nicholas Cooley, after which he secured a business education, attending nights at the Terre Haute Business College. He graduated from that institution and went to Bloomington, Illinois, where he secured a good position in a grocery store where he was employed nearly two years, when he came to Tuscola and accepted a similar position with Joseph J. Knox, formerly of this city, who was succeeded by F. M. Wardall & Co. He remained with this firm until he opened up a grocery business in company with J. F. Kerker in the building on Sale street, now occupied by T. J. McKee. On account of failing health he was compelled to give up the store and enter the real estate business, which he followed with success until January 1, 1897, when he was appointed deputy circuit clerk by the late Major Daniel A. Conover, which position he filled with credit and honor.

"Upon the death of Mr. Conover he was appointed protempore circuit clerk by the judges of this district, and he will certainly be elected to succeed himself, and fill out the unexpired term of the late lamented Major Conover."

W. L. WATSON.

W. L. Watson was born in Vermilion county, Illinois, on the 22d of December, 1837. His father was William D. Watson, in his early life an itinerant Methodist preacher who traveled extensively through Indiana, having been born in the neighborhood of Vincennes, and in Fountain county, of that state, married Mary Low. His health finally failed him, and coming to Illinois, he located above Georgetown in Vermilion county. William Watson, the grandfather, was born in Kentucky, and when a young man settled in the vicinity of Vincennes, Indiana.

W. L. was the oldest son and second child of the family. His father came to Douglas county, then Coles, in 1839, and located first on Brushy Fork, a short distance west of Newman. After a residence here of a year or two he moved to Camargo, and afterward to section 35, in township 16, range 9, where he resided till his death, which occurred in October, 1858. His wife survived him till April, 1866. They had nine children. W. L. Watson was between four and five years old when his father located southeast of Camargo. At this latter place he mainly received his education, partly under the instruction of his father, who taught school at Camargo and was one of his first teachers.

The old log school house stood about one hundred yards north of Alonzo Lion's store, on the road leading north from Camargo. In the winter of 1849-50, and also 1853-54, he attended the Georgetown Academy, in Vermilion county, then having the best reputation of any school of learning in this part of the state. At the death of his father in 1858, Mr. Watson, as the oldest son, took charge of the farm and managed it in the interests of the family till 1862.

The war of the Rebellion at this time had broken out, and in February, 1862, Mr. Watson volunteered. He preferred the cavalry service and being unable to enlist in an Illinois cavalry regiment, he went to St. Louis and enlisted in the Fifth Missouri Cavalry for three years. He was with the Fifth Missouri two years and a half, during which time he was mostly in the southern part of Missouri. In August, 1864, he re-enlisted in the Thirteenth Missouri Cavalry, and served to January, 1866. He was a non-commissioned officer. At the close of the war his regiment was sent out on the plains to fight the Indians. While in Missouri he was in the campaign against Price, and in the battles of Independence and Fort Scott. After receiving his discharge in January, 1866, he came home and commenced farming on the old homestead.

JOHN C. HOSTETLER.

John C. Hostetler, who is engaged in the agricultural implement business, including buggies and wagons, and recently elected alderman from the third ward in Tuscola, was born in Douglas county, August 27, 1866, and is a son of D. C. and L. M. Hostetler, natives of Indiana. The father settled in Bowdre township some time in the 'fifties, and died in Tuscola, in 1895, in the sixty-fourth year of his age. His mother is still living. Mr. Hostetler was married in 1889 to Miss Laura A., daughter of H. C. Jones, whose sketch is found on another page. They have one child, Leon.

Mr. Hostetler operated a planing and repair shop previous to entering into his present business, which he sold out in 1896. He was a member of the Masonic fraternity and the Order of Red Men, and is one of the popular and promising young business men of Tuscola.

JOHN L. GOFF.

John L. Goff served as sheriff of Douglas county from 1887 to 1891, and at the time of his death, in 1892, he held the office of supervisor. He was married to Miss Josie R. Rice, a daughter of Martin Rice, deceased, of Camargo (see sketch). Mrs. Goff owns a half section of land, part of which is in Camargo and a part in Tuscola townships. She resides in Tuscola.

THOMAS CRADDICK.

Thomas Craddick, a typical Kentuckian and a self-made man, now residing on his farm in Arcola township, was born in Montgomery county, Kentucky, April 13, 1856, and is a son of Michael Craddick and Catherine (Welch) Craddick, who were natives of Ireland. His father emigrated from Kentucky to Arcola township 1869 and died in 1890. His mother died in 1896, and they are both buried in the Arcola cemetery. Mr. Craddick's farm contains one hundred and fourteen acres of land. He has never been married. Socially he is very popular and in business one of the substantial men of the township.

GEORGE W. HENSON.

George Warren Henson, deceased, was born September 5, 1821, at Cynthiana, Kentucky. He was a son of Gideon and Nancy (Shumate)

Henson. He was the eldest of a family of six children and of Scotch-German descent. With his father's family he left the state of his nativity in 1834 and emigrated to Vermilion county, Illinois, and there remained until 1844, when he came into the section of country which is now Douglas county and immediately began the improvement of a farm.

He married Miss Eliza P. Sargent, a native of Illinois. To this union were born eleven children, six of whom are living, two sons and four daughters.

The county of Douglas, by the death of Mr. Henson, lost one of its most prominent citizens and honorable men. Politically he was a Democrat. He was a Mason, a pioneer of the county, and a man possessing a spirit of charity and enterprise. His death occurred May 9, 1881, at his residence near Camargo, Illinois.

FRANK W. HAMMETT.

Frank W. Hammett, cashier of the First National Bank of Tuscola, and one of the county's young men of recognized ability, was born on a farm in Camargo township, Douglas county, Illinois, February 12, 1862. (See sketch of his father, James R. Hammett.) Mr. Hammett grew to manhood on his father's farm and was principally educated in the University of Illinois. For some years after leaving college he was engaged in the manufacture of tiling at Camargo and Long View. In March, 1891, he accepted the position of bookkeeper in the First National Bank of Tuscola, and was promoted to cashier of the same bank in August, 1898.

He is a Knight Templar in Masonry; is a member of one of the oldest and most prominent families in the county, and will undoubtedly make his mark in the business world. He owns one hundred and sixty acres of land in Newman township

W. H. HANCOCK.

W. H. Hancock, who is one of the most successful broom-corn brokers and business men of Tuscola, was born in Chicago, March 29, 1864, and is a son of W. S. and Sarah (Bell) Hancock. His father was born in Oxford, Ohio, and his mother in Mifflintown, Pennsylvania. His father is now living a retired life in Chicago. W. H. Hancock was raised to manhood in Chicago and educated in the Cook county normal school. His first position of any importance was that of conductor on the Pullman car lines, and he continued as such for seven years, running over thirty-six different railroads. For seven years he was engaged in the broom-corn business with his father in Chicago.

In January, 1895, he was married to Miss Tillie Brogan, a highly accomplished young lady of Muscatine, Iowa. They have two children, John Henry and May.

In 1899 he associated himself in partnership with W. Avery Howard (a notice of whom is found elsewhere) in the broom-corn brokerage business with their office in Tuscola. The firm is one of the most active and responsible engaged in the business. During the last year they handled about fifteen hundred tons of broom corn. He and his wife stand high in the social circles of Tuscola, where they expect to make their future home.

WILLIAM A. WISEMAN.

William A. Wiseman, a well known physician of Camargo, where he has been in successful practice for several years, was born at Waterloo, Lawrence county, Ohio, January 1, 1853, and is a son of Abner and Martha J. (Irwin) Wiseman. His father was a native of Virginia and his mother of Ohio. Isaac Wiseman's grandfather was also born in Virginia and his maternal grandfather, George Irwin, was born in Virginia.

Dr. Wiseman was reared in his native county, where he attended the public schools and subsequently, in 1878, became a student at DePauw University, where he pursued a regular college course for three years and a half. In 1882 he commenced the study of medicine in the office of Dr. C. Patterson and in 1883 went to Jefferson Medical College, Philadelphia, and was graduated therefrom in the class of 1886. While at Philadelphia he took special courses in skin diseases and also in gynecology and gained practical experience at the Philadelphia Lying-in Hospital. In the spring of 1886 he located at Camargo in the practice of his profession and here he has built up a successful practice.

In political opinion the Doctor is a consistent Prohibitionist, and is also a member of the Modern Woodmen and Court of Honor. In 1875 he was married to Miss Emma C. Carrel, of Dennison, Ohio. They have three children: Eva C., Omer D. and Meda A.

IRA M. MULLIKEN.

Ira M. Mulliken, junior member of the well-known firm of Barr & Mulliken and one of the rising young business men of Newman, was born in Champaign county, Illinois, December 17, 1865. His father, James W. Mulliken, was a native of Johnson county, Indiana,

and removed to Champaign county in about 1852. His mother, Catherine, was a daughter of Rev. Samuel F. Miller, who was born in 1815, and at present resides in Arcola. (See sketch of W. H. Bush, of Hindsboro.) In about 1868 the father of I. M. Mulliken removed to a farm near Hindsboro, where the latter remained until he arrived at the age of twenty-one years, when he went to Arcola to reside, and there worked at the carpenter's trade. He attended Lee's academy at Loxa, Illinois, for six months, then subsequently attended the embalming college at Indianapolis. From 1893 to June 1, 1896, he was a member of the undertaking firm of Mike, Miller & Co., at Charleston, Illinois. In the latter year he removed to Newman to accept a partnership with James Barr (see sketch).

On September 4, 1893, he was married to Miss Ida A., a daughter of John W. Allison, of Arcola. They have one child, a daughter, Frances Marie. He is a member and noble grand of the I. O. O. F.; elder in the Christian

church. and superintendent of its Sunday school. He is also chief patriarch of the I. O. O. F. encampment; member of the Masonic fraternity and clerk of the school board of Newman. The firm of Barr &-Mullikin own two large stores in Newman, Mr. Barr superintending the furniture and undertaking establishment on the west side of the square, and Mr. Mulliken manages the hardware and tin shop and does the undertaking work on the north side. They carry a large stock and do quite an extensive business, drawing trade for miles around them.

ALBERT W. WALLACE.

Albert W. Wallace is president of the First National Bank of Tuscola, one of the leading banking institutions of central Illinois. The First National Bank was organized in November, 1869, with a paid up capital of one hundred and thirteen thousand dollars. Its first president was William P. Cannon (a brother of Congressman J. G. Cannon) and W. H. Lamb was the first cashier. Mr. Cannon remained president until 1872, when he was succeeded by Henry T. Caraway, who remained president up to January 1, 1898, when he was succeeded by Mr. Wallace. Mr. Lamb remained cashier up to July 1, 1898, when he was succeeded by the present cashier, F. H. Hammett. The bank was reorganized in the fall of 1890 and the capital stock reduced to sixty thousand dollars. The directors of this bank are among the wealthiest men of the county.

A. W. Wallace, who has been connected with the First National Bank for years, is a son of Andrew G. Wallace, whose death occurred in July, 1878. The ancestry of the Wallace family is traced back to Scotland. Andrew G.'s grandfather emigrated from Scotland to Ireland, and from there to America, settling in Pennsylvania near where the three states of Virginia, Maryland and Pennsylvania came together. He had five sons, three of whom moved away from their Pennsylvania home. One of these was William Wallace, the youngest child, who came to Hardin county, Kentucky, and from there removed to Davis county, Indiana, where Andrew G. Wallace was born March 31, 1824. He was the second child by his father's second wife, whose maiden name was Vashti Winkler. When two years old his father moved from Davis county to Vermillion county, Indiana, and there settled down as a farmer. After a residence of about ten years, the family, in 1833 or 1834, came to Coles county, and located on Gresey creek, just south of the line which now divides Douglas from Coles county. The country was thinly settled both in Vermilion and Coles counties, where Mr. Wallace's boyhood was spent, and but scanty advantages were afforded for obtaining anything like a good education. He was compelled to rely mainly on his own resources, but his quick perceptive faculties and industry enabled him to pick up a large amount of information, thus fitting himself for the duties of his after life. In 1841 the family moved north, in what is now Douglas county, and kept the widely known "Wallace stand,' west of Hickory Grove, which received its name from the family. In 1842 his father died. Mr. Wallace was then in his eighteenth year, and the charge of the family fell upon him, his older brother having previously left home. He remained on the homestead and continued to farm until 1854. On November 22, 1845, he married Harriet E. Busby, a native of Ohio, whose family had come to Illinois in 1836. At this time his younger brothers and sisters were grown up and were able to take care of themselves. His mother died in 1848. In 1854 Mr. Wallace removed to Camargo and began business there as a cattle dealer. After a residence of four years there he removed to Tuscola, then just springing into existence, the fourth house indeed having been built by Mr Wallace himself. Here he kept a hotel for about two years. From the inception of the plan of forming a new county out of the north of Coles, Mr. Wallace was deeply interested in it, and he may be said to have been the prime mover in the project. The petition presented to the Legislature during the session of 1858-9, in gaining which the bill was passed organizing the county, was drawn up by Mr. Wallace. He subsequently used all his influence to secure a favorable vote, on the question being submitted to the people of Coles county. In the spring of 1858 he was elected justice of the peace of Tuscola, the first ever elected in the town. In the year of 1859 he was elected first circuit clerk of the county. To this position he was re-elected in 1860, again in 1864 and again in 1868, thus serving four consecutive terms, performing the duties of the office to his own credit and the satisfaction of the people. In June, 1859, he was appointed master in chancery, a position which he still holds. For the last twelve years Mr. Wallace has been extensively engaged in the money loaning and real estate business. He possesses a complete set of abstracts and has every facility for the transaction of business in that line. Mr. Wallace was one of the pioneers of Tuscola and one of the founders of the town. With one exception he is the oldest resident. He was the first person in the town who could sing a religious song, the other inhabitants in some way being deficient in their musical acquirements. Mr. Wallace and his wife, with Mr. Thomas Woody and his wife, organized the Methodist church of Tuscola, of which he was a faithful and consistent member and for a long period class leader. To his exertions was largely due the building of the present church edifice. For twenty-five years in all Mr. Wallace served the people in various capacities—sufficient evidence of his popularity and the confidence reposed in him as an honest and faithful officer. He had ten children, all of whom are living. In his younger days he was a Whig. On the dissolution of that party he became a Republican, and was as steadfast in his adherence to the principles of that party as he was enthusiastic in its support. During the war he was active and liberal in the support of the Union cause, sacrificing both time and money. Few men were more closely associated with the progress of the county, and few were better citizens.

HENRY C. JONES.

Henry Clay Jones, the affable and genial treasurer of Douglas county, was born in Franklin county, Indiana, December 2, 1842, a son of Calvin and Hannah (Case) Jones. He was reared to manhood in his native county, and in 1860 removed to Douglas county. In 1862 he joined Company K, Seventy-ninth Illinois Infantry, and served as a private soldier in the Civil war until June 12, 1865, when he was honorably discharged at Nashville, Tennessee. He was wounded in the leg in the battle of Liberty Gap, which prevented him from keeping up with his regiment until the battle of Missionary Ridge, in which he participated. During the time between the battles of Liberty Gap and Missionary Ridge he caught cold in the wound and was confined in the hospital for three months. After his release he rejoined his regiment and was with it in every fight until the close. After the war Mr. Jones returned to Douglas county and engaged in farming, at which he continued for six years, when he removed to Arthur and bought grain. He then returned to his farm where he remained until 1894, when he became the deputy under his half-brother, James Jones (see sketch), who was then serving as county treasurer. He continued in this position during the regular term of four years. In the fall of 1898 he was elected to this office, when his half-brother, James, became deputy treasurer.

On February 25, 1866, Mr. Jones married Miss Harriet E. York, who was a native of Ohio, and a daughter of Abner York. To their marriage were born three daughters: Elizabeth, wife of R. C. Hostetter, of near Marshalltown, Iowa, Laura, who is the wife of John Hostetter, a brother of R. C., and resides in Tuscola, and Nettie. Mrs. Jones' death occurred in 1897. Mr. Jones is a member of the Grand Army of the Republic, also a member of the Methodist Episcopal church. He owns a beautiful farm of two hundred and fifteen acres just south of Tuscola. As an official and an every day citizen Mr. Jones' record in Douglas county is unimpeachable. His word is equal to his bond, which can be said of few, in this rumbling, blundering age of the almighty dollar.

JAMES A. WILLIAMS

James A. Williams, who has won his own way in the world and reached a degree of success beyond the average of men at his age, was born in Monongahela City, Washington county, Pennsylvania, August 1, 1862. He is a son of John S. and Elizabeth (Van Vorhis), natives of the same county. James Williams wedded Nancy Van Allen and they were among the early settlers of Washington county, the latter having been born in Allegheny county, Pennsylvania. His grandfather, Abram Van Vorhis, was one of the early farmers of that section and also traded in stock considerably. He was of Holland extraction.

James A. Williams grew to manhood on a farm and never attended school after he reached the age of thirteen years; at that age his mother died and he was thrown upon his own resources. In about 1885 he decided to try his fortunes in the west, and after arriving in Illinois settled in Tuscola township, where he became a farm hand; at this he continued until he was twenty-two years of age. By industry and good management he now owns two hundred and forty acres of well improved land in Douglas county, for which he has been offered eighty-five dollars an acre. Subsequently he bought the store at West Ridge, which he sold to W. H. Fry in December, 1899. He previously owned one at Allerton, which he bought in 1894 and sold in the following year.

In September, 1886, he was united in marriage to Miss Amy McGrath, and they have three children: Ida, Charles and Earle. Mr. Williams resides on one of his farms, a short distance south of West Ridge, where he gives his personal supervision to its management. He is a member of the Modern Woodmen of Camargo, and a Republican in politics.

SHILOAH GILL.

Shiloah Gill, an old Mexican soldier, and one of the pioneer settlers in Bowdre township, was born at Gill's Mills, Bath county, Kentucky, September 11, 1827, and is a son of Samuel C. Gill, who was a son of Capt. Thomas Gill, a Revolutionary soldier and a son of the Irish waif (see history of the Gill family in America, by Thomas F. Gill). Samuel C. Gill was born in the state of South Carolina November 22, 1783, and was reared on a farm. He was wedded to Sarah Malone, a daughter of Jonathan and Mary Malone, the latter of whom lived to be nearly one hundred years old. The family came from Tennessee and settled in Montgomery county, Kentucky, later removing to Boone county, Indiana, where she died. Samuel Gill and wife were very poor, their stock of goods consisting of one bay pony, one dollar in money and a feather bed. They packed all on the back of the pony and settled in Bath county, Kentucky. He built a mill, one of the first built in that section. He afterward entered large bodies of land in Putnam Montgomery, Boone and Henry counties, Indiana, and also entered several tracts in what is now Douglas county. It looks as if this old gentleman foresaw everything and selected the *creme de la creme* of the land. He became very prosperous. For twenty-five years he served as justice of the peace, and by virtue of that office he was also one of the justices of the Bath county court. His first wife died in 1847 and in 1849 he married Elizabeth Reed. In about 1845 Samuel C. Gill sold the old mill, but stipulated in the deed that the place should ever be known as Gill's Mill.

Shiloah Gill grew to manhood on the farm and while attending school volunteered for the Mexican war and was soon ordered to the front. He was in the ranks of Capt. James Ewing and served through the whole war, handling a musket in many of the principal battles of that conflict. He was in the ranks when Gen. Scott marched triumphantly into the city of Mexico, and after the treaty of peace of Hidalgo, Guadaloupe, he returned home with his regiment by way of the Gulf of Mexico to New Orleans.

On October 2, 1849, Mr. Gill married Sarah Ann, a daughter of William Anderson, of Bath county, Kentucky, where they remained until 1854, when they emigrated to Douglas county and settled on three hundred and twenty acres, where he now lives, and which was deeded to him by his father; he has since added two hundred and sixty acres more. His wife died about 1872. His second wife was Eliza Kensil. Her death occurred in 1874, and he was again married, September 1, 1875, this time to Mrs. Sarah (Dodge) Coots, who was born within six miles of Hamilton, Butler county, Ohio. The hospitality of Mr. Gill and his wife is well known and highly appreciated.

HARRISON GILL.

It is fitting that in the biographies of the early settlers of the county some mention should be made of Harrison Gill, who entered among the first land here and lived near Camargo.

The grandfather of Mr. Gill was born in Ireland. He came to America and settled in Virginia. His son, Samuel Cresswell Gill, removed from Virginia to Kentucky and settled in Bath county. Here, on the Licking river, he built Gill's mills, a noted point in that part of that state. He married Sarah Malone, by whom he had a large family of children, of whom Harrison Gill was the oldest, born in June, 1808.

On arriving at the age of twenty-one he found himself in possesion of a few hundred dollars, which his father advised him to invest in western lands. He accordingly traveled on horseback to Illinois, first to his uncle, Thomas Gill, in Cumberland county. He found his uncle busy shingling the roof of a house, and he told young Gill if he would help him finish the shingling he would go with him to Coles county in search of land. The first point above Charleston where they found any one living was Major Ashmore, at the mouth of Brushy Fork. North of that he came to an Indian camp, a French and Indian trading point, where Hugo, or Bridgeport, now is. His uncle mischievously informed the Indians that Gill was a young Kentuckian who had come for the purpose of taking to himself an Indian wife. He selected his land, the northwest quarter of section 35 and the west half of the southwest quarter of the same section. The railroad reservoir, east of Camargo, is now on these tracts. He returned immediately to Palestine and made his entry. The patents for the land, now in the possession of George C. Gill, of Camargo, were signed on the 8th of March, 1830, and bear the signature of Andrew Jackson. This was the first land regularly entered in the territory composing what is now Douglas county. Most of the land is still in his possession. He returned to Kentucky soon after selecting the land.

At the age of twenty-eight he married Georgia Ann Landsdowne, a native of Virginia.

Mr. Gill was elected sheriff of Bath county, Kentucky, in 1860, and from 1862 to 1864 was judge of the county court.

In early life Mr. Gill was a Whig. On the breaking out of the war he became a Union man. Mainly through his instrumentality the Twenty-fourth Kentucky Regiment was recruited at the Springs in 1862. In the fall of the same year the Springs was also the headquarters of Gen. Nelson, who ordered all the home guards of Kentucky to rendezvous at that point for the defence of the eastern portion of the state.

From the fall of 1863 to the fall of 1869 Mr. Gill resided near Kentucky, having been driven from his home on account of his Union sentiments.

P. H. MONAHAN.

P. H. Monahan, the father of the broom corn interests of Arcola and a highly esteemed citizen of that place, was born in county Galway, Ireland, February 19, 1837. His parents were John and Mary (Shiel) Monahan, natives of the same county. At the age of thirteen years young Monahan emigrated from his native land to America and settled in Pittsfield, Massachusetts. Later he came west and located in Arcola, which at that time was a mere hamlet. Here Mr. Monahan was married to Hannah Quirk, who was a native of Douglas county and a sister of the late John Quirk, of Arcola. To Mr. and Mrs. Monahan have been born four children: Marie, now residing in New Mexico; Thomas, the present mayor of Arcola, and Henry and Katie.

P. H. Monahan has served in the town council and was chairman of the board. His mother died in 1862, and his father died when Mr. Monahan was only three months old. He is one of the old landmarks of Arcola, having resided here nearly half a century, and is universally respected by everybody.

WALTER C. BLAINE.

Walter C. Blaine was graduated from the University of Pennsylvania, at Philadelphia, in the class of 1895. He commenced the practice at Murdock, where he remained until October, 1898, when he formed a partnership with Dr. William E. Rice, of Tuscola.

Dr. Blaine is a native of Champaign, Illinois, and was born June 2, 1866. He graduated from the Champaign high school, and after four years attendance was graduated from the University of Illinois, at Champaign, on certificate. He is a member of the Knights of Pythias, member of the Woodmen, and a member of the Douglas County Medical Society.

SAMUEL ERVIN.

Samuel Ervin, retired hardware merchant, large land owner, and a resident of Tuscola, was born in Hillsboro, Highland county, Ohio, in 1844. He was reared and educated in his native county and in 1865 came west and located in Tuscola. He and a younger brother were associated in business together up to

1893, when he retired. He owns five hundred and sixty acres of land that extends up to the corporate limits of Tuscola.

In 1871 Mr. Ervin was united in marriage to Miss Elizabeth Beach, who was born on Staten Island. She died in 1894. To their marriage were born two children: Pearl, who is the wife of C. S. Wardall. The other daughter is in college.

Samuel Ervin is a son of William B. Ervin, now deceased. The ancestry of the Ervins is traced back to the great-grandfather of Samuel, Thomas Ervin, a native of Ireland and member of the Presbyterian church, who was by occupation a bleacher of linen. He was a man of means, emigrated to this country in 1771, and purchased a farm in Chester county, Pennsylvania, residing there until his death. His wife was a daughter of the Scottish house of Monteith, which aided the mission of William Wallace so nobly and espoused the cause of Bruce. Jurad, the father of William B. Ervin, was born in 1758 and was thirteen years old when his parents came to America. He was a witness to many of the exciting incidents of the Revolutionary war. His education was limited and early in life he learned the hatter's trade and went to Rockingham county, Virginia. Here he followed his trade until 1813, when he removed to Huntingdon county, Pennsylvania, remaining there two years. He then emigrated to Highland county, Ohio, and was there engaged in farming until his death, which occurred at the ripe old age of one hundred and six years. His wife, Sallie Herron, of Harrisonburg, Virginia, was born July 4, 1776, Declaration of Independence day. Of this union there was a family of nine children, William B. being the second. He was born December 1, 1806, in Rockingham, Virginia, at nine years of age removed to Highland county, Ohio, and in 1865 came to Tuscola, where his death occurred.

Samuel Ervin during his thirty-five years residence in Douglas county has witnessed the wonderful transformation that has taken place, making this county one of the best in the commonwealth, and he has contributed his share to its improvement and development. His laudable business career has gained him the confidence of all with whom he has come in contact, either in a business or social way, and his friends throughout the county are many.

JAMES L. REAT, M. D.

James Lee Reat, M. D., one of the most distinguished physicians and surgeons of Illinois, and who has been long and honorably connected with the professional and industrial interests of Douglas county, was born in Fairfield county, Ohio, January 26, 1824. The Reat ancestors are traced back to Scotland, where the name was pronounced in two syllables, with the accent on the last. Two brothers emigrated to this country during the war of the Revolution, one of whom espoused the cause of the rebels, the term by which the patriot colonies were then known, and served through that struggle with Washington's forces. The other brother sided with the Tories, in consequence of which the two brothers became alienated and a total separation occurred between the two branches of the family. Dr. Reat is descended from the one who cast his fortunes with those of the patriots and who, after the war, settled in Frederick Town, Maryland. At this place James Reat (father) was born and subsequently found his way to Ohio, where he married Susanna Rogers, a Virginia lady, and with her settled in Fairfield county, Ohio. When our subject was five years old, his parents removed to Coles county, Illinois, where the father purchased a farm on which they resided for a time, then removed to Charleston and lived there up to the time of his death, in 1868.

Dr. Reat's early education was derived from the meager advantages offered in the neighborhood schools of that day and later attendance at the seminary at Charleston. That institution was conducted under eminent professors and here Dr. Reat received a good collegiate education and later took up the study of the languages, becoming familiar with Latin and German, and at the same time teaching school a number of terms. His natural taste and talent were those of his chosen profession and he soon thereafter took a regular course of studies at the Medical College at Cincinnati, where he was graduated in the class of 1858; he later attended the Rush Medical College at Chicago and there graduated. After leaving college, he was engaged for a time in the drug business at Charleston, but soon sold his interests and in 1859 took up his residence at Tuscola. In the fall of 1862 he received an appointment as assistant surgeon in the war of the Rebellion and was assigned to a post at Louisville, where he remained for some time in charge of a hospital. On March 1, of the same year, he was commissioned first assistant surgeon of the Twenty-first Regiment Infantry (Grant's old regiment). On July 22, 1864, he was promoted surgeon of the regiment. He returned to Springfield at the close of the war and was mustered out in January, 1866. He then returned to Tuscola and resumed his regular practice.

In 1861 he was married to Miss Sallie C. Callaway, of Jacksonville, a lady of fine literary attainments and of Christian virtues. She was born in Kentucky and was a graduate of Berean College. Her father was the late well-known Rev. S. T. Callaway, a Baptist clergyman. They have had three children, all of whom are living: A daughter Lois, who is the wife of Hon. Theodore Brantley, at present chief justice of the supreme court of Montana; Samuel C., who with his cousin, Harry R. Caraway, were proprietors and editors of the Tuscola Journal. He is now in Washington, representing a number of metropolitan newspapers. He is a graduate of Union Law School, at Chicago, and is taking a post-graduate course in literature. Fred, who graduated from the Illinois State University, and is now proprietor of the Tuscola Republican.

Dr. Reat is a member of the Military Loyal Legion of the United States and the Illinois Army and Navy Medical Association. He and wife are members of the Methodist Episcopal church of Tuscola. Both have taken an active part in the temperance cause. He has always manifested public spirit and through his entire life has been a man of abstemious habits and consistent morals. For three years he was clerk of the board of education of Tuscola and while occupying that office took deep interest in the erection of a public school building, which is surpassed by few in this section of the state. Dr. Reat is widely esteemed for his many good qualities of mind and heart.

JOHN J. JONES.

John J. Jones was many years previous to his death most prominently identified with the affairs of Douglas county. He was born in Virginia in about the year 1835 and died in Chicago in July, 1893. In early life he came to Illinois as a penniless orphan and located at Georgetown, in Vermilion county, where he resided with two of his cousins and with whom he remained until he was about grown, when he came and located in Camargo. Here he became a clerk for Alonzo Lyons, remaining with him for some time, when he, in partnership with Coleman Bright, who was manager for Mr. Lyons, started a little grocery store at Camargo. This was along in the '50s. The firm continued very successfully in business up until the fall of 1864. Then they sold out, came to Tuscola, and engaged in general merchandising, taking in a Mr. Wibly as a partner, under the firm name of Bright, Jones & Wibly. In about 1868 Mr. Wibly sold his interest to Bright and Jones, who continued together in business until Mr. Jones sold his interest to Mr. Bright; this was along about 1884 or 1885. Mr. Jones then gave his entire time to the management of his large farm near Tuscola. He was twice elected mayor of Tuscola. In the fall of 1890 he became the president of the banking house of Baughman, Orr & Co. and remained as such up to the time of his death.

Mr. Jones was united in marriage to Miss Lizzie Ketchum, a daughter of Dr. Ketchum, of Terre Haute, Indiana; she survives him. John J. Jones was of quiet and unassuming manner, a self-made man and his uninterrupted success and his character as a man were well worthy of the admiration of the entire people. He had the mind to conceive and the hand to direct his business affairs in such a way that brought him success in all of his undertakings. For many years he was a consistent member of the First Presbyterian church and a member of the Melita Commandery of Knights Templar of Tuscola.

A. C. SLUSS.

A. C. Sluss, the proprietor of the Tuscola Journal, a weekly paper published at Tuscola, and the present postmaster of Tuscola, has been for many years prominently identified with the business, social and political interests of his city and county, having served the city of Tuscola twice as alderman, three terms as city clerk and one term as mayor. He was born in Edgar county, Illinois, April 7, 1850, and is a son of Thomas S. and Martha (Hineman) Sluss. His father, who was born in Kentucky, removed to Tuscola in 1861, and there carried on his trade, that of a harness maker, up to the time of his death, in 1893, at the age of eighty years.

His grandfather, David Sluss, and his grandfather, John Hineman, were both natives of Kentucky, and were among the first settlers in Monroe county, Indiana.

A. C. Sluss learned the trade with his father, and received his education in the schools of Tuscola and the Chicago Business College. He was engaged in the manufacture of harness, etc., when, in 1889, he was appointed postmaster of Tuscola by President Harrison, and again received the appointment by President McKinley, which shows his popularity and efficiency as a public official. Mr. Sluss became the sole owner of the Tuscola Journal, the official Republican organ of Douglas county, in December, 1898. The Journal was founded by Siler & Lindsay in 1864, and has at the present time a paid circulation of about two thousand in the county. It is stanch Republican in its political views, and is one of the most progressive and up-to-date country newspapers in central Illinois.

In 1875 Mr. Sluss was united in marriage to Miss Minerva Higgins, of Highland county, Ohio. They have three children, Alfred H., Frank L. and Hattie E.

W. H. BASSETT.

Judge W. H. Bassett was born January 12, 1832, on a farm in Harrison county, Kentucky, and there grew to manhood, receiving a common-school education. He later attended a commercial college in Cincinnati, Ohio, graduating May 12, 1854. Afterward he engaged in the mercantile business in Cynthiana, Kentucky. He came to what is now Douglas county, Illinois, in 1857, and was engaged in farming until 1862. At this time he enlisted in Company K, Seventy-ninth Illinois Infantry, and served to the close of the war, filling all the company offices from corporal to captain.

Upon returning from his army service our subject engaged in merchandising and farming in and near Arcola until 1882, when he was elected county judge. He studied law and was admitted to the bar in 1889. Politically Judge Bassett is a Republican, and religiously is an adherent of the Methodist Episcopal church, having joined that society at Millersburg, Kentucky, in 1856.

In 1860 our subject was married to Miss Nellie M. Gruell, and two children are the result of this union: Jonathan H., residing at Arthur, Illinois, and Martin H., residing at Mattoon, Illinois.

MR. AND MRS. JACOB EPHLIN.

Mr. and Mrs. Jacob Ephlin are the oldest couple in Tuscola. They came here from Parke county, Indiana, April 4, 1858, when the number of inhabitants could be counted on the fingers of the two hands. They have lived here more than forty years, and out from the doorway of no home in Tuscola has come a kinder greeting to the wayfarer or a more hospitable reception to friends and relatives. Uncle Jake is closely related with the primitive town and the early county, having been among the first business men and serving as deputy sheriff under I. L. Jordan. Aunt Martha is best known for her charitable deeds that tell of missions of kindness and love and crown her with glory. To a life full of years and rich in experience they have added the greatest measure of affection for each other and love for mankind, two gems that shine with undimmed splendor in the crown of human possibility.

W T. PULLIAM, M. D.

W. T. Pulliam, M D., is one of Tuscola's leading physicians. The Doctor has been in practice for many years, and has, by his energy and efficiency, achieved a success and reputation in the healing art second to none. He is thoroughly educated, and a most honorable and congenial gentleman. He received a literary and scientific education at the University of Illinois, after which he studied medicine in the Indiana Medical College, from which he was graduated in the spring of 1882. Since that time he has been fully devoted to his chosen profession at Tuscola, where he now enjoys a lucrative and extensive practice.

GEORGE CALLAWAY.

George Callaway, a retired physician of Tuscola and a large land owner of Douglas county, is a native of Christian county, Kentucky, and was born May 4, 1848. In 1850 he removed to Illinois and was principally educated in the Illinois College at Jacksonville. After leaving school he read medicine with Dr. J. L. Reat, at Tuscola, Illinois, and subsequently entered the Ohio Medical College at Cincinnati, from which he graduated in the class of '73. Dr. Callaway commenced the practice of medicine at Virginia City, Montana, having gone first in 1871 to that territory as surveyor in the employ of the government. In 1875 he located in Tuscola, where he successfully practiced his profession up to within the last few years. At present he gives his entire attention to the management of his farm in Douglas county, owning in all over eight hundred acres of land.

In 1879 he was united in marriage with Miss Emma C. Wyeth, of Tuscola, daughter of L. J. Wyeth (see sketch). To their marriage have been born four children: Leonard, Katie, Ralph and Emma. Dr. Callaway owns one of the handsomest and most costly residences in Tuscola and is a large stockholder in the First National Bank of Tuscola. He is a son of Samuel T. and Mary (Means) Callaway, the former born in Clark county, Kentucky, and the latter in Christian county, in the same state. Samuel T. Callaway was a Baptist minister, and many years of his life were spent in the work of the church. For a time he served as county superintendent of schools of Douglas county. The Callaway family came from North Carolina, as did also the Means family, and settled in Kentucky, where they were contemporaries of Daniel Boone.

J. H. BASSETT.

J. H. Bassett is the editor and proprietor of the Arthur Graphic, which he bought and took charge of October 1, 1899. The paper was founded in April, 1887, by T. J. Haney, and was edited and owned by him until he sold it to Mr. Bassett. In 1883 he bought the Arcola Record, which he ran until 1886, when he sold it to P. L. Henry. Mr. Bassett was three years and a half in the public printing office at Washington, under the administration of President Harrison, at the end of which time he resigned and came home. In 1891 he and his father then again purchased the Record and ran it until 1895, selling to B. F. Wamsley. In 1897 he and his brother, M. H. Bassett, who owned the Mattoon Daily Journal, again purchased the Record and Mr. Bassett had sole charge of the paper until January 1, 1899, when the paper was sold to Nathan Collins and son. The Arthur Graphic was originally a five-column newspaper, but has recently been made six by the present proprietor, who has in other ways overhauled the paper and office and considerably increased the circulation.

Mr. Bassett was born in Arcola township, this county, July 19, 1861. In 1882 he married Miss Nora Perkins, who died in 1887. To this union was born one child, Nellie. He again married, in 1895, Miss Maggie Degnan, of Springfield, Illinois, becoming his wife. To them three children have been born, Bessie, Martin and Mary. The Arthur Graphic has a circulation of about five hundred, is well edited and is a very popular local newspaper.

W. W. SKINNER.

W. W. Skinner was born November 12, 1835, in Vermillion, Indiana. In 1839, with his parents, he moved to Coles (now Douglas) county, Ills., where he has since resided. When Mr. Skinner came to Douglas county there were only seven families in what is now Newman township, namely: Anson, Gaston, Robert Hopkins, E. J. Howell and three families by the name of Winkler.

Joseph Skinner, father of W. W. Skinner, burned a brick kiln on the banks of the Brushy Fork creek in 1839, it being the first kiln burned in that part of the state. For years after this he followed breaking prairie land, his boys aiding him until his death, which occurred in 1857. He raised a large family of children, ten boys and three girls, W. W. Skinner being the sixth child. From this large family of thirteen children only three are now living: W. W., John and Isaac, they being the three oldest sons. In the year 1862 John, W. W. and Anson Skinner, brothers, enlisted in the Seventy-ninth Illinois Volunteer Infantry. John and Anson were captured at the battle of Chickamauga. They were kept in prison seventeen months and nine days, and did not return to their regiment, but were mustered out at Springfield, Illinois, at the close of the war. W. W. Skinner remained with his company, was under the leadership of Sherman, and took part in eleven hard fought battles, besides skirmishing by the month. He was mustered out June 12, 1865, at Nashville, Tennessee, and discharged June 27, 1865, at Springfield, Illinois.

W. W. Skinner, being an early settler of the eastern part of Douglas county, Illinois, well remembers some of the incidents of its first settlers. Robert Matson, from Kentucky, settled here in 1839 or 1840. He first located near Coffee's Grove, in Sargent township, and in a few years removed one and one-half miles northeast of Newman. He was a wealthy man, owning a large plantation in Kentucky and a number of slaves. He brought nine slaves to Illinois with him. In 1847 his slaves were spirited away to Charleston, the county seat of Coles county, they claiming their freedom under the laws of a free state and being protected in their project by Rutherford and Ashmore. Mr. Matson, fearing the loss of his human property, followed them to Charleston and brought suit for the rights of property. He employed for his attorney the Honorable Abe Lincoln, who was at this time but twenty-nine years old, while the defendents employed the Honorable O. B. Ficklin. It so happened that Matson lost his slaves, while he himself returned to Kentucky, from which place he never returned to the free state of Illinois.

JOHN W. McKINNEY.

John Wright McKinney was born near Springfield, Clark county, Ohio, June 17, 1825, and died at Camargo, Illinois, July 31, 1897, aged seventy-two years, one month and twenty-four days. His father and family moved from Ohio to Montgomery county, Indiana, in 1830, where the deceased lived until his twenty-first year. During the following two years he taught school in Montgomery county, studying medicine meanwhile with an energy and avidity so characteristic of his nature.

Mr. McKinney and Mary Roll were joined in matrimony October 12, 1848, at Pleasant Hill, Indiana. Soon after his marriage he moved to Hillsboro, Indiana, and began the practice of medicine. In 1851 he moved to Camargo, Illinois, and continued the practice of his chosen profession. Later he attended lectures at the Jefferson Medical College of Philadelphia, graduating therefrom in 1855. In 1858 he moved to Centralia, Illinois, but removed to Camargo the following year. September 15, 1862, he enlisted in the Sixty-second Regiment Illinois Volunteer Infantry, but was shortly transferred to the Sixty-third Illinois Volunteer Infantry and appointed surgeon of the regiment, with the rank of major, in which capacity he served during the remainder of the war, most of that time in Gen. John A. Logan's corps—the notable Fifteenth Army Corps. He was mustered out April 9, 1865. Before the Sixty-third joined General Sherman's army, it was engaged in the battles of Vicksburg, Mississippi, Mission Ridge, etc. After joining Gen. Sherman's army his regiment was active in the attack on the Ogeechee Canal and Miller's Station, and participated in the long list of famous battles of Sherman's army during his famous "march to the sea." During its active service the Sixty-third regiment traveled some six thousand, four hundred and fifty-three miles.

After the war Dr. McKinney resumed his practice of medicine and surgery at Camargo with marked success. He was author of the bill granting the formation of Douglas county, and gave the county its name in honor of the "Little Giant," Stephen A. Douglas. The deceased served several terms as supervisor of Camargo township. In politics he was a Democrat. While he did not belong to any church, he possessed strong convictions of man's duty to his God, his country, his family and himself, and practiced doing good and being honest all the days of his life.

September 25, 1870, Mary, his wife, died at their Camargo home, respected and beloved by her husband and all who knew her. September 10, 1871, Dr. McKinney and Minnie A. Coykendall were joined in wedlock and lived happily together until death separated them. The Doctor was a prominent member of the A. F. & A. M., Camargo Lodge, No. 440; Knights Templar; Frank Reed Post, G. A. R.; County and State Medical Societies, and was a prominent and respected citizen of his township, county and state, being considered one of the most capable and successful physicians and surgeons of central Illinois. He was a member of the local or county pension examining board, serving in that capacity two terms.

During Dr. McKinney's late illness—general physical relaxation—he was attended constantly by his wife and children. His express wish, that his family nurse and care for him, was gratified. During these two months all of his family and children were able to be at his bedside and administer to his wants, night and day. His strong will power and remarkable energy coupled with the desire to recover his health, no doubt, prolonged his days. During this last illness the Doctor was ever mindful of the wants of his family, prescribing rest and medicine for them if at any time he fancied they needed it. Dr. McKinney died in the same house he had lived for almost half a century—forty-six years. He died as he lived, loving and beloved by his family, neighbors and friends. His leading characteristics were his honesty in his dealings with his fellow men and his integrity as a physician and citizen. He possessed an indomitable will and a conviction of purpose that won him many a battle in the fights for life for his patients. He was courageous as a lion, yet withal tender and sympathetic as a woman. He was liberal and generous, administering to the poor as skillfully and carefully as to the rich.

SAMUEL L. HOPKINS.

Samuel L. Hopkins, one of the most successful farmers and stock raisers in Newman township, was born south of Newman on the old Hopkins homestead in the year 1849. In 1884 he was united in marriage to Miss Hattie Bell, and is the father of six children. Mr. Hopkins owns four hundred and twenty-seven acres of land which extends nearly to the corporation line of Newman. His mother was, before her marriage, Elizabeth Thomas, and was born in Indiana. His father was James Hopkins, who was one of the earliest settlers along the Brushy Fork timber. He was born in Pickaway county, Ohio, February 12, 1815. At the age of nine years he, with his family, removed to Vermillion county, Indiana. Here, on January 21, 1838, he married Elizabeth Ann Thomas, who was mentioned above. In October, 1841, he came to Illinois and located in section 5, township 15, range 14, where he resided until his death. He first bought one hundred and thirty acres of land at seven dollars an acre, and at the time of his death he had accumulated many more acres. He was the father of ten children, three of whom were born in Indiana. Two of his sons, John William and Eli Thomas, enlisted in the Twenty-fifth Regiment Illinois Volunteers at the commencement of the Civil war and both died in the service, the former on the 13th of December at a hospital in St. Louis, and Eli Thomas in the latter part of August, 1862, near Iuka, Mississippi.

DANIEL RODERICK.

Daniel Roderick is one of the oldest settlers now living in Douglas county. He came to near Danville, Illinois, with his father, Samuel R., sixty years ago. The latter died in Vermilion county, and soon afterward Daniel came to what is now Garrett township and kept generally about twelve yokes of oxen. He was born July 16, 1816, and his education was almost entirely neglected, but he is known as "honest, old Dan Roderick."

SEGLER H. LESTER.

Segler H. Lester (deceased) was born in Virginia October 29, 1804, and died in Garrett township May 22, 1864, and married Parthenia Cassaday May 14, 1833. Mrs. Lester, who is known among her neighbors as Grandma Lester, still survives. She was a daughter of Daniel Cassaday, of Virginia, where she was born July 9, 1811, and spent her early years in Kentucky. In 1829 she came with her parents to Edgar county, Illinois, where she met Mr. Lester, whom she subsequently married. Immediately after her wedding she moved with her husband to a place on the Springfield or State road, where there were about four families, of whom Mrs. Lester is the only survivor. In the autumn of 1834 she moved to the site of her present residence, where a round-log cabin, 16x18 feet, was built, and the new family began the difficulties of pioneer life, with little more capital than willing hands and stout hearts. There were no cabins nearer than ten miles north and seven miles south, the site being chosen by Mrs. Lester because the Indians had once made it their camping ground. Here five children were born, and here was laid the foundation of a handsome competence; here also the homestead still shelters the welcome guest. There was no open road to fortune for the pioneers; the nearest market for surplus produce was at Chicago, where corn was sold for six and one-half cents per bushel; pork from one dollar and a half to two dollars per hundred and wheat at thirty-seven and one-half cents per bushel. Supplies were only to be purchased at the expense of a tedious trip to Charleston, Terre Haute, Georgetown, Eugene or to Monticello, a round trip taking a week to accomplish. Each family could not afford this expense and some went for the whole neighborhood. This involved the use of a wagon and three yoke of oxen; the loan for a whole neighborhood of those times would not now be considered large, but owing to the condition of the roads three yoke of oxen barely sufficed. The accumulation of property under such circumstances was a difficult matter. Mr. Lester worked two years to earn money enough to enter his first eighty acres, where the homestead stands, and in 1837 he went to Rock River and broke prairie for two months, earning enough to enter one hundred acres. When the coming of winter closed the season's work on the farm Mr. Lester turned his skill as a hunter to good account, in one winter earning enough from the sale of deer's hind-quarters to discharge a debt for his rifle, for which he had contracted to pay twenty-five dollars. It was by such slow and arduous efforts that he accumulated some one thousand acres of land, of which he died possessed. In 1874 a fine frame dwelling, which had been erected by him at the cost of twenty-seven hundred dollars, was destroyed by fire, but was at once rebuilt at a cost of fifteen hundred dollars.

Nine children have been born to Mr. Lester: Eliza J., wife of James Howe; Harriet A., wife of William Howe; Almeta J., wife of Elbert S. Crowley; John D., now in the agricultural implement business in Tuscola; Louisa E. A., wife of Daniel C. Johnson; Orlando B., occupying an important position in the patent office at Washington, D. C.; Lemuel P., now a resident at the homestead; Mary E. died November 6, 1845, aged one year; Margaret C. died April 25, 1855, aged three years. Lemuel P. Lester was married February 27, 1872, to Luvina Rice, a native of Kentucky, who, when a child, came to Douglas county with her parents. They have had seven children, six of whom are living, Perl D., Bert, Paul, Otto W., Gertrude and Martin. Orwell died in his sixth year.

W. E. PRICE.

W. E. Price, a resident of Camargo, and the present county surveyor, who has efficiently served in this capacity for twelve years, was born in New York city July 8, 1849. He was a son of William Edward and Mathilda M. (Wilson) Price, natives of Ireland. His father was a cabinetmaker by trade, an Episcopalian in religious belief and died in New York city. Mr. Price came to Douglas county in 1860 and was bound out to a Mr. McNair, going through all the hardships that generally befall a poor orphan.

In 1873 he was married to Miss Ella Drummonds, of this county. He is the present nominee on the Republican ticket for re-election to the office of county surveyor.

GEO. O. MOORE.

Geo. O. Moore was born December 1, 1858, on a farm near Muncie, Indiana. He is the third child of the family of Mr. and Mrs. Louis Moore, and migrated with them to Douglas county when only five years old, locating near the county seat, Tuscola. His early education was attained in the schools of Tuscola and adjoining districts. He also took a classical and scientific course in the Normal College at Danville, Indiana, from which he graduated in 1881, paying his tuition and way through the school by the sweat of his brow as janitor. He was principal of the schools at Russellville, Indiana, in 1882, giving entire satisfaction. He then held the chairs of music and higher mathematics in the Campbell Normal University at Holton, Kansas, in 1883. In August of the same year he went to Troy, Ohio, where he was united in the holy bonds of matrimony to Miss Lillie Conway, a resident of that city, whose acquaintance he had formed at college. He and his amiable wife took up their abode at Middleton, Virginia, where Mr. Moore had accepted the associate principalship of the Shenandoah Normal College, which position he held for three years. Owing to the declining of his wife's health Mr. Moore returned to Illinois, stopping at Tuscola, where Mrs. Moore passed away in August of the same year. To this union was born one son, Louis C. In the fall of 1886 he accepted the principalship of the Newman schools, which he held for three years. In the spring of 1890, being solicited by his many friends, he made the race for the Republican nomination for superintendent of schools of Douglas county.

A. A. ARMSTRONG.

Archie A. Armstrong, one of the progressive, intelligent and well-known young farmers of the county and Camargo township, was born in Lawrence county, Ohio, September 10, 1861. He is the son of John Armstrong, who is also a native of Ohio and now a resident of Champaign. He came to Douglas county in 1879, and bought several farms in Tuscola township and in other localities. He resided for some years on one of his farms, when he removed to the city of Champaign. He is now living a retired life in the sixty-fifth year of his age.

Archie Armstrong owns one of the most beautiful and attractive farms in the county, which he has well stocked with Aberdeen Angus cattle. In 1886 he wedded Miss Nora Rice, of Champaign county. They have one child, Floyd, ten years of age. Mr. Armstrong is a director of the Douglas County Fair Association, and a member of the Masonic lodge at Camargo.

WILSON S. BURGETT.

Wilson S. Burgett, a native of Sargent township, and a son of I. W. Burgett, whose sketch is found on another page, was born December 23, 1863. He was reared in Sargent township, where he continued to live until eight years ago, when he removed to his present farm two miles south of Camargo.

In 1886 he was married to Miss Kate May, a daughter of Judge Brown (see sketch). They have three children: Ray Brown, Burley Sumner and Wayne Brenton.

W. S. Burgett owns two hundred and ten acres of land, on which he lives, and is one of the intelligent and representative young business men of the county. In politics he is an enthusiastic Republican and has served two years as township committeeman.

JOSEPH B. PETTY.

Joseph Bradley Petty, one of the successful business men of Tuscola, engaged in merchandising and identified with several other enterprises of the city, was born in Hendricks county, Indiana, August 24, 1855, and is a son of Nathan and Ann Mariah (Wood) Petty, the former born in Chatham county, North Carolina, and the latter in Mercer county, Kentucky. Mr. Petty was engaged in farming for several years in Champaign county, and from 1884 to 1891 he resided at Iantha, Missouri, where he was engaged in blacksmithing and hardware merchandising. In the atter year he returned to Illinois and settled in Tuscola, where he has since worked at his trade, and in 1898 opened up a general store in connection with his other business.

In 1881 he was united in marriage to Miss Priscilla Mars, of Champaign county. They have five boys: Earle Shirley, Byron Talmage, Clara Marrs, Virgil Ira and William Nathan. He owns his own home and store buildings, is a hard working man, and is one of the honorable and representative citizens of Tuscola. He is a member of the Methodist Episcopal church and of the Court of Honor. Mrs. Petty, a lady of good intelligence and fine business tact, is a daughter of William and Mary Jane (Sutherland) Marrs, the former a native of Bourbon county, Kentucky, and the latter of Ohio. At the age of four years William Marrs, with his father, John Marrs, moved to Shelby county, Ohio, where William was raised. He moved to Macon county, Illinois, in 1859, and there engaged in agricultural pursuits. Priscilla Marrs taught school seven years in Champaign county, Illinois, then became Mrs. Petty. She has the agency and is field manager for the Viavi Company for Douglas county, and has also the agency and field management for the Magnetic Shield Company, of Chicago, in her county. Viavi is a purely vegetable compound, the outgrowth of a physician's prescription. To his years of experimenting was added an incredible amount of patience and money, and Viavi in its present form is the result. It is virtually predigested food and is used with most perfect safety by the most delicate, young and old. This remedy is world famed, and is successfully used by every nation. The motto of the Viava worker is "The higher physical life of woman," and thus preserve the health of the race. Mrs. Petty has, in her six years' agency, done a business of over $4,600. She is thoroughly capable, and with the time that she has given to her special work she has been remarkably successful.

SAMUEL B. LOGAN.

Samuel B. Logan, one of the very oldest of the pioneers now living in Douglas county, and the first sheriff, was born near the village of Washington, Mason county, Kentucky, April 30, 1816. He is a son of Joseph and Mary (Morris) Logan. The former was a native of Mason county and the latter of the state of New Jersey. John Logan (grandfather) was one of the early settlers from Pennsylvania, and after his arrival in Kentucky he lived in a fort. Joseph Logan (father) was a soldier in the war of 1812 and was in the battle of the Thames. John Morris (grandfather) was a native of New Jersey and in the opinion of Mr. Logan was a soldier in the war of the Revolution. His father and mother, in 1837, removed to Coles county and located within two miles of where Mr. Logan now resides. The first year his father raised a crop, renting his land of old Jacob Moore.

Samuel B. Logan enjoys the honor of having been the first sheriff of Douglas county, and has lived a long, honorable and beautiful life in his adopted county. In 1848 he was married to Miss Leah Fuller, a native of Virginia, whose death occurred in 1896. To this marriage were born twelve children. Of this number six are living, viz: Samuel F., Albert W., Harriet J., Hannah C., Mary E. and Stephen.

GEORGE C. JEFFERS.

George C. Jeffers, member of the firm of Bragg & Jeffers, engaged in general merchandising and banking at Camargo, was born in Adams county, Illinois, in 1858, and is a son of Samuel P. and Rachel (Orr) Jeffers. Samuel P. Jeffers was born in Clermont county, Ohio, June 9, 1834, and is a son of Elijah and Hannah (Pine) Jeffers, natives of Clermont county, Ohio, and New Jersey respectively. Hannah Pine was a daughter of William Pine, who, an orphan, emigrated from England to this country and first settled in New Jersey, thence removing to Ohio and later to Pike county, Illinois, where he died. He served in the war of 1812. Elijah was a son of William Jeffers, a native of the north of Ireland. Samuel D. Jeffers came to Camargo township in 1869, from Adams county, this state, where he farmed up to within the past ten years, since which time he has kept the meat market at Camargo. On February 22, 1855, he was wedded to Rachel J. Orr, a daughter of Thomas and Elizabeth Orr. In the beginning of 1865 he volunteered in the Forty-seventh Illinois Infantry, and was in service till the close of the Civil war.

George C. Jeffers, after leaving school, taught for one year, and in 1879 became a clerk for A. W. Bragg, in the latter's store at Camargo, in which capacity he continued till 1893, when he became a partner, with one-half interest, and the firm name became Bragg & Jeffers. The general store and banking house of Bragg & Jeffers containing two departments, carries a stock of general merchandise valued at about $20,000, requiring a corps of four clerks, and does an annual business of from $35,000 to $40,000. George C. Jeffers is a clear headed and able business man whose industry and comprehensive grasp of details has to a great extent made this one of the leading mercantile firms of central Illinois.

In 1884 Mr. Jeffers married Miss Carrie, a daughter of W. H. Hall, an old and highly respected citizen and merchant of Camargo.

WILLIAM W. REEVES.

William W. Reeves, of Tuscola, one of the youngest members in active practice at the Douglas county bar, was born on a farm near Villa Grove, Camargo township, December 25, 1870, and is a son of George R. Reeves. The latter, who was a native of Delaware county, Indiana, was born in 1836, and his death occurred in 1881. He removed to Douglas county in 1865, and was engaged in farming up to the time of his decease. W. W. Reeves' mother was before her marriage Miss Nancy E. Wilson. She was born near Urbana, Ohio, and was a daughter of John O. Wilson, a native of Pennsylvania, who emigrated in 1861 to Illinois, first locating near Paris, and later came to this county, where he died at the age of seventy-nine years. Elijah Reeves (grandfather) was born near Culpeper Court House, Virginia, and subsequently emigrated to Kentucky. At one time he was the owner of quite a number of slaves, but later became convinced that slavery was wrong and freed them all in the year 1836 and moved to Indiana, a free state.

William W. Reeves remained on the farm until he had arrived at the age of seventeen years, when he entered Wesleyan College. He continued his studies in this institution until he had finished the sophomore year. In 1896 he commenced reading law in the office of John H. Chadwick, and was graduated from the Bloomington (Illinois) Law School in the class of '98. He was immediately admitted to the bar and opened an office in Tuscola. He is a member of the Masonic order and is a Knight of Pythias. In politics he is a Democrat and takes an active interest in the success of his party.

J. L. AVERY.

J. L. Avery, editor and proprietor of the Arcola Weekly Herald since April 1, 1893, was born four and one-half miles southeast of Arcola, in Coles county, Illinois, November 25, 1866. The Herald was founded in the year 1883 by H. H. Moore, who conducted it until about the year 1891, when Willis S. Scales bought it and published it until he sold it to Mr. Avery. The paper is in a flourishing condition, strictly Democratic in politics and full of local news, with a circulation of about fifteen hundred.

J. L. Avery was educated in the common schools, the Arcola high school, and took a teacher's course of two years. Afterward he taught school for seven years in Douglas and Coles counties. In 1892 he was married to Miss Nellie I. Fancher, of Charleston, Illinois. They have one child, Paul Kenneth.

Mr. Avery is a member of the Knights of Pythias and the Woodmen. He is a splendid news gatherer, a pungent writer and a young man of splendid reputation.

J. W. BOYER.

J. W. Boyer, a well known farmer of Sargent township, and the present census enumerator for the same, was born in the vicinity of Ashmore, Coles county, Illinois, on the 11th day of April, 1850. For twenty-five years he has been identified with the industrial growth of his township, and is well and favorably

known as an intelligent and upright citizen. He is the son of James and Susan (Mack)

Boyer, the former a native of Virginia, and the latter was born in Kentucky. As early as 1835 James Boyer came and settled with his father, Joseph, who was also born in Virginia, and who settled in the neighborhood of Ashmore. Here Joseph Boyer became one of the first settlers and afterward went to Missouri, where he died. William Mack (maternal grandfather) was also one of the early settlers in the same vcinity. James Boyer (father) is at present residing in the state of Kansas, at the age of seventy-nine years, and his wife is still living in the same year, of her age.

Jospeh Boyer was reared on a farm in Douglas county, where he received a very good common school education, and went to Westfield College four terms. His farm of two hundred and nineteen acres, which lies in the northeast part of the township, is well improved and valuable. Nearly ever since Mr. Bower's residence here he has served efficiently as school director, and in 1900 was appointed census enumerator of Sargent township. In 1875 he married Josie, daughter of William Hopkins (see further notice of the Hopkins family on another page), who was one of the pioneer settlers in this section of the county. Mr. and Mrs. Boyer have seven children living: Mamie, Robert, Belva, Clinton, Maggie, James and Floyd

REV. J. V. MARTIN.

Rev. J. V. Martin, pastor of St. John the Baptist church at Arcola, Illinois, was born in Champlin, Minnesota, November 22, 1857. He was educated in the St. Francis College, Milwaukee; St. John's University, Minnesota, and subsequently completed the six-years' divinity course at the Grand Seminary, Montreal, Canada, where he was ordained December 18, 1886. His first charge was at Springfield, Illinois, where he did hospital service for two months; from there he was transferred to Shipman, laboring for two and a half years as the regular pastor; thence to Neoga, where he remained two years, when, in 1891, he came to Arcola. The church here was built about thirty-three years ago, with Father Manganas as first pastor. The present membership of the church is about three hundred, situated in the town and in the southwestern part of Douglas county. The church is out of debt and is in a prosperous condition.

Father Martin is a conscientious worker in his church; he is a thorough Christian gentleman and a devout worshiper of Christ.

WILLIAM H. FISHER.

William H. Fisher, a retired farmer and an ex-soldier of the Civil war, came to Douglas county in 1877 and located on a farm two and a half miles southeast of Arcola, which he purchased and resided on for four years, when he removed to Albany, Oregon. In 1882 he returned to Douglas county and located on a farm in Tuscola township, remaining here for two years. He then purchased a farm east of Galton, which he owned and resided upon for ten years, when, in 1893, he moved to Tuscola, where he at present resides.

He owns one hundred and sixty acres of land, northwest of town.

Our subject was born in Ohio county, Indiana, January 7, 1839, and was a son of Andrew and Eliza (Hunter) Fisher, the former a native of Butler county, Ohio, and the latter of Switzerland county, Indiana. His paternal grandfather, Jacob Fisher, was a Pennsylvanian by birth. His maternal grandfather, John Hunter, was born in Ireland, and subsequently emigrated to Switzerland county, Indiana, and then to Ohio county, Indiana. Mr. Fisher's paternal great-grandfather was a Revolutionary soldier, and several other members of the Fisher family were in the Indian and other early wars.

William H. Fisher was reared in Jefferson county, Indiana, on a farm, and in August, 1862, he volunteered in the Eighty-third Indiana Infantry and served until the close of the war. He belonged to the Second Division, Fifteenth Army Corps, which was organized and commanded by Gen. Sherman, and later by Gen. Logan. He was in the battles of Chickasaw, Miss., Arkansas Post or Hindman, Jackson, Mississippi, was through the siege of Vicksburg, at Missionary Ridge and Atlanta; also at Jonesboro, Bentonville, North Carolina, was with Sherman on his sweep to the sea, and was present at the grand review, Washington, at the close of the war.

In 1869 he was wedded to Miss Nancy J. Beatty, of Ohio county, Indiana. They had four children: James Edward, Rosanna B., Eliza B., and William Franklin, the latter deceased. Mrs. Fisher is the daughter of George and Rosanna (Smith) Beatty. Her father was a native of Pennsylvania, and her mother was born in Ohio county, Indiana. Her grandfathers were Hugh Beatty and George Smith, who came from Pennsylvania. Mr. and Mrs. Fisher are members of the Presbyterian church; he is also a member of the Grand Army of the Republic, and Independent Order of Odd Fellows.

T. M. RICHARDS.

T. M. Richards, a leading merchant and grain buyer of Hayes, Illinois, was born in Douglas county, Illinois, August 7, 1864, and is a son of Thomas Y. Richards, who was a native of Hardin county, Kentucky, where he was born in 1818. The latter moved to this county in the 'forties and was engaged in farming. He was three times married and was the fa-

ther of nine children, of whom all are dead excepting T. M. and G. R. Richards. His last wife was Hester A. Reat, and she was the mother of the above named boys (see sketch of Dr. J. L. Reat). Thomas Y. Richards died in 1872.

T. M. Richards has been twice married, first, in January, 1889, to Miss Dove E. Donnals, daughter of R. T. Donnals, of Tuscola, Illinois. She was born December 16, 1866, and died November 20, 1894. Their marriage was blessed with two children: Beryl E., born September 28, 1889, and Theodore T., born February 16, 1892. Our subject was again married, in October, 1897, to Mrs. Effie M. Doty, of Effingham county, her maiden name being Baker. She was married to W. Doty in 1891. He died December 3, 1893. They had one boy, Daniel I. Doty. Mr. and Mrs. Richards also have two children: Ralph H., born August 4, 1898, and Lee M., born December 27, 1899. Mr. Richards is the grain agent at Hayes for O. L. Parker, of Tuscola, and handles about three hundred thousand bushels of oats and corn yearly. He is a member of the Modern Woodmen of America, and is a hustler.

WILLIAM S. HAMMETT.

William S. Hammett, retired farmer residing in Tuscola, was born in Montgomery county, Virginia, December 9, 1823, and is a son of John Hammett (see sketch of James R. Hammett). He came with his father from Bourbon county, Kentucky, in 1829. He was for many years a leading farmer of Camargo township and prominent in the early affairs of the county.

JAMES S. REEDER.

James S. Reeder, postmaster at Garrett, to which position he was appointed in July, 1898, located in Bourbon in 1856. He is a son of John A. and Mary B. (Harter) Reeder. John A. Reeder was born in Ohio in 1815 and died in 1891. David Harter (maternal grandfather) was a native of Virginia. James S. was in the Civil war as a private, enlisting in Company G, Seventy-ninth Illinois Regiment Volunteer Infantry. Going in in August, 1862, he remained out for two years and ten months.

G. R. RICHARDS.

G. R. Richards, who is associated in business with his brother, T. M. Richards, was

gaged in the livery business in Tuscola, and in born in 1865. He was for several years en-

1899 removed to Hayes and became associated with his brother. In 1896 he was married to Miss Myrtle Johnson, a daughter of William T. Johnson, of Tuscola. They have no children. George is known as a ball player all over central Illinois.

STEPHEN S. HENSON.

Stephen S. Henson, a highly respected citizen, belonging to the old school of gentlemen, and who is probably as well and favorably known as any man in the county, was born near Cynthiana, Harrison county, Kentucky, in October, 1827, and is a son of Gideon and Nancy Shumate. His father was a native of Virginia and his mother of Kentucky. The former emigrated from Kentucky to Vermillion county, near Indianola, in 1834, and, with his wife and children, located in the vicinity of Villa Grove, where he entered a large tract of land. His children were: George W. (see sketch), Stephen S., and two daughters, who were the wives of James Richards and Coleman Bright, respectively. All the children are now dead except Stephen S.

Mr. Henson was about fifteen years old when he arrived in Douglas county. He has always been engaged in farming and at present owns a beautiful farm of two hundred and eighty acres, part of which is in Douglas county and part in Champaign. In 1853 he was united in marriage to Miss Nancy E. Williams, who was a native of Vermilion county, Illinois, and a daughter of Elijah Williams, an early settler in Vermilion county. Mrs. Henson was born in 1830 and died in 1893. Of this marriage there are seven children living: Franklin, who resides just across the road from his father; Mantie, who is the wife of Dr. E. S. Smith, of Urbana; Lula, wife of Charles Ammon, of Carthage, Missouri; Ward, who resides east of Villa Grove on a farm; Burt, deceased; Flora, at home, and Kitty B., wife of S. W. Love, of Urbana, editor of the Daily Courier. Mr. Henson is a consistent member of the Methodist Episcopal church at Villa Grove, in the affairs of which he takes an active interest.

COLEMAN BRIGHT.

Coleman Bright came to Douglas county in 1850 and engaged in retail merchandising, and in about 1860 removed to Tuscola and remained a member of the firm of Bright & Jones until his death on July 20, 1881.

W. AVERY HOWARD.

W. Avery Howard, who has recently become a partner in the broom corn business with W. H. Hancock, is a native of Fultonville, New York, and was born February 26, 1846. His early years were spent at Fort Hunter and later he engaged in the manufacture of brooms here with his uncle, E. Howard. In 1888 W. A. Howard withdrew and associated himself with Henry Herrick, of Amsterdam, New York, and acted in the capacity of superintendent of factory and broom corn purchaser. In 1894 he went to St. Louis and for three years superintended the broom corn business for Cupple's Wood and Willowware Company, the largest in the world. In August, 1898, he located in Tuscola and engaged in the broom corn brokerage business.

He is a son of Silas and Julia A. (Avery) Howard. In 1872 he was wedded to Miss Emma A. Howe, a daughter of Allen M. Howe, who resides in the town of Florida, Montgomery county, New York. Mr. Howard is a man of culture and education and the city of Tuscola has gained in him a representative citizen and a thorough student in business affairs.

N. S. MONROE.

N. S. Monroe, of Arthur, and the well-known road-machine manufacturer, is a native of Shelby county, Indiana, having been born eight miles from Shelbyville, the county seat, January 8, 1851. His parents were Andrew J. and Julia Ann (Huffman) Monroe, who were also natives of Shelby county, Indiana. His father was a farmer and came to Illinois in 1856 and settled in Richland county, thence in 1866 to Coles county, and three years ago moved to Arcola, where he is living a retired life. N. S. Monroe's grandfathers, Samuel Monroe and Jacob Huffman, were both Virginians by birth and were pioneer settlers in Shelby county, Indiana. His grandfather Monroe resided in Shelbyville sixty years. John Raynes (maternal great-grandfather) was born in Maine. John Monroe (paternal great-grandfather) was born in Virginia and was engaged in the Methodist ministry for about sixty years, living to be ninety-six years old; he also had several brothers who were preachers in the Methodist church. N. S. Monroe grew upon the farm and received only a common-school education. He removed to Douglas county and in 1876 he located on a farm in Bourbon township, where he continued to farm up till 1896. The farm upon which he resided he still owns; it contains three hundred and seventeen acres.

In 1876 Mr. Monroe was married to Miss Martha A. Leggett, who was born in Terre Haute. Seven children have blessed their union: Charles W., Andrew J., Margaret M., George W., Julia E., Ora B. and Alice J. He is a member of the Methodist church and the Masonic fraternity. In 1894 he founded his present road-machine manufactory at Arthur, and it promises to be one of the leading industries of its kind in the country. His building is 132x35 feet in size. The advantages of the Monroe road-machine when working on a pike are that you do not have to put one horse in the ditch while cutting off a shoulder, as the bars extend out so that the team and machine can travel on the road. The fact that the Monroe road-machine will do so much more work than other machines with the same power lies simply in the construction of the machine. The bars acting against each other there is no wide draft and no power lost, and the machine will not slide into the ditch. The bars work independently of the upward and downward action of the frame caused by the unevenness of the road.

Under date of February 23, 1900, the Arthur Graphic copies from the Southern Review of Commerce, of Louisville, Kentucky, dated February 7, 1900, the following: "As a result we find that 'The Monroe Road Machine,' a product of N. S. Monroe, Arthur, Illinois, who is the patentee and manufacturer of this machine, is the best on the market. In an editorial like this it is impossible to give all the details of our recent investigation of this subject, but we wish to state that the above named machine is vastly superior to all other makes because it is made of the best material regardless of cost; it is constructed strictly on scientific and mechanical principles; is strong and durable and every machine sold by Mr. Monroe is fully guaranteed.

"This machine scrapes ten to twenty feet at a time, leaving a perfectly smooth road and one free from all ridges. It is a practical road machine for successful work on either dirt or gravel roads, and those who have used it pronounce 'The Monroe Road Machine' the finest that is on the market, while practical mechanics say it is the acme of perfection in this line of invention, and that any man of ordinary judgment can operate it with ease and safety and perform perfect work with it. Its efficiency, durability, simplicity and the cheap price at which it is put on the market certainly recommend this machine to all who desire to secure perfect roads.

"We advise our inquirers, or all interested readers, to write Mr. Monroe direct for further and detailed information. He is a gentleman well known for his business tact and enterprise, his commercial rating is of the highest order and all parties dealing with him can rest assured that he will make good every representation that he may make.

"This unsolicited editorial endorsement is made in strict accordance with the policy of the Review, which is to give credit where credit is due in every investigation that we make for our readers, whose interests alone we seek to serve. The Monroe system of road work should be given careful investigation as it should be adopted to obtain the best results when the machine is used."

JACOB MOORE.

Jacob Moore, the pioneer of the family of Moores in the county, was a native of Kentucky. His wife, Amanda Rice, was also born in Kentucky. They came to Douglas county in the spring of 1834. In the same year he purchased from Sigler Lester forty acres of land, and afterward added about two thousand more. He died in 1860, and his wife in 1863. They had ten children; the eldest of whom, William T. Moore, was born in Park county, Indiana, September 5, 1830.

ALVY J. PARKE.

Alvy J. Parke is one of the hustling, go-ahead, young business men of the county, located at Hindsboro, engaged in the grain and implement business, was born on a farm in Sargent township March 11, 1876, and is a son of B. F. and Harriet (Wierman) Parke. Both of his parents were born in Champaign county, are living, and for the past year resided in Shelby county, Tennessee. Mr. Parke was reared to manhood on the farm and received his education in the high school of Oakland. In 1897 he married Miss Myrtle Lewis.

A. J. Parke started up in his present business in November, 1898, and is doing an immense business solely on his own account. Last year he bought in the neighborhood of eighty thousand bushels of corn, besides other grain, and finds a market at Terre Haute, Indiana. He has just completed a building 32x60 feet, and has it filled with the best grade of the Columbus, Ohio, buggies, the celebrated Mitchell wagon and farm machinery of all descriptions. Mr. Parke's future in the business world seems unusually bright, and his characteristic push and his reputation for square dealing will undoubtedly bring him just results.

JESSE R. BEGGS.

Jesse R. Beggs, president of the First National Bank of Arcola, doubtless enjoys the distinction of being the youngest national bank president in the state. He has occupied this important position since the death of his father, whom he succeeded in February, 1895. He was born in Arcola, August 19, 1868, and was educated in the public schools of the village. His father, James Beggs, was born in Clark county, near Charlestown, the old county seat. He came to Arcola in 1858, where he followed a most successful business career up to the time of his death. His wife was Amanda Brentlinger, who was also born in the same town. On the organization of the bank, in 1874, he was chosen its first president, though he had had banking experience since 1866. The present capital of the bank is fifty thousand dollars, with a surplus of ten thousand dollars, and one hundred and twenty thousand dollars average deposits. Under its present management it is doing a flourishing business, and is one of the most substantial banking houses in central Illinois.

In 1892 our subject was married to Miss Florence M. McMillan, of Arcola. Mr. Beggs has many substantial and devoted friends and no young man is more favorably known throughout the county than he.

MARION WATSON.

Marion Watson, of Arthur, after reading law under the instruction of William H. Whittaker, of Sullivan, was admitted to practice law before the supreme court of the state in 1896. He was born on a farm near Bloomfield, Greene county, Indiana, October 29, 1864. His education was received in the common schools, and he afterward attended a short term at the normal at Danville, Indiana. He remained on the farm in his native county until 1883, when he came to Illinois, locating in Douglas county, and spent two seasons as a common work hand on the farm, working one winter during this time for his board and attending school. Subsequently he taught school for six years in the county. In 1892 Mr. Watson succeeded W. H. H. Reeder in the insurance and real estate business, since which time he has been very successfully engaged in this business in connection with his law practice. He has a most complete law library, and one as varied as those generally found in cities.

On September 5, 1892, he was united in marriage with Miss Ivy J., daughter of James and Belle Gamron, of Edgar county, Illinois. They have four children: Esther Marie, Ralph Waldo, Gladys and Grace.

Marion Watson is the son of Dale and Quintilla (Payne) Watson, who were probably born in Virginia. Dale came to Indiana with his father, John Watson, and they were among the early settlers of Greene county. His maternal grandfather, William Payne, was a native of North Carolina.

Mr. Watson has served one term as president of the village board of Arthur; served a part of a term as justice of the peace, and one term as assessor of Bourbon township, and is a member and trustee of the Baptist church. Mr. Watson has fought his own way to the front over many obstacles, and occupies at present an enviable and honorable position among his professional brethren of the county, having the confidence of the entire community in which he lives. In political opinion he is a stanch believer in the tenets and principles of the regular Democracy as laid down in the Chicago platform of 1896.

SAMUEL W. SMILEY.

Samuel W. Smiley, grain buyer at West Ridge, and member of the firm of Smiley & Watson (B. T. Watson, of Bourbon), is one of the wide-awake and energetic business men of the county. He came to Douglas county in 1889, and located in Bourbon township, where he was engaged in business. Subsequently he and B. T. Watson formed their partnership, and Mr. Smiley located at West Ridge. This firm bought at this place from July 1 to November 10, 1899 130,000 bushels of corn and oats.

Samuel W. Smiley was born at Greencastle, Indiana, February 11, 1855, and is the son of Jonathan and Mary (Warner) Smiley. They are both dead. Mr. Smiley's parents removed from Greencastle to Stanford, Kentucky, where he was principally reared and educated. In 1876 he was married to Miss Elizabeth Hester Hasbarger, and six children have been born to their marriage. Mr. Smiley's grandfather, Jonathan Smiley, was a native Virginian; his maternal grandfather was Samuel Warner. Mr. Smiley is postmaster at West Ridge, owns one hundred and sixty acres of land in Camargo township, and is rapidly coming to the front as one of Douglas county's most successful business men.

WILLIAM E. ATWELL.

William E. Atwell was born in Bracken county, Kentucky, in the year A. D. 1831, and there grew to man's estate, when he moved to a farm in Pendleton county in the same state. He wedded Miss Nancy Barrett, of near Cynthiana. She died in June, 1897. They had twelve children, all of whom are living and doing well in the world. Mr. Atwell is a son of William and Ursla (Fields) Atwell, who were natives of old Virginia. His grandfathers were Hugh Atwell and Leban Fields, the former born in Virginia and the latter in North Carolina. Mr. Atwell, who is a warm hearted gentleman, for which his state is noted, has for several years made his home with one of his daughters, Mrs. Elizabeth M. Wyeth, in her beautiful country seat in Garrett township.

CHARLES A. HAWKINS.

Charles A. Hawkins, the present gentlemanly county clerk, was born in Pickaway county, Ohio, May 25, 1860, and is a son of William and Sarah (Hard) Hawkins, natives of the same state. His father died in 1866. Mr. Hawkins was principally educated at Danville, Indiana, and spent two and a half years teaching. He served his township (Newman) as tax collector and supervisor, and in November, 1898, was elected county clerk.

On October 7, 1884, Mr. Hawkins married Louisa J. Curtis, of Newman, and they have four children: Claude A., Opal B., Pearl L. and Jay M.. Our subject is a Mason and a Knight of Pythias and is active in Republican politics.

ALEXANDER McNEILL.

Alexander McNeill, farmer, was a son of Alexander and Nancy (Montgomery) McNeill, and was born in Ireland March 10, 1808. The first twenty-six years of his life he spent in his native land. In 1834 he emigrated to America, landing in Philadelphia. Thence, two months later, went to Paris, Bourbon county, Kentucky, where, upon letters of introduction from his uncles in the old country, he obtained a situation as clerk in a cotton establishment. After a year he accepted a position as clerk in a dry goods store at Owensville, Bath county, Kentucky, where he remained six years, then sold goods on his own account in the same town, having been saving and diligent during his seven years' clerkship, which enabled him to engage in business for himself. Owing to ill health, after about four years in mercantile pursuits, he bought a large farm in Bath county, Kentucky, and began farming, which has been his principal pursuit since. It is proper to here note the causes which induced his removal from Kentucky to Illinois. Soon after coming to America he became a Whig, then a Republican and the breaking out of the Civil war found him a Union man. Bath county, his home, was the constant scene of guerrilla warfare, and men like Mr. McNeill lived in a state of constant jeopardy. In 1863 his home was invaded by a party of fifteen men, whose enmity Mr. McNeill had incurred by his outspoken, patriotic sentiments. The inmates were overpowered, Mr. McNeill shot three times in different parts of the body and left for dead. His wife was shot once through the feet, and the child in the nurse's arms had a bullet sent through its clothing. In consequence of this and the intoleration of free speech, in 1864 he sold his farm of five hundred and sixty-six acres and came to Douglas county and located on the large farm where he afterward resided, then little developed, but later finely improved, with large two-story residence and surrounding adornments. January

30, 1844, he married Miss Minerva Iles, of Bath county, Kentucky, an intelligent Christian lady, to whose encouragement and frugality Mr. McNeill largely attributed his success. Mr. and Mrs. McNeill were members of the Methodist church, and had the confidence and esteem of all who knew them.

KIMBALL GLASSCO.

Kimball Glassco was born November 19, 1819, in Hardin county, Kentucky, three miles from the birthplace of Lincoln. His father, Enoch Glassco, a farmer, moved to Coles county, Illinois, in 1828, and there died in 1835; his wife was Rachel Carlton. The family of Enoch Glassco was the sixth that settled in Coles county, and located there while yet the Indians were quite numerous and wolves present by the thousand, and to reach a mill they had to go twenty-eight miles. Kimball Glassco had no school advantages for four years after coming to Illinois; then, with but few books, such as could be borrowed, he attended a subscription school and hoed corn to pay tuition. His clothing was one pair of shoes a year, made out of home-tanned leather, buckskin pants and linsey shirt. When Kimball was sixteen years old his father died; then he worked out by the month for three years to support the family, he being the eldest son at home. He then learned brickmaking and plastering, worked at contracting and building seventeen years in Charleston, then went into mercantile business in Charleston for four years, then went to farming, owning one thousand acres of land. In 1862 he moved to Greencastle, Indiana, to educate his children. His sons enlisting in the war of 1865, he returned to Douglas county, Illinois, and again engaged in farming. He was married February 1, 1844, to Margaret Reat; she died December 26, 1880. His second wife was Hester Richards, formerly Hester Reat, sister of his first wife. Mr. Glassco was well acquainted with the Lincoln family, and often went to the grist mill belonging to Tom Lincoln, the father of Abe. He knew Abe from the time he was three years old and sat on juries in cases Lincoln was trying. Although Mr. Glassco was a life-long Democrat, he always voted for Lincoln when that lamented martyr was a candidate for office.

JOHN N. OUTCELT.

John N. Outcelt was born March 4, 1839, in Muskingum county, Ohio, his father, John, being a farmer and a native of Pennsylvania. His grandfather, Jacob Outcelt, came to the United States from Scotland and settled in Bedford county, Pennsylvania. His mother was Mary McClain, of Bedford county, in the same state. He was the youngest child, and at sixteen left home, came to Illinois and for two years sold lightning rods and saved his earnings, with which he paid tuition and other expenses in attending school one year in St. Louis. Up to the time of leaving home he had constantly attended school. After leaving the St. Louis school he sold tombstones for a St. Louis firm for three years, then worked on a farm on Fort Harrison prairie, north of Terre Haute, for a short time and in July, 1861, came to Douglas county. In February, 1862, he went to St. Louis, enlisted in Company I, First Missouri Volunteer Infantry, and in 1864 veteranized. Five months after veteranizing he went into Company F, Thirteenth Missouri Cavalry, and in December, 1864, was promoted to a lieutenancy and assigned to Company L, same regiment. After the surrender of Lee Mr. Outcelt went on an Indian campaign into Colorado and New Mexico. He received his final discharge from the service in June, 1866. At the battle at Independence, Missouri, he, with four companions, unexpectedly ran on to a masked battery of three cannons and eight or ten confederate soldiers, which they succeeded in capturing, being immediately re-enforced. For this service he was promoted. At the close of the war he returned to Douglas county and farmed three years. He then was appointed deputy county clerk, which position he held up to 1880, and was then appointed clerk for a term of four years. He was formerly a Democrat, but at the fall of Fort Sumter became a Republican. He was a Mason and a member of the Christian church.

JAMES R. HAMMETT.

James R. Hammett, named for his father, whose full history and plate is on another page, was born in Camargo township, Douglas county, Illinois, December 26, A. D. 1870. He was principally educated in the Northwestern University at Evanston, Illinois, where he remained three years. In 1897 he married Miss Conchita Kelley, of the state of Chihuahua, Mexico. They have two lovely babies: Helen and Blanche. Jimmie and his family live happily in their beautiful home, which constitutes a part of the old homestead.

THOMAS S. WYATT.

Thomas S. Wyatt, ex-sheriff of Douglas county, was born in Todd county, Kentucky, January 13, 1838. His father, Needham Wyatt, a blacksmith, was born in Tennessee. Thomas Wyatt, the father of Needham, was born in North Carolina; was a Revolutionary soldier, and was at the surrender of Lord Cornwallis. The mother of Thomas S. Wyatt was Mrs. Martha A. (Mann) Wyatt, sister of Rev. William W. Mann, a prominent member of the Methodist church of Kentucky. Thomas S. Wyatt's early life was spent in his father's blacksmith shop. He received but ten months' schooling, yet became a fair scholar through studious habits. At the age of nineteen years he began business for himself as a carpenter, which trade he followed for two years in Muhlenburg county, Kentucky; he next followed farming; then, in 1865, came to this county and built a blacksmith shop seven miles northeast of Camargo, which he conducted until 1880, when he was elected sheriff. In 1882 he was re-elected by a majority of six hundred and forty. He had previously, while engaged in his trade, been a justice of the peace for nine years. In youth he united with the Methodist church; has been a class leader and Sunday school superintendent, and was licensed as a preacher in 1875, since when he has preached often. He organized a society in Jordan schoolhouse, Camargo township, which society afterward built a large church, wherein he preached his first sermon. He is a Mason and a Republican, and voted for Abraham Lincoln in Kentucky. December 30, 1857, he married Cascinda Smith, of Muhlenburg county, Kentucky.

JAMES H. HOWE.

James H. Howe was born June 1, 1832, in Bourbon county, Kentucky. April 5, 1838, he came with his mother to Vermilion county, Illinois; he was reared and educated in Vermilion and Champaign counties. In his youthful days he traveled considerably, and, in 1854, came to Douglas county; two years later he bought the Williams farm, which he improved and afterward sold. He was largely engaged in the live stock business, handling as high as one hundred thousand dollars in a year. In the spring of 1882 he was elected justice of the peace and was also highway commissioner. He was married in 1857 to Eliza J. Lester, who was born in Garrett township.

JOHN C. BARNES.

John C. Barnes, physician and lumber dealer, was born in Jefferson county, Indiana, September 27, 1835. His grandfather, John, came from Culpeper county, Virginia, to Indiana in 1800. McGannon Barnes, father of John C., was born in Jefferson county, while his wife, Rebecca Fouts, was a native of Clark county, Indiana. John C. Barnes was the eldest in a family of ten children; he was given a thorough educational training, attending first the common schools, then Hanover Academy in Jefferson county, Indiana, and in 1855 graduated from Scott's Commercial College, Indianapolis. At twenty years of age he began for himself, clerking in a store and post office at Hanover four years. April 24, 1860, he married Mrs. Elizabeth Coombs. After marriage he took a course of lectures at the Eclectic Medical Institute, Cincinnati. In 1866 he came to Douglas county, first landing at the present site of Hindsboro, then a waste prairie, but went direct to Coles county; after a year there he bought a farm three miles west of Hindsboro, which he improved and superintended in connection with his practice of medicine until 1883, when he sold out, came to Hindsboro and engaged in keeping a lumber yard in connection with his practice. He is a member of the Masonic lodge, of Arcola, and Odd Fellows lodge, No. 571, of Hindsboro. Politically, he is a Democrat and in 1882 was candidate for Congress on the Greenback ticket; he was a member of the convention at Indianapolis that nominated Benjamin F. Butler for president in 1884. He stands high socially and is one in whose opinions the community has great confidence. His charity and generosity are marked traits of his character. Mrs. Barnes was born and reared in Clark county, Indiana, and is a daughter of Absalom and Nancy Bower. Her grandfather, Adam, was born on the ocean while his parents were enroute for America from

Germany in 1754. Her father came to Indiana from North Carolina with his parents in 1806. Mrs. Barnes was educated at the seminary at Washington, Indiana, and remained at home until her marriage to Jesse Coombs, a farmer of Clark county, Indiana, who died December 8, 1853. After the death of her husband she attended and taught school until 1855, when she began the study of medicine for which, from early childhood, she had a natural inclination and talent. After preparatory study in the office of Dr. Joseph Hostetler, she attended lectures at and graduated from the Eclectic Medical Institute of Cincinnati in 1857, then settled in Clark county, where she practiced till her marriage to Dr. Barnes. Since coming to Illinois she has constantly practiced until quite recently and has an eminent standing professionally and socially.

JAMES S. REEDER.

James S. Reeder was born March 4, 1840, in Darke county, Ohio, and came with his parents in 1856 to this locality, where he engaged in farming. He enlisted August, 1862, in Company G, Seventy-ninth Illinois Infantry, and served three years. At the battle of Stone River, December 31, 1862, he was wounded and taken prisoner; after being in the enemy's lines twenty-seven days he was exchanged, and participated in the battles of Liberty Gap and Chickamauga; at the latter, September 19, 1863, he was captured and taken to Richmond prison, thence to Andersonville, Charleston, South Carolina, and Florence, making seventeen months in all spent in prison. At the close of the war he returned and engaged in farming. He was married December 2, 1865, to Mary M. Kelly, who was born in Winchester, Indiana. He resides in Arthur.

J. B. RIGNEY, M. D.

J. B. Rigney, M. D., was born in Paoli, Orange county, Indiana, and is the son of William H. Rigney, who held the offices of sheriff, treasurer and collector. At about the age of sixteen he, with his family, moved to Terre Haute, Indiana, and for three years resided on a farm. Finding rural pursuits distasteful, he turned his attention to medicine. He commenced his studies under Dr. James H. Sherwood and continued with him for three years, when he went to Chicago and attended the Rush Medical College, from which he graduated in 1863. He then enlisted as hospital steward, serving until January, 1866, when he returned and practiced medicine eleven miles south of Terre Haute, and in 1867 came to Arthur, where he has since resided. In 1868 he married Miss Ora F. McDonald, of Mattoon.

JOHN WHITAKER.

John Whitaker was born in Vigo county, Indiana, March 12, 1833, and is the son of William and Elizabeth (Taylor) Whitaker, who were natives of Kentucky. His father was born in 1803 and died in 1846. John Whitaker came to Douglas county in 1856, located on section 13, Bourbon township, where he bought a farm of eighty acres, on which he lived five years; this property he then sold and purchased eighty acres later on. At present he owns in all two hundred and forty acres; this farm he has improved with buildings at a cost of about two thousand dollars. He has been township commissioner for about five years. In 1860 he married Hannah Davis, who was born in Vigo county, Indiana. She died and he subsequently married Mrs. Yeager, of Arcola. In 1898 they commenced the construction of the Douglas hotel and on April 19, 1899, it was swung open to the general public. This hotel is by far the best in every way of all other public inns in the county.

WILLIAM B. CHANDLER.

William B. Chandler, a well-known stock buyer of the county and a resident of Bourbon township, was born in Douglas county, Illinois, March 6, 1852. He is a son of Lemuel Chandler (for the ancestry of the family, see sketch.) When yet a boy, William B. Chandler entered the University of Illinois at Champaign and was graduated therefrom with a degree of B. S. in the class of 1876. In 1885 he served in the capacity of clerk to the Indian commission at Yankton and continued in this capacity for four years. He then went to Pueblo, Colorado, where he engaged successfully in the practice of law for three years. On account of the sickness of his father and business interests at home, he returned in 1892, since which time he has been quite extensively engaged in farming and stock buying.

In 1883 Mr. Chandler was united in marriage to Miss Belle Augusta Bailey, of Tuscola. They have no children. Our subject is a Democrat in politics and the only office he ever held was that of town clerk of Bourbon township soon after he reached the age of manhood. Mr. Chandler is well and favorably known throughout the county, is a man of good business ability and devoted to the highest and best interests of Douglas countians.

W. D. REED.

W. D. Reed, the assessor of Bowdre township, was born on the old Reed homestead in the same township March 14, 1852, and is a son of the gallant B. Frank Reed, who fell at the battle of Chickamauga, and for whom the G. A. R. Post at Tuscola is named, and whose portrait adorns this page. He was born in Bourbon county, Kentucky, and emigrated with his father, Daniel, to Edgar county, when he was but eight years old. Daniel Reed founded the old tavern or road house at Hickory Grove between Newman and Indianola. He volunteered in the Civil war and became captain of Company D, First Illinois Regiment. He was united in marriage to Catherine, a daughter of William Barnett, who lived in Camargo and was one of the early settlers.

W. D. Reed has been assessor of Bowdre township continuously for five years. He was married in 1874 to Ida L., a daughter of J. H. Bagley. They have had five children, of whom Ward, Clark, Fred and Mary are living, and Maud is dead. Mr. Reed is a stanch Democrat in politics, as was also his father, Captain Reed.

WILLIAM BRIAN, SR.

William Brian, Sr., was born May 6, 1806, in Ross county, Ohio, and in 1837 he came to Coles, now Douglas, county; he entered about one thousand acres of land when coming here, and has owned as high as three thousand acres. He had learned the blacksmith's trade in Ohio, and followed it about twenty years here. On one occasion, when shoeing a Methodist preacher's horse, he nailed the shoes on with the toe-corks behind. The preacher remonstrated with him for doing so; his reply was, "The devil takes after these Methodist preachers, and I thought I would make him take the back track." He was married October 1, 1829, to Anna Lewis, who was born in Pike county, Ohio, May 4, 1805. They had nine children, six of whom are here named: Thomas, James, Mary (wife of R. E. H. Westfall), William T., Taylor W. and Samuel. His death occurred a few years since.

JOHN W. KING.

John W. King, of Newman, who has for several years been prominent in the politics of the county, and at present is associated with the Newman bank, was born in Bourbon county, Kentucky, October 13, 1841. He is a son of David A. and Jane Elizabeth (Mitchell) King, who were natives of Clark and Montgomery counties, Kentucky, respectively. His father, who was born in 1818, followed the occupation of farming, removed from Kentucky to Champaign county, Illinois, in 1855, and there his death occurred in 1896. His mother died in 1882, aged fifty years. His paternal grandfather, Robert Cass King, was a native of Virginia, and his maternal grandfather, John W. Mitchell, was also born in Virginia, in Culpeper county.

John W. King was reared on his father's farm and attended the public schools of the neighborhood. In 1862 he joined Company G, Seventy-second Illinois Volunteers, as a private, and served three years and four months, part of the time as a non-commissioned officer. After the war he entered the state normal school, where he remained for three years. Leaving there he attended Bryant & Stratton's Business College at Chicago, where he remained one year. He then taught school for some years in Champaign county, when, in 1872, he came to Newman, and for three years held the principalship of the Newman schools. In 1875 he was elected to the office of county superintendent to fill a vacancy, which he held up to the next general election in 1877, when he was re-elected and served up till 1881. In April of the latter year he resigned to accept the appointment of postmaster of Newman, which position he held under the administrations of both Garfield and Arthur. At the expiration of his term he accepted the position of bookkeeper in the Newman Bank, which position he held up till 1890. In that year he was elected county clerk, and was re-elected in 1894, serving in that office up until 1898, when he re-entered the Newman Bank. In 1872 Mr. King was united in marriage to Miss Kate C. Fry, of near Champaign. They have five children: Blanche, Earl G., Katie W., Roscoe W. and Harry T. Mr. King has been collector of Newman township some four or five terms; is a member of nearly all the secret societies, is trustee of the Methodist Episcopal church at Newman, and a stanch Republican in politics. Both as a soldier, officer and citizen Mr. King has been faithful in the discharge of his regular duties and the performance of any special work assigned to him.

THOMAS W. ROBERTS.

Thomas W. Roberts, the bright young lawyer of Tuscola, attorney for the I. D. & W. R. R. Co. and city attorney, has from the humble walks of life pressed his way to the front and to-day stands among the leading and most successful lawyers at the bar.

Thomas W. Roberts was born in Owensburg, Green county, Indiana, May 1, 1866, and soon thereafter came with his parents to Douglas county, and located at Camargo, where young Robert attended school until sixteen years of age. In 1882 his father removed to Tuscola, and there the young man learned the tinner's trade. But that was only a means to an end, and in 1886 he was appointed to a clerkship in the treasury department at Washington, where he worked day time and attended school at night, and for four years continued in the preparatory department of Georgetown University, after which he took a four-years' course in the law department of the same institution and was graduated in 1892. Mr. Roberts was at once admitted to the bar of Illinois, and entered upon his chosen profession, becoming the partner of the late C. W. Woolverton (see sketch), with whom he continued until the death of his associate in 1895, since which time Mr. Roberts has continued in the practice alone. He is attorney for the I. D. & W. R. R. Co. in Illinois, attorney for the Corn Belt Building & Loan Association, attorney for the bank of Baughman, Bragg & Co. and this along with his other practice makes him a very busy man.

Mr. Roberts is a son of Henry Clay and Anna Elizabeth (Sleet) Roberts, both natives of Kentucky. Henry Clay Roberts came to Douglas county in 1870, and here resided for some years; later he removed to South Dakota, where he at present lives. He was a member of the Ninety-seventh Regiment, Indiana, in the Civil war, volunteered in 1861, and was mustered out in 1865. Thomas Roberts (grandfather) was one of the early Virginia settlers in Boone county, Kentucky, as was his grandfather Sleet.

In June, 1888, Mr. Roberts wedded Mrs. Jennie Sharp, a daughter of R. H. B. Madison, of Tuscola. Two children have blessed their union: Irene Elizabeth and Ralph Henry. In Masonry he is a Knight Templar, a stanch Democrat in politics, and is popular and influential in the county.

WASHINGTON D. BOYCE.

Washington David Boyce was born at the foot of Blue Ridge near Leesburg, Lee county, Virginia, in the year A. D. 1802 and died in

Camargo township in February, 1882. He was among the first settlers in that township, where he entered forty acres of land. He established the first blacksmith shop at the village of Albany.

ROBERT McKAIG.

Robert McKaig is one of the pioneer settlers of Tuscola township, who came in 1857. He and his wife are members of the Presbyterian church and highly respected in their neighborhood.

J. T. BUTLER.

We copy from a recent issue of the Tuscola Review:

"J. T. Butler, of this city, secretary and manager of the Corn Belt National & Loan Association, had received intelligence from his brother in California, that he had struck a gold mine of unparalleled richness, and that our fellow citizen was a half owner in the new wonder.

"The editor knowing that Mr. Butler was a man who shunned notoriety and would be loth to give out information that would bring him into such prominence as an article of this kind necessarily will, approached him on the subject. He was at first disinclined to talk on the subject, but learning that it had become generally known throughout the city, he consented to make a statement, in order that the public might get the facts and facts only. As Mr. Butler is a man of unimpeachable character and known to be a truthful and conservative man, we have the fullest confidence in his statement.

"The following facts have been given us by Mr. Butler, and his host of friends in this city are happy to know that he has suddenly become, or will soon become, the wealthiest man not only in Tuscola, but probably in the state of Illinois.

"He states that he has a brother, Dr. Thomas Butler, a prominent and reputable physician of San Diego, who has been in the gold regions of that and other states for thirteen years, and who has always prospected more or less. About three months ago his brother visited the great Dewey mine in what is known as the "Grapevine" district, sixty miles east of San Diego. This range of mountains is probably a spur of the San Barnadino range and are called the Vulcan mountains. The Dewey mine is a late discovery and was recently capitalized at one million dollars. It is regarded as a wonder."

WILLIAM T. BRIAN.

William T. Brian, one of the old and favorably known citizens and a member of one of the pioneer families of the county, was born in 1845 in Douglas county, and is a son of William and Anna Lewis Brian, who were born in the same county. William Brian (father) located in what is known now as the Brian neighborhood in about the year 1843, where he entered a large tract of land at one dollar and twenty-five cents an acre, and adding to that later considerably more at thirteen dollars per acre. At the time of his death, in 1888, at the age of eighty-one years, he was one of the biggest land owners in the county. Lewis Brian was his paternal grandfather. His maternal grandfather, John Lewis, settled in the same neighborhood, from Ohio, in an early day and is buried at the Hickory Withe cemetery.

William T. Brian was married in 1868 to Miss Sarah Bundy, a daughter of Caleb Bundy. The latter was born in North Carolina and settled early in Douglas county, three miles north and one-half mile west of Tuscola. Mr. and Mrs. Brian have one child, a daughter, Ellanor, who is the wife of John Lathrop. Mr. Brian owns at present eight hundred and sixty-two acres of land, lying in one body, and is one of the biggest tax payers in the county. He is a stanch free-silver Democrat and is universally respected by all who know him.

OLIVER H. PARKER.

Oliver H. Parker, grain buyer at Hayes and Humboldt, and a son of Lines L. Parker, of Bowdre township, was born in Vermilion county, Illinois, in the year A. D. 1860. He resides with his family in Tuscola. In 1881 he was married to Miss Angie Wallace, a daughter of Joseph and Mary Ann (Breezley) Wallace. Joseph Wallace was a pioneer settler in Bowdre township. To Mr. and Mrs. Parker were born four children: Burt I., Fred Earle, Minnie Pearle and Everett Dewey. Mr. Parker is one of the substantial business men of the county.

THOMAS CRUZAN.

Thomas Cruzan was born in Douglas county January 15, 1836, and is a son of the two oldest citizens now living in the county who were born in it. He is a son of Robert Cruzan and Jane Crawford, who settled early in the Brown neighborhood, coming from Indiana. Our subject owns two hundred and forty acres of land.

CALEB GARRETT.

Among the oldest residents of Douglas county, is Caleb Garrett, of Tuscola. His ancestors early made their home in America, his father's great-grandfather, John Garrett by name, and an Englishman by birth, having settled in Virginia. He had a son, John Garrett, and a grandson, Welcome Garrett, who was the grandfather of the subject of our sketch. Welcome Garrett was born in Virginia, and when a young man moved to Surry county, North Carolina. He served in Tennessee during the Indian wars prior to the Revolution. He married Phœbe Sumner, a Pennsylvanian by birth. The Garretts were a strong, vigorous race of men. Joshua Garrett, a brother to Welcome, was killed at the battle of Brandywine, during the Revolutionary war. Lewis, another brother, was shot by the Tories before enlisting. William was with Marion in South Carolina through the war, and after the conclusion of the struggle died of disease contracted in the service. This William Garrett was a man of powerful build and of great strength. He weighed two hundred and forty pounds, and was called the strongest man in the state of North Carolina.

Welcome Garrett became a member of the society of Friends. In 1824 he moved to Wayne county, Indiana. He died in Hamilton county of that state, at the age of eighty-four. Isom Garrett, Caleb Garrett's father, and the son of Welcome Garrett was born in Surry county, North Carolina, in 1796. In 1814 he married Mary Puckett, and the same year moved to Clermont county, Ohio. After a residence there of a year he went to Clinton county, Ohio, where his son Caleb was born. In 1819 he moved to Randolph county, Indiana, and in 1823 to Vigo county of the same state, where he lived till his removal to Illinois, with the exception of part of the year 1839, when he resided in Texas.

The date of Caleb Garrett's birth, in Clinton county, Ohio, was the 16th of July, 1816. He was consequently seven years old when the family moved to Vigo county, Indiana, in the vicinity of Terre Haute. His early opportunities for securing an education were very limited. One of the schools which he attended was about three miles and a half from his father's residence near Honey Creek bridge. Here school was sometimes kept for three months in the year, an unusually long period at that day. Another school was afterward established nearer home under the care of Joel Butler, of the state of New York, which for a time afforded excellent advantages. The next school he attended was taught by one Joel Thayer, an excellent teacher, but so confirmed and inebriate that the children soon discontinued attendance on his instruction. His father was a man of considerable education, and under his care he learned rapidly. According to Isom Garrett, his father, obedience to his parents was one of his marked traits. His mother died in 1830, and for a period of nine years succeeding this event, the father and the sons, Caleb and Nathan, kept house for themselves, and did their own cooking, besides attending to their usual occupations. During part of this period Mr. Garrett was in the employment of Chauncey Rose, of Terre Haute, and now one of the wealthiest and most liberal citizens of Indiana. He drove an ox team for Lucius H. Scott, now of Philadelphia. He dropped corn for twenty-five cents a day, and split rails at from twenty-five to thirty cents a hundred, averaging one hundred and fifty for a usual day's work. For a long time he worked for a wealthy Scotchman, William Walker, at six dollars a month. At twenty-one he was probably the strongest man in all the country round. Although full of life, he had no intemperate habits. He was a favorite in the community. "He could do as big day's work as anyone," says his father, "and at a country frolic could play a tune on the fiddle second to none."

In the period from 1834 to 1839 he made several trips down the river on a flat boat, and thus became well acquainted with the Ohio and Mississippi rivers. The greater part of one winter he remained in New Orleans. On a return trip at one time with Captain Shallcross, of Louisville, he was stuck in the ice near Paducah, Kentucky, and the men were reduced to two crackers a day. On this same trip, in coming home, he walked from Evansville to Terre Haute through snow eighteen inches in depth Out of the forty boatmen who started at the same time, only Mr. Garrett and a companion succeeded in going through, the others falling behind and giving it up before they had gone far.

In 1840, on the day succeeding the exciting presidential campaign of that year in which Mr. Garratt voted for General William Henry Harrison, he took a steamer for New Orleans on his way to Texas. The steamer stuck fast in the rapids below Terre Haute, the pilot became intoxicated, and Mr. Garrett, in company with two other young men bound for points south, procured a rough spring wagon in which they journeyed from Mt. Carmel to Evansville on the Ohio river, when the three took a steamer and continued their voyage. One of his companions left him to go up to the Cumberland and the other up the Tennessee river. At New Orleans he secured a passage on a steamship for Galveston, Texas. When out on the Gulf of Mexico the vessel encountered a terrific gale, and for seventy-two hours the ship and crew were in danger of going to the bottom. At Galveston a steamer was taken for Houston. But the steamer stuck fast on the bar, and for a day or two the passengers had time to amuse themselves by fishing in the shallow water for oysters. Mr. Garrett was aiming to make his way first to Independence, in Washington, county. To this point he traveled on foot, with the exception of thirty or forty miles before reaching the town, when he had opportunity of riding. At Independence he obtained a mustang pony, and continued his journey to Austin City. The route led two hundred miles through a frontier country inhabited by hostile Indians. At Austin City, on his arrival, the Congress of the Republic of Texas was in session. Texas had then achieved its independence from Mexico, and formed a separate republic, of which Lamar was president. Sam Houston was one of the prominent members of the Congress. Mr. Garrett remained several weeks in that section of the country, and was frequently in attendance on the sessions of the Congress, on one of which occasions he heard Houston deliver his speech on sectionizing and selling the lands of the Cherokee Indians. Mainly for the purpose of seeing the country, he joined a surveying party, and was absent for some time on the exposed frontier. On his return a company was organized for a buffalo hunt and general exploring expedition, which Mr. Garrett joined, still animated by a desire to see something further of frontier life before he should leave Texas. The party consisted of nine men and two boys. They were attacked by a party of Indians, between thirty and fifty in number. The horse of a young man named Osburn was shot under him, the rider having received a spear wound in the back. The unfortunate man, after being knocked insensible with his own gun by the Indians, was scalped within sight of the remainder of the party, and left for dead on the field. He was afterward rescued, and finally recovered from his wound. The whole party effected their escape to a block-house.

Mr. Garrett's visit to Texas had for its end an object different from any yet described in a record of these incidents. On the 20th of December, 1840, he had been married to Irene Puckett, a native of Vigo county, Indiana, but who at that time resided on the Colorado river, twelve miles below Austin City. He had previously been acquainted with her in Indiana. In February, 1841, he, with his wife, set out on his return home. In company with three or four others they journeyed by an ox team to Houston, where they took a steamer, and ran down the Buffalo Bayou, and thence across the bay where the vessel struck an old ship anchor, tore off part of the planking, and was in danger of sinking. Remaining some days in Galveston, they took passage on the steamer New York for New Orleans. From here they proceeded up the Mississippi and Ohio to Evansville, Indiana, and there took stage for Terre Haute, at which place they arrived on the 5th of March, 1841.

Mr. Garrett now engaged in farming and stock raising, at first renting a farm five miles south of Terre Haute. He was soon called upon, however, to discharge other duties. In August, 1842, he was chosen to represent the county of Vigo in the Indiana Legislature. He took his seat in December, 1842, and served the following winter. The next year he was re-elected, and served another session, performing his duties with credit to himself and satisfaction to his constituents. He was only twenty-six at the time of his first election. Like his father before him, Mr. Garrett was a Whig, and it was as a candidate of the Whig party that he was elected to the Indiana Legislature. At the conclusion of his second term of office he declined a re-election, and devoted himself more assiduously than ever to farming and stock raising. He bought a small farm six miles south of Terre Haute, but sold it after making improvements upon it. He continued to reside in Indiana till 1849. His business operations were attended with success. He desired to invest his surplus funds in new land, and in consequence resolved to settle in Illinois.

He had visited Illinois in company with three others in the fall of 1833. He traversed the state from Edgar county to the Mississippi, passing through Sadorus Grove, Springfield and Beardstown, to Quincy. His course was then up the river for a considerable distance, when, leaving it, he journeyed southeast to the Illinois, and thence through Springfield by the old Springfield trace, across the Okaw, through what is now Douglas county by the Wayne stand, to Paris in Edgar county, and thence to Terre Haute. There were no settlements on the route traveled through Douglas county except at the Shaw stand.

About 1846 Mr. Garrett bought one hundred and sixty acres of land near William Brian's in what is now Douglas county. The next spring he came out with an ox team and began improving it. In 1849 he removed with his family to Douglas county for the purpose of making a permanent residence. He had previously been accustomed to driving cattle from Indiana, and herding them in Douglas county. He located on section three, of township fifteen, range seven. He devoted his whole attention to farming and stock raising. In 1856 he and his wife revisited Texas. They were absent about three months, during which they traveled extensively over the northeastern part of the state. His farm of eight hundred and sixty acres, on which he lived till recently, was sold in May, 1875. He now resides in Tuscola. For two or three years following 1868 he was in the grocery business at Tuscola in partnership with Mr. John M. Maris.

Mr. Garrett served on the first grand jury

that ever convened in Douglas county. In 1854 he was elected justice of the peace and held that office until his resignation. On the organization of the county into townships, Mr. Garrett was chosen a member of the board of supervisors from Garrett township. His public trusts he has discharged with fidelity, and few citizens of the county have gained a larger share of the popular esteem.

WILLIAM H. FULTON.

William H. Fulton located in the village of Camargo in 1852, began merchandising in a small way, and is now the oldest merchant in active business in the county. He was born at Clinton, Indiana, August 17, 1827, and is one of the well-known and respectable citizens of the village.

JAMES GILLOGLY.

James Gillogly, dry goods and general merchant at Newman, is a native of Pennsylvania, where he was reared on a farm and acquired a common school education. He followed farming in Pennsylvania and Illinois until the war, when he enlisted in Company D, Twenty-first Regiment Illinois Infantry, under General then Colonel) Grant. He was wounded at the battle of Stone River, Tennessee, having a leg broken, and was discharged soon after. He then engaged in merchandising at Jacksonville, Ryerson's Station and Ninevah, Pennsylvania, thence coming to Illinois and locating at Newman, where he has since been engaged in his present business. Mr. Gillogly occupies a fine brick store room, 30x70 feet, centrally located and well stocked with the best goods, and is doing a business of twenty-five thousand to thirty thousand dollars yearly. He was married to Miss H. L. Atkinson, and six children have blessed their union: J. C., H. B., Emma J., Lotta, Benton (deceased), and Lewis (deceased). Mr. and Mrs. Gillogly are members of the Cumberland Presbyterian church, and he belongs to the Masonic fraternity and the I. O. O. F.

A. TAYLOR.

A. Taylor, real estate dealer at Newman and a man universally popular and esteemed by everybody around Newman, was born in Tippecanoe county, Indiana, April 8, 1836, where he was reared and educated. He has been a resident in Newman since 1876 and has negotiated many important real estate deals in Douglas and adjoining counties. In 1856 he wedded Miss Alice Beezley, of Indiana. They had three children: A. A.; Charley, who is the present census enumerator of Newman township, and Belle. They are highly respected and counted among Newman's best people.

WIL .. M H. HALL.

William H. Hall, one of the oldest merchants in the county, was born in Bourbon county, Kentucky, September 1, 1831, and was the only son of William and Elizabeth (Hooe) Hall, natives of Kentucky and Virginia respectfully. In 1837 the family came and settled in the neighborhood of Brushy Fork and for two years lived in the family of General Robert Matson, who was a cousin of Mrs. Hall. In 1865 Mr. Hall engaged in the harness business and later engaged in general merchandising. He is still engaged in the same business and is a thorough gentleman of the old school, whose religion consists in doing good to himself and his friends and neighbors.

INDEX.

	PAGE
CHAPTER I.—EARLY SETTLEMENT OF THE COUNTY	7
Cabin, The	18
Farm, The	19
Indian, The	11
Inhabitants, Original	7
Life on the Prairie	17
Markets	20
Mills	20
Mound Builders	7
Natural Resources	16
Pioneers, The	12
Prairie Travel	21
CHAPTER II.—HISTORICAL SKETCH OF COUNTY	25
Agriculture	40
Assessor, First	32
Circuit Clerk, First	31
Circuit Court, First	33
County Clerk, First	31
County Judge, First	31
County Seat	32
Court, First meeting of County	32
Court House, The	33
Geology	38

	PAGE
Officials, County, from organization to date	84
Organization, Act of	27
Organization, Supplementary Bill	30
Origin	26
Railroad, Danville, Tuscola & Western	44
Railroad Indebtedness Assumed	44
Railroad, Illinois Central	42
Railroad, Indianapolis, Decatur & Western	43
Railroad, Toledo & St. Louis	44
Railway, Illinois Midland	44
Recorder, First	31
Sheriff, First	31
Surveyor, First	32
Surveys, System of	35
Swamp Lands	39
Topography	38
Treasurer, First	32
CHAPTER III.—MILITARY RECORD	47
Cavalry, Thirteenth	64
Company, First full	49
Infantry, Twenty-first	49
Infantry, Twenty-fifth	52

	PAGE
Infantry, Fifty-fourth	54
Infantry, Seventy-ninth	57
Infantry, One Hundred and Thirty-fifth	62
Infantry, One Hundred and Fifty-ninth	63
Public Sentiment and Civil Action	47
CHAPTER IV.—TOWNSHIP HISTORICAL SKETCHES	69
Arcola City	109
Arcola Township	107
Atwood Village	86
Bourbon Township	73
Bowdre Township	77
Camargo City	72
Camargo Township	69
Garrett Township	80
Hindsboro Village	79
Murdock Township	91
Murdock Village	92
Newman City	116
Newman Township	113
Sargent Township	88
Tuscola City	109
Tuscola Township	98

BIOGRAPHICAL SKETCHES.

	PAGE
A.	
Armstrong, Archie A	270
Ashurst, Joseph	240
Atto, Daniel	135
Atwell, William E	281
Avery, J. L	273
B.	
Bailey, Capt. David	244
Baker, S. H	141
Barnes, John C	285
Barr, James	181
Bartholomew, Michael D	136
Bassett, J. H	264

	PAGE
Bassett, W. H	263
Beggs, Jesse R	280
Black, Robert M	236
Blaine, Walter C	259
Boyce, Washington David	289
Boyd, W. P	166
Boyer, J. W	273
Brian, William, Sr	288
Brian, William T	290
Bright, Coleman	277
Brock, George W	230
Brown, Judge John	233
Burgett, Carl S	214
Burgett, I. W	234
Burgett, Scott	209
Burtnett, William H., M. D	133

	PAGE
Butler, J. T	290
Bush, William H	179
C.	
Cahill, Eli F	142
Callaway, George	264
Calvin, Edward W	228
Campbell, Allan	227
Carnahan, Clarence H	217
Chadwick, John H	147
Chandler, Lemuel	157
Chandler, William B	287
Conover, Daniel A	221
Cooper, David	128
Covert, I. N	215

INDEX.

	PAGE		PAGE		PAGE
Coykendall, D. F.	165	Howard, W. Avery	277	Mulliken, James W.	253
Craddick, Thomas	251	Howe, James H.	285	Murdock, Judge John D.	145
Cruzan, Thomas	291	Howe, William	202	Murphy, Wiliam F.	152
Culbertson, Charles M.	220	Hunt, Oliver T.	194	Myers, O. V.	158

D.

I.

N.

Dever, Frank C.	177	Iles, William	148	Newport, William H.	285
Drake, Israel A.	147	Irwin, John T.	125	Niles, Henry C.	174
Drew, James	204				

E.

J.

O.

Ephlin, Jacob	263	Jeffers, Emmor W.	248	Outcelt, John N.	283
Ephlin, Mrs. Jacob	263	Jeffers, George C.	272		
Ervin, Samuel	259	Jenne, Charles F.	186	### P.	
		Jones, Henry C.	256		
		Jones, James	133	Parke, Alvy J.	279
### F.		Jones, John J.	262	Parker, Lines L.	169
		Jones, Malden	225	Parker, Oliver H.	291
Fidler, Albert F.	246	Jones, Owen E.	242	Pepper, W. W.	223
Fidler, Levi	246	Jordan, John V	173	Petty, Jo eph B.	270
Finney, E. C.	164			Phillips, J. W.	225
Finney, Joseph H.	175			Price, W. E.	269
Fisher, William H.	274	### K.		Pulliam, W. T., M. D.	264
Foster, R. S.	132				
Fry, William H.	134	Kincaid, James A.	135	### Q.	
Fulton, William H.	295	King, John W.	288		
				Quinn, John	209

G.

L.

R.

Garrett, Caleb	200	Lester, Segler H.	268		
Garrett, Caleb	291	Lindsey, John	127	Reat, James L.	260
Gere, Benjamin W.	190	Logan, Samuel B.	271	Records, Jasper S.	168
Gill, Harrison	258	Long, Stroder M.	198	Redden, Stephen	124
Gill, Shiloah	257	Loose, Frank E.	122	Reed, Daniel W.	191
Gillogly, James	295	Lowry, John	159	Reed, W. D.	287
Glassco, Kimball	283	Lyrla, N. C.	174	Reed, Winfield S.	156
Goff, John L.	251			Reeder, James S.	276
Goodspeed, James M.	170	### M.		Reeder, James S.	286
Greenman, Anson H.	137			Reeder, John A., Jr.	191
Greve, C. D.	237	McCarty, Francis A.	231	Reeves, William W.	272
		McGee, J. Park, M. D.	185	Rice, Eugene	206
### H.		McGown, J. A.	241	Rice, Martin	162
		McKaig, Robert	290	Rice, William Edgar, M. D.	140
Hall, William H.	295	McKinney, John W.	266	Richards, G. R.	276
Hammett, Frank W.	252	McMasters, Charles L.	126	Richards, T. M.	275
Hammett, James R.	158	McNeer, V. C.	218	Richman, James A.	192
Hammett, James R.	284	McNeill, Alexander	282	Rigney, J. B., M. D.	286
Hammett, Richard Clyde	168	Madison, John M.	242	Roberts, Thomas W.	289
Hammett, William S.	276	Magner, D. N.	143	Roderick, Daniel	268
Hance, Alexander	239	Martin, Rev. J. V.	274	Rogers, John E.	139
Hancock, James W.	159	Martin, W. S., M. D.	188	Root, D. O.	206
Hancock, W. H.	252	Means, Rev. William E.	123	Root, Lawrence E.	216
Hapke, Adolph	182	Milligan, Robert E.	191	Rutherford, Dr. C.	222
Hawkins, Charles A	282	Monahan, P. H.	259	Rutherford, Thomas H.	187
Hawkins, John	161	Monroe, N. S.	278		
Hawkins, J. M.	183	Moore, Abram H	184	### S.	
Hawkins, Samuel	176	Moore, Edw. McC.	184		
Hayward, A.	210	Moore, George O.	269	Sanford, Charles S.	211
Heaton, James P.	121	Moore, Jacob.	279	Sawyer, Albert S.	214
Heaton, William	197	Moore, Jacob R.	229	Siders, George W.	178
Henson, George W.	251	Moore, Morris L.	185	Skinner, Isaac.	238
Henson, Stephen S.	277	Moore, William T.	189	Skinner, John	171
Hockett, Oliver O.	224	Morrow, James	151	Skinner, W. W.	265
Hopkins, Samuel L.	267	Moser, George H.	241	Sluss, A. C.	262
Hostetler, John C	250	Mulliken, Ira M.	253	Smiley, Samuel W.	281

	PAGE		PAGE		PAGE
Smith, Moses S	155	Todd, James G	219	Williams, James A	256
Summers, William T	155	Todd, John T	212	Williamson, Joseph S	199
Swigart, T. W	228			Wilson, Charles W	248
				Wiseman, William A	253
		W.		Woodford, J. P	167
T.				Woolverton, Charles W	129
		Wallace, Albert W	254	Wright, James H	247
		Watson, Marion	280	Wyatt, Thomas S	284
Taggart, Col. Wesford	143	Watson, W. L	250	Wyeth, Clarence L	161
Taylor, A	295	Whitaker, John	286	Wyeth, Joseph S	188
Thompson, R. R	163	White, George	238	Wyeth, Leonard J	149

www.ingramcontent.com/pod-product-compliance
Lightning Source LLC
Chambersburg PA
CBHW030545080526
44585CB00012B/262